The Music Producer's Survival Guide
Chaos, Creativity, and Career in Independent and Electronic Music

Brian M. Jackson

Cengage Learning PTR

CENGAGE Learning®

Professional • Technical • Reference

Australia • Brazil • Japan • Korea • Mexico • Singapore • Spain • United Kingdom • United States

CENGAGE
Learning

Professional • Technical • Reference

The Music Producer's Survival Guide: Chaos, Creativity, and Career in Independent and Electronic Music
Brian M. Jackson

Publisher and General Manager, Cengage Learning PTR: Stacy L. Hiquet

Associate Director of Marketing: Sarah Panella

Manager of Editorial Services:
Heather Talbot

Senior Marketing Manager: Mark Hughes

Acquisitions Editor: Orren Merton

Project Editor: Kate Shoup

Technical Reviewer: Michael White

Copy Editor: Kate Shoup

Interior Layout Tech: MPS Limited

Cover Designer: Arnold Steiner

Cover Archivist: Mike Tanamachi

Indexer: Kelly Talbot Editing Services

Proofreader: Kelly Talbot Editing Services

Library of Congress Control Number: 2013944583

ISBN-13: 978-1-285-19892-7

ISBN-10: 1-285-19892-1

Cengage Learning PTR

20 Channel Center Street

Boston, MA 02210

USA

Cengage Learning is a leading provider of customized learning solutions with office locations around the globe, including Singapore, the United Kingdom, Australia, Mexico, Brazil, and Japan. Locate your local office at: **international. cengage.com/region**

Cengage Learning products are represented in Canada by Nelson Education, Ltd.

For your lifelong learning solutions, visit **cengageptr.com**

Visit our corporate website at **cengage.com**

Printed in the United States of America
1 2 3 4 5 6 7 15 14 13

Dedicated to 8, ∞, 0, 1.61803398875, 011235813213455,
r > 3.57, Z = Z² + C, and especially 7.83 Hz.

Preface

The most damaging phrase in the language is: We've always done it this way.

–Grace Hopper

Reality is not composed of things or processes; it is not composed of atoms or quarks; it is not composed of wholes nor does it have any parts. Rather, it is composed of whole/parts, or holons.

–Ken Wilber

Chaos is what we've lost touch with. This is why it is given a bad name. It is feared by the dominant archetype of our world, which is ego, which clenches because its existence is defined in terms of control.

–Terence McKenna

Welcome. I truly hope you enjoy this book, on multiple levels. *The Music Producer's Survival Guide* is as much a creative project for me as any track or record I've produced. Obviously, I think I have something significant to share with the world, or I wouldn't be writing a book such as this. At the same time, this book ultimately is not about me. It is not an autobiography of a music producer. That said, on multiple occasions I do share biographical stories and anecdotes when it serves a purpose—giving background on my thinking, using my personal history to contextualize the present, to illustrate a point, and especially when I think you can learn something from my successes and mistakes.

I love what I do for a living. My professional passions are the intersections of music, audio, technology, education, culture, and consciousness. Between my students, collaborators, and clients, I have literally worked with people at all levels of the industry—total beginners, legendary DJs, multiplatinum heavy-metal legends, movie stars, multiple Grammy nominees and winners, brilliant software developers, and countless otherwise-accomplished musicians, artists, and thinkers. This variety of experiences with such a diverse amalgam of people sparked the inspiration for this book.

After consistently being asked the same sorts of questions from a nice sample of the aforementioned people, I realized I needed to write a music-production book. After answering their questions, there was no one website, no one book, no one written source to which to refer them for follow-up. Many of these questions were contextual or relational in their nature, meaning that it was my synthesis of information that clarified the issues. So, in addition to my technical, creative, and cultural knowledge, I knew that my philosophical and intellectual perspective would have to be a significant aspect of the project.

A Philosophical Survival Guide

Survival guides are practical by definition because they help ensure you are prepared via pragmatic expert advice and a slew of utilitarian lists. Some intend to prepare you for unexpected, dangerous situations, be they hurricanes, getting lost in the wilderness, the zombie apocalypse, while others emphasize navigating common difficult non-emergency scenarios, such as help with popular technologies or personal finances. If not a survival guide for reading philosophy, "philosophical survival guide" may seem like an oxymoron or the premise for a lost scene from Monty Python's *The Meaning of Life*.

Unlike the typical survival guide that underscores immediate concerns, life as a technical-creative professional is an odyssey. Accordingly, this book is equal parts practical and philosophical. In many ways, what really sets this book apart from all the many other books on music-production topics is the perspective of your author. I do not claim to be the smartest, best-educated, most-talented, most-successful, most-experienced, or most-knowledgeable person to write a music-production book. I am certainly nowhere in the vicinity of the most famous or richest. However, it is my sincere belief that you have a unique book in your hands (and/or on your screen)—one that I hope you find equally useful and inspiring.

I don't blame you if you are already thinking something along these lines:

Oh, great. Another Gen X electronic musician who thinks he's some sort of thinker or philosopher. So he's read some Kurzweil, Bey, Stephenson, Baudrillard, Pinchbeck, and his fill of books by Disinformation and RE/Search. He's had his share of 5 a.m. discussions with other psychonauts about holographic cyberspace chakras and the sound of one hand clapping as it relates to a post-apocalyptic, hyperdimensional, culture-jamming, open-source, raw vegan–induced singularity while listening to the CD release of Alien Dreamtime: Space Time Continuum with Terence McKenna.

Okay, sure. Maybe I've had a few such discussions. Who hasn't? But in all seriousness, to put your mind at ease, I *do* have a few actual degrees from respectable, accredited American institutions of higher learning. Although I've been active in music and music culture nearly my whole life, I have a BS in sociology and philosophy (1994) and an MA (nearly ABD) in East-West psychology (1999). In fact, the focus of my master's thesis largely provides the philosophical and intellectual framework for the practical aspects of this book. It was the late 1990s, and I was in my late 20s, so with a complete, self-aware, ironic academic pretentiousness, I wanted to have the longest title in the printed program at the graduation ceremony: "Complex thinking, perceiving, and meaning-making: The evolution of integral consciousness and the paradigm of complexity." (Actually, it turned out to be the second longest title.)

Enough on my *bona fides.*

This is a big-picture book that includes a ton of specific, practical, detailed discussion. I intend to clear up common confusions, bring clarity to frequently murky topics, and provide context for many aspects of modern independent and electronic music production. As you will see, there are many aptitudes and skill sets involved, and understanding how they overlap and relate to each other requires a solid intellectual framework. There are many books on software, audio engineering, music composition, music business, music production, record producers, and promoting your band, for starters. Many of them are quite good. Yet they primarily address only pieces of the puzzle—a necessity for any in-depth discussion. So, to talk about how all the puzzle pieces fit together, we must need a "holistic" approach, right?

According to Ken Wilber, if part-ism is "gross reductionism," then holism is "subtle reductionism." French thinker Edgar Morin breaks it down for us: "Holism is a partial, one-dimensional, and simplifying vision of the whole. It reduces all other system-related ideas to the idea of totality, whereas it should be a question of confluence. Holism thus arises from the paradigm of simplification…" (*Journal of Social and Evolutionary Systems,* 1992). Required is a discussion not only of the parts and the whole, but also the relationship of the parts to each other and to the whole, to other wholes and their parts, and so on and so forth. Fortunately for us, Integral philosophy is perfectly suited to such an ambitious goal, and therefore I am taking an *integral* approach to this book.

Integral Philosophy and This Book

In December of 1994, after one semester of grad school at Western Michigan University, I walked away from a full ride (with stipend) and moved to San Francisco to pursue music. Thanks to my friend Naomi, another recent transplant from the Kalamazoo DIY music scene, I quickly landed a job at Royal Ground Coffee on Polk St. A few blocks down I found Fields Book Store, an amazing shop that was in the same location from 1932 until February of 2013, when the new digital landscape forced it to go online only (fieldsbooks.com). There, I discovered countless mind-opening books, including a few by psychiatrist Stanislav Grof, MD. Grof pioneered LSD psychotherapy starting in 1955 (when it was still legal), which directly led to his co-founding of the field of transpersonal psychology in 1969 with psychology pioneer Abraham Maslow.

After a few years as a barista in the wonderful freak show that is Polk St., in 1996 I started looking into grad schools to continue my formal education. While looking through a Learning Annex pamphlet, I saw that Grof was lecturing at a school just a few blocks away, the California Institute of Integral Studies (CIIS), and he also taught there! That fall, I became an East-West psychology PhD student at CIIS, where I remained until the summer of 1999. While at CIIS, I had amazing professors for a wide variety of courses. Excluding the most traditional and alternative, they ranged from Mahayana Buddhism and Vedanta, to transpersonal psychology and consciousness studies, to chaos theory and linguistics. There, I was exposed to the works of many great thinkers and researchers, but only four of them became the focus of my thesis: Robert Kegan, Jean Gebser, Edgar Morin, and Ken Wilber. Again, I left grad school for music, which is why I do not have a PhD, just a master's. From 1996 to 2000, I was also in I Am Spoonbender (GSL, MINT), a band I co-founded with a friend from Michigan—but that is part of another story.

CIIS: The American Academy of Asian Studies was founded in San Francisco in 1950 by Stanford professor of religion Frederick Spiegelberg (a friend of Carl Jung) and Alan Watts, an influential British East-West philosopher, speaker, writer, and self-described "spiritual entertainer." They wanted an Indian scholar on faculty at this newly founded East-West graduate school, and wrote a letter to the highly regarded Indian sage Sri Aurobindo for a recommendation. One of Aurobindo's students, Haridas Chaudhuri, chair of a philosophy department in Bengal, soon joined them in California. In 1974 they changed the name to the California Institute of Asian Studies, and then in 1980 to the California Institute of Integral Studies. In 1981, CIIS was accredited by the Western Association of Schools and Colleges. It continues to draw more and more students from around the globe.

What Is Integral Theory?

We live in a complex world that places an unprecedented combination of demands on us. In his 1994 book *In Over Our Heads: The Mental Demands of Modern Life*, Harvard psychologist Robert Kegan summed up his research on this point. Kegan tells us that these demands may "require a qualitative transformation in the complexity of mind every bit as fundamental as the transformation from magical thinking to concrete thinking…or the transformation from concrete thinking to abstract thinking." Just a few years after making this statement, Kegan would become a major player in the emerging field of Integral psychology.

What are some of these demands on professional independent and electronic music producers in the 21st century? You need musical and technical skills, of course, which means you need to know how to learn. People must know who you are and want to work with you, which means you are part of social scenes and require professional social skills. How do you know that the styles you want to produce are relevant? To answer that question, you need to be immersed in culture. You need to stay motivated and inspired, which means knowing yourself and evolving as a person. To take care of your mind, you need to take care of your body. Add all of those together, seeing them as simply different dimensions of the same thing, and you can start to get an idea of what integral means.

The word integral has two basic definitions:

▷ Necessary for wholeness or completeness
▷ That which integrates

The first notable appearances of the word "integral" in 20th century philosophy are found in the works of two intellectual giants: Sri Aurobindo (India, 1872–1950) and Jean Gebser (Poland/Switzerland, 1905–1973). Building on the works of these two geniuses, Ken Wilber (USA, 1949–) burst on the scene with the 1977 publication of his book *The Spectrum of Consciousness*, establishing himself as the premier theorist in the field of transpersonal psychology. By the 1990s, he'd evolved beyond one field and into the most prolific thinker, teacher, pandit, and writer on Integral theory. An expert meditator, needing just a few hours of sleep a night, and a true polymath, able to effectively speed-read a few books a day, his knowledge is accurately described as encyclopedic.

Currently, Integral theory is primarily associated with Wilber. Although he was not the first Integral philosopher, he was the first to develop a comprehensive theory that synthesized knowledge from almost every major field. Certainly, he has his detractors and critics, but fans of his writing include massage therapists, psychoanalysts, rock stars like Billy Corgan and Serj Tankian, Hollywood notables like Sharon Stone and the Wachowskis, and even Bill Clinton and Al Gore. In 1998, he founded Integral Institute with dozens of respected experts and professionals from numerous fields: psychology (including Robert Kegan), business, politics, medicine, education, law and criminal justice, art and music, ecology, and spirituality. On the front page of Integral Institute's website (integralinstitute.org), they offer the following definition.

> Integral theory is an all-inclusive framework that draws on the key insights of the world's greatest knowledge traditions. The awareness gained from drawing on all truths and perspectives allows the Integral thinker to bring new depth, clarity and compassion to every level of human endeavor—from unlocking individual potential to finding new approaches to global-scale problems.

Lofty goals, for sure. I don't pretend for a second that this book is going to solve global problems in any direct way. But I am working with the same intellectual framework, and I want you to know why. A serious study of Integral theory has numerous positive, practical side-effects, such as sharpened critical-thinking skills, tools for addressing common logical fallacies, and enhanced clarity when wading through ostensibly nebulous issues. I am not attempting to formally apply Integral theory as the central focus of this book. I only emphasize a few aspects and some not at all. In fact, other than a few mentions here and there, unless you know what to look for you will barely even notice Integral theory's influence on this book. You do not need to focus your energy on learning it. If you are interested in knowing more about Integral theory make sure to check out Appendix B, "Integral Theory Primer."

While Integral theory is mostly supporting architecture, topics of chaos and complexity are plainly visible elements. We will soon talk about tipping points, fractals, the butterfly effect, and other aspects of chaos and complexity. Integral theory is more expansive and inclusive of perspectives and ways of knowing than chaos theory and complexity studies. As such, a serious study of Integral philosophy ensures that a passion for science does not cause a devaluation of domains it does not adequately address, namely the world of subjective and inter-subjective experience. So, now that we have a basic idea of what is meant by "integral," let me tell you a story about a dragon and a dragon slayer. And no, heavy-metal lyrics are not the inspiration here.

Chaos, Dragons, and Fractals?

I love chaos. It is beautiful, especially if you learn to perceive its ubiquitous patterns and rich nuances. Chaos is often conflated with confusion or complication, or often solely to its pejorative connotation of destruction. Historically, you can trace our civilization's problematic relationship with chaos back to an ancient Babylonian myth (c. 1900 BCE). In this myth, the "hero" Marduk slays a dragon, the ocean goddess Tiamat, and order rules over chaos—the second version of the myth, by the way. In the earlier version of the myth, Tiamat was the peaceful creator of the cosmos, which is more in line with our current understanding of chaos as equally a creative process. The post WWII computer revolution isn't just responsible for the tech we use to produce music; the raw number-crunching power of computers made it possible to discover the fundamental role that chaos has in shaping the physical universe. Chaos theory, fractal geometry, cybernetics, systems theory, 3D computer-generated imagery, astronomy, and various schools of psychology and medicine are just a few examples of fields rife with research and results saturated with chaos.

Deborah Tussey is a law professor at Oklahoma City University who specializes in intellectual property and copyright law. Her 2012 book *Complex Copyright* applies complexity concepts to a future vision of a more flexible and adaptive copyright law. A few years earlier, in 2005, she published a paper on chaos and file sharing, called "Music at the Edge of Chaos: A Complex Systems Perspective on File Sharing" and published in *Loyola University Chicago Law Journal*, which included as succinct a summary of all key elements of complexity theory as I could find. What follows is an academic quote that I think will help you understand precisely where I am coming from:

> *A brief foray into the basic concepts of complexity theory is an obvious prerequisite to application of those concepts to the music system. Complexity theory posits that complex adaptive systems universally possess certain characteristics: they are composed of multiple, interconnected components; change cascades through them in a nonlinear manner; they evolve and coevolve over time in a pattern of punctuated equilibrium; and they produce emergent behaviors. These qualities make system behavior unpredictable over the long term and, where humans intervene in such systems, their actions are likely to produce unintended consequences. The most robust systems exhibit a property sometimes referred to as self-organizing criticality or positioning at the 'edge of chaos'—the ability to maintain a productive internal tension between order and chaos.*

So what does music production or being a music producer have to do with chaos and complexity? Chaos and complexity are fundamental characteristics of the natural world, and we are part of that world, so they not only influence music, art, culture, technology, psychology, and careers, but life in general. The more fluid and dynamic a given system, the higher the tendency toward turbulence, and the more likely we will notice chaotic behavior. Artistic and entertainment industry careers are much more fluid than most fields, with various flavors of instability being a common state of affairs. Why do some people's careers take off, and other's not? Why do new genres blow up, when they blow up? Chaos and complexity also shed light on everything from the creative process to social scenes, the evolution of music styles and genres, and dynamics in pop culture.

> **NOTE:** Complexity studies is the broadest intellectual umbrella for the fields interested in the ideas mentioned in the preceding quote. In popular language, chaos theory is synonymous with complexity studies, though it is just one of many approaches to complexity. Technically speaking, chaos theory is a subset of dynamical systems theory, and is the mathematical study of non-linear, unpredictable behavior of complex deterministic systems.

Moreover, the concept of complexification helps to explain many of the massive changes in our industry that make this book possible in the first place. From a complex systems theory perspective, we are reaping benefits of the complexification process, which is illustrated via numerous relevant examples throughout this book. For right now, let's just work with Ervin Laszlo's succinct explanation from his 1991 book, *The Age of Bifurcation: Understanding the Changing World*:

> *In sum, the processes of evolution create initially comparatively simple dynamical systems on particular levels of organization. The processes then lead to the progressive complexification of the existing systems and, ultimately, to the creation of simpler systems on the next higher organizational level, where complexification begins anew. Thus evolution moves from the simpler to the more complex, and from the lower to the higher level of organization.*

Throughout this book, to help explain certain concepts and relationships, I rely on various aspects of complexity studies, especially key concepts from chaos theory such as unpredictable outcomes and fractal geometry. Regarding the latter, we are going to talk quite a bit about branching structures and self-similarity in a number of the chapters. Sometimes I apply ideas and concepts in line with the science as it is currently understood. At other times I take poetic license, using them as metaphor, analogy, muse, and/or inspiration. In either case, I do not get into the mathematics underlying the science. In addition to sidebars mixed in with the chapters, the aptly named Appendix A, "Chaos Theory and Complexity Studies Primer," serves as a primer on chaos theory and complexity studies.

One of this book's meta-goals is to formally introduce these ideas into our field. They are already utilized in psychology, sociology, biology, education, and numerous other academic fields, but also video game development, digital visual arts, and other fine arts. Many of today's scientific givens, which are regularly discussed in audio engineering and the more technical aspects of music production, were once deemed too "off topic" in the context of music (for example, the Nyquist-Shannon sampling theorem). Some of you may find it odd that I am putting so much time and energy into integrating chaos and complexity ideas into the world of independent and electronic music production. Just as talking about computer networks and IP addresses would have been fringe topics in music production curricula back in the 1980s, talking about music production, chaos, and complexity one day will seem like a no brainer.

Down the Rabbit Hole

I know for a fact that some of you will really appreciate and enjoy the science and philosophy contextualizations in this book. But, if you are concerned that this book might be too intellectual or academic for your taste, don't fret. Although I do not hold back when I think there is something worthy of deeper consideration, I guarantee that you will also find a lot of perfectly straightforward, practical, immediately useful information. It took years to digest the fundamentals of chaos theory, complexity studies, and Integral theory, and new layers of understanding continually dawn on me. You do not need to know all of this stuff for *The Music Producer's Survival Guide* to be useful. If you do decide to take a deeper look into the ideas presented here, you may just find an endless source of inspiration and intellectual stimulation, as I have. If not, no worries. This book is designed in such a way that there are levels of understanding to take away from it, so there is something in here for everyone.

To sum up the intuitive foundations of my thinking better than any words can convey, this preface concludes with pretty photos of self-similar, fractal shapes found at all levels of the physical world. (See Figures P.1–P.6.)

NOTE: For full-color versions of the images in this book, be sure to visit this book's companion website, www.iempsg.com.

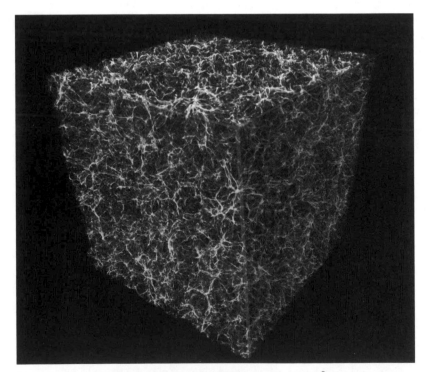

Figure P.1 NASA-generated simulation of 13 million³ light-year sliver of our universe. The texture is created by the "filaments," which represent dark matter in the space between galaxies.
Source: Public domain via NASA.gov.

Figure P.2 A satellite photo of the Lena river delta in Siberia, with fractal structures similar to a sponge, cardiovascular system, or "filaments" as seen in Figure P.1.
Source: Public domain via NASA.gov.

Figure P.3 Lichtenberg figure in plexiglass caused by high-voltage current. Created and photographed by Bert Hickman of Stoneridge Engineering (capturedlightning.com).
Source: Public domain via Bert Hickman.

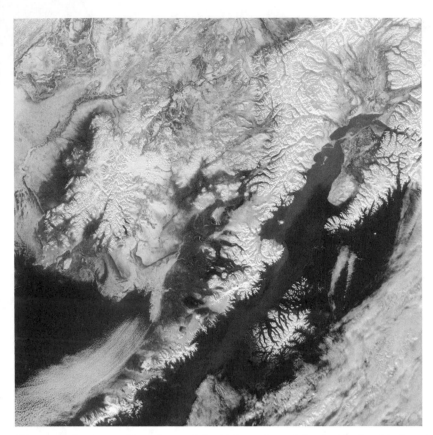

Figure P.4 A satellite photo of the Yukon river delta in Alaska. Notice the coastline's and mountain ranges' fractal branching structures.
Source: Public domain via NASA.gov.

Figure P.5 A Hubble satellite photo of the M13 Galaxy nucleus. (Photo by NASA/STScI.)
Source: Public domain via NASA.gov.

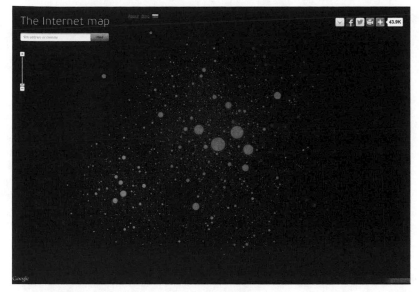

Figure P.6 Screenshot of internet-map.net depicting a map of the Internet in 2011. Each dot represents a website, and the overall image displays self-similarity.

Source: internet-map.net.

Acknowledgments

The Music Producer's Survival Guide: Chaos, Creativity, and Career in Independent and Electronic Music represents a culmination of experiences and knowledge from the past 25 years or so. This brain dump was a group effort, so there are a lot of people that I need to thank for making it possible. There is one group that must be thanked above all others: my students. They say that the best way to learn is to teach, and I couldn't agree more. If not for students asking me questions, this book would not exist.

A big, heartfelt thank you also goes out to all of the following: Orren Merton, my acquisitions editor, for believing in this project and making it happen. Michael White, the technical editor most uniquely qualified for this book, not only for his technical knowledge and decades of industry experience, but also his knowledge and wisdom on many of the other topics found herein. Kate Shoup, my project editor, for her editing chops and helping me make sense. Alexandra Ricciardi, for putting up with my barrage of fair use and public domain questions. Mark Hughes, for promoting this book. Mark Garvey, for originally bringing me into the Cengage Learning universe back in the day, and for crafting the cover copy and Web copy.

Thanks also go to: David Zeitler, for his expertise on all things Integral theory. Jean-Luc Cohen, Daniel Gould, and Chris Buono, for additional help or feedback on a few key topics. Arnold Steiner, for the awesome cover art. The wonderful strangers from around the globe who answered "yes" to my out-of-the-blue requests to use their math, science, synth, Integral, or history images gratis: Shevy Shovlin (Vintage King LA), Brad Berry (Perfect Circuit Audio), Paul Bourke (paulbourke.net), Bert Hickman (capturedlightning.com), Chris Skirrow (Lindos Electronics), Ruslan Enikeev (internet-map.net), David Giovannoni (firstsounds.org), Steve Self (formlessmountain.com), Georg-Johann Lay, and Lutz Pietschke.

Any factual, intellectual, or philosophical mistakes in this book are mine, and not the fault of anyone else.

Thanks to Hank Shocklee for the amazing interview found in Appendix C, and to everyone who honored me with an interview (originally intended for this book but now to be found in a forthcoming companion book): Chris Baio, Laura Escudé, Jason Drummond, John Jansen, Shawn Hatfield, and Erik Magrini. Thanks also to Adelaide Matthews for saving my wrists by transcribing all four hours of those interviews. Thanks, too, to Dennis DeSantis, Dave Hillel, Huston Singletary, Tony McCall, and everyone at Ableton; Dave Hill; Joe DeStefano (IK Multimedia); James Coker (Five12); Przemek Gocyla and Sebastian Bachlinski (D16 Group); Stefano Daino (i3 S.R.L); Jo-Ann Nina; Jason Koons (Sweetwater); and Bob Power.

Thanks to the Jackson, Meyer, and Greenwald families.

Thanks to Phoenix Perry, Margaret Schedel, David Last, and everyone else at Devotion Gallery.

Thanks to Tony Grund, Dion Roy, Jon Margulies, Jon Mack, Dave Greenberg, Todd Sines, Michael Doyle, Bethany Shorb, Adriano Clemente, Ellen Pearlman, A.J. Tissian, Mark Ephraim, Eric Hoegemeyer, Jesse Smith, Dave Tate, Dan Storchan, Phil Eichhorn, James Hayes, Lee Marvin, Cleve Pozar, Ronnie Shingelo, Richard Luchese, Bill Appel, Adam Silk, Mike Swartzstein, James Marvel, Naut Humon, Jennifer Jass, Lenny Gonzalez, Anna Sitko, Tom Rollison, J.C., David Rishel, Paul Grove, Smelly Mustafa, Benjamin Chance, 550 Ashbury St. (1998–2002) and 516 McCourtie St. (1992–1994). Richard Termini, Karl Wenninger, Jeff Humphrey, Michael Marcucci, and everyone else at DMX NYC. Stacey Van Buskirk, Robert Daniels, Dave Walker, Dimitri Vandellos, and everyone else from the Bryant Street days at Rocket Network. Sean Kelly, Alfonso Montuori, Richard Tarnas, Steven Goodman, Carol Whitfield, and numerous other professors and peers at CIIS, including all my NYCIIS alumni peeps.

Finally, thanks to anyone else who deserved to be mentioned but was somehow left out.

About the Author

Brian Jackson is a musician, audio engineer, music producer, teacher, and philosopher. He is co-owner and director of education at Devotion, an art gallery and community space in Brooklyn that also serves as his Ableton Certified Training Center. Brian's involvement in DIY, independent, and underground music culture started in Detroit more than two decades ago. He has produced various styles of electronic music, played bass in bands, promoted club events, attempted a record label, and DJed after-hours parties. From award-winning experimental video to TV shows such as *24*, his sounds have been heard worldwide. He uses the pseudonyms Infinite Volume and Cyphony for solo works and remixes, was half of the conceptual retro-future electro synth A/V duo Memory Systems, and co-founded the genre-bending band I Am Spoonbender (1996–2000). He is the author of multiple tutorial DVDs on Ableton Live and technical editor of books on Live and Pro Tools, among others. Brian is also a creative-technical consultant with clients including Ableton, Access, and multiple Grammy nominees/winners. With a B.S. in Sociology and Philosophy already under his belt (WMU, 1994), Brian went on to earn an M.A. in East-West Psychology (1999) from the California Institute of Integral Studies in San Francisco. He lives in Brooklyn, NY, and is reachable through his website, www.formlabsnyc.com.

Contents

Chapter 5 The Social Scene 81

Chapter 6 Producer Tips 91

Chapter 7 Creative Process   115

Chapter 8 Selecting Your Tools   145

Chapter 9 Lifestyle Tips   173

Chapter 10 Dénouement 199

Appendix A Chaos Theory and Complexity Studies Primer 203

Appendix B Integral Theory Primer 209

Appendix C Interview with Hank Shocklee 215

Index 225

Introduction

As technology advances, it reverses the characteristics of every situation again and again. The age of automation is going to be the age of "do it yourself."

–Marshall McLuhan, 1957

The technology at the leading edge changes so rapidly that you have to keep current after you get out of school. I think probably the most important thing is having good fundamentals.

–Gordon Moore (co-founder of Intel)

None of us ever got into it to strike it rich, let's put it that way. I think anybody who wants to start a band...specifically to make money...it's kind of a fool's dream in a way.

–Thurston Moore, Sonic Youth (*Innovators in Music*, 2010)

I could use the industry to try and further my own career or get records signed to major record labels but that's not what I'm about....I'm just so happy to be traveling around with my friends and to play records for people in clubs....It's not about success or money for me, it's about shared experiences.

–Ellen Allien (owner, BPitch Control)

DIY.Independent.Electronic.Music.Producer.

Like most of you reading this book I started out as a music fan and musician. Production and audio engineering came later, initially as a way to help better express musical ideas without having to depend on costly recording studios and later as a way to help pay the bills. I love computers, production, and audio engineering, but first and foremost I am a music fan. Although we all have our favorite styles and genres, I can appreciate something about most any one of them. If an artist truly has something to express, it doesn't matter if the music is released on a major label, an imprint, a boutique indie, self released, or simply just performed live. The music can be techno, electro, house, rock, metal, punk, jazz, hip hop, pop, bluegrass, Afrobeat, funk, gospel, classical, experimental, or unclassifiable. It can be from Detroit, Berlin, London, Morocco, Ghana, Iran, Israel, Tibet, China, India, Brazil, Mexico, or parts unknown. Having said all that, this is not a music-appreciation book, *per se*. Rather, it is about music production—independent and electronic music production. Moreover, it is as much about *being* an independent/electronic music producer in the 21st century, and being able to do it yourself, being DIY, as it is about music production.

If I had started writing this book in 1992 and not 2012, the main title would simply be the *Electronic Music Producer's Survival Guide*. Back then, electronic musicians were the only ones you would find toiling away for hours by themselves making music with computers, synths, samplers, and sequencers. The Internet's role in the spread of information and connecting the like-minded from anywhere, at any time, cannot be understated. So this book talks about the computer revolution and the resulting home-studio boom. How they have inexorably changed the game for everyone, given that making high-quality music at home using computers is no longer just the domain of arty rock stars and electronic music producers. We'll deal with the implications of powerful, sophisticated, affordable (and even free) software putting once-expensive, state-of-the-art capabilities from just a few decades past in the hands of anyone looking for it.

What Is the Goal of This Book?

The Music Producer's Survival Guide is no slacker. It is ambitious and has a lot of goals. It wants to help you become smarter and wiser. It wants to help those who are committed to their craft rise above the distracting, incessant, low-level noise generated by marketers, shills, haters, posers, followers, clowns, oafs, trolls, and parasites. It aims to give you tools that you will need to survive, and better yet, to have a fulfilling career as an independent and/or electronic music producer in the 21st century.

We live in the Information Age. There is a vast amount of information readily available to you about most all aspects of music and production. Largely absent is readily available knowledge about how all this information fits together. Even more rare is readily available knowledge about how all these aspects connect to other areas of life and career that are equally important for survival and success. As a teacher, I am motivated to share information and knowledge. So in many ways, this book aims to fill in many of the gaps that an aspiring producer would learn only from many years of experience or a few less years of mentoring from established professionals. I do not claim expertise in every area discussed in this book, and I regularly seek out knowledge from others, but I have more than enough expertise and competence across the board to help you perform a metaphorical decryption of cipher text into plain text.

Rapid advancements in technology are changing most every aspect of our lives, not just audio and music. For music producers, the narrow context is music technology's piggyback ride on the exponential ascent of the communication, computing, and information revolutions instigated by Alexander Graham Bell, Nikola Tesla, Thomas Edison, Claude Shannon, and Alan Turing. Given the complexity of the modern world, and our field in particular, there is a need for clarity. Not only is our industry evolving and changing at a very rapid pace, but it is also exposing us to knowledge once privy only to specializations and crafts unto themselves. How do various aspects of music production relate to each other and what does it mean for somebody trying to do it all himself or herself? For example, there are few aspiring young producers who understand the differences and relationships between composing, sound design, mixing, mastering, audio technology, creative process, and technical skill.

I want to get you thinking—about the big picture and about very specific topics. At the same time, there are a lot of questions that everyone needs to ask themselves—in other words, contemplations. I am not so deluded as to think that I have all the answers, or that I even know all the questions, but I know a lot of the questions that every aspiring technical creative professional should ask himself or herself. As a *philosophical* survival guide, this book puts the onus on you to pave your own road.

As a philosophical survival guide, this book is also very practical. I want you to have immediate takeaways, and each chapter provides these in its own way. Here are a few examples of topics that feature tips and pointers:

▷ Planning your career
▷ Learning your craft
▷ Networking and navigating social scenes
▷ Organizing your sessions for maximum productivity and creativity
▷ Dealing with creative blocks
▷ Making decisions about equipment
▷ Avoiding common lifestyle pitfalls
▷ Protecting your hearing
▷ Staying healthy

How Is This Book Structured?

If this book were an analog synthesizer, you could say it is semi-modular. Each chapter provides different functionality to the system and its user. Each chapter also offers guidance regarding key components of a music producer's survival. Various themes are woven throughout, and I do refer to other chapters' topics here and there, but each one can stand on its own. I certainly didn't write this book in order, so a non-linear read seems as logical as not. Read it straight through, or jump around to make it suit your needs.

Each chapter includes a combination of loosely definable section types: quotes, context, theory, contemplations, definitions, practical topics, and anecdotal items. There is no set order for these sections, but I always start out with a few quotes. Usually what follows is prose about the big picture to provide context before moving on to theory or topics designed to provoke contemplation about your specific needs and situation. When I say big picture, I mean it, and I know a lot of you are going to appreciate these sections. But, I realize a broad context may not be useful for some beginners or those who are already feeling a bit lost or overwhelmed by the sheer amount of options and information. (If you suddenly wake up on the corner of Broadway and Astor Place on a rainy day, having never been to NYC, and you ask someone where you are, being told that you are toward the outskirts of the Milky Way galaxy is not very helpful.) Every chapter also includes useful definitions and/or highly practical sections to make sure there is something to immediately apply. To illustrate key points or to ground seemingly abstract ideas, I often use personal anecdotes, so you can learn from my experience and mistakes or simply avoid reinventing the wheel.

Depending on your personal entry point to the subject matter or your mood that day, you may be more or less interested in different sections or chapters. While moving through different chapters out of order will work for some of you, I do recommend approaching most of the chapters in a more linear fashion—at least on the first read. Whether you go from start to finish or take a more circuitous route, as you circle back through material, previously read sections will take on new meaning and eventually you will put it all together in a way that makes sense to you.

Toward the back of the book you will find three appendixes. Appendix A, "Chaos Theory and Complexity Studies Primer," is additional background on complexity studies and chaos theory. Appendix B, "Integral Theory Primer," offers additional background on Integral theory. Appendix C is an interview with legendary music producer Hank Shocklee.

NOTE: Look for the companion book to *The Music Producer's Survival Guide*, which features interviews with a variety of music professionals.

What This Book Is Not

The Music Producer's Survival Guide is not trying to be trendy. It is not overly concerned with what is currently hot. It is not going to show you a bunch of screenshots of this year's latest software. Therefore, it is not going to slowly leak relevance with each new update and GUI overhaul or with the rise and fall of genres, styles, or artists. A survival guide must have a decent shelf life.

This book is not an in-depth technical manual. It does not shy away from technical discussion when it is relevant, but it does not attempt to give you technical training. You will find out about what you should learn, tips on how to learn it, and suggested directions on where to learn it.

This is not another "how to make it in the music industry" book. What you may learn here can help you to meet your goals, whatever they may be. I do want you to make a living doing what you love, but the goal of this book is not to help you get rich and famous (although it is a guide that may help you reach those goals should a fulfilling career require them). That said, I hope you find fame and fortune so you can drop my name in interviews and hire me to hang out in your entourage. (You never know. You may just need someone who can explain the differences between dither and aliasing and between minimal techno from Detroit or San Francisco at your next private after-hours party.)

Whom Is This Book For?

This book is custom-tailored for people interested in the intersection of music, sound, audio, technology, creativity, culture, science, philosophy, and consciousness. You may even notice that many of the concepts are also relevant to other creative-technical trades and professions. There is something in here for almost anyone interested in the topics named on the cover, but I expect it will be most appreciated by five loosely defined groups:

▷ If you are an aspiring young producer or musician and just getting started in music production or have yet to pursue a career path, this book is for you.
▷ If you are an experienced DJ or serious hobbyist with some production experience and want to make a go at it, this book is for you.
▷ If you are a student or teacher at a college or school with a music-production or audio-technology curriculum, then this book is perfect for you.
▷ If you are a professional and/or are established in one of the four major aspects of music production (music, sound design, audio engineering, or tools; see Figure 4.1 in Chapter 4, "Master Your Craft") and are looking to expand your creative and career options, there is a lot in this book for you. (Although, it is equally likely I have a lot to learn from you in your area of specialization.)
▷ If you have a home studio, are a hobbyist, are a serious music fan with interest in technology, or are someone who is simply trying to make sense of all of the options available for working on music in the computer-centric world, there is something in this book for you.

Can I Get a Venn Diagram?

The terms DIY, independent, indie, and electronic music are defined and briefly discussed right after Figure I.1. First, this diagram is not to scale in any way, and only attempts to clarify the focus of the book in your hands, not all possible relationships. We are concerned with the circles labeled "indie music" and "electronic music," primarily where they overlap. In total, there are seven circles: one huge, one large, three medium, and two small. The huge one that encircles the other six represents music in general, which has been around for a very long time—at least 42,000 years (but possibly millions). The large circle on the right represents music business, which includes all the aspects of music related to commerce. There is commercial music, traditionally dominated by major labels, and artists concerned with getting on a major label. This industry is really young—only about 125 years old. There is/are indie music, indie artists, and independent labels, which may or may not consciously appreciate the DIY ethic. In this diagram I am using "indie" in its broadest sense and not showing any delineation from DIY. Electronic music can be indie or commercial.

> **NOTE:** The terms *producer* and *professional* are defined and discussed in Chapter 2, "Plot Point on the Space-Time Continuum." A sidebar later in this introduction ruminates on the word *produce*.

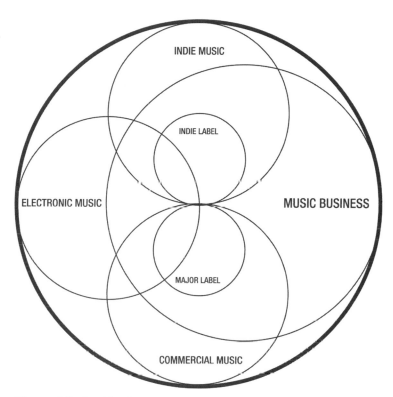

Figure I.1 In this diagram, the largest circle is music, with the circles representing electronic music and indie music as this book's focus.

© 2013 Brian Jackson. Graphic design by Arnold Steiner. All Rights Reserved.

DIY

Don't hate the media; be the media.

–Jello Biafra, founder of Dead Kennedys and Alternative Tentacles Records

Do-it-yourself is a philosophy. "Yourself" is not limited to one person; it can be groups or even collectives of people who share the same sensibility. It implies consciously chosen freedom from dependence on institutional structures for your creations and productions. This choice usually involves a tradeoff of less financial or material resources for absolute creative control. There was a time when this tradeoff resulted in poor production quality and lack of sonic fidelity, leading to a common and fair criticism of DIY/indie productions. Nowadays, due to more readily available information, overall production quality is improved, and fidelity is no longer a serious concern because of lower technology costs, increased computing power, and the maturation of digital audio. Note that DIY implies being independent, but not necessarily vice versa.

Independent (Indie)

Independent labels take nothing and make something out of it. Major labels buy that something, and try to make more out of it.

–Tom Silverman, CEO Tommy Boy Records

By independent, I mean music that is not part of the major label, multi-national corporation music business (as briefly discussed in the next section). I am not referring to a specific style or aesthetic of music. Although indie music can be very popular and commercially successful, commercial viability is not normally the primary motivation. The modern indie label mold is most associated with the DIY punk counter culture movements of the late 1970s/early 1980s, the electronic music and adventurous/experimental labels of that same period and into the early 1990s, and later labels following in the footsteps of the aforementioned. (More discussion on this topic is in Chapter 1, "Musica Universalis."

How is indie different from DIY? If you are DIY you are in all probability indie, but not necessarily the other way around. For example, there are artists on indie labels who play on the smaller-venue music circuits, but essentially use smaller, cheaper, less-commercial versions of the traditional project workflows, production processes, and commerce infrastructures. They are indie, but not very DIY. Also, indie labels are often stepping stones for artists hoping to sign with a major label, so they are indie only by definition and DIY only by necessity, not philosophy, until they get signed (if they get signed, and it works out). There is nothing necessarily wrong with this fact; it is what it is.

Electronic Music (EM)

Electronic music is not easy to precisely define, but it is safe to say that it is music primarily created with electronic instruments such as synths, samplers, drum machines, and sequencers. Electronic music production (EMP) is easiest to DIY from a logistical point of view because it can literally just be you and your computer. Yes, there is mainstream, major-label, electronic pop and dance music, but the vast majority of electronic music is aptly part of the DIY and independent music world.

Chapter 1, "Musica Universalis," and Chapter 7, "Creative Process," discuss historical relationships and evolutions of various genres. Here I offer a super short history of EM for context, but know that most of the following is further covered throughout the book. Although electronic instruments first appeared in the 1870s, electronic music didn't really get going until the 1950s with pioneering academics such as Karlheinz Stockhausen and Max Matthews. Then, in the 1960s, with the synthesizers of Don Buchla and Robert Moog in particular, various composers and experimental musicians fertilized the ground for the major-label, progressive rock artists of the early 70s along with the German Krautrock movement that birthed Kraftwerk. By the late 1970s, the U.K./U.S. led new wave and proto-industrial music's paralleling of synth pop, Zapp and Roger's electro funk, and Giorgio Moroder's chart-topping Italo-disco productions solidified electronic music in the pop and club worlds. Jamaican Dub and Roland's legendary x0x series of drum machines and synths were the final ingredients needed for the largely African-American innovations of house, techno, electro, and hip hop that spawned most of the countless genres thought of as EM today.

> **NOTE:** From a production point of view, hip hop is for all intents and purposes electronic music (as it is a close relative of electro, or "break-dance music"). The exact same technology is used to make beats or produce tracks. If this doesn't make sense to you, just listen to "Planet Rock" (1982) by Afrika Bambaataa or "Jam On It" (1983) by Newcleus. The record industry separates hip hop and other "urban" styles from the rest of electronic music for marketing and distribution purposes. Mainstream hip hop and other styles of electronic music do inhabit different cultural niches, so this separation is understandable.

A Few Words on Major Labels and the Corporate Media Business

> **NOTE:** While reading this section, keep in mind that "independent" is in this book's title for a reason. Accordingly, it is written from the perspective that, not only can you have a fulfilling and successful career without the major labels and/or corporate media companies, but that moreover, such a career is a commendable goal unto itself.

There are numerous obvious cases of creative and artistic successes by popular major-label artists, yet it is important we never forget that the commercial music business is first and foremost profit driven. In most industries, competition between companies is good for consumers, while monopolies are not good for the public because they can fix prices, offer limited products, and control access to opportunities. In 1998, there were six major label groups—"The Big 6"—which included Dutch, German, British, American, Canadian, and Japanese financial interests. As of 2012, there was only "The Big 3": Universal Music Group (35+ labels), Sony Music Entertainment (10+ labels), and Warner Music Group (20+ labels). All of these are subsidiaries of larger corporations. Combined with the predatory domination of various media by Clear Channel (discussed next), these four entities basically control the large-scale, commercial music industry (and much more).

Clear Channel in particular is quite problematic. For starters, its Live Nation Entertainment subsidiary includes a 2010 merger with Ticketmaster, who already had a famously troubled relationship with musicians and fans alike due to its fees and control over access to venues. Clear Channel also has major interests in TV (including news), talk radio, outdoor advertising (billboards), and performance venues. In fact, Clear Channel owns more than 99 percent of the top 250 broadcast radio markets. In 2008, its primary shareholder, Bain Capital, took it from a publicly traded company to a privately owned subsidiary of CC Media Holdings, Inc. In addition to other industries, Bain also has significant financial holdings in Guitar Center, AMC Cinemas, Warner Music Group, and D&M Holdings, a merger of Japanese companies Denon and Marantz, which also now owns U.K.-based Allen & Heath. (Yes, Bain is the same private-equity company founded by the losing 2012 Republican presidential nominee Mitt Romney.)

> *Clear Channel will do anything they can, threaten me, go to my clients directly, anything to get control of the markets. And once they've got that control they can do whatever they want, including raise the rates. They're a clear example of what can happen with deregulation. They've ruined radio, as far as I'm concerned. And now they're licking their chops to be able to control more of what the public sees and hears."*
>
> –Anonymous owner of a southeastern advertising agency (in Eric Boehlert's
2003 article "Clear Channel's Big, Stinking Deregulation Mess" on Salon.com)

Universal Music Group, until recently part of France's Vivendi Universal Entertainment, was sold to GE (80 percent in 2004 and the other 20 percent in 2011), owner of NBC, to form NBC Universal with Comcast in 2011. As of February 2013, Comcast bought GE's remaining shares to become full owner of NBC Universal. Comcast is a huge company and, as the largest cable operator in the U.S., also has significant control over Internet access.

So, when we talk about the *commercial music business,* we are referring to an industry controlled mainly by just four entities in only two countries (as of February 2013): Comcast (U.S.), Time Warner Inc. (U.S.), Bain Capital (U.S.), and Sony Corporation of America (U.S./Japan). Media corporations have a lot of vested interests, including those of their parent companies. To support their financial, political, and/or ideological goals, they make decisions on what to say, print, and release, and what to omit. (To be fair, most corporations do not have political and ideological goals, and therefore primarily make decisions based on revenue and their mission statement.) As a generalization, we can say that misinformation and censorship are the most pressing concerns about mainstream, corporate-owned media's control of information flow.

> *A famous middle-aged rock-and-roller called me last week to thank me for speaking out against the war, only to go on to tell me that he could not speak himself because he fears repercussions from Clear Channel. "They promote our concert appearances," he said. "They own most of the stations that play our music. I can't come out against this war."*
>
> –Tim Robbins, actor (in Eric Boehlert's 2003 article "Habla usted Clear Channel?" on Salon.com)

Everyone has a point of view, so all media has a bias of some sort, but I think the most problematic forms manifest in specific ways: with mainstream right-leaning media, it is what they do say (profit interest misinformation) and don't allow (ideology and morality censorship), while with mainstream left-leaning media it is what they don't say (corporate interest censorship). There are significant implications for bands, artists, and music producers. Who controls what you can sell, where you can sell it, what you can say, how you can say it, where you can play, and how you are heard? In other words, who controls your freedom of expression and ability to make a living doing it? These are not new issues or questions. In fact, these issues are precisely why DIY and independent exist in the first place. Moreover, there are more opportunities than ever for self-motivated DIY and independent artists and producers.

NOTE: Chapter 2 discusses the evolution of the record industry and the huge changes that have transpired in the last decade due to the digital revolution.

Let me be very clear. For a few people, major labels are a good choice. When you have a substantial following and have outgrown the capacities of smaller labels, then considering working with a major label can make sense—should it be an option and the deal is right. Just remember that although the A&R person who signs you may be your friend, to their boss, you are just numbers on a spreadsheet, profit or loss, nothing more, nothing less. If your buddy in A&R is let go, you likely depart with him or her. It happens all of the time. If "getting signed" is your goal, just make sure to do your research and get a really good music-business lawyer. (Check with your local musician's union for a referral.) That said, you should have a good lawyer for any deals, and don't assume that independent labels won't screw you over just because they are "indie."

Music business is not covered in this book because there is a lot of material out there already and it is not my area of expertise. But I have four pieces of hard-learned advice that are important when dealing with strangers, acquaintances, and even friends:

▷ Get financial agreements sorted out before any money is involved.
▷ Put agreements in writing.
▷ Do your research. Don't make decisions based on assumptions.
▷ If it sounds too good to be true, it probably is.

Magic Might Make Machine Mechanism, *Moegen Macht*

"Any sufficiently advanced technology is indistinguishable from magic."

–Arthur C. Clarke

Whether before or after one chooses and commits oneself to a life of intellectual, technical, and/or artistic pursuit, there comes a time to recognize a lineage. Who and what carved the pathways that created this option for you and your peers? Although the most immediate and obvious forerunners are important to recognize, beyond that, the breadth and scope of this lineage can vary greatly from person to person and career to career. A musician may simply see himself or herself as following in the footsteps of the modern greats in his or her genre, while another might understand that he or she is also part of a broader artistic movement that also includes the writers, filmmakers, dancers, and painters of his or her day. Other musicians will further see themselves as participants in long arcs of intellectual traditions that include not only the arts, but also whole cultural movements including technology, science, politics, religion, and social change. It is not unreasonable to even include streams of thought or traditions dating back hundreds or thousands of years, such as shamanism, the philosophers of ancient Greece, or the artists of the Italian Renaissance.

We are committed to producing music using modern electronic and computer technology, so what is our lineage? There is no right answer, and I am not going to offer one. I'm sure you can figure out the music part for yourself, but for the big context, I offer the following paragraphs for your consideration.

A brief scan of various dictionaries tells us that the verb *produce* means to make, to create, to bring forth, to bring into being, to give form or shape to, to oversee the making of. The word *technology* stems from the Indo-European root, *tek,* which means to shape or to make, and the later Greek *tekhne*, which refers to arts, skill, craft, methods, or techniques, combined with *-logy*, meaning the study of or language of. Jean Gebser (1949) pointed out that all the terms in this section's heading stem from the same Indo-European root, *magh*. In German, *moegen* means *to want*. *Macht* means *power*, as in might or willpower (though not unrelated to energy, as in a power station or *ein kraftwerk*).

The tree-like branchings that stem from the primal root words *magh* and *tek* point to an archetypal constellation that permeates our craft. Christopher Nolan's film *The Prestige* (2006) brilliantly re-imagines the late 19th century's crossfade from mechanical trickery to electrified technological wizardry via the bitter adversarial competition between two popular magicians: one driven by want, the other by will. David Bowie makes an appearance as Nikola Tesla, who is regularly referenced as a wizard or magician. Thomas Edison, inventor of the phonograph (1877), was known as the "wizard of Menlo Park," and released a silent film called *The Magician* in 1900. Magicians present a variety of illusions, with the most common known as a *production*—wherein they produce something from nothing, such as a rabbit from a hat.

Welcome to the Future

We truly are living in amazing times. I'm not exaggerating when I say that you have more freedoms and opportunities than any creative person living at any time in human history. It is unquestionable that technology is largely responsible for this state of affairs. But as with all technological progress, there are also new challenges. Just because you have more opportunities does not mean they are easy to grasp because anybody can readily choose to compete for those same opportunities. The Internet and the democratization of computing technology enables everyone to have their own media outlet. Even if you've never explicitly thought about the DIY ethos, these challenges include implicit responsibilities and demands on each of us to do more for ourselves. Whether you produce house, techno, hip hop, dubstep, indietronica, or even independent movie soundtracks, we are all in the same boat. Those who refuse to accept the new technologies are being left behind. Those who are too dazzled by all of their possibilities and wonder are ultimately distracted.

Frank Sinatra sang on over 1,000 recorded songs, but is credited as a composer on fewer than 10 of them. Have you heard of Motown? What about the Funk Brothers? The Funk Brothers were the in-house session musicians who played on all the classic Motown recordings from 1959–1972. Even if you are not a fan of that era's music, every producer should see the 2002 documentary *Standing in the Shadows of Motown*. It was not that long ago that recorded music was a process accomplished only by a whole team of specialists. First, there was the producer who put the whole team together, including the composers, lyricists, and arrangers—the songwriters. Commonly, studio musicians played the accompaniment. Finally, you had the performers and singers—the ones whose name was on the cover of the album. Additionally, there was the A&R person, a recording engineer, mixing engineer, pre-mastering engineer, mastering engineer, manager, and publicist, to name just the most obvious.

The Accidental Producer

Now it is expected, often unrealistically, for the independent musician/artist to accomplish or plan, and pay, for the whole production—in other words, to play every role and be the whole team. For the moment, let's just consider the writing, recording, and mixing. Most electronic music producers are comfortable wearing all these hats, although they often get assistance in the mixing area. For other independent music producers, whether hip hop or indie rock, writing and recording is often the main goal. Regardless, each of these areas takes years to master, and musicians who want to produce their own music are often thrown right into the deep end of the audio-technology pool. So here you find yourself interested in pursuing a creative-technical profession that demands a high level of DIY—buying all your own tools of the trade, learning how to use them, and learning the industry, all by yourself. It may sound crazy, but it is a common expectation, whether fairly placed or not. There are many reasons for this situation, but the advancement of technology and equally drastic decreases in its cost are at the center of it.

Faster, Smaller, Cheaper...Easier?

In 1979, Tascam released a groundbreaking affordable tape recorder: the Teac Model 144 Portastudio, for about $1,200. Mix Online's TECnology Hall of Fame describes it as "an integrated 4-track cassette recorder with Dolby B noise reduction, 3.75 ips operation and a 4 × 2 mixer with pan, treble and bass on each input." Just 25 years later, in 2004, Apple's top-of-the-line Power Mac G5 2.5 GHz DP retail price was $2,999. That same year, Apple released the iLife '04 software suite, which included GarageBand, iTunes, iMovie, iPhoto, and iDVD. In 2002, Apple had acquired Emagic, makers of Logic Audio. Dr. Gerhard Lengeling, Emagic's founder, directed the development of GarageBand. Upon its release, iLife '04 was included *free* on all new Macs, and for another $49, anyone could purchase it. Counting for inflation, $1,200 in 1979 is equivalent to $3,100 in 2004.

Yes, there have been huge advances in interface design and functional simplification, but it is a mistake to assume that technology is easier to understand or use simply because it is more affordable and accessible than before. As somebody who is a musician, electronic or otherwise, why would you expect to quickly understand how you're supposed to use all the tools you have at your disposal? Nearly every major piece of audio software is standing on the shoulders of a century's worth of history and technology. Just because current smartphones have more computing power than a desktop computer with an Intel Pentium 4 or PowerPC G4 processor, that certainly does not make you think you understand what is inside it any more than the more expensive, larger, older computer.

It is fair to say that somebody just getting into music production might be a little confused and overwhelmed with all the options and information presented by numerous sources of varying reliability. One reason for all this confusion is the separation of the technology from their various trade crafts. Just a few decades ago, if you wanted to learn how to use a recording console, you would have gotten a job or internship in a major recording studio because those audio desks often cost many hundreds of thousands of dollars. A piece of equipment that expensive is not trusted to just anyone, so engineers were brought up in a pseudo-apprenticeship situation. Subjective sonic characteristics aside, you basically have most of the same functionality of the $500,000 consoles in your personal computer. Why should you be expected to know how to use it professionally without significant training just because technology's advance has made it smaller and cheaper?

From Musician to Producer: An Author's Version

The following personal anecdote illustrates dynamics of decisions and outcomes related to career evolution and should be especially eye-opening for those who are just starting down the path. Although a lot has changed since the 1990s, the underlying structural elements are largely the same. Most of the themes are topics worthy of in-depth discussions, which are found spread throughout chapters in this book. For your convenience, they are noted when relevant.

In late 1995, I decided I didn't want to be dependent on other musicians for my creative expression. I was going to create a bedroom studio using some "extra" student loan money. I went to Guitar Center on Mission St. and bought a Tascam Porta07 four-track cassette tape recorder for about $300 (see Figure I.2) and a used Alesis SR-16 drum machine. (I didn't keep either of them for long). I had my Music Man bass, drum machine, tons of Boss and DOD FX pedals, and my all-in-one home stereo as a mixdown deck. This setup was a lot of fun, but I very quickly outgrew its capabilities. I started looking at eight-track recorders but realized that without spending way more money than I had, I would not overcome the limitations causing the creative frustrations.

In 1995, the World Wide Web was only a few years old, and there were not yet many audio forums. Using my state-of-the-art 28.8 Kbps dial-up modem and taking advantage of new free AOL trial offers every 30–60 days (they sent CDs to everyone like junk mail back then), I found a few useful forums. I noticed a lot of discussion (flame wars) about all the advances in digital audio on the Mac. By the summer

Figure I.2 An ad for the Tascam Porta07 in *Guitar World* magazine, 1993.
© Tascam, All Rights Reserved.

of 1996, I sold my Performa 6116 (60 MHz) and 14-inch CRT monitor, upgraded to a used Power Mac 7600 (120 MHz) with a used 17-inch CRT monitor, and decided to get into this fairly new thing called Pro Tools.

Most of my friends either didn't know what I was talking about or thought I was crazy for embracing computer-based audio. One of them had spent a lot of time in recording studios (his previous band was signed to Metal Blade Records), so I asked him to meet me at Guitar Center for the purchase. Skeptical of making a computer the center of my studio, he tried to convince me that I would be better off with the new Roland VS-880 digital multitrack recorder ($2,900). My gut told me that Pro Tools was the future, and that it might even lead to paying work at some point down the road. Fifteen minutes—and $1,500—later, I was the proud owner of Pro Tools v3.4 w/DAE PowerMix and an Audiomedia III PCI card. (For more information on related topics, see Chapter 3, "What Is Your Plan?" and Chapter 8, "Selecting Your Tools.") Looking back, I can say without hesitation that it was the single best career decision I ever made.

> **NOTE:** FYI: Accounting for inflation, $2,900 in 1996 is more than $4,200 in 2012, and $1,500 in 1996 is more than $2,100 in 2012.

Ancient Pro Tools: Pro Tools w/DAE PowerMix was the short-lived native, non-TDM precursor to Pro Tools LE (which appeared with version 5 in 2000). Depending on your CPU speed, you could play back eight tracks of audio using the Audio Media III card in a PCI slot, and had access to a few, very basic, real-time EQs. Or, you could use your built-in sound card and play back 16 tracks with no EQ. AudioSuite plug-ins didn't show up until version 4 in 1997, and RTAS not until version 5. Needless to say, it was extremely limited compared to any DAW of this century. The AM III card had two RCA jacks for analog in, two RCA jacks for analog out, and another RCA pair for S/PDIF digital I/O, and there were no preamps. Also, there were no virtual instruments. Pro Tools could only play back MIDI files at that time, and was not even able to record or edit them until version 5.0. So, I had to sync Cubase to PT via OMS and an IAC bus (more on OMS and IAC in Chapter 6, "Producer Tips"). Even with all those limitations, it was still very good at multi-track audio editing. And honestly, it was a lot of fun. I had plenty of hardware synths, drum machines, and effects boxes to play with, in addition to file-based sound-processing software such as SoundHack and dearly missed pre–MacOS X only apps such as Thonk and SoundMaker (of course with Michael Norris' SoundMagic FX plug-ins). By the way, to play back 16 full tracks of audio, I needed two hard drives. Each external 9 GB SCSI drive (Digidesign qualified) cost more than $1,300 in 1997. Up hill, both ways, in the snow.

One Thing Leads to Another: Positive Chaos

We are all agreed that your theory is crazy. The question which divides us is whether it is crazy enough to have a chance of being correct.

–Niels Bohr

Getting into Pro Tools ahead of the curve was my most important career decision from a trade-craft point of view. Inspired by a tip from a friend, the most consequential decision was the selection of my part-time job during freshmen year at college in 1990. At that job, I established important relationships, which are key to any fulfilling career (and of course life in general). The second-best career decision was adding Ableton Live to my repertoire shortly after moving to Brooklyn in 2002. (The previous paragraph includes key topics from Chapters 3, 4, and 5.)

These three decisions and their combined outcomes beautifully illustrate sensitive dependence on initial conditions, what is commonly known as the *butterfly effect*. Seemingly small changes in the system amplified each other to produce unpredictable results, a system with radically different characteristics. In this case, the different characteristics are appreciated opportunities and positive outcomes, not a tornado in Texas set off by Lorenz's hypothetical butterfly flapping its wings in Brazil. Each opportunity opened the way for subsequent ones, but this deterministic process did not resemble a cascade of falling dominoes or even a Rube Goldberg machine. In hindsight, a visualization of the process more resembles the fractal, branching patterns emphasized in the preface's images. (More on the butterfly effect in Chapter 3 and Appendix A.)

For now, I am omitting stumbles, dead ends, sacrifices, and questionable decisions with variable outcomes, so what follows is a simplified, sanitized, bare-bones yet accurate description of one thing leading to another. Learning Pro Tools helped lead to a job at Harmony Central, which directly led to a job at Rocket Network, which certainly led to a teaching job immediately upon landing in NYC in 2002, which directly led to a better one in 2003 (working for Richard Termini). Also, knowing Live directly led to writing an online article about using ReWire with Live and Pro Tools for the now-defunct *DigiZine* in 2005. This in turn led to authoring Ableton Live tutorial CDs for Thomson Learning's CSi CD-ROM series, and then starting in early 2008 to work as a technical editor for their Course Technology division (mostly Pro Tools– and Ableton Live–related books).

In tandem with developed professional relationships, the previous gigs led to an invitation to the very first Ableton Certification testing event in the summer of 2008, hosted at SAE NYC. I was the only one not sent there on behalf of an existing school, and therefore the only one paying out of their own pocket to get certified—a no-brainer DIY decision. After two days of presentations and tests, I became the first person on the planet to be handed an Ableton Certified Trainer certificate—an honor for which I will be eternally grateful. (The four other attendees were also certified at that inaugural event, as was Laura Escudé shortly thereafter in L.A., who helped design the program for Ableton.)

After the Thomson Corporation and Reuters Group merged in 2008, they spun off Thomson Learning to a new company, Cengage Learning, the publisher of this book. Orren Merton, the acquisition editor who made it possible for this book to happen, was the technical editor on the very first Ableton project I did for Thomson Learning in 2005.

Conclusion: If you like this book, make sure to thank my long-time friend Dave. I am a fan of *non sequiturs*, but the previous statement is not one of them. Although he was living in Bloomington, IN, while attending Indiana University at the time, Dave mentioned that when I moved to Kalamazoo, MI, I should check out this music club that his band had played at while on tour. It was well respected nationally by booking agents for its "new music" Monday nights and all-ages weekend matinees. A few days after moving into the dorms, I went into the club to see if they were hiring. One position had just unexpectedly opened up. I worked there part time as a doorman (ID checker) and occasional bouncer during my freshmen year at Western Michigan University. With such a high-visibility job, I was able to meet and socialize with everyone of significance in the regional music scene and beyond….

Translation: If not for being told about that club before moving there, I likely would not have applied in time to get the job, since there was just one opening at the time and it was a highly desirable job. I would not have come to know many of the people who led to all the things that made it possible for me to write this book, and therefore for you to be reading it wherever and whenever you may be. So be sure to thank Dave if you like *The Music Producer's Survival Guide*.

Companion Website

One more thing: If, after reading this book, you're interested in learning more about the topics presented or accessing a list of the resources cited herein, please visit this book's companion website, located at www.iempsg.com.

Musica Universalis

Let us begin with music itself. Its history could be written from the viewpoint that music consists of a continuous discovery of new harmonies, of novel consonances and harmonic possibilities.

–Joachim-Ernst Berendt

To unify recent insights in physics and in the life sciences into a coherent description of reality, a conceptual shift from structure to rhythm seems to be extremely useful. Rhythmic patterns appear throughout the universe from the very small to the very large.

–Fritjof Capra

In the final analysis, it is a matter of interpretation whether we experience the numerical proportions that are found in so many phenomena of the organic and inorganic world as harmony or as rhythm. Harmony is rhythm is harmony is rhythm.

–Joachim-Ernst Berendt

I AM MAKING ONLY ONE ASSUMPTION ABOUT EVERYONE INTERESTED IN THIS BOOK: You love music. There are many reasons for choosing music and music production as a career, but one of those reasons is that your passion for music is strong enough that it is what you want to do with your life. Even if we do not share taste in any artists, styles, or genres, all of us at least have that one thing in common. This book is about being an independent and/or electronic music producer, but this chapter is largely about music. It is about the significance of music in our lives and culture. It is about the cultural cross-fertilization in the evolution of music and its proliferation of genres and styles as seen through the lens of chaos theory. It is about the rise of indie labels and a brief history of electronic music.

> **NOTE:** The terms DIY, independent, and electronic music are defined in the book's introduction, which also includes a brief summary of the extraordinary consolidation of major labels in recent years. The next chapter defines "producer" and briefly discusses the record industry from its inception to present and the impact of the digital revolution and the Internet on the music industry as a whole.

Music Is Universal

All human cultures and civilizations develop their own particular customs, artifacts, and social systems. When we compare them to each other, the differences add up to a mind-boggling variety and diversity of human creativity and problem solving. Even given the astounding differences between them over long historical arcs, vast geographical separations, and layered socio-economic strata, these differences appear as unique manifestations of universally shared human enterprises. In many ways, what defines each culture is its characteristic manifestation of these domains, including but not limited to language, cuisine, art, social structure and norms, religion and creation myths, spiritual and/or mystical practices, ritualistic/ceremonial mind-altering substances, distilled and/or fermented libations, martial arts, and music. To say that music is the universal language is of course a cliché, but all clichés are true, which is why they are clichés. And although it could be argued that food is also a universal language, music nonetheless has a unique and uncanny ability to successfully communicate across all known cultural barriers like no other cultural creation.

Identifying a significant culture or civilization without its own music and musical instruments, from at least the last 6,000 years, is not an easy task. Some expression, manifestation, or integration of music, song, and/or chant is found in most significant human endeavors. Music is everywhere, from songs of celebration, to the chants in a rain dance or meditative mantra, to pub songs, party anthems, and a romantic candle-lit-dinner-for-two piano music. It is present at weddings, bar mitzvahs, funerals, and protest marches. It is heard as the beat of war drums and in the traditional music performed during the Wai Khru Ram Muay ceremony as Muay Thai fighters enter the ring. Music is central to collective experiences at concerts, modern music festivals, and "raves." Music is ubiquitous.

Music Is Diverse

Music can express any emotion. It can capture any mood or state of mind. Music can be affectionate, aggressive, angry, annoying, banal, bombastic, calming, depressing, devotional, disgusting, eccentric, egotistical, elevating, energetic, entertaining, ethereal, evocative, fantastical, flippant, fun, grounding, hateful, humorous, incomprehensible, inspiring, institutional, insulting, ironic, irreverent, jittery, kinky, lethargic, malicious, manipulative, motivating, mysterious, nihilistic, painful, ominous, outlandish, profane, provocative, psychedelic, quirky, rebellious, revolutionary, sacred, sensual, serious, somber, soothing, strange, surprising, transcendent, transformational, uplifting, vibrant, whimsical, weird, xenophobic, zany…the list goes on. Artists create music that reflects their experiences and those of the surrounding culture. People gravitate toward music they relate to or that connects to them in some way.

Given that music is so diverse and pervasive, it is not surprising that whole cultures and communities develop around specific styles of music. This is particularly obvious when we look at the subcultures that developed in the latter half of the 20th century, such as punk and hard core, B-boy, industrial, goth, indie rock, metal, rave, and various other electronic music scenes. Although it is hard to imagine now, there was a time not that long ago when every one of these scenes was almost totally isolated from the others. Rockers didn't go to techno parties or vice versa. Punks and metal heads acted like the Hatfields and McCoys. Goth and industrial made a perfect pair, and although they occasionally hung around some of the more arty punks and metal heads, they literally occupied different cultural universes from B-boy scenes. House and garage were primarily urban, black, and gay, while indie rock was primarily suburban, white, and straight. Although most of the scenes that birthed these styles still occupy recognizably similar cultural niches, the social boundaries between them are significantly more porous, and any boundaries pertaining to the cross-fertilization of musical influences, ideas, and aesthetics are non-existent.

Music Is Technological

Music's fundamental status in culture is illustrated by how quickly new technologies are applied to it. Many musicologists argue that musical instruments became commonplace for the first time right after we learned how to make hunting tools, and therefore not only had new craft knowledge but also regular exposure to naturally resonant animal parts such as ram's horns. Yet, we have evidence of rudimentary tools from millions of years ago and our oldest physical evidence of a musical instrument is from about 42,000 years ago. Fast forward to 1874, when, while working on inventing the telephone, Elisha Gray demonstrated the Musical Telegraph, the very first synthesizer. While working at Bell Labs, Max Matthews applied computers to music recording and synthesis in 1957, 20 years before the Apple II.

Apple and other significant entrepreneurs and hackers emerged out of the Homebrew Computer Club in Silicon Valley. The release of the MITS Altair 8800 spurned the creation of this club, and although it was almost useless and had no operating system, the fact that an individual could have a computer at home in 1975 was the stuff of nerd legend. About a month after the founding of the club, no one had yet figured out what to do with the Altair. Then, Steve Dompier demonstrated a lengthy switching program that modulated AM radio interference, which produced a cover version of the Beatles' *Fool On The Hill*. Shortly thereafter, inspired by this musical hack, other members got the idea to create add-on boards for the Altair, and the personal computer industry was born. Shortly after microprocessors became commercially available in the early 1970s, it only took a few years before they found themselves in digital music systems and synthesizers. The MIDI spec was published in 1983, and by 1984–1985 Steinberg, MOTU, and Opcode had released commercially available music software for home computers. Within months of the iPad's April 2010 release, developers offered audio and music production software. That same month, Propellerhead re-released ReBirth-338—its flagship title circa 1997 and discontinued since 2005—for iPhone and then quickly updated for the hottest gadget around.

Music Is Personal

The combination of artists and styles one most enjoys says a lot about a person. Our individualized palate of musical tastes can influence what people think about us, and what we think about who we are. Many cultural signifiers are attached to music, which are interpreted to imply everything from social scenes, to political views, to attitudes toward authority, and even intelligence or education. Moreover, the music in someone's personal collection often represents memories, feelings, and experiences from specific times and places in one's life. Although these collections are often organized with playlists on an iPod or the like, in the past personal attachments extended to the actual "record," with its full-color cover art and pages of liner notes, whether vinyl album, cassette tape, or CD.

A million people listening the same song are part of a shared experience, but there can be millions of interpretations. Some songs carry an extra special personal meaning to many because of life experiences associated with that song. Like sports, politics, or religion, people get emotionally involved with their music. It is no coincidence that The Beatles' emphasis on personalized lyrics, not yet common to upbeat music, helped them set the standard for huge frenzied international followings—what was known as "Beatlemania." With titles like "Love Me Do," "Please Please Me," "From Me to You," and "I Want To Hold Your Hand," it is no wonder that fans felt like John and Paul were singing right to them. They had a personal connection, even while surrounded by other crazed, crying, screaming, and even fainting fans in the crowd. These crowds were unprecedentedly loud—to such an extreme that The Beatles could not hear themselves on stage. This famously caused them to mistakenly play two different songs at the same time, a gaffe that went unnoticed until the band figured it out backstage after the show. Those were simpler times, but even today, commercial pop songs still load up on personal pronouns in the hope of selling more records. How many songs combine "you," "me," "us," "I," "we," and "baby," with some mix of "all night," "tonight," and/or "love"? Such examples from the dawn of the modern pop era to today clearly show that music is very personal.

Why is it that consumer music products are commonly marketed with slogans containing the words "your music"? Generally speaking, the music in question was made by someone else, and many millions of others might have the same song. So why "your music"? Why did "I Want To Hold Your Hand" set off the British Invasion of the 1960s? As painfully contrived as this common approach to consumer marketing may be, the fact remains that music is very personal, and marketers understand the deep and powerful emotional relationship we have with the music we enjoy. We don't like it when others mess with our music. If it is dissed, exploited, or commoditized in a way that cheapens or lessens our experience, we feel personally insulted or disrespected to an extent that does not occur in relation to other products, such as cars, home appliances, or clothing. When profit motives influence those products, how they are designed, marketed, and sold will bother some people, but not in the same way as when it influences their music. Certain artists who give into such commercialization (or are perceived to have done so) are referred to with some version of the pejorative phrase "sell out"—as in, "They sold out," "What a sell out," "They were great before they sold out," or "Why did they have to go and sell out?" This gets at why numerous communities have issues with big labels—or more precisely, with what often happens to certain types of artists after they mistakenly sign with one of them. (Chapter 2, "Plot Point on the Space-Time Continuum," talks more about the pros and cons of the major label sector of the music industry.)

Music Is Vital

Without music, life would be a mistake.

–Friedrich Nietzsche

Without music to decorate it, time is just a bunch of boring production deadlines or dates by which bills must be paid.

–Frank Zappa

Music is a moral law. It gives soul to the universe, wings to the mind, flight to the imagination, and charm and gaiety to life and to everything.

–Plato

I do not think that is an overstatement to say that music literally saves lives. Many individuals over the years have credited music with giving them a sense of hope and direction when life seemed pointless or meaningless. Music was their antidote to the variety of negative experiences, feelings, and thoughts so fully described and elucidated by the existentialists and absurdists.

The serious issues in existential philosophy regularly found themselves repurposed in the brilliant comedy of Monty Python. There is no better example of existentialist humor than their 1983 sketch comedy musical movie *The Meaning of Life*. The movie's theme song is heard during the closing credits, but is first performed about halfway through the film by troupe member Eric Idle. To console Mrs. Brown after witnessing her husband's gory death by premature organ donation due to a bureaucratic mix up, he leaps out of a closet and leads into the very whimsical, vaudeville-esque song. A brief prelude is directed at Mrs. Brown, as he lets her know that when life is hard or people are bothersome, and she's had enough of it all, to remember that she is on an evolving planet.

The first verse of this song, called "The Galaxy Song," is a lengthy astronomical description of the Earth's location in our enormous galaxy and universe, with the second verse of the song telling us how the universe is continually expanding at the speed of light in all directions, the fastest speed possible, before reminding Mrs. Brown that her unlikely birth is no less amazing regardless of how insecure or small she feels. The song then concludes with a punch line about intelligent life in space but not on Earth. Though intended to cheer up the newly widowed character by pointing out to her that it is amazing she is here in the first place, to make that point he first must explain how tiny we are in a vast expanding universe. Monty Python's comedic genius is on display here as they make existential despair funny. It is almost impossible to appreciate how they do this if you've never seen the movie, so do yourself a favor and watch it sometime, or at least find "The Galaxy Song" scene on the MontyPython YouTube channel.

Feeling small and feeling insignificant are classic existential maladies, ones that can be cured by comedy and music. Countless alienated, angst-ridden teens and young adults have stated that music was a positive influence that helped through rough patches by giving them hope and allowing them to feel like they were part of something bigger than themselves. Beyond the powerful emotional impact of the music itself, there is also a connection to the artists and music scenes full of others with similar dispositions and experiences, which creates a shared sense of cultural identity. This dynamic is especially noticeable when considering the various subcultures that once defined the "underground," such as goth, punk, industrial, metal, techno, house, rave, and B-boy, which are now the foundations of many current-era styles.

Personally speaking, deep involvement in underground music culture starting in my late teens was incredibly formative and for the most part full of positive experiences. An intense passion for music that was commonly frowned upon definitely helped me to get through very rough, rebellious, angry high-school years. In the mid to late 1980s, punk, metal, industrial, and what was then called "hard core" rap offered powerful distractions from the homogenous, conformist, superficial, and otherwise dull high-school years common to American suburbs like those north of Detroit. Additionally, a lot of this music was the target of national-level censorship campaigns by various religious fundamentalists or secular "concerned parent" groups like the PMRC—the latter of which instigated the now-legendary Congressional hearings that, in 1985, resulted in the RIAA giving in to pressure to place "Parental Advisory" stickers on all records with "offensive" content. Because music is so personal, especially to those who already feel like they must operate outside of the mainstream, these perceived attacks galvanized music communities and made involvement in such scenes that much more meaningful and motivating.

Music has this powerful positive effect on all kinds of people, not just angst-ridden teens and other fans of intense, aggressive, angry music. In 1982, Indeep released the post-disco-funk-pop-new-wave-R&B club hit "Last Night a DJ Saved My Life," which inspired the 1999 book *Last Night a DJ Saved My Life: The History of the Disk Jockey* by Bill Brewster and Frank Broughton. Not only a history, this book also discusses the reverence that club and festival goers have for A-list DJs. This reverence stems from their consistent ability to create transcendent, life-altering experiences for those in the room or crowd. The meaning-giving power of music is potentially that much more powerful for artists, musicians, and producers because they are not only fans and listeners, but also creators. As producers, we can experience additional levels of connection to music not only during the creative process, but also as fans give back energy, either in the crowd or through other common fan/artist interactions.

"Music Saved My Life": Three great examples of highly successful musicians on the record for how music saves lives are Mike Borden, Mary J. Blige, and Cee Lo Green.

> ▶ In the August 2007 issue of *DRUM!* is an interview with drummer Mike Borden, co-founder of Faith No More, about joining Ozzy Osbourne's band. He tells us, "It's no joke that Black Sabbath saved my life. I always dreamed of meeting Ozzy and telling him that."
> ▶ In an October 2, 2010 NYDailyNews.com interview with nine-time Grammy winner Mary J. Blige, she is quoted as saying, "Music makes us want to live. You don't know how many times people have told me that they'd been down and depressed and just wanted to die. But then a special song caught their ear and that helped give them renewed strength. That's the power music has."
> ▶ Before singer/producer Cee Lo Green co-founded Goodie Mob in the early 1990s, before he partnered with Danger Mouse to form Gnarls Barkley in the early 2000s, he was another teenage troublemaker heading down a bad path. In a July 14, 2011 article on Metrolyrics.com, Green is quoted as saying, "I was angry about being an outcast. I would have liked to fit in and have tons of friends, but I didn't. So I'd cut school, drink beer and end up making examples of people. After a while I became so comfortably numb with violence I felt that my only purpose in life was to be a rudeboy. So really, music saved my life. I have always said that if I wasn't famous, I would be infamous."

There is no need to look up quotes by famous musicians. Just do a simple Web search on the topic. You might run across the posts from about 300 users who joined the group on experienceproject.com, "I Know Music Has Saved My Life." You might also find dozens of positive responses to "How Downloading Music Has Literally Saved My Life," an article posted to pitchforkreviewsreviews.com by a once morbidly obese teen. It is not a rare statement.

Music Is Fundamental

Of all the art forms, music more than any of the others is found in mixed forms that cater to multiple senses—for example in theatre, film, TV, dance, and even fireworks displays. There is something about music and sound that connects to us on all levels, from the primal and instinctual to the most sophisticated and evolved. Not only can we perceive sounds that are out of view, but we can also perceive the source's direction and distance from us. This ability is refined to mimic echolocation as used by other animals, such as bats and dolphins. This cultivated skill is best exemplified by Daniel Kish, founder of World Access for the Blind, an organization that teaches blind people how to use echolocation to navigate the world without the usual cane. Kish himself is completely blind, yet he gets around by himself completely unassisted, including riding mountain bikes, because of his developed echolocation skills.

Not only can hearing at times fill in for vision, but we also "feel" music and sound—not just emotionally but literally, through physical and kinesthetic sensations. This latter point helps explain why there are so many hearing-impaired individuals who still appreciate music. Famously, Ludwig van Beethoven continued to compose even after he lost his hearing, but it goes much further than that one anecdote. It is now common for big music festivals to have people doing sign language in front of the stage and projected onto the big screens. These "signers" allow the hearing impaired who are feeling the music to also perceive the lyrics. For a brilliant and entertaining example of a signer at a recent music festival, do a Web search for a video of ASL signer Holly, 2013 Bonnaroo Festival, Wu Tang Clan. Beyond genius composers and concert goers, how about a deaf professional DJ? Just look up Robbie Wilde, "That Deaf DJ," online; there are a number of good interviews and mini documentaries floating around. You might also check out the 2004 documentary *Touch the Sound*, "which explores the connections among sound, rhythm, time, and the body by following percussionist Evelyn Glennie, who is nearly deaf (IMDb.com)." Given such diverse examples of the hearing-impaired involved in music, there must be something more to it than just audible sound.

Nature Is Musical

Many characteristics of music share patterns, relationships, and structures with the physical world around us. In addition, musical idioms pervade our language. ("It is time to face the music." "Let's play it by ear." "Does that ring a bell?" "Your story rings hollow.") Even more significantly, many musical terms are found in our language. When describing elements or structure in the composition of visual art, it is common to talk about their rhythm or harmony. Interpersonal relationships have rhythms; they can be harmonious or full of tension. The slang term "vibe" is short for vibrate or vibration. ("We just don't vibe," "I vibed to that song," "That place gave me weird vibes," or "That club has a nice vibe.") It goes much further than colloquial language. All the quotes at the top of this chapter are from Joachim-Ernst Berendt's 1991 book *The World Is Sound: Nada Brahma: Music and the Landscape of Consciousness*. A successful European jazz producer, Joachim-Ernst Berendt (1922–2000) had more than 200 album credits, including with legends like Don Cherry and Eric Dolphy. In the book, Berendt covers some of the material we are about to go over, but there is a lot more that is worthy of your attention. It's just too much of a tangent to cover here, so check it out if you are interested in the subject matter that follows.

Music is sound, and sound is vibrations that correspond to pitches and timbres. In audio, we talk about a sound wave's periodicity as cycles per second (cps) and use hertz (Hz) as our unit of measurement. The higher the frequency, the shorter the wavelength, and vice versa. The timbre of a sound is largely determined by the sum of its partials, each of which is essentially a sine wave with an amplitude and hertz measurement. Musical pitches are largely determined by the fundamental frequency, the lowest frequency partial. And just as the notes in a chord determine whether it is harmonious (consonant) or disharmonious (dissonant), the combination of partials determines whether any given timbre produces an identifiable note or an atonal sound. Analysis of the natural world reveals that such relationships are found everywhere and understood as combinations of mathematical ratios.

Music Is Mathematical

The golden ratio and its fraternal twin, the Fibonacci series, appear in patterns at all scales of the physical world, recognizably in spiral shapes ranging from pine cones to galaxies. For thousands of years, composers and architects have used these ratios to structure the harmonies and proportions in their compositions and designs. In 1995, HarperPerennial published *A Beginner's Guide to Constructing the Universe: Mathematical Archetypes of Nature, Art, and Science* by math professor Michael S. Schneider. In 2007, Schneider posted an article to his website, www.constructingtheuniverse.com, entitled "The Amen Break and the Golden Ratio." The six-second long drum solo from The Winston's 1969 song "Amen, Brother" is the most sampled drum break of all time, and is known as "The Amen Break." To figure out why that sample is so popular, Schneider analyzed its structure mathematically and discovered relationships with major similarities to the golden ratio (1.61803398875). He summarized these findings as follows:

> *The major wave peaks of the Amen Break, and many of its smaller ones, seem reasonably close to being an expression of the fractal nature of the wonderful Golden Ratio. Maybe it's just an apparent coincidence or maybe it's like thousands other approximations of the Golden Ratio that are not consciously planned but do appear in human designs....*

The direct connection between music, math, and nature dates back at least to Pythagoras circa 500 BCE, who was one of the many great minds to ponder the Golden Ratio. This great interest in proportion and ratio led Pythagoras to historical experiments with a very simple instrument, the monochord. The monochord had one metal string attached to a hollow resonating piece of wood with a moveable bridge that was used to change the pitch. He figured out that the intervals—the relationships between notes—had precise ratios. For example, a perfect octave is a 2:1 ratio and a perfect fifth is a 3:2 ratio (see Figure 1.1). So if the string's 1:1 ratio was the note A, with the modern 440 Hz tuning, by moving the bridge exactly to the middle, we get 880 Hz, a 2:1 ratio or octave, which is the most consonant interval there is. If we move the bridge to create a ratio of 16:15, we get a minor 2nd, which is a very dissonant interval. Consonance and dissonance, or harmony and disharmony, are largely explained by the character of their ratio. Pythagoras then applied these insights to astronomy and cosmology to explain the movement of the planets. Believing they followed similar harmonic ratios, he coined the phrase "harmony of the spheres." Fast forward 2,500 years, and string theory (also known as M-theory), which is at the forefront of theoretical physics, posits that the fundamental particles comprising atoms are actually like incredibly tiny one-dimensional vibrating strings. Just as different notes are created by different vibration patterns on the same string, so too are the different subatomic particles, according to string theory.

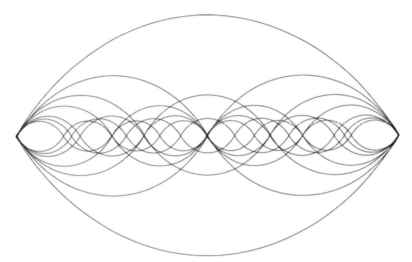

Figure 1.1 Ratios in the harmonic series. This image shows 1:1, 2:1, 3:1, 4:1, 5:1, 6:1, and 7:1. For example, the 5:1 wave also includes the 3:2 ratio (perfect fifth).

Let's travel back to about 150 years after Pythagoras. As Socrates' star pupil, Plato is certainly one of the most important philosophers of the ancient Greek era, the foundation of classical Western thought. He is also well-known for identifying five unique geometrical shapes, known as the Platonic solids. If you think that the shapes found in role-playing dice with four, six, eight, 12, or 20 sides are a product of the early 1970s, think again. Plato singled out those five polyhedrons from all the others for their unique mathematical properties. The Platonic solids form the foundation of classical geometry to this day.

Yet, by the early 20th century, geometry was actually frowned upon by many mathematicians. In *Chaos,* James Gleick describes this state of mind among the elite mathematicians behind Bourbaki, a secret society of mathematicians that formed in 1935, when he tells us that "above all, Bourbaki rejected the use of pictures.... Geometry was untrustworthy. Mathematics should be pure, formal, and austere." This attitude largely faded away over the last 50 years, not only because of the discovery of fractal geometry by Mandelbrot (who fled to the U.S. because of Bourbaki), but also because of other advances in chemistry pertaining to atomic and molecular structures. We've regained an appreciation for the shapes that seemed relegated to dungeon masters. We now know that the Platonic solids are the most efficient geometric shapes in nature. For example, near-perfect hexagonal shapes are found in honeycombs, the once-mysterious rock formations in Ireland, the Giant's Causeway (featured on the cover of Led Zeppelin's 1973 *Houses of The Holy*), and the 15,000 mile wide hurricane at Saturn's north pole. The intersections of soap bubbles display all of these shapes, depending on the number of bubbles, and salt crystals are known to grow in perfectly cubic crystals. Other than Saturn's storm, all of the above examples are well documented in part 2 of the three-part BBC Two documentary series from 2011, *The Code: Shapes.* Why do we care about Platonic solids when discussing music?

Almost 1,800 years after Plato, Johannes Kepler used the Platonic solids as the mathematical basis for his *Mysterium Cosmographicum* (1596), which showed how all of the planets could form orbits around the sun (see Figure 1.2), a radical idea proposed just a few decades earlier by Nicolaus Copernicus. Kepler's "music of the spheres" used the harmonic ratios discovered by Pythagoras and his "harmony of the spheres" to figure out the mathematics underlying the planets' distance from the sun and their orbital periods, which became Kepler's Third Law of Planetary Motion. He noted that all the orbits fell within a certain harmonic range except the interval between Mars and

Jupiter, which was the most dissonant of them all. Incredibly, it was not until a few decades later that we had empirical evidence to prove that the sun, not the Earth, was the center of the known universe. Moreover, the asteroid belt orbiting between Mars and Jupiter was not discovered until 1801, about 182 years later, and is believed to be the remnants of a failed planetary formation process. So the basic math of harmony and musical ratio spelled out by Pythagoras, with the geometry of Plato, allowed Kepler without a telescope to make incredibly good predictions about planetary orbits, and also to partially explain the asteroid belt between Mars and Jupiter. It is almost as if Kepler were able to analyze a hidden chord in a silent scale. Harmonic relationships are so fundamental to our universe that Kepler's theories, though now mostly obsolete, paved the way for where we are now. (Indeed, NASA's mission to find habitable planets in our galaxy is named after Kepler.) As to exactly where that is, and when, we get to those questions in the next chapter as we discuss the digital revolution and its implications for us as music producers in this new era.

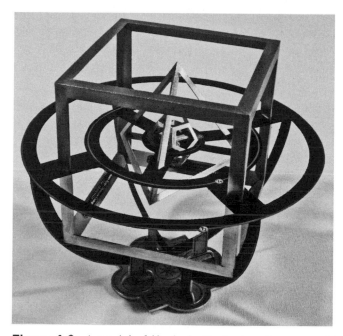

Figure 1.2 A model of Kepler's *Mysterium Cosmographicum*. In 1596, it was the best model of the solar system, based on Pythagorean harmony and the Platonic solids.

Music Is Evolving

Now that we have a baseline understanding of music's central and important status in human culture, let's dig a bit deeper and focus on how styles and genres evolve. Although our focus is indie and electronic music, the core ideas are best illustrated when considering all music.

Music as a fundamental human form of expression mirrors the time and culture of artists. So, when considering the evolution of modern music styles in the last 125 years, we need to emphasize two variables characteristic of this time period: the simultaneous influences of modern technology and cultural cross-fertilization. Keep in mind that I am just touching on ideas that could easily be the focus of a few musicology graduate degrees.

Trying to make sense out of all the different forms of music through sorting and categorization is a chaotic affair. If you agree that music is universal, personal, and fundamental, then the following statement should sound reasonable: The exploration of new possibilities, expressions, and combinations of musical ideas is a natural incessant process. In other words, if we think of music as a continuous flow of water running over a creek bed, then just like water, it will flow into any hole, nook, crevice, and channel not already occupied. If we start with this idea, then making sense of how music evolves and how new styles are born becomes a lot easier. To further help in this endeavor, I am employing some of the basic concepts underlying chaos theory and complexity studies.

Music's Evolution Is Chaotic

I am going to try to keep things as simple as possible when talking about complexity, so if you are interested in more details, be sure to check out Appendix A, "Chaos Theory and Complexity Studies Primer." For present purposes, we are interested in three related topics that are used to both explain and model many aspects of natural and synthetic systems. Each of these is based on very simple non-linear equations that iterate (repeat), with one of them additionally being recursive (feedback): bifurcation theory, L-systems, and fractal geometry.

It should not be surprising that one of the first people in the modern era to write about creative processes was also arguably the first chaos theorist: polymath Henri Poincaré. We will return to his thoughts on chance, the unconscious, and creativity in Chapter 7, "Creative Process." Of immediate relevance is the term bifurcation, which he coined in the 1880s from *bi* (meaning "two") and *furcation* (meaning "dividing into branches"). The top image in Figure 1.3 is an example of a bifurcation diagram—in this case, one that plots period-doubling bifurcation. What starts as one branch becomes two branches, then four, then eight, then 16, so on and so forth, with the rate of bifurcation also doubling at each split. Even with such simple math, complex and chaotic behavior quickly arises due to the non-linearity of the equation.

Figure 1.3 This image shows a bifurcation diagram (top) and the fractal Mandelbrot set (bottom). They are great visual metaphors when considering the evolution of musical genres.
Source: Georg-Johann Lay. Public Domain.

Fast forward to 1968, when Hungarian biologist Aristid Lindenmayer created a formalized algorithmic language to model the growth of plants known as L-systems. As you can see in Figure 1.4, both of the computer-generated plant-like structures are simply iterations of the same shapes. In Figure 1.5, you can see how this process is like a computer-generated imagery version of sound going through a delay effect. The top spectrograph shows just a single tone at ¼-note intervals, with each spike representing the sound's partials. The bottom spectrogram shows the same tone run through a multi-tap delay effect. Delay effects also use linear feedback to evolve the sonic structure, but over very short durations of time—in this case, iZotope's Insight plug-in is set to have a history time of 15 seconds (from right to left). Different furcation maps are like various tempos and rhythms of simple branching algorithms growing through space. L-systems are the same except they include more variables, which makes them well-suited to their role as a basic foundation of modern computer-generated nature imagery. In the real world, shapes grow with similar geometry but with much, much, much slower tempo stretched out over days, years, or even decades.

Figure 1.4 Two different L-systems generated with relatively simple math, outlining the basic structure of an algae (left) and a leaf (right).

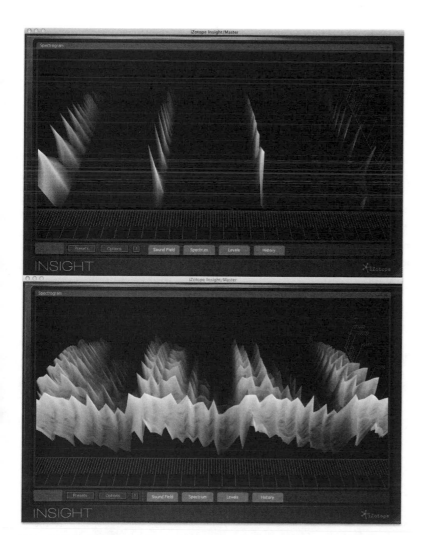

Figure 1.5 The top spectrogram is a simple tone. The bottom spectrogram is the same tone run through a delay plug-in. The feedback creates self-similar patterns.

Source: iZotope Insight.

As amazing and complex as are the results of bifurcation and L-systems, they pale in comparison to the undisputed king of chaos geometry. At the bottom of Figure 1.3, you can see the characteristic shape of the Mandelbrot set, the most complex mathematical object known to humanity. When rendered on a computer, you can "travel" through its endless vistas by zooming in forever because its non-linear equation is also iterative. The output feeds back into the input on an infinite loop until stopped by the programmer. That means if you attempt to perfectly trace its outline you will never finish unless you arbitrarily decide to stop iterating/zooming in and ignore further details. This is much like our attempts at categorizing music into genres, with some of them being more or less concerned with precision and therefore more or less zooming in to make out the detailed edges. In essence, we are talking about what is known as the "the coastline paradox," which was finally solved by the creator of the Mandelbrot set.

Mandelbrot: Mandelbrot shared his discoveries in a 1982 book, *The Fractal Geometry of Nature*. Although full of math, it was targeted at popular audiences, not just academics. If you have seen any Pixar movie (or any other major digital animated movie in the last few decades) and marveled at how realistic it might seem, you can thank Benoît Mandelbrot. His book gave those animators new algorithms to try, and it revolutionized computerized graphics.

Mandelbrot was a genius, maverick mathematician who started working at IBM in 1958. There, he had access to mainframe computers, which he used to solve various problems such as getting rid of the noise that was present in the transmission of computer data over phone lines. His research into solving such problems resulted in a discovery of a revolutionary new mathematics that greatly expanded our understanding of the natural world.

Although he introduced the term *fractal* to the public in 1975, the ideas were spelled out almost a decade earlier in his landmark article on the topic from the May, 1967 edition of *Science* magazine, "How Long Is the Coast of Britain? Statistical Self-Similarity and Fractional Dimension." The abstract to this article was as follows:

"Geographical curves are so involved in their detail that their lengths are often infinite or, rather, indefinable. However, many are statistically 'self similar,' meaning that each portion can be considered a reduced-scale image of the whole. In that case, the degree of complication can be described by a quantity D that has many properties of a 'dimension,' though it is fractional; that is, it exceeds the value unity associated with the ordinary, rectifiable, curves."

There are two amazing insights here: Objects in nature often have fractional dimensions, and self-similarity is everywhere. In plain English, most shapes in nature do not have integral (whole number) dimensions, such as two or three. Rather, they have fractional dimensionality and therefore surfaces that are difficult to measure with standard math. Mandelbrot's discovery of fractals fully explains "the coastline paradox," also known as "the Richardson effect." Although it seems counterintuitive at first, the fact remains that the measured length of natural features goes up as the unit of measurement gets smaller. If you measure the coast of England with a 200km or a 100km ruler, the measurement using the 100km ruler will be longer. Such infinite or indefinable curves also display self-similarity, which means that as you zoom in, you see similar patterns as when you are zoomed out. They repeatedly show up at different scales. So relatively speaking, if it looks like the same pattern but the zoom level if different, it is only natural to use a measuring standard according to the scale.

What happens if we define musical genres according to small differences between them because we are zoomed in and hyperaware of every little variation? We end up with more genres than if using the comparatively larger differences perceived when we are zoomed out. The level of zoom changes according to the desired level of precision when making distinctions. Does this not explain why there are so many micro genres of electronic music that seem indistinguishable from each other to the uninitiated? Does this not explain why all metal or punk bands sound the same as each other to the uninitiated? But, once people "get into it," they start to notice the differences, which over time become clear as day and seem totally obvious.

Basic Dynamics of Genre Evolution

Each genre has defining characteristics—how it combines any of the following elements to give it its personality: instrumentation, rhythms, harmonic structures, tempo, meter, lyrical content, and other cultural references. We can think of these traits as different genes found in DNA. In the most simplistic sense, modern Western music is largely a result of the mixing of musical DNA of African rhythm and

European harmonic structures. Of course, there are many other elements commonly at play in modern music that integrate melody, harmony, rhythm, and timbre from Asia, Oceania, Africa, the Middle East, the Caribbean, Central America, and South America. However, our focus is electronic music and modern independent music, so we are not going to get lost in a full musicology exploration.

Let's use two metaphors to help us make sense out of the proliferation of musical genres and styles. The first metaphor is evolution itself. Musical styles are like species that fill a niche, which is appreciation by a group or groups of people. Like evolution, music tries out as many combinations as possible through random mutation, and the ones that have the best traits for survival (appreciation) continue to pass on their DNA. (We return to the misunderstood notion of "random" in Chapter 7.) This constant experimentation occurs naturally for many reasons—not simply the desire for commercial success or widespread appeal, as an evolutionary metaphor might imply—and can be motivated by personal exploration or for small scenes or peer groups. Some musical genres are more dominant than others, some are antagonistic and compete over the same niches, while others are symbiotic and support each other. Most species have recognizable characteristics within their phylogenic family, though there are many cases of rare, bizarre, unique, or downright alien-looking life forms, such as the barreleye fish or, to a lesser extent, the platypus. In similar regards, most music is easily placeable within a family of similar traits by average music fans but some of it is *sui generis*, such as The Residents or to a lesser extent U.S. Maple.

The tree of life is a metaphor used in evolutionary biology to categorize and map related life forms with branching lines. Our second metaphor, then, is that of a tree, its branches, leaves, and connecting nodes. Branching shapes are the most efficient way for trees to maximize surface contact to sun, air, and water, their life-giving sources of nutrition. Some do this by growing bigger, thicker trunks with a few substantial branches and large leaves (fewer subgenres), while others cover equal area with many more smaller bifurcations and countless smaller leaves or needles (many sub or micro genres). The bifurcation diagram in Figure 1.3 shows how quickly simple binary splitting results in an incredibly complex structure, while the L-systems in Figure 1.4 show more tree-like geometry (although both of them are a bit too static to really capture what is happening). Things get more interesting if we represent these dynamics with the Mandelbrot set as seen at the bottom of Figure 1.3. This shape in our metaphor could represent budding instead of simple branching, which is that much more powerful when viewed as a dynamically evolving computer animation (as is easy to find online or in free software for your computer). In either case, let's place all these genres in a dense, vibrant jungle that is teeming with life, with each tree representing a major style of music, such as classical, blues, rock, funk, soul, jazz, reggae, *avant-garde*, or electronic. Each music form that is the base of a tree is also a root style, one that has spawned variations and new genres. Let's consider a few simplified examples:

▷ Blues spawned a few styles, including rock 'n' roll, which then spawned numerous subgenres, such as progressive rock, punk rock, Krautrock, post rock, math rock, and of course, eventually, the neologism of classic rock.
▷ Rock 'n' roll also spawned hard rock, which retained key elements of blues and mutated into heavy metal, that then spawned numerous subgenres such as progressive metal, thrash metal, speed metal, technical metal, black metal, death metal, and industrial metal.
▷ Disco mutated into house (Chicago) and garage (NYC), which then spawned numerous subgenres such as acid house, tech house, micro house, progressive house, Dutch house, French house, fidget house, U.K. garage, speed garage, two-step garage, U.K. funky, and countless others.
▷ Detroit techno emerged on the tail of house as a futuristic mixture of electro, funk, and new wave, which then spawned numerous subgenres, such as minimal techno, acid techno, ambient techno, and dub techno.
▷ Coming out of NYC on the tail of electro funk, rap, and B-boy culture was hip hop, which spawned numerous subgenres such as West Coast, Dirty South, G-funk, gangsta, abstract, turntablism, trip hop, and trap.

Each of these genres and subgenres forms the raw materials not only for countless micro genres but also whole new styles. As one of them catches on and blows up, what was once a small leaf can more resemble an acorn that grows its own roots and marks a new beginning in the iteration process. Sometimes this process is initiated by a specific artist or small scene of musicians who cut out recent complexifications in a genre and return to the fundamentals. This revisit to a style's essential musical elements is usually referred as "going back to the roots." Sometimes this return to musical origins is simply an enjoyable retro pursuit, but other times whole new branches emerge from it. These roots can be fairly close, such as when a current dance music producer finds inspiration from the first acid tracks such as those of Phuture 303. An exploration of the roots might also imply a much deeper journey and even include a "pilgrimage" to Jamaica, Haiti, Cuba, or Africa to meet native musicians steeped in the origins of our modern rhythms and other seminal stylistic innovations.

As musical styles diverge and converge to and from their parent branches and cross-fertilize with other branches, a few things tend to happen. As they diverge, they tend to get more extreme, complex, refined, or idiosyncratic, as is best illustrated in the many micro and niche genres found in electronic music and metal. As they converge, they tend to simplify and include more classic motifs. Sometimes traits skip a generation, while other times the energy and foci simply shift to accentuate other musical elements, such as transferring emphasis from drums to bass or exploring significantly slower of faster tempos. In either case, regardless of their current vector, once ideas have played themselves out, they either shrink down to small core followings, cross-breed with new growths closer to the roots and find new life, represent a dead end, or even go extinct, waiting to be dug up in a dusty record bin. Some styles and genres slow down their evolution to no more than small incremental changes and stabilize to become traditionals, standards, "folk" music, or a perennial favorite for long periods of time. Regardless of the evolutionary vector, there are now so many styles of electronic music that even *Ishkur's Guide to Electronic Music v2.5* leaves off at the end of the 1990s, as can be seen in Figure 1.6. *Ishkur's Guide* is the most ambitious project of its kind to be found on the Internet and is regularly cited on blogs about data visualization. There is no notable close second to be found, and although it is not perfect or 100% accurate in all cases, it is very fun, entertaining, and educational.

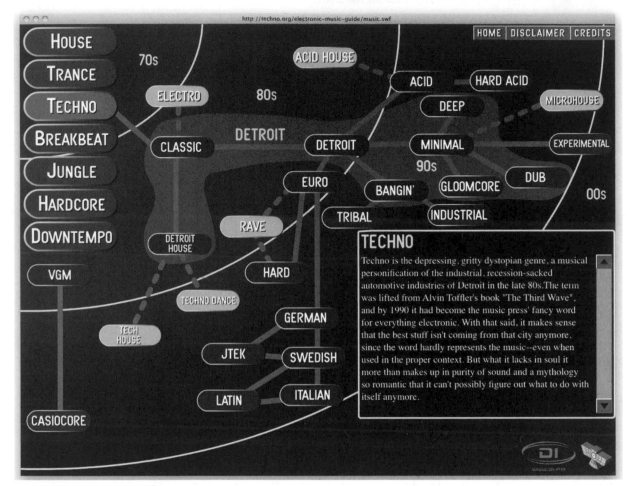

Figure 1.6 The Techno page from *Ishkur's Guide to Electronic Music v2.5* (techno.org/electronic-music-guide), an ambitious interactive multimedia taxonomy.
Source: techno.org.

Baker's Transformation

Can you hear James Brown's influence in the psychedelic trance genre? The answer surely is no—unless you are overdoing the psychedelic part, as it is no more apparent than the influence of Ada Byron on the computer I'm using to write this book. Yet that genre, at the opposite end of the musical spectrum from funk, has core elements that evolved out of house and techno, which have roots in electro funk, electro, and Kraftwerk, all influenced by James Brown. This isn't a game like "Six Degrees of Kevin Bacon"; it is more like researching a family tree. Although it is possible to trace many of a current artist's direct influences or some key elements that make up a current genre, at some point the elements of the older styles are so mixed up that it is impossible to tease them apart.

This mixing of styles is not unlike the experience of any kid who plays with finger paint until the whole sheet of paper is covered in that certain shade of green/brown, or at its best, like the delectable creations of a master pastry chef with no resemblance to the original separate ingredients. In physics, there are numerous mathematical tools that describe such irreversible mixing processes. One of these is commonly employed in chaos theory and is known as a *baker's transformation*. The name comes from the process of kneading bread, as the dough is first rolled out, then folded over, then rolled flat again, then folded over, again and again. Once the elements have completed this topological mixing process, the results are irreversible. The equations that describe the process leading to the mixture are solvable even though the final pattern of the elements is unpredictable. In other words, even if we know the initial position of every paint molecule, there is no way to predict their final position. Yet, we can mathematically describe how they got there once the process is complete. This weird reality is known as *deterministic chaos*, and is one of the most important discoveries from chaos theory.

In this sense, as music evolves, the genres that define themselves are the ones that have survived a baker's transformation to more resemble the metaphorical fine baked good than the kid's green/brown finger-paint mixture. These self-defining genres grow into a significant branch, occasionally even becoming a root to new subgenres that continue the process. Styles that are too complex, weird, or idiosyncratic are like exotic foods or odd paint colors, although they may attract a small hard-core following. Unless tastes evolve to appreciate these fringe, left-field, or "accident of nature" styles, which does happen from time to time, they are likely to be evolutionary dead ends with no more than a cult following. However, a lot of great music is very idiosyncratic with only small cult followings, and certainly has its place in the music ecosystem. The best-case scenario for such fringe styles or artists is that they are later rediscovered, a "hidden gem" that passes on some of their musical DNA as an obscure influence. Occasionally, an artist is so talented and interesting that his or her idiosyncratic uniqueness is a plus that sets him or her apart from all the rest. These artists are self-defining. Either they "transcend the genre" or are genre defying. There are of course numerous additional factors that influence music's evolution, and we will discuss many of them throughout *The Music Producer's Survival Guide*.

The Global Village and the Noosphere: The Information Age and the Internet perfectly fit predictions made in the 1920s by Pierre Teilhard de Chardin (1881–1955), and again in the 1960s by Marshall McLuhan (1911–1980). Their ideas help us to understand not only the ways music has evolved over the last 100 years, but also what is ongoing. Although very different in biography and intellectual approach, the common thread in their work is a global perspective. The cultural cross-fertilization and exchange of customs, ideas, and perspectives so common now were just emerging in their day.

Canadian-born Marshall McLuhan was information theory's first philosopher and a pioneer in what is now called *media theory*. The core of his essential ideas were first spelled out in his landmark books *The Gutenberg Galaxy: The Making of Typographic Man* (1962) and *Understanding Media: The Extensions of Man* (1964). He famously stated that "the medium is the message" to explain how new communication media change social interactions. People tend to notice only superficial incremental changes in information technologies and fail to recognize the big changes caused by such technologies. The effects of the medium are essentially invisible, taken-for-granted facts of life, so in that sense the message is a part of the social structure created by the medium, according to McLuhan.

As well-known as is that widely misunderstood phrase, the term *global village* is certainly his most popular linguistic invention. McLuhan considered media as extensions of the human senses just as a hammer is an extension of the human arm. The combined total of all information networks and media technologies, then, are like an extension of the human nervous system that surrounds the planet. So the term global village emerged from this concept of a planetary nervous system that allowed for the sharing of information as if in a small village. McLuhan did not necessarily consider a global village in the same positive light we tend to these days, in part due to the many unintended consequences resulting from global media. But his thoughts on the future of media technology were quite prescient. He posited that the next advances in media would be like an extension of human consciousness, which is a common way of thinking about the Internet. McLuhan was definitely ahead of his time, but he was not the first to discuss global information systems as leading to an evolution of consciousness.

Pierre Teilhard de Chardin, or simply Teilhard, was a French Jesuit priest who was also an accomplished geologist and paleontologist. In addition to his role with the 1920s expeditions that discovered the 400,000-year-old "Peking man" in China, he is equally famous in intellectual circles for his posthumously published book, *The Phenomenon of Man* (1955). This classic was actually completed in the 1930s but was published posthumously to prevent his excommunication from the church due to his belief in evolution. In this epic book, he traces the evolution of life on Earth through increasingly complex stages. First there is the *geosphere* (sphere of Earth), the geological foundations for the *biosphere* (sphere of life), which is the thin layer of living organisms covering the planet. The biosphere complexifies to support intelligent life, and humans spread out radially to surround the planet. Once *homo sapiens* (Latin for "wise/knowing man") complete this encompassing diaspora, evolutionary energy is tangentially directed away from the biosphere to form a new sphere that allowed consciousness to feed back on itself. Teilhard states in *The Phenomenon of Man*, "By a tiny 'tangential' increase, the 'radial' was turned back in on itself and so to speak took an infinite leap forward" (p. 169). This leap forward is manifested in the information networks that surround the geosphere and biosphere. To describe this evolutionary emergence of a "sphere of mind" superimposed on the two more fundamental spheres, he coined the term *noosphere* in 1925, from the ancient Greek *noos* for "mind," or "knowledge." When he coined the term, we had the telegraph, phonograph, telephone, and radio, but not yet even TV, the epicenter of McLuhan's work, let alone computers, cell phones, or the Internet. As such, it is understandable that Teilhard is widely considered the first person to essentially predict the Internet.

> **NOTE:** From this point on, the material that follows significantly overlaps topics and discussion found in Chapter 6, "Producer Tips," Chapter 7 "Creative Process," and Chapter 8 "Selecting Your Tools."

The Technology

The history of electronic music mirrors the history of the 20th century. Staying close together while swirling around the primary trunks of our modern civilization are the branches that represent the evolution of science, electrical engineering, computing, communication technology, music, and music culture. Over the last 150 years or so, most branches of knowledge underwent their own baker's transformation, creating new technologies that appeared at a blistering unprecedented rate, with music and music technologies doing their best to keep pace. The appearance of the phonograph, microphones, analog tape recorders, mixers, audio effects, synths, samplers, drum machines, MIDI, personal computers, the DAW, and plug-ins are all concurrent with the various stages in the evolution of music production and electronic music. Although there are now many great products, amazing musicians, and brilliant producers from all over the world, most of the primary elements we take for granted today emerged roughly between 1880 and 1980 from just a handful of countries.

Question: Which countries were the source of the majority of the last century's technological innovation?

Answer: U.S., U.K., Germany, Japan, France, and honorable mention for Switzerland.

Comment: We will discuss some of the major innovations here and there, but in-depth discussion is beyond the scope of this book.

Question: Which countries were the source of the majority of electronic music innovation?

Answer: U.S., Germany, U.K., France, and honorable mention for Jamaica.

Comment: Later in this chapter and elsewhere in this book, we cover a lot of ground on this question—which, when combined with the next Q&A, should be more than sufficient to make this point very clear (although a comprehensive discussion is beyond the scope of this book).

Question: Which countries are most responsible for the equipment and technology we most use in electronic music, music production, and pro audio?

Answer: U.S., Japan, Germany, U.K., and honorable mention for Northern Europe.

Comment: Later in this chapter and elsewhere in this book, we will hit a lot of key points on this topic, which should be more than sufficient to make this point very clear. A rudimentary perusal through any gear site or catalog easily shows that each of these countries is best known for manufacturing and developing certain electronic music and music production products. The following list is not meant to be comprehensive and emphasizes fortés:

 ▷ **Northern Europe:** Loudspeakers, audio software, and digital synths
 ▷ **U.K.:** Mixing consoles, EQs, compressors, loudspeakers, and analog synths
 ▷ **Germany:** Microphones, loudspeakers, analog tape recorders, digital synths, and audio software
 ▷ **Japan:** Analog and digital electronic musical instruments, microphones, loudspeakers, analog tape recorders, digital recording systems, personal computers
 ▷ **U.S.:** All of the above (see the following note)

> **NOTE:** It is often suggested that the U.S. is so innovative because of its cultural diversity. The mixing and blending of cultures and ideas from so many places and cultures presents that many more opportunities for evolutionarily useful and successful baker's transformations.

x0x

Elsewhere in this book, we talk about all sorts of gear, software, and instruments with significant impacts on 20th century music and production. Roland deserves its own section, especially pertaining to what many think of as its golden era of influential electronic musical instruments and effects. There are others worthy of note, but the items in the following list are hands down the most important ones to the history of modern electronic music production in particular.

▷ 1974 RE-201 Space Echo
▷ 1980 TR-808 Rhythm Machine
▷ 1981 Jupiter-8 synthesizer
▷ 1982 TR-606 Drumatix
▷ 1982 TB-303 Bass Line
▷ 1982 Juno-60 synthesizer
▷ 1983 SH-101 synthesizer
▷ 1984 TR-909 Rhythm Composer
▷ 1985 TR-707 Rhythm Composer

"Nothing Sounds Quite Like an 808"

The reason there are quotes around "nothing sounds quite like an 808" is that it is from the lyrics of the Beastie Boys' 1998 song "Super Disco Breakin." Although each of the listed classics are worthy of further research, one is revered above all the others for the reasons just stated. Roland's "Transistor Rhythm" model 808 is the most sampled drum machine of all time. Japan's Yellow Magic Orchestra (YMO), co-founded by EM icon Ryuichi Sakamoto, was the very first band to use an 808 in 1980. The documentary *Planet Rock and Other Tales of the 808* is due out sometime in 2014. One of the producers of this documentary is Arthur Baker. Baker produced the landmark 1982 single "Planet Rock," the first known American release to use an 808 (followed about five months later by its first use in a certified platinum release, Marvin Gaye's "Sexual Healing"). On the IMDB.com page for this documentary, Baker is quoted as saying, "The day we recorded 'Planet Rock,' I went home that night and told my wife, 'We've made musical history tonight.'"

In a February 10, 2010 editorial on KMAG's website (kmag.co.uk), "Tunes That Shaped: Afrika Bambaataa—Planet Rock," Dr. Khan stresses the historical importance of "Planet Rock." This importance stems not only from the fact that "Planet Rock" "ushered in a whole new era for the fledgling genre of hip hop," but also because the way they approached the production took "the whole culture into an entirely new direction."

In the November 2008 edition of *Sound On Sound* magazine, writer Richard Buskin introduced that month's "Classic Tracks" section with the following:

Man and machine, transporting rap to electro. That, within the historical context of popular music, was what the 1982 single 'Planet Rock' was all about, transforming rap by blending break beats, a vocoder and one of the first Fairlight synths in America, to create computerized, futuristic, robotic funk that paved the way for dance, trance, techno and house, whilst also being the first hip-hop/R&B track to utilize a Roland TR808 drum machine.

"Planet Rock" comes in at #240 on RollingStone.com's 500 greatest songs of all time list. On that page, they include a quote from the Tommy Boy compilation album *Looking for the Perfect Beat 1980–1985*. The discussion between producer Arthur Baker, artist Afrika Bambaataa, and keyboard player John Robie went as follows: "'Can you play stuff like Kraftwerk?' asked Bam, who played their records at DJ gigs. Baker worried about stealing the melody from 'Trans-Europe Express,' but Robie said, 'I'll tear that s... up.'" Why did *Rolling Stone* include that quote? Read on for the answer.

Arthur Baker's Baker's Transformation

Arthur Baker produced the landmark 1982 Tommy Boy Records release of "Planet Rock" by Afrika Bambaataa and the Soulsonic Force. Depending on your taste in musical styles, if you have never heard this song before, you might wonder why it is such a big deal. Whether or not you appreciate its aesthetics 30 years after its production, this classic record nonetheless perfectly illustrates cultural cross-fertilization of musical styles with technology from around the globe. As a quintessential example of a successful baker's transformation, we have a perfect case study of different branches combining to form a new tree able to support new genres and styles. So as to not get sidetracked into a few other fascinating threads, let's simply consider the ingredients that went into this mixture. The following details were sourced from interviews with Arthur Baker in *Sound On Sound* magazine (June 1997, November 2008) and Red Bull Music Academy's website (redbullmusicacademy.com, Toronto 2007 transcript and 4/4/2013 Key Tracks).

From the onset, mixing elements from different styles was fundamental to the intended goal of the track's production, which was to appeal to fans of both Talking Heads and The Sugarhill Gang. Moreover, it was also intended to have international appeal, so the whole theme was "global." The planet theme goes beyond the song's title; it was rapper MC G.L.O.B.E who wrote most of the lyrics, which were inspired by a list of countries from all over the world they generated as an internationalized version of U.S. cities James Brown would call out at performances. In addition to James Brown, other stated background influences for the composition included fellow New Yorkers Kurtis Blow (U.S.) and Kool Herc (Jamaica/U.S.), with Yellow Magic Orchestra (Japan), Gary Numan (U.K.), and Kraftwerk (Germany) guiding the most obvious aesthetic elements that were combined with Bambaataa's Bronx stylings. This cluster of influences represents a full circle of sorts, as YMO cites significant influence by Kraftwerk, who cite significant influence by James Brown.

"Planet Rock" was produced in about 30 hours for about $900 at Intergalactic Studio in NYC, which is known for many classic records by artists such as The Ramones, Swans, and Tibetan Monks of the Dalai Lama, and was the inspiration for the title of that famous Beastie Boys' song. Intergalactic's equipment list included a Neve console (U.K.), a Studer 24-track analog tape recorder (Switzerland), Urei monitors (U.S.), Sony Reverb (Japan), and a Lexicon PCM41 digital delay processor (U.S.) that was used to create the robot voice effect (not a vocoder). They also had one of the few Fairlight CMI Series II computer musical instruments (Australia) in the U.S., which was used for the explosion sounds and the song's signature orchestra hits. (We talk a lot about the CMI in Chapter 8.)

They decided early on that they wanted to use a drum machine and not sampled breaks or live drums so as to emulate the electronic drum sounds on Kraftwerk's 1981 album *Computer World*, specifically the song "Numbers." Once they heard an 808, they knew immediately it was the right tool for what they wanted to do. They saw an ad in the *Village Voice* for a guy offering his drum machine services for $20 or $30 per session (both are stated in interviews), which is where they found the Roland TR-808 drum machine (Japan) used on "Planet Rock." Keyboardist John Robie brought in his Micromoog (U.S.) and the Sequential Circuits Prophet-5 (U.S.), the latter of which was one of the few polyphonic analog synths on the market. (We talk a lot about the Prophet in Chapter 6.) The characteristic keyboard line from Kraftwerk's 1977 "Trans-Europe Express" was not sampled; it was performed by John Robie. Baker's concern about replicating that classic keyboard lead was well-founded. After its release drew attention from Germany, Tommy Boy Records agreed to avoid legal proceedings and pay Kraftwerk $1 per single sold, which in the end worked out well for everyone. And as they say, the rest is history.

A Very Brief Intro to the History of Electronic Music

Here we are not talking about the use of electronic musical instruments in existing music forms, such as the electric guitar, Theremin, Mellotron, or synthesizers that started to appear in rock music and jazz in the 1960s. This brief history pertains to a music form that emerged in the 1950s and exists only because of electronic musical instruments and sound-reproduction technologies. Electronic music (EM) as defined here is a music form that broke ground in human musical history with innovations not found elsewhere. What music innovations might these be? Given the vast and diverse styles of music from many cultures all over the world over many thousands of years, what was left for EM to innovate? Let's consider a short list of non-electronic music forms, styles, and composers, in no particular order, before we answer this question.

Classical, big band, jazz, blues, funk, soul, rock, metal, punk, reggae, blue grass, dub, disco, salsa, meringue, tango, and shamanic/ritual music; traditional music from India, China, Tibet, Japan, the Middle East/North Africa, and West Africa; and the works of Beethoven, Bach, Wagner, Strauss, Mahler, Debussy, Bartok, Mussorgsky, Vivaldi, Stravinsky, Ligeti, Penderecki, Satie, Shoenberg, Gershwin, Barber, Charles Mingus, John Coltrane, Eric Dolphy, Ornette Coleman, Bob Marley, Fela Kuti, James Brown, Parliament, Ohio Players, The Beatles, The Beach Boys, The Rolling Stones, Pink Floyd, MC5, Black Sabbath, Black Flag, The Birthday Party, Slayer, Sonic Youth, Einsturzende Neubauten, The Police, Johnny Cash, Tom Waits, etc., etc., etc.…

When considering all of the harmonies, melodies, rhythms, compositional structures, and timbres found in those styles and works of those artists, it doesn't seem like there is much left for EM. Even while EM was emerging in the 1950s, 20th-century classical composers were busy deconstructing all conventions with acoustic instruments and further laying the foundations for EM to build upon. Many of these purely acoustic musical explorations dating back to the turn of the previous century are now echoed in modern EM. Some amazing mid-century examples of acoustic parallels to early electronic music include the numinous atonality of György Ligeti's *Lux Aeterna* (1966) for 16 solo singers, or the serialist polyrhythmic explorations of cyclic harmonic structures found in Steve Reich's *Music for 18 Musicians* (1976). Moreover, some 20th-century classical composers like John Cage, Toru Takemitsu, and Iannis Xenakis also pioneered early electronic music, and along with some transitional-era composers who emerged in the 1950s, such as Stockhausen, represent exceptions to some of the following generalizations about EM.

So, as of 2013, we can say with certainty that modern EM is not known for melodic innovation. In fact, it generally is quite simple and no further along than the pop music up to about 1980 in those regards. EM is not known for new harmonic structures either, as the chords, scales, and progressions generally are no further along than the pop music up to about 1980 in those regards as well. In modern electronic music post 1980, we also don't find much innovation in terms of rhythm, although there are a few genres from the 1990s that serve as exceptions and demonstrate some integration of the innovations made by early *avant-garde* electronic music composers, such as Bernard Parmegiani. In regard to the latter point on rhythm, an example of early electronic music composers' influence is discussed in the sidebar about Stockhausen that appears later in this chapter. So what is left after mixing together all of the musical encyclopedia? In short, leaving aside a period of rhythmic innovation, EM's most significant contributions to music are innovations in timbre and creative process. Chapter 7 is titled "Creative Process," so we will just focus on timbre for the moment.

Even considering all of the timbres available with instruments from around the globe, electricity opened up completely new vistas. This innovation in timbre is a big deal, and every bit as important as the major innovations in rhythm, harmony, and melody from the previous thousand years. With analog, digital, and computer-based tools, EM pioneers offered up truly new sounds. Additionally, they invented completely new composition techniques and creative processes, many of which are related to the recent explosion of the democratization of music production. In EM we find rhythms, harmonies, and melodies from all over the world carried and modulated within new timbres. Consider electronic dance music, which is founded on repetitive trance-inducing ancient percussion rhythms and simple harmonic structures. When listening to the synthesized leads and basses in this music, we can hear the instrument's modulation capabilities creating rhythmic shifts in timbres and harmonic relations, which similar complexity in the acoustic realm would require at least an ensemble of musicians. Even with that ensemble of musicians, EM still offers a sound palette all its own.

EM's Two Timbral Sources

Because one of EM's two major innovations is in the domain of timbre, it makes sense to look closer at sound genesis methods. We can think of EM as having two basic schools that are defined by the primary source of sound generation, both of which are possible only with electricity. As we will discuss in the next chapter, recorded music and synthesized tones appeared around the same time. Yet, recording technology took off right away and it would take about another six decades before synthesis made its mark.

Source 1: Sound Reproduction

Turntables and analog tape machines were the original sound-reproduction media used in EM. These storage technologies served as the first sound sources for electronic music composition. When considering the manipulation of audio recordings as an art form, we find two parallel roots of equal significance—one starting in the 1940s and the other in the 1970s. The artists working with this source are responsible for most of the significant innovations in creative process.

AMERICAN AND EUROPEAN INTELLECTUAL *AVANT-GARDE* SCENES

As we will discuss in more detail in Chapter 7, the very first forms of EM emerged out of France, Germany, and the U.S. in the late 1940s and early 1950s. Pierre Shaeffer's first public *musique concrète* performance in 1950 France used only multiple turntables, a mixer, and a PA. Soon thereafter, Schaeffer founded GRM and worked with many influential composers such as Varese, Boulez, Parmegiani, and Karlheinz Stockhausen. Stockhausen was right there at the beginning and almost immediately settled into the now-famous, but new at that time, NWDR studio in Cologne, Germany. Evolving right alongside *musique concrète* was tape music, which included a variety of additional sound sources such as field recordings, tone generators, and acoustic instruments (out of this milieu emerged electroacoustic music). The Columbia-Princeton Electronic Music Center popped up in NYC around this time, associated with notables such as John Cage and later also Bob Moog. Then, in 1962, the San Francisco Tape Music Center was founded by Pauline Oliveros and a few others. Meanwhile, a completely different approach to working with existing sound recordings was bubbling up independently in Jamaica.

JAMAICAN DUB, SOUND SYSTEMS, AND AMERICAN DJ CULTURE

As an outgrowth of reggae, dub appeared in the 1960s and 1970s when King Tubby and Lee "Scratch" Perry became the very first remixers. At the same time, people began to build mobile sound systems, which by the 1970s were massive walls of speakers and amps attached to truck beds, vans, and other autos. As it is now, New York City was home to a lot of Jamaican immigrants, including Kool Herc, the originator of hip hop. (The New York State Office of Parks, Recreation, and Historic Preservation officially recognized Herc's home on Sedgwick Avenue in the Bronx as the "Birthplace of Hip-Hop" on July 5, 2007.) By the late 1970s, Jamaican sound systems found their place in NYC's emerging DJ culture. The modern DJ was born there as artists figured out how to play just the drum breaks off of records by juggling two turntables, thus giving break dancers an endless soundtrack. Thus was the birth of break beat and sampling.

While all of this was going on up in the Bronx, Larry Levan was pioneering club culture downtown on the West side of Manhattan at the Paradise Garage, the birthplace of garage, NYC's version of what was being called "house" in Chicago. This venue didn't sell food or drinks and was first to put the DJ at the center of attention. Although Levan was born in Brooklyn, he is credited as the person who introduced elements of Jamaican dub music to electronic dance music. He was exposed to those styles through the remixes he did for Island Records, including releases by the legendary dub production team of Sly and Robbie.

> **NOTE:** The syncopated rhythm characteristic of the guitar parts in reggae/dub is now heard in a lot of modern electronic music. Instead of a guitar hitting on the up beat, also referred to as the "and" (as in 1 and 2 and, etc.), we hear a "pumping and breathing" synth. The rhythm is created by a compressor that ducks the synth each time a kick drum triggers its side chain's detector circuit, or what is commonly known as "side-chaining."

Source 2: Sound Synthesis

Electronic music as we know it did not exist until synthesis was added to the composer's toolkit. Synthesis is largely responsible for the electronic generation of sounds and timbres, and therefore the artists and inventors working with this source are responsible for most of the significant innovations in timbre. It is important to note that most drum machines were basically sequenced synths until the early 1980s, including all of the sounds produced by the TR-808.

ADDITIVE SYNTHESIS

Of all the major figures in early EM, Stockhausen is the only one who made an equal mark with both sound sources—although his invention of the additive synthesizer in the early 1950s puts him at the vanguard of pure electronic music (see the following sidebar). Due to its complex and over-wieldy nature, additive synthesis would not become common until the digital era decades later.

SUBTRACTIVE SYNTHESIS

Synthesis did not find its way into popular music until subtractive synthesis was invented, about a decade after Stockhausen invented additive synthesis. Subtractive synthesis is significantly more user friendly than is additive synthesis. We discuss the invention of subtractive synthesis in detail in Chapter 8, "Selecting Your Tools." In the early 1960s, Bob Moog was hanging around the Columbia-Princeton Electronic Music Center while Don Buchla was making friends at the newly founded San Francisco Tape Music Center. Based on discussions with composers at each of those centers, Moog and Buchla were inspired to simultaneously, independently invent the modular subtractive analog synthesizer. When people say analog synth, they mean subtractive synthesizer.

FM SYNTHESIS

While Moog and Buchla were busy creating the most popular synthesis method of all time, a few miles down the peninsula from San Francisco, John Chowning was inventing FM synthesis at Stanford in 1967. FM offers timbral capabilities not possible with any of the previous methods, but didn't appear in a commercially successful product until 1983. We will talk about John Chowning and the significance of that successful 1983 product in Chapter 6.

MISC. SYNTHESIS

Numerous other methods emerged once digital synthesis was viable in the 1970s and into the early 1980s, such as wavetable synthesis (Wolfgang Palm, PPG, Waldorf), granular synthesis (Iannis Xenakis, Curtis Roads), vector synthesis (Dave Smith), physical modeling synthesis, sample and synthesis, spectral resynthesis, and other variations on the above.

Karlheinz Stockhausen (1928–2007)   Stockhausen was interviewed for the Nov/Dec 1977 issue of *Synapse Magazine*. Interviewer Janet Henshaw Danielson starts the interview with the following question: "What I'd like to know is something about your past career. What originally attracted you to electronic music?" Stockhausen replied: "The question is wrong, because I started the electronic music."

No one ever accused Stockhausen of humility, but his assertion is only a slight overstatement. In 1953, he composed and produced *Studie I*, which he claims is the first true electronic music composition. Stockhausen's invention of the additive synthesizer was an application of one of Joseph Fourier's theories, known as Fourier analysis. Fourier analysis states that all periodic functions, such as found in sound waves, can be deconstructed into a series of sine waves, each with a measureable frequency and amplitude. By implication, Stockhausen realized that sounds could be synthesized by generating a lot of sine waves, each with their own sine wave oscillator and amp. Although others previously utilized electronic instruments and tape recording, when it comes to synthesized electronic music, Stockhausen is in fact the single-most seminal composer, since *Studie I* is the first known composition using synthesized sounds.

The unimaginable horrors Stockhausen experienced as a teen in WWII Germany help explain his serious demeanor and reputation for obsessive control over every detail of the performances of his compositions. Every bit in the same league as other 20th-century intellectual giants, and like many German intellectuals of his era, Stockhausen was heavily influenced by Oriental philosophy (now just called Eastern or Asian philosophy). After the war, at the age of 20, he was so unsure of his future direction he started writing letters to Herman Hesse, author of *The Glass Bead Game*, *Siddhartha,* and *Steppenwolf*. They developed a serious pen-pal relationship that lasted for more than two years, with Hesse taking a role almost like that of master to apprentice, pushing Stockhausen to focus his life efforts on whatever it was that made him unique. In a 1950 letter to Hesse, Stockhausen thanked him for his help in forming his personality, and I paraphrase, in transforming him from tears of salt to crystalline stone. A few years later, after establishing himself as a serious composer, the writings of Indian sage Sri Aurobindo are a cited major influence on the realization of *Kontakte*, completed in 1960. This is considered as one of the most important works in the evolution of electronic music.

Not only a serious composer, Stockhausen was also quite elegant when speaking about music. During a lecture to the Oxford Union on Four Criteria of Electronic Music in May 1972, he stated, "Whenever we hear sounds we are changed, we are no longer the same after having heard certain sounds. And this is the more the case when we hear organized sounds, organized by another human being…music."

It is easily argued that Stockhausen is the most seminal figure on the timbre side of the EM equation. Chapter 7 spends a lot of time talking about an American composer of equal importance on the creative-process side: John Cage. And just as the preceding quote resembles ideas found in Asian philosophy, so too are many of the deep insights of this American pioneer—but manifested and applied to music and life in a completely different way. In the flowing current that is the evolution of electronic music, if Stockhausen was the positive charge, then John Cage balances things out as the negative charge. When you get to Chapter 6 and Chapter 7, make sure to check out Figure 6.6 and Figure 7.7, which show significant connections to and from Stockhausen.

Earlier, I mentioned innovations in rhythm from electronic music composers such as Stockhausen. *The Wire* magazine's November 1995 edition asked Stockhausen what he thought about a number of current electronic music artists he had recently been asked to critique. Stockhausen replied:

> I heard the piece Aphex Twin of Richard James carefully: I think it would be very helpful if he listens to my work Song of the Youth, *which is electronic music, and a young boy's voice singing with himself. Because he would then immediately stop with all these post-African repetitions, and he would look for changing tempi and changing rhythms, and he would not allow to repeat any rhythm if it were varied to some extent and if it did not have a direction in its sequence of variations.*

After publication of that issue, Aphex Twin responded: "I thought he should listen to a couple of tracks of mine: 'Didgeridoo,' then he'd stop making abstract, random patterns you can't dance to."

Richard James was already recognized as a serious electronic musician upon the release of *Selected Ambient Works 85–92* in 1992, ambient music that picked up where Eno left off. And although he was producing other interesting music under a variety of pseudonyms, it was not until Aphex Twin that he really hit his stride with a trio of Warp Records releases widely considered to be his most groundbreaking and influential works outside of the ambient genre: *Richard D. James Album* (1996), *Come To Daddy* (1997), and *Windowlicker* (1999). It is interesting to note that these three releases are not only full of influential and innovative timbres and rhythms, but also abstract and random patterns you can't dance to. Aphex Twin is one of the cornerstone artists of the Intelligent Dance Music (IDM) genre, which got its unfortunate name from the *Artificial Intelligence* compilation, released by Warp Records in 1992 and then licensed by Wax Trax for release in the U.S. in 1993.

Independent Label Pioneers

As more genres appeared, more labels appeared. There is a close synergy between the branching dynamics of genres and labels, since labels cater to the audiences of niche genres and subgenres. Some labels even define a genre's identity such that certain artists are best described to those who have not heard them by mentioning their label. This last case is even more obvious when considering any of the boutique labels owned by established DJs or producers, which are often known for very small variances between artists on their label. In many cases, such labels mostly release music by the artist/owner and perhaps a few of his or her friends or collaborators. On the other hand, there are indie labels not as concerned with specific aesthetics and styles, and release a diverse assortment of music and artists based on commonalities in their approach to music or other shared cultural artistic inclinations, philosophies, or attitudes.

Most labels started out as independent labels. By the 1950s, numerous mergers and acquisitions created what we now think of as the major labels. Although independent labels such as Chess, Sun, and A&M continued to pop up in the 1950s and 1960s, by the early 1970s most of them had been acquired by the increasingly larger major labels. The modern indie label emerged in the 1970s and grew to such an extent in the 1980s that by the early 1990s, indies became standard feeding grounds for big-label A&R. This created a new dynamic in the industry wherein some musicians began to think of indies as no more than a stepping stone in their career on the way to getting signed by a major.

Major labels exist to make money, but there are a lot of different motivations for starting an indie label. These motivations are generally a combination of want and/or need along with any of the following: to serve as an alternative to big labels; to feed DJ and club scenes; music loving entrepreneurship; DIY passion; to be an impresario/curator expression of personal taste; to support a niche community or subculture; out of necessity for academic, experimental, *avant-garde* music with no commercial potential at all; or just foolishly hoping to make money on indie music.

Let's consider some of the most important indie labels related to the focus of this book. (If I omitted a label of significance, it was not on purpose.) It is important to point out a few things about all of the labels in the following list. All of them started out as indie labels, although many are now part of major label groups (and some of those later escaped and returned to indie status), while others are no longer around at all. I also chose to stop at 1990 because accounting for the proliferation of labels that began after that year would take up a whole chapter, and moreover, most of those essentially follow in the wake of the mentioned pioneers. The grouping is loosely according to similar genres, styles, and branches of influence. For those of you who are interested, and have a lot of time on your hands, looking into each of these labels and their roster of artists will reveal a universe of amazing influential music.

Jamaica, U.K., and New York

Labels include the following:

▷ Island Records (1962)
▷ Wackies (1974)
▷ West End Records (1976)
▷ Sugar Hill (1979)
▷ On-U Sound Records (1979)
▷ Tommy Boy (1981)
▷ Def Jam (1983)
▷ Relativity Records (1985)
▷ Axiom (1989)

> **NOTE:** Island Records was the largest indie label in history until it was sold to Polygram in 1989, which is now Island Def Jam Music Group, part of the Universal Music Group. Axiom was started as part of Island when it was still indie.

American Punk, Metal, and Aggressive or Alternative Rock Styles

Labels include the following:

▷ SST (1978)
▷ Alternative Tentacles (1979)
▷ Discord (1980)
▷ Epitaph (1980)
▷ Touch and Go (1981)
▷ Metal Blade (1982)
▷ Combat (1983)
▷ Amphetamine Reptile (1986)
▷ Lookout! (1987)
▷ Matador (1989)

Various Styles of Adventurous Rock, Underground Metal, and "Industrial"-Related Genres from Germany, U.K., U.S., and Canada:

Labels include the following:

▷ Ohr (1970)
▷ Brain Records (1972)
▷ Sky Records (1975)
▷ Factory (1978)

▷ Mute (1978)
▷ Rough Trade (1978)
▷ 4AD (1979)
▷ Waxtrax (1980)
▷ Noise (1981)
▷ Ryko (1983)
▷ Nettwerk (1984)

Electronic Music Labels from U.S., Canada, Germany, and U.K.

Labels include the following:

▷ Trax (1984)
▷ Metroplex (1985)
▷ Transmat (1986)
▷ Warp (1989)
▷ Plus 8 (1990)
▷ Ninja Tune (1990)
▷ Basic Channel (1993)

NOTE: Basic Channel is the only label listed here that was founded after 1990. Moritz Von Oswald and Mark Ernestus are a Berlin-based production team known as Rhythm & Sound. They epitomize DIY to the extreme. After starting the Basic Channel label in 1993, they opened Hardwax, a record store and distribution company under the same name. They also have their own dub plate–capable mastering studio. Additionally, they run a few labels as part of the Basic Channel family, including their own Chain Reaction and Rhythm & Sound labels. Moreover, they have resurrected the Wackies label as an imprint under Basic Channel and reissue many of the seminal dub releases that have long been out of print.

Music Is Cybernetic

Cybernetics is the study of feedback loops, how inputs to systems influence their output that then influences the next input. Any time we are talking about networks and feedback loops, we are in the domain of cybernetics. Cybernetic concepts are applied in the study and practice of everything from behavioral psychology, to robotics, to communications networks, and beyond. Norbert Weiner coined the term in the 1960s from "cybernaut," the ancient Greek for "helmsman," the person who steered a ship to keep it on course by reacting to feedback from the water and then making adjustments. Cybernetics, then, is very useful when describing and understanding the behaviors of the Internet, which consists of numerous overlapping and interlinking networks rife with inputs and outputs. The term cyberspace was coined by science-fiction writers in the early 1980s and most popularized by William Gibson in his 1984 novel *Neuromancer*. So *cyber* is quite an old word, and it is only because of the postmodern sci-fi genre known as *cyberpunk* that its futuristic hi-tech connotations are so prominent. Now that you know a little bit about cybernetics, let's consider the prominent role feedback loops play in the creation of music.

We can literally think of music as transmission of energy. As discussed, music can express any emotion and capture any mood or state of mind. Given our discussion on the lead role that cultural cross-fertilization plays in the evolution of musical genres, we can make a few statements about factors that influence the creation, production, and performance of music. These factors of influence include complex, multidimensional fractal networks from all domains of human experience, including but not limited to personal history and psychology, tools and the scientific knowledge used to create them, shared cultural meaning, and commercial markets. It is useful to view many of the interactions through the lens of cybernetics, feedback loops that each artist and producer experiences in his or her own way. As all of these influential factors set off the urge to create, there are correlated patterns of electrical impulses in the brain. Once we decide what we want to do, our brain sends electrical signals through our nervous system to set muscles into action.

Recordings are a result of unique combinations of a producer's and artist's life experiences and personal history. Transducers change energy from one form to another. So with those two givens, let's consider this cybernetic process starting with the playback of a digital recording. Digital is a binary code that must be converted to a continuously variable (analog) alternating current. Once all those ones and zeros are a stream of variable voltages traveling through a metal wire, they can manipulate magnetic fields. Speakers use electromagnetism to drive electromechanical motors that create mechanical movement that pushes acoustic wave energy through air. These pressure waves are collected by the outer ear, which resonate in the ear canal to boost certain frequencies. As the wave energy hits the ear drum, three tiny bones act like pistons and match impedance for energy transfer from air to fluid. This then vibrates thousands of little nerve hairs that act like microphones and convert energy to electrical signals for flow through the auditory nerves to the brain. The brain processes these patterns of electrochemical activity that our consciousness perceives as sound, and thus music. Upon hearing music, additional electrical patterns in the brain translate it into emotions, thoughts, and feelings, thus influencing our life experience and personal history.

Cadence

Hopefully, this chapter adequately conveyed how astounding, extraordinary, and amazing the processes and dynamics of musical history are that have brought us to where we are today. It is easy to lose sight of the big picture when we get too caught up in the latest trends, the newest plug-ins, the most complex LFO modulations, or the hottest venues and DJs. It happens to all of us at some point. When you notice it happening, just remind yourself what it is all about in the first place. As we gain more knowledge, learn more about influences and styles, and develop our skills, our taste changes in such a way that it is harder to be impressed or inspired by the mass of available music. Simultaneously, as the years go by our exposure to the negative sides of the business, being on the receiving end of raw deals, and run-ins with hacks, leeches, and other undesirable people can drain motivation and inspiration. Combined, these two dynamics increase the risk of becoming jaded or cynical. We all go through rough spots in life, but those should be temporary. Don't become that person on the scene who lets it become permanent and either always hates on "music these days" and/or goes on about all of their should'ves, would'ves, and could'ves.

There is a fine line between having a high threshold to be impressed and being bored or cynical about music in general. People obsessed with music have a lot more knowledge about it, which means they appreciate things others don't—but are also often harder to impress because they have seen or heard most of it before. A few years ago, while watching an indie electronic act at a small venue in Brooklyn, one of my good friends asked me what I thought of them. I said they were good at what they were doing, but nothing special in any way. She then said I was jaded. My snarky response, "I'm not jaded, I'm just over informed." We both laughed, but later I realized it was the perfect response from a music professional that addresses the difference between jaded and simply having a different frame of reference, although with no less enthusiasm, passion, and excitement for music in general.

Even if we do not share taste in one single artist, we at least share a passion for music. As we dig into more grounded, practical, and technical topics, it is crucial we never lose sight of this passion. With intense focus on the music industry, career planning and development, mastering technical skills, networking, people skills, file management, creativity, gear, and lifestyle, it is easy to lose perspective and forget what got us interested in dedicating our lives to music in the first place. Think about those moments when music changed your life. As producers, we are also on the other side of that equation, creating the music that does that for others. No matter what kind of music you want to produce, you have the potential to create powerful experiences that can resonate long after you're gone.

Plot Point on the Space-Time Continuum

The whole of life is just like watching a film. Only it's as though you always get in ten minutes after the big picture has started, and no one will tell you the plot, so you have to work it out all yourself from the clues.

—Terry Pratchett

THIS CHAPTER SETS THE STAGE FOR THE REST OF THIS BOOK. To do this, it will traverse a few interwoven story arcs about the expansion of human knowledge. These arcs pertain to the technological advances that enabled music production and birthed the record industry, and then how the progression of those same arcs crossed a few others to radically alter their trajectory and bring us to where we are now.

Attempting to trace all the significant vectors that point to the ever-increasing access to the means of production and consumption of music can seem like trying to solve a jigsaw puzzle without the picture on the front of the box. Fortunately, a big piece of the puzzle is framed by Deborah Tussey in her 2005 *Loyola University Chicago Law Journal* article, "Music at the Edge of Chaos: A Complex Systems Perspective on File Sharing." She offers up the useful term "music system," which greatly simplifies things for us as we proceed. As she states:

> *The system for producing and distributing music recordings (hereinafter 'the music system') can be described as a complex adaptive system in which legal, political, economic, socio-cultural, and technological subsystems converge, interact, and coevolve. Digitization and global networking introduced disruptive perturbations into the workings of this system, requiring an evolutionary response to the new environment.*

Taking a lead from Deborah Tussey, I am going to borrow her use of the term "music system" when addressing our industry as a whole. We explore this "evolutionary response" as we delve into the implications of the digital revolution and the Internet through topics ranging from the cyclic nature of historical revolutions; to the RIAA, piracy and Napster; to defining what is meant by the terms "producer" and "professional." This chapter is very important for anyone that wants to fully understand the big picture; if you are anxious to get into the more practical and immediately employable subjects in this book, you might be inclined to do so and come back to this chapter at a later time. That said, there are very good reasons for this chapter's placement so early in the book, since an understanding of the disruptions and evolutionary responses to the music system antecedes this book's *raison d'être* and is therefore likely why you are now reading it.

Putting Things in Perspective

The more things change, the more they stay the same.

—common idiom

I hated history class in high school—mainly because the teachers were boring, but also because the stories just didn't feel quite right. That feeling was correct. Many of us now know that the official canon, which was pervasive in those days, was a highly simplified, sanitized, incomplete, culturally biased version of the past. Nonetheless, the past *is* prologue. History is about why things are the way they are. And while history does not actually repeat itself, it does spiral through cycles with similar archetypes, themes, and events popping up like Spirograph patterns in a kaleidoscopic tapestry. If this seems like no more than abstract philosophy to you, please humor me and hang in there for a bit; I promise that there is a payoff at the end. I get very specific about how these ideas directly pertain to the music industry as I trace the evolution of the music system from inception to present.

Consider the word "revolution," which refers to motion around a central point, such as the rotation of Earth on its axis. Although it also implies a radical change in the status quo, it originally referred to the revolving patterns of celestial bodies (planets), such as the sun around Earth. This *geocentric* view of the universe was the accepted "truth" based on the works of Aristotle and Ptolemy dating back to 300 BCE. In 1543, Nicolaus Copernicus published *On the Revolutions of the Heavenly Spheres*, which suggested that Earth actually revolved around the sun. This *heliocentric* model of the universe solved the perplexing problem of epicycles caused by the apparent retrograde motion of planets in the sky, but was also a heretical idea punishable by death in some parts of Europe. It took another 140 years, and the ideas of Tycho, Kepler, Galileo, and finally Newton, for the Copernican Revolution to be complete. So the very word that we most associate with significant change is also inseparable from our idea of cycles. The Copernican Revolution represented a seismic paradigm shift in our understanding of the solar system and the universe. It literally inverted what was the central point and what was in motion revolving around that center.

NOTE: Our solar system was the known universe until Galileo employed a telescope in 1610 and discovered that the Milky Way was in fact a galaxy full of more stars. The Milky Way galaxy was the known universe until Edwin Hubble employed the largest telescope of his day and discovered other galaxies in 1923. That our universe is one of many universes in a multiverse is an increasingly mainstream conjecture, particularly since the launch of the Hubble telescope in 1990 and the WMAP in 2001.

History is composed of the stories we tell ourselves to describe events from the past to help us make sense of the present. There are good storytellers and bad storytellers. No matter their storytelling abilities, benevolent or malevolent motivations, some are honestly trying to tell a tale, while others shade the truth or outright lie to advance an agenda. Any attempt to define history resembles the "coastline paradox" that lead Mandelbrot to coin the term "fractal." Even assuming honest intentions and good skills, all stories are subjective and limited in their point of view. As a coast's measured length depends on an arbitrary choice of the unit of measurement, so too are versions of history dependent on how the story is told and who is telling it. All histories are therefore partial and incomplete. With this understanding in mind, know that being helpful and accurate to the best of my abilities is the motivation behind this chapter. But what is the motivation behind the stories being told by the corporate record industry?

Music Is More Than the Recording Industry

The Recording Industry Association of America (RIAA) describes itself on its website, in part, as "the trade organization that supports and promotes the creative and financial vitality of the major music companies." It is part standards organization, part research institution, part copyright administrator and protector, part legal defense and free speech advocate, but also part political lobbyist (it is based in Washington D.C.). Sometimes we really like what they do, such as when they are standing up for free speech and against censorship, and protecting intellectual property from international bootlegging operations. Sometimes we are not fans at all, such as when they lobby for legislation that would limit the free exchange of information on the Internet, or mistakenly file big-dollar "copyright infringement" lawsuits against a 66-year-old grandmother on dialysis living off of Social Security checks (2003), a deceased 83-year-old grandmother (2005), and another grandmother who had just been displaced from her home by Hurricane Rita (2007).

All of us have to imagine what life was like without recorded music, in the same way that someone born now will have to imagine life before the Internet. The recording industry predates everyone alive today, so it is easy to ignore the fact that it has not been around for very long—about the same duration as the automobile. It is an undeniable fact that the early record companies, which evolved into what we now call major labels, played the leading role in the evolution of music technology, recording, and distribution for many decades. It is therefore understandable that the RIAA and the major labels it represents not only act like they're cultural institutions that have been around forever, but also that everyone owes them something. As if we just wouldn't have music if it weren't for them, they'd like you to believe. Leaving aside the obvious facts that they are dependent on talented musicians and composers, or that independent labels provide an alternative to their goods, they also don't appear to understand the nature of change and revolutions. They seem oblivious to the fact that they are dependent on technology that is part of a long arc of progress. These technologies have evolved to a point that they offer most of the same capabilities to the masses. Does not the RIAA realize that what allowed it to exist in the first place is now also allowing others to not need it anymore?

In ancient Greek mythology, a pantheon of gods ruled from atop Mount Olympus. To their dismay, the titan Prometheus created humans. Worse, he stole fire and gave it to humanity. Once humans had fire, technological progress and the birth of civilization were set in motion. To punish Prometheus for this theft, Zeus sentenced him to eternal torture. The archetype of Prometheus represents not only technological progress, but also revolutions and rebellion against authority in general. Just as the gods once had a monopoly on fire, the RIAA and its associates once had the monopoly on the means of music production and distribution. Just as the gods wanted to punish Prometheus for stealing fire and liberating humans from divine dependence, the RIAA wants to dish out punishment, too. In the real world Prometheus is represented as the Internet and the digital revolution, so the RIAA must look elsewhere to bring down its wrath. Is it moving past this spitefulness and trying to evolve? Before I can answer this question, we first need to explore a few other topics.

Yo Ho Ho, and a Bottle of Rum

The British New Wave band Bow Wow Wow released "C30 C60 C90 Go" on EMI in 1980. It was the first ever cassette single. The song's title is a reference to the fact that blank cassette tapes were sold with different lengths, with 30 minutes, 60 minutes, and 90 minutes being popular formats. The lyrics tell a tale about using blank cassette tapes to record songs off of the radio, and then subsequently being stopped by the police and put under arrest for such "illegal" activity. Singer Annabella Lwin then tells us how she shoves the officer, blows his whistle, and states she gets to keep her loot because she's a pirate. These silly but poignant lyrics were a rebellious, youthful response to a legendary British record industry "anti-piracy" campaign, which is discussed in the following paragraph. Moreover, the band's infamous manager, Malcolm McLaren, paired the single's release with a clever publicity stunt: The back side of that cassette single was left blank so buyers could use it to record a song off the radio. EMI refused to promote the single because it promoted piracy and dropped the band shortly thereafter. Decades before the golden age of the CD and its file-sharing nemesis, the industry decried music sharing and copying as "piracy" that would ruin music. Yes, music...not that it would ruin the music industry.

The British Phonographic Industry (BPI) is the UK's equivalent of the RIAA and works with all the same major labels. Its 1980 anti-copyright infringement campaign stated "Home taping is killing music. And it's illegal." Figure 2.1 is a photo of a retro (not vintage) T-shirt that includes the 1980 campaign's first sentence below a graphic based on their design, which I bought sometime around 2003 at the height of the industry's freak out over file sharing. As you can see, the cassette and crossbones graphic alludes to the "Jolly Roger" flag with skull and crossbones, which was flown on the mast of pirate ships to indicate their intentions to other ships. Once they hoisted a Jolly Roger up the mast, your only choices were to surrender or to be subject to a merciless assault. As such, the term "piracy" historically refers to the acts of dangerous and violent criminals who steal property for financial gain, as is now a huge problem in the shipping lanes off the east coast of Africa. When it comes to theft of intellectual property and copyright infringement, piracy also accurately refers to criminal acts committed for financial gain, such as the many large-scale music, video, and software bootlegging operations that are prevalent in Russia and China. While piracy always implies theft (or another more serious crime like kidnapping or hijacking), the opposite is usually not the case.

Figure 2.1 Photo of T-shirt purchased in 2003, based on the BPI's 1980 campaign. The industry tried to warn us that blank cassette tapes could "kill music."

The key words in either definition of piracy are "financial gain," not simply failure to pay, as in the case of shoplifting. The BPI campaign of 1980 set a precedent in its tenuous use of the word. There is an argument to be made for using the word "theft," but applying the label of "piracy" is very problematic when referring to regular people in their homes who are obtaining copies of music without paying for that copy, but with no intention to sell it for financial gain. To consider the taping of a song off the radio an act of piracy is not only hyperbolic, but such usage undermines the term when applied to real piracy. Actual piracy of intellectual property is a serious problem with real consequences. But here we are, 33 years later, and the RIAA is still following the lead of the BPI. On its website, under the section "Who Music Theft Hurts," it states: "It's commonly known as 'piracy,' but that's too benign of a term…." They make it sound as if President Obama should send in the Navy Seal snipers, as happened in 2009 to three Somali pirates holding a freighter's captain hostage, to take out P2P users. Not only did "home taping" fail to kill music, on the contrary, the major labels continued to grow and thrive for another 20 years thanks to the CD. According to the RIAA's own U.S. sales figures, in 1980, the industry shipped about 440 million albums, and by 1999 it shipped nearly a billion units. Of course, it is no longer worried about cassette tapes, a sonically inferior and obsolete format. Before I get into how the digital revolution changed the trend beginning in 2000, we need some more information.

Bow Wow Wow, Adam and The Ants, and The Sex Pistols: When Bow Wow Wow released "C·30 C·60 C·90 Go" in 1980, lead singer Annabella Lwin was just 14 years old. How did she become the singer of this pop band?

Here's the story: Malcolm McLaren was a truly infamous and very successful British impresario, fashionista, and boutique owner. McLaren is best known for creating the Sex Pistols to help promote the boutique he owned with his girlfriend, fashion designer Vivienne Westwood. The shop was named SEX, and there they defined the fashion and styles that became synonymous with 1970s U.K. punk. After the Sex Pistols (EMI records) self destructed in 1978, sending frontman John Lydon off to form the critically acclaimed post-punk band Public Image Ltd (PiL), McLaren was in need of a new band to help promote his fashion boutique. Adam Ant approached McLaren to manage Adam and The Ants. In response, McLaren essentially dumped Adam and took The Ants (bass, guitar, and drums) to form Bow Wow Wow, minus a singer. During the singer search, one of McLaren's friends overheard Lwin singing while at her part-time job. The rest was history.

What happened next? After McLaren's "home taping" publicity stunt led to EMI dropping the band, it got picked up by RCA in 1981. In 1982, the band released a single and music video for a cover version of The Strangeloves' 1965 hit "I Want Candy." MTV had just launched in 1981, and by 1982 had become the new force in the music industry. The video for "I Want Candy" was in heavy rotation for years and is considered one of the defining videos of the early MTV era (along with videos by the likes of Devo, Cyndi Lauper, Duran Duran, Michael Jackson, Pat Benatar, The Cars, Phil Collins, The Vapors, and The Buggles, among many others).

Context Is Everything

There are a lot of good historical books about the music industry, electronic music, musical instruments, computers, music producers, and musicians. There is no way to cover everything here, so if you are interested in digging deeper, check out some of the recommendations on this book's companion website, www.iempsg.com. The goal of this chapter is largely to provide a little bit of context so we all have a shared sense of where we have been, where we are now, and where we might be going. What exactly is context, and why should you care? According to Merriam-Webster online, context is "the interrelated conditions in which something exists or occurs." Everyone understands how that definition applies to language. The phrase "let's get out of here" has significantly different connotations if you have just paid your bill at a restaurant than if that restaurant is on fire. Context defines meaning.

Anything you can name can be thought of as a "holon," a whole/part that is embedded in a complex web of whole/part systems (as further discussed in the next sidebar, "Complexification"). Because a holon might be considered as a whole and/or a part in any given example, context largely determines the borders and texture of any topic under discussion. Without some context to define the scope and scale of the subject matter, anything can be everything, and wallowing in murkiness is not a recipe for success. Some degree of clarity is required to be a nimble professional in the current era. Context is information, and information can give you an advantage. Without some knowledge of historical context, you are not only leaving it up to others to define the wholes and parts, but you may be unaware of the story elements they have decided to include and omit that best advance their position.

History...zzZzz...What's in It for Me?

What follows are some reasons why you might care about history and context:

▷ With a sense of context you are less likely to lose perspective about what you are doing and what is important.
▷ Knowledge of cyclical aspects of history can help you to better understand trends and their significance. Trends emerge in a context, so with that better understanding you will have more information for deciding which ones you should care about and possibly even for positioning yourself ahead of the curve.
▷ Understanding that change is inevitable can help you avoid becoming jaded or cynical. If you don't like what's going on now, you know that you just have to wait for something to emerge that excites you.
▷ Career professionals often care a lot about the history of their vocation, so being able to demonstrate such knowledge can help separate you from the rest of the pack at the onset of your career.
▷ You can impress your friends at parties.

A (Very Incomplete) Brief History of Everything

To put everything in context, let's take a little trip from Genesis to the present. The following timeline is not meant to be comprehensive, but it hits enough key points to invoke the texture of our terrain. Herman Hesse won the 1946 Nobel Prize for Literature for his 1943 novel, *The Glass Bead Game*. One of the characters in the book tells us, "Studying history, my friend, is no joke and no irresponsible game. To study history one must know in advance that one is attempting something fundamentally impossible, yet necessary and highly important. To study history means submitting to chaos and nevertheless retaining faith in order and meaning." I couldn't agree more.

Epoch 1: Back in the Day

▷ **13,770,000,000 years ago:** A Big Bang occurs.
▷ **4,600,000,000 years ago:** The sun ignites.
▷ **4,540,000,000 years ago:** Earth is born.
▷ **3,600,000,000 years ago:** The oldest known life on Earth appears.
▷ **200,000 years ago:** Anatomically modern humans appear.
▷ **80,000 years ago:** Modern *homo sapiens* appear in Africa.
▷ **50,000 years ago:** Humans appear in North America.
▷ **42,000 years ago:** The approximate date of the oldest known musical instruments.
▷ **14,000 BCE to 2585 BCE:** Agriculture, the wheel, first civilizations, etc., etc.
▷ **2584 BCE:** Construction begins on the Great Pyramid of Giza in Egypt.
▷ **570 BCE:** Pythagoras is born (harmony of the spheres, musical ratios and harmonic relationships; refer to Figure 1.1).
▷ **500 BCE to 1449 CE:** A lot happens.

NOTE: Keep in mind that these dates from pre-history are estimates based on the best current information.

Epoch 2: Recent History

▷ **1450:** Gutenberg invents the printing press, allowing for printed sheet music…and with it, the birth of the music industry.
▷ **1492:** Columbus gets lost looking for India and lands in modern-day Hispaniola.
▷ **1600:** William Gilbert's *De Magnete*, the first modern book on electricity and magnetism, is published.
▷ **1687:** Newton publishes "Principia," which asserts that gravity is a predictable force of nature (among other breakthroughs).
▷ **1747:** Benjamin Franklin discovers the electricity principle of "charge conservation."
▷ **1809:** The first known telegraph appears.
▷ **1843:** Ada Lovelace writes the first computer algorithm, for Charles Babbage's Analytical Engine, to calculate Bernoulli numbers.
▷ **1857:** Édouard-Léon Scott de Martinville patents the phonautograph, the first known sound-recording device (see Figure 2.2).

Figure 2.2 The phonautograph is the first known sound recording device. Drawing of 1859 model in Franz Josef Pisko's, *Die neuere Apparate der Akustik* (Vienna, 1865).

Source: Public domain, courtesy of the David Giovannoni Collection (firstsounds.org).

▷ **1874:** Elisha Grey publicly demonstrates the Musical Telegraph, the first synthesizer.

▷ **1876:** Alexander Graham Bell patents the telephone, and has better lawyers than the other inventor, Elisha Grey.

▷ **1877:** Thomas Edison invents the phonograph.

▷ **1877:** Emile Berliner patents the "flat disc" gramophone, paving the way for replication.

▷ **1892:** GE is founded at the end of the "current wars" with Nikola Tesla's AC and Thomas Edison's DC.

▷ **1892:** Emile Berliner founds the United States Gramophone Company (later called the Victor Talking Machine Company/RCA).

▷ **1896:** Guglielmo Marconi patents radio (see 1944).

▷ **1888:** American Gramophone Company (formerly Volta Gramophone Company, later Columbia/CBS) is the first to sell pre-recorded records.

▷ **1889:** The first jukebox appears, created by Louis Glass, manager of Pacific Phonograph Company in San Francisco.

▷ **1898:** Fred Gaisberg becomes the first ever "producer" and A&R exec, for London Gramophone Company (later HMV and EMI).

Epoch 3: The 20th Century

▷ **1903:** The Wright brothers accomplish the first successful airplane flight.

▷ **1905:** Albert Einstein publishes a paper with his famous equation $E=mc^2$, asserting that matter and energy are the same thing.

▷ **1906:** Lee De Forest invents the Audion amplifying vacuum tube.

▷ **1914:** Germany's Merck patents 3,4-methylenedioxy-N-methamphetamine, commonly known as MDMA.

▷ **1922:** The Motion Picture Association of America (MPAA) is founded.

▷ **1923:** Edwin Hubble not only discovers that the Milky Way is not the only galaxy, but is in fact one of many, but also that the universe is expanding at an accelerated rate.

▷ **1924:** Bell Labs is founded.

▷ **1928:** Philo Farnswarth demos the first working television system.

▷ **1931:** Alan Blumlein develops stereophonic sound at EMI.

▷ **1931:** RCA Victor releases the first "long-play" records, at 33⅓ RPM.

▷ **1933:** Harvey Fletcher and Wilden A. Munson publish a paper defining "loudness."

▷ **1936:** Alan Turing defines computers as being able to calculate any calculable function, what is commonly referred to as "Turing complete."

▷ **1938:** Swiss chemist Albert Hofmann synthesizes D-lysergic acid diethylamide, commonly known as LSD.

▷ **1939–1945:** World War II. Computers are developed to crack the Nazi's "Enigma" code.

▷ **1941:** Grace Hopper creates the first compiler for a computer programming language.

▷ **1942:** RCA awards the first gold record to Glen Miller for "Chattanooga Choo Choo."

▷ **1944:** The U.S. Supreme Court rules that 15 of 16 radio patents filed in 1896 by Guglielmo Marconi infringed on Nikola Tesla's patents.

▷ **1946:** The ENIAC, the U.S. Army's first digital and Turing-complete computer, is revealed.

▷ **1947:** Bell Labs creates the first working transistor.

▷ **1948:** Claude Shannon at Bell Labs publishes a paper that launches the field of information theory, making the digital age possible.

▷ **1948:** Les Paul invents "sound on sound" and pioneers overdubbing, a multitrack recording technique essential to modern production, in his home studio.

▷ **1952:** The Recording Industry Association of America (RIAA) is founded.

▷ **1957:** Max Matthews at Bell Labs invents computer-based audio recording.

▷ **1962:** Philips invents the compact cassette tape format.

▷ **1964:** The Stereo 8 consortium develops the 8-track tape format (based on RCA's magazine loading cartridge from 1958).

▷ **1969:** The first message sent via ARPANET, the precursor to the Internet.

▷ **1969:** Neil Armstrong becomes the first human to walk on the moon.

▷ **1971:** Intel releases the first commercially available microprocessor, the 4004.

▷ **1975:** Apple Computer and Microsoft are founded.

▷ **1980:** Sony and Philips publish the "Red Book" outlining the CD-DA format.

▷ **1983:** The MIDI spec is published.

▷ **1984:** Steinberg, Digidesign, MOTU, and Opcode (1985) are founded.

▷ **1988:** The Moving Picture Experts Group (MPEG) format is created as part of ISO.

▷ **1990:** NASA launches the Hubble Space Telescope into orbit.

▷ **1992:** CERN's HTTP protocol and the World Wide Web (WWW) join the Internet.

▷ **1993:** Fraunhofer's MPEG ISO Layer-3 is given a file extension, .mp3.

▷ **1999:** Napster is born.

▷ **1999:** This year marks the historical peak of CD sales, according to the RIAA.

▷ **2000:** The Y2K scare, a.k.a. the Millennium Bug, quietly comes and goes.

Epoch 4: The New Millennium

▷ **2001:** NASA launches the Wilkinson Microwave Anisotropy Probe (WMAP); the age of the universe is no longer a mystery. (See Figure 2.3.)

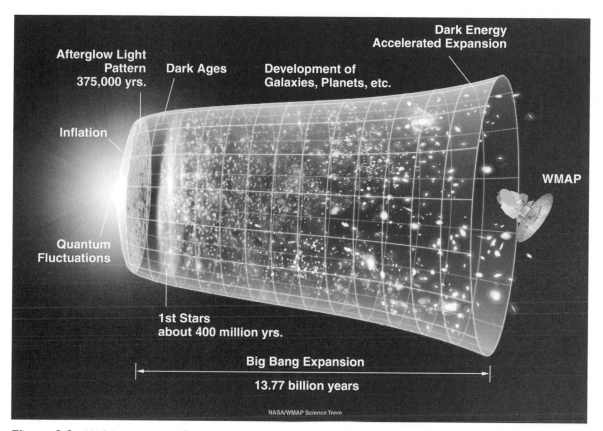

Figure 2.3 NASA-generated "Timeline of The Universe," based on WMAP measurements of cosmic background radiation.

Source: Public domain, courtesy of NASA.

▷ **2001:** Apple releases iTunes and the iPod.
▷ **2003:** Apple launches the iTunes Music Store (now called the iTunes Store).
▷ **2003:** RIAA launches the first 261 file-sharing lawsuits of 30,000+.
▷ **2004:** SpaceShipOne is the first successful private manned space flight.
▷ **2004:** RIAA includes sales of downloaded music toward certification.
▷ **2007:** Apple Computer changes name to Apple, Inc.
▷ **2010:** Apple releases the iPad.
▷ **2011:** Apple (temporarily) surpasses Exxon as the world's most valuable company.
▷ **2012:** The Higgs boson is detected at CERN, arguably the biggest scientific discovery since $E=mc^2$.
▷ **2012:** The end of the Mayan calendar quietly comes and goes.
▷ **2013:** *The Music Producer's Survival Guide* is published by Cengage Learning.

NOTE: Determining who was really the "first" to invent or do something is not as easy as it sounds, especially before the media age. When there is no obvious public documentation of a first, "history" usually remembers the first notable example, the first in the lineage that has most directly contributed to our current civilization's widespread technologies, or the one who was awarded the patent. To illustrate the last reason, I would wager that while you've likely heard of Alexander Graham Bell, you've not heard of Elisha Grey until now (see 1874 and 1876 above). There are many other such examples of *multiple independent discovery* (as is discussed in Chapter 8, "Selecting Your Tools," with regard to the invention of the subtractive modular analog synthesizer by two people).

Complexification (Dynamics of Holon Evolution): What do each of the following word pairs have in common?

- ▶ cell–organism
- ▶ planet–galaxy
- ▶ perception–concept
- ▶ individual–society
- ▶ computer–the Internet
- ▶ musician–band

These pairs represent just a few examples of holons—wholes that are also parts of more complex wholes, or whole/parts. Chapter 4, "Master Your Craft," includes a more in-depth discussion of this incredibly useful concept, as does Appendix B, "Integral Theory Primer."

To fully understand how our industry evolved to what it is today, we need a basic understanding of the process of complexification. Specifically, we are interested in the term complexification as it is used in systems theory. Systems theory is the transdisciplinary study of any self-regulating system, such as inquiries found in thermodynamics, meteorology, electronics, computing, biology, psychology, ecology, economics, sociology, and history. Systems theory emphasizes the significance of interrelationships and is often considered the first "holistic" modern field of science, dating back to Ludwig von Bertalanffy in the 1930s. We might consider systems theory as a scientific approach to understanding context. As you may recall from a few pages back, Merriam-Webster.com defines context as "the interrelated conditions in which something exists or occurs." We are not only interested in considering systems as they are, but also how they evolve. Complexification is used to describe a ubiquitous dynamic found in evolving systems. It describes how dynamics that commonly emerge as simpler systems become parts of more complex systems, including the implications for parts and the new whole. In other words, what happens to holons as they become parts of a more complex holon, and how is that emergent more complex holon different from all of its parts?

The parts are fundamental to the wholes, which have emergent abilities and capacities that the parts by themselves do not have. Yet, the new whole cannot exist without the parts. For example, the Internet can do a lot more than an individual computer. If you disconnect a few computers it doesn't matter, but if you disconnect all of them from the network, there is no more Internet. Although each individual computer loses the emergent functionality that exists only when connected to the network, individual computers can still continue to function as they did before gaining such additional capabilities. That is, unless a computer's basic functions were designed after the emergence of the Internet in such a way that they are dependent on a network connection, such as with the so-called "netbooks" like Google's Chromebook.

Complexification sheds a lot of light on how it is that we can now produce music at home and then access it most anywhere. The functional complexity of the many parts becomes simplified in the new whole. In plain English, as systems evolve into a new larger system, there is a simplification in overall system function. For example, while sitting in front of your home computer, you have most of the same basic functionality and capabilities that used to require a full recording studio system. While sitting in front of that same computer, you can buy music, which was produced in someone else's home while sitting at their computer, instead of having to leave your house and find transportation to a store. Talk about a simplification of system function! At the same time, the complexity of the software and hardware on which it runs, though physically smaller, is substantially higher, thanks to decades of technological advancement from numerous fields and industries. A recording engineer working in a studio in the 1980s could repair many equipment breakdowns himself, while not one of us knows how to fix the microprocessor in our computer that makes everything we do possible (although you might be able to replace it).

The common idiom "the whole is more than the sum of its parts" perfectly describes wholes and their emergent properties. But that is not the whole story. In *Method Vol. 1* (1992), leading systems theory philosopher Edgar Morin points out that not only is the whole more than the sum of its parts, but also that "the whole is less than the sum of the parts." According to Morin, this is due to the fact that some qualities, properties, abilities, or characteristics of the parts are suppressed, inhibited, or constrained by the systemic relationship to the whole. This last point is easily illustrated when considering musicians and bands. Collaboration in a band can lead to results not possible by the individuals alone; yet, each individual cannot fully express himself or herself when working together to enable the emergent properties of group behavior.

You do not need to fully understand the content in this sidebar to get a lot out of this chapter, but the basic ideas do add another potential layer of insight to those of you who do. If you are particularly interested in these ideas, without question, the best source for further reading is Ken Wilber's 1995 magnum opus *Sex, Ecology, Spirituality: The Spirit of Evolution* or his more user-friendly condensed version from 1996, *A Brief History of Everything.* You will also find more in-depth discussion of holons in Chapter 4 and Appendix B.

Where Are We Now?

Humans surely have been making music at least as long as we've been *homo sapiens*. Recent discoveries in Germany of flutes made from bird bone and mammoth ivory date back more than 42,000 years (*Journal of Human Evolution*, June 2012). It is safe to assume that music was around before we started making musical instruments, but for argument's sake, let's use that time as our most conservative estimate. As 1888 was the year that pre-recorded records first went on sale, we can think of it as the birth year of the record industry. So as of 2013 the industry is about 125 years old. Using common construction measurements, if we think of 42,000 years as the equivalent height of a 12-story building, we could represent the music industry with a human hair. The record industry is a blip in the history of music. Yet, that blip marks the shift from the one era of music to another.

As our global civilization evolves, so too does our relationship to music and to the whole music system. This relationship includes many facets, such as our personal experience of music as a listener or a musician, the prevalence of music in general, its means and methods of production, its distribution, and its sale and purchase as a product. And just as we have identified complexification in biological, social, and technological systems, so too can we see that complexification is radically altering our relationship to music, primarily for the better. It appears that we have recently entered a new era of music in human culture.

Making and experiencing music used to be much more difficult and rare. Both the production and consumption of music is more prevalent than at any other time in human history, largely due to recent and significant instances of complexification in our social, economic, and technological systems. And as with all cases of complexification, there are gains and losses as wholes become parts of larger more complex wholes. Although most of the older and simpler parts are retained, they also lose some of their significance and prominence. Trains are still important parts of our economic and transportation systems, but they lost their dominant position as automobiles, interstate highway systems, and jet airplanes appeared. As we now briefly discuss each music era, notice how the "new" is commonly layered around or built on top of the "old."

Era 1: Local and Exclusive (? to 1887)

During this era, the only way to hear music was to be there while it was performed (or as performer), which meant being at a specific location at a specific time. All instruments were acoustic and there was no way to record performances. Access to music from different cultures was rare and difficult, both in terms of geographical separation but also often socio-economic class structure. Just as someone in Asia would not be able to hear music from Mexico, the poor and working class rarely heard the music performed at the halls and theaters attended primarily by the wealthy and privileged. The next era began to emerge as the first industrial revolution offered a plethora of new manufacturing techniques powered by the steam engine.

Era 2: Transmission and Storage (1888 to 2000)

During this era, audio transmission and storage technologies proliferated on the tail of the second industrial revolution, which included widespread distribution of electricity after GE's founding in 1892. In tandem with other landmark breakthroughs, reliable, safe, and plentiful electricity enabled the proliferation of countless world-changing technologies characteristic of the 20th century's unprecedented rate of change. In addition to the introduction of broadcast radio in the 1920s, people could now also buy pre-recorded music, which could be listened to anytime and anywhere one could connect a playback system to an electrical outlet (including car batteries). This era might be considered as the "golden age" of the recording industry. The first real signs of this era evolving into the next one emerged in the 1980s with the advent of portable playback devices, such as the Sony Walkman, and the introduction of the CD. By the 1990s the rising popularity of digital technologies, most notably personal computers and the Internet, began to unravel the need for the physical distribution systems put in place by the recording industry and music retailers.

Era 3: Global Information Networks (2001 to 2045[?])

This era is just coming into its own as we adapt to the repercussions of the digital revolution and the nascent Information Age. So far, it is characterized by the Internet and by digital means of production and distribution. Music flows like any other information over our digital networks, which include wireless transmission technologies as much as hard-wired connections to local networks and the Internet. Sound reproduction systems are ubiquitous in most modern people's lives—at home, in cars, in elevators, in lobbies, in clubs, at restaurants, in movie theatres, in bars, in stadiums, in airplanes, on portable computing devices, and on cell phones, for starters. And although the same could be said for a lot of places in the last half of the 20th century, the source of the music no longer must exist on a physical medium in that location.

Yes, before this there was radio, and yes, you could take a Walkman with you anywhere in the world, but your music selection was limited to the available stations or how many tapes or CDs you could carry with you. Not only can current portable music playback devices store more than 10,000 songs, they can easily swap out music from other common portable storage devices able to hold hundreds of thousands of songs. Moreover, music is now commonly stored on servers with practically unlimited capacity, which is accessible to these players, and therefore speakers, via the Internet and even satellites in geosynchronous orbit around our planet. So not only can we access music anytime, anywhere, but the available selection theoretically includes every song ever recorded in the history of humanity. This emergent system that allows us to access virtually unlimited amounts of music, anytime, from anywhere in the world, is now being referred to as a "celestial jukebox." Are we already seeing the beginnings of the next era, so soon?

Era 4: Biotechnology Network Integration? (2045[?] to ?)

When is this next era going to emerge? It might be sooner than we think. Just consider the following examples of the accelerating rate of change. From the time of the first known music instruments, it was about 42,000 years until we started recording music. Only 63 years separates the Wright brothers' first successful airplane flight until Neil Armstrong took that famous first small step on the moon. Philips introduced the compact cassette tape in 1962; only 18 years later, the industry was worried about "home taping." Officially, the World Wide Web joined the Internet in 1992, and the MP3 showed up in 1993; it only took about six years for Napster, in 1999, to mark the most significant transformation in the record industry in many decades.

Scientists employ the term "singularity" when describing something they do not fully understand or cannot "see" beyond, such as the singularity at the center of black holes. In his 2005 bestseller, *The Singularity Is Near: When Humans Transcend Biology*, Ray Kurzweil employs the term in reference to a time in the near future when our technology evolves past our ability to understand it. He predicts that this will happen sometime around 2045. At that time, only those who merge with technology will be able to understand and keep up with it. This merger is already well underway, as is exemplified in already common medical procedures such as heart pacemakers, the latest generation of artificial limbs, lab-grown replacement organs, and any variety of new retinal implants being tested for those with vision problems.

When the ENIAC was revealed to the public in 1946, it was the most powerful computer on the planet, and the first Turing complete one at that (see 1936 in the previous section "Epoch 3: The 20th Century"). It used almost 18,000 vacuum tubes for its calculations, weighed more than 25 tons, took up about 1,800 square feet, and cost of about $6 million in today's money. Transistors replaced vacuum tubes in the 1960s, which were in turn replaced by even smaller microprocessors in the 1970s. Microprocessor specs regularly include the number of transistors on them. Intel's first processor in 1971, the 4004, had 2,300 transistors and fit in your hand, costing about $300 in today's money. By the 1990s, the processors in cell phones had about 1,000,000 transistors. These were standard mobile phones, not smartphones! Today's smartphones are more powerful computers than top-of-the-line PCs from the pre-smartphone era. By 2013, Intel's 61 core Xeon Phi 7100 series, had exceeded 19,000,000,000 transistors on a slightly larger chip and costing about $3,800. To put that in perspective, based on dollar-per-transistor cost, 19 billion of them on a chip in 1971 would have cost more than $145 billion. How long before we really can safely implant computers into our bodies? When that happens, it is possible that all information will be immediately accessible. In that case, could unlimited music be piped directly into our awareness? Any good futurist understands that predictions tend to overshoot the short term but way undershoot the long term. Many of us will be alive in 2045, so who knows? We'll just have to wait and see.

What Goes Around Comes Around

The record industry is only possible because of the scientific breakthroughs and subsequent technologies that make music production possible in the first place. And although music has a really long history, sound recording didn't start until the phonautograph in 1857. A mechanical device designed as an analog to the human ear, it is widely believed to be the first known sound-recording device (although it was originally intended simply to draw sound waves, not sonically reproduce them).

Music production was not yet possible even millennia after humans created sophisticated civilizations with large-scale engineering projects like the Great Pyramids and the Great Wall of China. We still had to learn enough about electricity, magnetism, and physics to build the devices capable of transducing, transmitting, storing, and reproducing sound. The necessary scientific knowledge sufficiently accumulated over a 300-year period that finally culminated in the last half of the 19th century with the inventions of such notables as Alexander Graham Bell,

Thomas Edison, Nikola Tesla, and Emile Berliner. Geniuses from the first half of the 20th century like Alan Turing and Claude Shannon paved the way for exponentially powerful technological advances in the form of computing technology and digital signals, which finally crossed over into the commercial world in the 1970s with the emergence of Silicon Valley in California. Without these innovators and their inventions, among many others, we would not have our amazing recording technology, and therefore no record industry.

Industry Expansion and Limited Access to Technology

From the beginning of the industry until the 1990s, quality record production was really only possible with the financial backing of labels. Simply stated, it cost too much money for individuals to have access to the equipment and facilities required for commercial quality releases. This state of affairs also meant that only professionals with a lot of training and knowledge would have access to working these facilities. Logically it follows that to become an audio professional, one had to work in such commercial facilities as interns or assistant engineers to gain the necessary skills and experience. In most cases, much like with film production, whole teams of people with specialized skills and expertise were involved in record production. Even into the 1960s, there are famous stories about Beatles sessions that required techs in white lab coats be the only ones to touch and set up the mics. Musicians would rehearse material, often written by other composers, and then go into the studio to record the songs under the direction of a producer who was largely unknown to the masses. By the 1960s a few record producers, including Phil Spector and his "wall of sound," gained superstar status on par with Hollywood movie directors. There was no place for amateurs or even serious hobbyists in such a world, for at least a few more decades.

Phil Spector made his name at a time when the technology, though high quality, was relatively primitive compared to what would emerge in the following two decades. As with famous Motown recordings from the same era (and many others), Spector was working with a 3-track tape recorder, and although stereo had been around for a while, most releases at this time were still in mono. It was not until the late 1960s that stereophonic releases became the established norm, and moreover, that 8- and 16 track tape machines were to be commonplace. Then it was another few years before the industry saw recognizably modern inline consoles such as the Harrison MCI JH-400 in 1972, the Neve 8048 in 1973, and the SSL 4000 B in 1977. By the 1990s, a fully decked out 96 input SSL 9000J would cost about $750,000 or more, depending on requested mods or add-on options. As the industry expanded and evolved, increasingly sophisticated and expensive equipment offered many new creative possibilities. Artists started using the studio itself as an "instrument" and creative tool. For an amazing example of this emergence, check out the 1974 documentary *Pink Floyd: Live at Pompeii*, which intersperses concert footage shot in the ruins of Pompeii (sans audience) from 1971, but most relevant to our purposes, amazing footage of them in the studio creating *The Dark Side of the Moon* (1973).

It is to be expected that increasingly expensive equipment translated into more costly studio time. Not only did studio time become more costly, but it became common for bands to actually write the album in the studio, not just go in to record. This new creative tool resulted in lucrative extended "lockouts" for the studios, and multi-million dollar budgets for the bands and labels. For the most successful bands, the budgets were essentially open ended, which created the perfect environments for eccentric behavior and excessive drug use during these productions. In fact, sometimes the "tape" budget was purposely inflated to account for something else often cut with razor blades at that time. (Thanks to my tech editor, Michael White, for this tidbit of historical trivia from that bygone big studio era!) Fleetwood Mac's *Rumors* (1977) is widely considered one of the best rock albums of all time. The 1976 sessions at the Record Plant in Sausalito, CA are legendary examples of excess. Those session are known for such copious amounts of cocaine consumption that, even into the 1990s, visiting engineers would ask about all the marks on the consoles arm rest, only to be told there were razor blade nicks that had all been there since the *Rumors* sessions. Redeemingly, that album would go on to sell more than 25 million copies, and the band members successfully completed rehab a few years later. By the early 1990s it was not uncommon for labels to spend many millions of dollars on such productions, even growing totally out of control. According to a March 6, 2005 *New York Times* article, "The Most Expensive Album Never Made," Guns N' Roses accrued more than $13 million in production costs for a record they started in 1994 and that, by 1999, was still incomplete. In early 1999, a few years after Seagram purchased their label, Geffen Records, the project was cancelled and the album was never finished or released. Is it more than an interesting coincidence that 1999 was the year that production on the most expensive album never released was cancelled and also the high water mark in record sales for the major label industry?

Industry Contraction and Expanded Access to Technology

What else was going on in 1999? We will talk about trends in record releases, sales, the Internet, and "illegal" downloading in a bit, but there is a lot more to the story than CD sales and MP3s. The home studio boom really started in the 1980s with the introduction of relatively affordable 4-track cassette tape recorders such as the TEAC Model 144 Portastudio (1979). Now musicians did not have to go into the studio just to record a "demo"; they could put their ideas together in their own studio. These demos were most often used to get a record deal or as a preproduction step to sketch out ideas that were to be more fully realized in a costly studio. As MIDI evolved from 1983 on, composers could write full scores with the sequencers on their home computers and then even record them themselves with any number of the 4-tracks that were hitting the market. By the early 1990s, the Alesis ADAT 8-track digital tape recorder (1991) paired with a Mackie analog 8-bus console (1993) offered big studio functionality for a fraction of the cost, albeit with some sonic sacrifices. It was now possible for indie studios and artists to fully mimic the same workflows and techniques that were prohibitively expensive to all but the big studios just a few years earlier.

As a follow-up to the successful Sound Designer and Sound Tools platforms, in 1991, Pro Tools 1.0 made its debut. Although it was not until version 5, in 1999, that Pro Tools was used to produce a #1 hit (*Livin' la Vida Loca*), indicating that it was well on its way to becoming the industry standard it is today. On the project or home-studio level, users could run Pro Tools LE with native real-time RTAS plug-ins and the new 001 interface with 18 channels of I/O, all for about $1,000. The top-of-the-line TDM-based Pro Tools|24 MIX system was highly scalable, and even their largest stock bundle with three DSP cards connected to three of their flagship 888|24 I/O interfaces would cost only about $30,000. This was quite a bargain, considering that by themselves, the high-quality 24-track analog tape machines found in commercial studios easily cost that much, and moreover, at this time many studios were also using DASH recorders (digital tape machines), such as the Sony 3348 series, which cost from eight to 12 times more than the aforementioned Pro Tools system. In addition to challenges to their dominance of distribution networks, the majors would now also have to deal with the fact that the trending in lower costs, more power and quality, and widespread availability of these technologies had ended their monopoly on access to the means of production. Although they attempted to take advantage of these new fast workflow technologies by normalizing smaller advances for less studio time, the cat was already out of the bag.

A Parallel Teachable Moment from Recent History

With origins traceable to the 1880s, IBM (International Business Machines) is one of the world's most important companies in the history of computing. As of 2012, it had more than 430,000 employees and revenue exceeding $100 billion. For most of its history it's been a hugely profitable company, in large part due to its numerous innovations, breakthroughs, and inventions ranging from the guidance computers used in NASA's Gemini space flights (1965), to Mandelbrot's discovery of fractal geometry (1967), to computers used for NASA's first moon landing (1969), to relational databases (1970), to the floppy disk and speech recognition (1971), and of course, the IBM PC (1981). By 1985, "Big Blue" had more than 400,000 employees, but soon thereafter, massive nightly news–making layoffs became the norm. By 1995, IBM was down to just over 225,000 employees. What happened, and why should we care?

There were a lot of factors that had IBM on the ropes, but one that best symbolizes the nature of the company's bad decisions during that period is the story of the PC and Microsoft. IBM was a major player in the mainframe world. When it introduced the PC, the company was sure that only business people and scientists would want one. Of course, up to this point, these were the only people who had access to the powerful mainframe computers, so IBM assumed the market consisted of essentially the same types of professionals. IBM approached an upstart company called Microsoft to help it write an OS for its new "personal" computer, as Bill Gates had just made a name for his new company by writing software for the practically useless but historically significant Altair 8800. Because IBM failed to see the future of personal computing, it decided not to buy the OS from Microsoft, but instead to license it and pay a royalty on each copy sold. That very bad decision by IBM turned Bill Gates and his partners into billionaires. The personal computer revolution was well underway, and the rest is history. The computing power once only available via mainframes was now in the hands of anyone who could afford a home computer, such as those by Apple, Tandy, Atari, Commodore, and all of the companies making IBM PCs that were running an OS licensed from Microsoft. Around 1995, IBM began to right its course by refocusing its vast resources on super computers and other innovations in high tech other than personal computers, which was demonstrated to the world with the historic "Deep Blue Versus Garry Kasparov" chess matches in 1996 and 1997.

Where Is the RIAA's Equivalent of Deep Blue?

Let's relate this to the record industry. Just as we all have access to incredible computing power once only affordable to institutions and companies, we now also have access to the incredibly powerful record-production technology that was once affordable only by the big labels and their clients. Would it have made sense for IBM to blame its decline on Apple and other personal computer makers? IBM failed to see the future that the company itself had played a major role in creating, and it cost the company dearly for over a decade. Imagine if IBM continued to behave as if it were the only source of quality computing power and never refocused when it did. Does it make sense for the RIAA and its associates to blame the project studio boom and the Internet for its decline? The recording studio industry has legitimate gripes, but the record industry as a whole, not so much. Is it fair to say that they are still acting like they are the only source of quality music production and distribution? We will soon consider the arguments for and against their stance.

Complexification, as discussed in the previous sidebar, helps to explain these dynamics. Just as single-cell organisms were once the pinnacle of complex life on Earth, the major-label record industry was until very recently the pinnacle of the music system. And just as a variety of single-cell organisms are still around and common parts of more complex organisms, the record industry and other media/entertainment industries are part of a more complex global culture and economy characterized by the digital revolution and the Internet. As more complex wholes emerge, there are gains and losses—gains in terms of the emergent properties of the new system and losses for aspects of the parts (listed momentarily). The record industry was the whole game; now it is a part of the emergent global information network. The music-production and distribution system has complexified. It is no longer dependent on corporate channels and capital. The big labels are like an organ in an organism that could survive without it. The record industry is now much more than just the major labels; it also includes the chaotic jungle of new indie producers and distribution networks that have evolved over the last 30 years.

Gains from Complexification

Gains from complexification include the following:

▷ **More music.** We can now hear more music from more places, cultures, and times than at any point in the history of the world. In addition, there is more indie and DIY music than ever.

▷ **Personal empowerment.** More people can explore and express a fundamental human urge: to make music.

▷ **Creative freedom.** High-quality, sophisticated productions are possible for a fraction of the cost a few decades back, diminishing the need for funding from labels that often place limitations on creative expression.

▷ **New opportunities.** Decentralization in a transitioning record industry means that many people can carve out new niches for themselves. It is much easier to be an independent professional now due to lower costs of production.

▷ **More jobs.** The crash of the big-label industry had a cascading effect that forced a lot of the big studios to go out of business, and the ones that survived had to trim down. In their place appeared many more jobs in burgeoning private and project "prosumer" studio scenes. Unfortunately, these new jobs usually lack good pay, long-term stability, and/or advancement opportunities, and the quality of the work environment varies wildly.

▷ **Information everywhere.** If you know where to look, you can learn from people all over the world, including once well-guarded tradecraft secrets.

Losses from Complexification

Losses from complexification include the following:

▷ **More music.** We now have to sift through an unprecedented flood of amateur, inane, poorly produced, and/or just simply bad music, most of it indie and DIY. The new system has a lot of noise in it.

▷ **Less expertise.** The lower threshold of entry and easy distribution systems allow amateurs and hobbyists to get in the game even with the lower production values resulting from lack of experience, training, and skill.

▷ **Fewer jobs.** The crash of the big-label industry had a cascading effect that forced a lot of the big studios to go out of business, and the ones that survived had to trim down. So now there are not only significantly fewer jobs in "world class" commercial recording studios, there is also a lot less stability in the jobs that do exist. Moreover, the downward pressure on rates from project studio competitors (as discussed previously) negatively affects a lot of good, veteran audio engineers.

▷ **Less apprenticing.** Because there are fewer big studios and therefore fewer entry-level positions, learning from high-level experts or mentors on the job has become much more rare.

▷ **Record store experience.** The experience of going into a record store to discover new music is very enjoyable—if you can find one, that is. The sounds, smells, and tactile experience of flipping through aisles of records and CDs, with full-size, full-color artwork, is not possible online. Although there are still a few stores here and there, most people rarely get their music from small specialty shops with knowledgeable staff. The experience of being condescended to by the pretentious clerk behind the counter, and the subsequent exposure to amazing new indie or underground music, is now a rare experience unless you are in a big city or college town lucky enough to have a few survivors still around.

The Argument for the Industry

The cutthroat, take-no-prisoners, survival-of-the-fittest reputation of the music business is nothing new, and the tarnished reputation of the current major label corporate media controlled record industry is well earned. Yet, we do owe a lot to the industry as a whole. Not only did it help to make a lot of great music widely accessible, but it also deserves credit on two other major points: technology and economics.

Technology

The industry's size, scope, and significant profitability drives advances in audio technology and music-production capabilities. This point is most directly attributable to many of the labels, since they either owned their own studios or had significant relationships with major studios. Historically, the major labels, the production facilities, and the motion-picture industry were by far the primary market for developers and manufacturers. These innovations also paved the way for the project and home studio booms, indie labels, and the widespread distribution of a diverse assortment of non-commercial music.

Increasingly since the 1990s, the industry's prominence in those regards has diminished significantly. It should also be noted that, as discussed in the book's introduction, nearly every historically significant label is now owned by only four corporations with financial interests in many different industries. As such, much of the credit due to those labels for their innovations is more for historical and posterity's sake than current credit due to their new corporate owners of which they are now a subsidiary. That said, though diminished, their role in driving new technologies still exists.

Economics

The industry provides job, income, and career opportunities for creative artists and other professionals. The large-scale, big-budget productions create a lot of work for skilled professionals, including audio engineers, musicians and music techs, stage-lighting companies, and the electrical and software engineers who design the equipment and software. Major labels are a good choice for some artists. If an artist has a large enough fan base, or the potential to develop one, then the big labels can facilitate large-scale and expensive PR campaigns, lucrative licensing deals, global distribution, studio productions, and world tours. That being said, only an elite few fully benefit from these resources, as you have never even heard of most artists signed to a major label. These days, many of them are dropped quickly if their first album is not hugely successful, and sometimes even before any music is even recorded or released. The industry still has huge potential to offer a lot more in these regards if it ever changes its business model.

> **NOTE:** The unprecedented deal between Jay-Z, his Roc Nation label, and Samsung for the release of his July 4, 2013 album, *Magna Carta Holy Grail*, is a hugely significant example of such innovation. Also appearing on July 4, 2013 was the article "Jay-Z's $5 Million Samsung Deal Will Change Music Forever" on www.businessinsider.com, which was a reposting of an article from www.theguardian.com.

The Industry's Weak Argument

According to the RIAA's own website, "RIAA members create, manufacture and/or distribute approximately 85% of all legitimate recorded music produced and sold in the United States." What does it mean by "legitimate" recorded music produced? Does that not lend credence to the argument that it still acts like it has a monopoly on access to means of production? Legitimate sales, sure. There is piracy. But legitimate production? To be fair, there is a lot of amateur-induced noise out there now, but there is also a wealth of amazing, high-quality indie and DIY productions that are not under their banner. Upon closer scrutiny, as you will soon see, much of the industry's behavior could easily be interpreted as contempt for its customers. It is not trying to innovate its way out of its predicament. Survival instinct seems to be driving its primary adaptation strategy, which explains its conservative decisions, defensive posturing, aggressive litigation, and victim mentality. (Note: I am primarily referring to the RIAA and corporate executives, not the assortment of talented professionals and independent businesses that have suffered in the economic fallout.)

P2P and CD Sales (Correlation Does Not Imply Causation)

The phrase "correlation does not imply causation" is a central scientific understanding when comparing statistical variables. Without question, more than any other cause, the RIAA blames peer-to-peer (P2P) file sharing for the drop in record sales. Record sales peaked in 1999, Napster appeared in 1999, sales began to drop in 2000, so the obvious conclusion is that file sharing caused the drop in record sales, right? Napster, Kazaa, Hotline, Audio Galaxy, LimeWire, BitTorrent, and Pirate Bay must be responsible for industry's revenue losses, and therefore the downsizing and consolidation that had to occur in order to maintain big profits, it would like us to believe.

Found in the "Online Piracy" section of the RIAA's website, under the heading "Scope of the Problem," the first bullet point states: "Consider these staggering statistics: Since peer-to-peer (p2p) file-sharing site Napster emerged in 1999, music sales in the U.S. have dropped 53 percent, from $14.6 billion to $7.0 billion in 2011." The RIAA has trotted out numerous charts over the years that show correlated trends of increases in P2P downloads and drops in record sales, such as found in the previous quote. There are also numerous expertly prepared charts that accurately show that rates of juvenile delinquency rise and fall in tandem with ice cream sales. Yet, clearly increases in ice cream sales do not cause more juvenile delinquency. The common factor in both variables is summer break, when it is hot outside and kids are off from school without adult supervision. Summer is the causative variable on both of the correlated variables of ice cream sales and juvenile delinquency rates. Is it possible that the correlation between rises in P2P file sharing and drops in record sales is also spurious? There is no doubt that file sharing played a big part in the recent transformation, but it is not even close to the whole story.

In 2004, Felix Oberholzer-Gee (Harvard University) and Koleman Strumpf (University of Kansas) co-authored an article, "The Effect of File Sharing on Record Sales: An Empirical Analysis," that was published in the *Journal of Political Economy*. It is easy to find online if you would like to sort through their methods and statistics, but I've included their conclusion for brevity's sake.

> *We find that file sharing has no statistically significant effect on purchases of the average album in our sample. Moreover, the estimates are of rather modest size when compared to the drastic reduction in sales in the music industry. At most, file sharing can explain a tiny fraction of this decline. This result is plausible given that movies, software, and video games are actively downloaded, and yet these industries have continued to grow since the advent of file sharing. While a full explanation for the recent decline in record sales is beyond the scope of this analysis, several plausible candidates exist. These alternative factors include poor macroeconomic conditions, a reduction in the number of album releases, growing competition from other forms of entertainment such as video games and DVDs (video game graphics have improved and the price of DVD players*

and movies have sharply fallen), a reduction in music variety stemming from the large consolidation in radio along with the rise of independent promoter fees to gain airplay, and possibly a consumer backlash against record industry tactics. It is also important to note that a similar drop in record sales occurred in the late 1970s and early 1980s, and that record sales in the 1990s may have been abnormally high as individuals replaced older formats with CDs (Liebowitz, 2003).

Other Factors

Piracy, real piracy, is a problem. When people illegally sell knock-offs and bootlegs of a company's product, it does result in a direct loss of revenue. Since there is a direct transactional exchange of money for the pirated goods, though difficult to measure, it is measurable. On the other hand, executives can only guess at the losses resulting from freely exchanged digital information via P2P file sharing and downloading. Making use of such an obvious scapegoat has allowed them to ignore their own mistakes. Beyond glaring examples of the wasteful excesses that peaked with the $13 million GN'R record that was never even released, or alienating customers with expensive CDs containing just a few good songs and a lot of filler, there are many other variables to consider.

MIT- and Harvard-educated Dan Bricklin knows numbers. He is considered "The Father of the Spreadsheet," having co-created VisiCalc in 1979, one of the apps that helped launch the Apple II and establish Apple as a major player in the burgeoning home computer market. In 2002, he posted an article to his website (www.bricklin.com) entitled: "The Recording Industry Is Trying to Kill the Goose That Lays the Golden Egg." In that article, he explores a slew of other economic and consumer trends, including the rise of the cell phone as a new source of monthly expenses for an increasing number of people—disposable income that now went to the phone companies and not the record companies. With regard to the rise of the cell phone as concurrent with the drop in CD sales, he states: "The entertainment industry is trying to turn peer-to-peer into a bad name. This is wrong. Fax machines are peer-to-peer. Telephones are peer-to-peer. Email is peer-to-peer. Cell phones are peer-to-peer. As we see here, maybe the peer-to-peer systems they should be complaining about are sold by AT&T Wireless, Verizon, and Voicestream." If you think that Bricklin's example is just a spurious correlation, and that Napster really did cause the drop in record sales, please keep reading.

The Argument for Self-Destruction

Steve Knopper's brilliant 2009 book, *Appetite for Self-Destruction: The Spectacular Crash of the Record Industry in the Digital Age*, offers a mountain of evidence that the RIAA and friends have themselves to blame more than anyone else. Over the course of a well-researched 250 pages, he supports his central thesis with eight case studies of "Big Music's Big Mistakes":

▷ **"The CD Longbox."** Starting in the early 1980s, to get labels to switch formats from LP and cassette, they needed to satisfy stores' visual placement requirements. Thus, the incredibly wasteful packaging known as the CD longbox was developed. This was seen as useful for marketing purposes, but annoyed consumers, and cost the labels many millions of dollars. It finally came to an end in 1993.

▷ **"Independent Radio Promotion."** The famous payola scandals of the 1960s didn't end the practice of "pay to play." A network of independent radio promoters became powerful go-betweens between the labels and radio stations. Essentially, they put pressure on radio programmers to play certain songs based on payments from the labels—as much as $80 million per year. Some estimates claim even as much as 30% of their pretax profits went to these indie promoters. This dubious practice finally came to an end a few years after the Telecommunications Act of 1996 deregulated markets and allowed companies like Clear Channel to dominate the radio markets (as discussed in the book's introduction).

▷ **"Digital Audio Tape."** Originally presented to the labels in the mid 1980s, Sony's DAT format was sonically superior to cassette, and on par with or better than CD. Concerned about piracy—specifically, the ability to make crystal-clear copies of CDs—the labels insisted that DAT machines include a copy-protection scheme that made it possible to produce one copy, but not copies of copies. The industry also insisted that there be a royalty paid for every DAT machine sale. Sony walked out of negotiations. As part of the 1992 Audio Recording Act, computer manufacturers, such as Apple, insisted that there be no royalty or legally mandated technical limitations to CD-R drives in their computers, and they got their wish written into the legislation. A few years later, optical read-write drives were standard on nearly every home computer. Anyone could "rip" a CD and then burn a perfect copy, or convert the files to the new MP3 format.

> **NOTE:** Although DAT never took off as a consumer format, it found a home in professional production environments as an evolutionary improvement over earlier Sony systems that used the larger Betamax video tape format, and was ubiquitous through most of the 1990s and into the early 2000s. DAT was the pinnacle linear 2-track audio tape format for a variety of reasons, but its 48 kHz limitation ultimately ended its usefulness beyond access to archival projects. Unlike DAT, S/PDIF, which was developed by Sony and Philips as a high-quality consumer digital audio transfer protocol, still lives on in the production world. S/PDIF's data steam is very similar to that of the "pro" AES/EBU digital format. The biggest differences between them are cabling and impedance specifications, and S/PDIF's copy protection bit, which is no more than an unused historical remnant.

▷ **"Killing the Single."** The huge profit margins from CD sales in the 1980s and 1990s led executives to the conclusion that selling singles was not in their best interest. Why sell one good song for $4 when you can sell two good songs plus another 10 mediocre songs for $15? Singles used to be sold to promote records; consumers could then decide to buy the record if they liked the single. By the 1990s, the labels determined that singles didn't help sell records, so they forced fans to buy whole albums, mostly full of filler. Knopper quotes producer/songwriter Terry McManus on this trend: "Here is where the North American music industry made its greatest mistake of the twentieth century." In essence, they were forcing people to pay for songs they didn't want to buy in the first place.

> **NOTE:** The term "one hit wonder" exists for a good reason. If they are lucky, big-label artists are known for a hit song or two. If they are particularly successful, they may have a few hits off of a few different albums. It is the minority of big-label artists who consistently release whole albums full of good songs and/or hit the top of the charts year after year. For knowledgeable music fans with good taste who do not pay attention to the charts, it is easy to think only about all of the classic albums released over the years. Therefore, unlike the average music consumer who listens primarily to Top 40, it can be challenging to appreciate the implications of forcing people to buy full albums full of songs they don't like.

▷ **"Pumping Up The Big Boxes."** In the 1990s, big-box stores like Wal-Mart and Best Buy emerged as major CD retailers, and were able to sell music for tiny profit margins because they made most of their money by selling other consumer goods. By 1996, as their share of total U.S. RIAA-tracked CD sales hit 25%, they started to make demands of the labels. Wal-Mart's morally conservative demands equated to censorship of lyrics and cover art as part of a necessary tradeoff to be in their store, while Best Buy demanded huge chunks of change for prominently placed in-store promotional displays. Music-retail chains like Tower and Sam Goody, as well as local mom-and-pop stores, could not compete with these low prices. In addition, being long-time loyal customers, most refused to demand money for in-store placement. In an effort to respond to the threat from the big-box stores, they were able to compel the labels to implement a minimum advertised pricing (MAP) policy. This, however, led to an FTC charge of price fixing, which forced the abandonment of the MAP policy, reopening the door for the big-box stores to offer music at super low prices. Unable to compete with these big-box stores, it wasn't long before most of the music retailers went out of business, causing the music retailer industry to collapse.

> **NOTE:** If all of the independent record stores closed shortly after Wal-Mart moved into your town (as happened to countless mom-and-pop businesses over the last 20 years), making Wal-Mart the only music retailer in your vicinity, would you be more likely to look to the Internet as a source of music?

▷ **"The Secure Digital Music Initiative."** In 1998, the industry formed a think tank, called the Secure Digital Music Initiative, or SDMI, to figure out how to copy-protect digital music. After a few years, it developed an encryption scheme and put out a public challenge to hackers. If they could crack the scheme in less than three weeks, a $10,000 prize would be paid out. A team of eight people from Princeton University cracked it in one night. When the team planned to give a technical presentation on how they did it, the RIAA threatened legal action but backed off after the Princeton team fought back on grounds of free speech. After four years and millions of dollars spent, the SDMI disbanded with only one flawed product on the market that attempted to implement a copy-protected music-playback system. Its plans to include an inaudible watermark in every recording so only authorized songs would play back had failed miserably. Apple was invited to take part in the SDMI, but since Apple was not yet involved in the music industry, the company kept its distance and was not involved in the details of the failure. From the SDMI, Apple learned what *not* to do.

▷ **"The RIAA Lawsuits."** In 2003, The RIAA decided it needed to make examples of people and clearly demonstrate to the world that downloading music without paying via P2P services would not be tolerated. By 2006, more than 6,000 suits against college students and other random individuals for hundreds of thousands of dollars were mostly settled out of court for about $3,000–$6,000 per case—a lot of money for most people. In many cases, the RIAA demanded $750 per song, which for some people resulted in the RIAA bringing multi-million dollar lawsuits against them. By 2006, Apple's iPod and newly named iTunes Store were well on their way to dominance in the retail music market, and the RIAA was well on its way to making enemies out of a large portion of its consumer market.

> **NOTE:** Of the 30,000-plus cases brought by the RIAA between 2003 and 2008, *Sony BMG Music Entertainment et al. v. Tenenbaum* stands out. In 2003, the RIAA sent a demand of $3,500 to the home of then–20-year-old college student Joel Tenenbaum for sharing music via Kazaa. His settlement offer of $500 was declined. Then, in 2007, Tenenbaum was sued for statutory damages that could

potentially exceed $1,000,000. He then offered to pay the original demand, which was refused, and countered with an even higher settlement amount. Finally, the case went to trial in 2009. Tenenbaum was found guilty of sharing 30 songs, for which the jury awarded the plaintiffs $675,000 ($22,500 per shared song). In 2010, another judge held that such arbitrarily huge damages violated due process and reduced the amount to $67,500. Upon appeal in 2012, yet another judge reinstated the $675,000 fine, which was upheld again in a higher court on June 25th, 2013.

▷ **"Sony BMG's Rootkit."** The industry perceived the CD burners in personal computers as the primary source of shared music. In 2005, Sony attempted to nip that problem in the bud. Without informing consumers, Sony BMG released 52 titles totaling about 4.7 million CDs that included hidden software that would install itself on computers when inserted into the commonplace built-in optical drives. Essentially, Sony was installing malware, called a rootkit, on its customers' computers in the hope that it would enable the company to curtail piracy. Unfortunately, not only did Sony's rootkit make it harder to rip music off the CDs, but it opened up security holes in the OS that made it easier for other malware to do its dirty work. Needless to say, people who legally purchased CDs only to be treated like potential criminals and have their computers crashed by label-supplied malware were not rushing out to hand over more money to Sony BMG (or the rest of the major label industry due to guilt by association). The RIAA finally gave up on hardware-based digital rights management (DRM) schemes at this point.

RIAA Failures + Apple Computer = Apple, Inc.

In 2008, the Electronic Frontier Foundation posted a white paper on their website (www.eff.org) entitled *RIAA v. The People: Five Years Later*. In section VI, it asks, "Are the lawsuits working? Has the arbitrary singling out of nearly 30,000 random American families helped promote public respect for copyright law? Have the lawsuits put the P2P genie back in the bottle or restored the record industry to its 1997 revenues? After five years of threats and litigation, the answer is a resounding no." The paper then goes on to advocate for a "voluntary collective licensing regime as a mechanism that would fairly compensate artists and rightsholders for P2P file sharing" along the lines of ASCAP, BMI, and SESAC. Another five years have passed since the EFF's five-year retrospective in 2008, and no such model exists, so it is safe to say that this idea fell on deaf ears.

It is important to keep in mind that the RIAA represents the industry as a whole, but each label had to decide for itself how it was going to adjust to the new digital age. The labels are competitors, after all. Collectively, they failed to implement legal online downloading alternatives to P2P file sharing systems, while they simultaneously treated their whole customer base like potential pirates, focusing primarily on copy protection schemes and lawsuits. The RIAA was suing grandmothers and college students for file sharing at the same time that Sony was installing malware on the computers of its paying customers.

When the lawsuits started in 2003, Apple's stock was at about $10 per share (having just returned to profitability in 1998 after Steve Jobs returned to the company he founded and saved it from the brink of bankruptcy). If each label had invested the same amount of money in Apple stock that they paid for lawyers and lawsuits against a random assortment of average people who just happened to get caught file sharing, how many billions would they each have made by the time AAPL hit $700 per share in 2012? If these companies had invested $13 million, the cost of the never-released GN'R record, in 2003, each would have made about $1.8 billion by 2012. Of course, if they had been smarter with their resources, Apple, Inc. might still be known as Apple Computer. Just as IBM basically conceded many billions of dollars to Microsoft and the PC clone manufacturers, the RIAA and the labels it represents, too, conceded many billions of dollars in revenue to Apple and other new services. They refused to evolve and failed to recognize the opportunity in front of them, leaving a vacuum open that was filled by Apple and other new services that better catered to the new desires of music buyers.

No one is arguing that "illegal" downloading has not affected the industry, including musicians and producers, only that its impact is overstated and/or misunderstood given all of the other factors. Some argue that much of the music that is downloaded would never have been purchased in the first place—a valid point when arguing the accuracy of the RIAA's stats and numbers pertaining to hypothetical loss of revenue. In the early Napster days, there was a lot of music on the site that was not even available for sale because it was out of print and often very rare to begin with. Accessing these previously hard-to-find gems illustrates one of the driving motivations behind downloading habits. Music lovers always want to hear more music, especially when they are a fan of the artist. While for some people avoiding payment for music is a motivation for their downloading habits, for others it is more about convenience and some combination of the preceding eight big mistakes just discussed.

Not even counting movies and books, Apple brought in more than $25 billion from music purchased and downloaded through the iTunes Store in about a 10-year period. Its sale of 25 billion songs in that period is hard evidence that people *are* willing to pay for music. Don't get me wrong: I am not saying that the iTunes Store is perfect. Until 2009, all music was low-quality 128 kbps and was DRM-protected in a frustrating and simply annoying fashion, even for owners of iPods and iPhones. Although Apple dropped DRM from about 80% of the available music and finally started to offer higher-quality 256 kbps files for an additional $0.30, the iTunes Store still has downsides. For users looking to purchase music either not available from the iTunes Store, in higher-quality formats (320 kbps, WAV, or FLAC), or without DRM, there are also services such as eMusic, Beatport, CD Baby, and even Amazon MP3 (although possibly with watermarks in the metadata). Regardless of where people are buying their music online, the conclusion is the same. Simply stated, music lovers want to easily download and listen to more of the music they enjoy.

The record companies should have adopted new systems before the vacuum was filled by Apple and other new players in music sales. A decade after Napster, the industry's most symbolic nemesis, access to legally downloaded music from all over the world is easy and affordable through a variety of Internet services. From the consumer's point of view, the industry arguably has never been better. Additionally, users increasingly can store their purchased music in "the cloud," essentially making it available anywhere and anytime.

Thank You, Internet: All I can say is, thank goodness for the Internet. If you live in a democratic society, you also likely take for granted Net neutrality. Net neutrality is the technical term that refers to an Internet in which all data is treated equally. ISP bandwidth throttling issues aside, for the most part, we still have it at the time of this writing, although Internet freedom is threatened from a few angles. It is no coincidence that the Recording Industry Association of America (RIAA) and the Motion Picture Association of America (MPAA) spend many millions of dollars every year on powerful lobbyists in Washington D.C. to influence legislation, including laws that would change the Internet to their benefit at the expense of Net neutrality. The Stop Online Piracy Act (SOPA) and Protect IP Act (PIPA) are perfect examples of such legislation that was proposed in 2011. Thanks to widespread organized public hullabaloo, they were shelved in January of 2012 and never came up for a vote.

New York Times writer David Carr moderated a panel discussion at the Sundance Film Festival's Cinema Café series in January of 2012. Participating in the panel were MPAA chairman Chris Dodd and John Fithian, chairman of the National Association of Theatre Owners (NATO), among others. They discussed their recent defeat during this discussion. In his January 24, 2012 hollywoodreporter.com article, "Sundance 2012: MPAA's Chris Dodd Calls Piracy Defeat a 'Watershed Event,'" Jay A. Fernandez quotes Dodd talking about how, in his 30 plus years of public office, he had never see such "ability to organize and communicate directly with consumers" as displayed by the opponents of the legislation. Fernandez then quotes Fithian describing the situation as "the greatest backlash I've ever seen."

Chris Dodd accepted the job as chairman and CEO of the MPAA in March of 2011, immediately following five (six-year) terms as a U.S. Senator (D-CT). Part of his new job description is chief lobbyist, so he now lobbies his former colleagues in the U.S. Congress. The annual salary of a U.S. senator in 2009 was $174,000, while the estimated annual salary of a CEO for the MPAA is $1,500,000. Revolving-door politics at its finest.

But I digress.

If you care about issues of Internet freedom, Net neutrality, and individual rights in the digital age, start by checking out the Electronic Frontier Foundation (eff.org), Save The Internet (savetheInternet.com), and Demand Progress (demandprogress.org).

We make our living producing intellectual property, so if there was any doubt in your mind, I am not endorsing piracy in any way. For additional discussion on file sharing as it relates to the industry, you, and your career, see Chapter 8, "Selecting Your Tools."

Emergence of the "Celestial Jukebox"

The previous section talked briefly about singles. The record industry began by selling singles in 1888. In 1889, in San Francisco, Louis Glass and William S. Arnold created a coin-operated phonograph, and the first jukebox was born. The jukebox was the first system designed to offer a preloaded selection of songs from different artists in one device—the first of its kind in the historical lineage of the iPod, etc., as illustrated by the plethora of vintage-looking jukebox docking stations available. (Just do a Web image search for "iPod jukebox" and you'll see what I mean!) Whether then or now, mechanical or digital, sizeable or portable, jukeboxes and singles are inextricably linked. By the 1950s, jukeboxes were so prevalent that today they still define the classic diner experience from that era, and retro diners often include a mini-jukebox in each booth. Although the jukebox has declined in popularity since the 1970s, they live on in the form of digital multimedia systems commonly found in bars and restaurants. Not only were full-length albums ubiquitous by late 1960s, but increasingly so were double albums and "concept" records such as The Who's *Tommy* (1969), Miles Davis' *Bitches Brew* (1970), and Pink Floyd's *The Wall* (1979). Yet, even as the "album as art form" established its prominent position in 20th century culture, the labels continued to release singles for another few decades.

As the labels placed their bets on more expensive full-length CDs, and singles disappeared, the Internet and digital revolution made itself known. The explosion of P2P file-sharing services allowed fans to listen to the one or two good songs from an album and avoid paying for bad, uninspired, filler songs. With the introduction of the iPod and other such devices, all of these downloaded singles on one device signified the return of the jukebox. But these were not huge appliances with perhaps a few hundred songs. These devices fit in the palm of your hand and could store thousands of songs with customizable playlists. This was a space age super jukebox that would have been futuristic science fiction less than two decades earlier. In his January 7, 2010 article on guardian.co.uk, "What Does the Return of the Single Mean for Music?," Tom Ewing notes that 2009 was the first year in decades that single sales exceeded album sales. Singles are back big time, but now they are distributed in a new music system, digitally and over networks, via streaming services, file download shops, or even increasingly in a "cloud" account.

The story of the jukebox is a perfect example of a revolution—one that exhibits the telltale signs of complexification. We started with mechanical jukeboxes playing singles off of phonographs, and more than 100 years later we have an unlimited virtual jukebox comprised largely of singles, organized with playlists, and searchable with meta tags or "sounds like" neural pattern-recognition algorithms. It is also a sweet synchronicity for this author that "celestial jukebox" is the term being used to describe this new emerging distribution system. As I discussed at the top of this chapter, the term "revolution" stems from astronomical observations of the planet's circular motions around Earth, and then after the Copernican Revolution, around the sun. Dictionary.com defines *celestial* as "pertaining to the sky or visible heaven, or to the universe beyond the earth's atmosphere, as in celestial body." As the telescope is to revolutions in astronomy and cosmology, the Internet and the digital revolution are to revolutions in the music system.

These revolutions in the music system and subsequently induced reorganizations of the record industry might simply be another case of the widespread and rapid changes we can file under the broad heading of "globalization." Industries rise and fall, ebb and flow; history progresses; and technology continues to accelerate the rate of change. No matter the causes, we are where we are. And the fact is that at this point in time, there would not be a shortage of music without the multinational corporate owned commercial music industry. That also means there is no shortage of people producing music. On the contrary, there are more now than ever. Given all of the huge changes, which include a significant increase in the number of amateurs entering the fray, what does it now mean to be a producer? And further, to be a professional producer?

What Is a "Producer"?

"A producer is either/and/or…a really good musician. Someone that's not a musician at all but has instincts. Someone that has neither of those things but knows how to navigate through a record label. Someone who's a great engineer. Someone who doesn't know a fader from a hole in the wall. Someone who has a lot of money. Someone who has a megalomaniacal personality."

—Bob Power

Grammy- and Emmy-nominated Bob Power is a New York–based producer, musician, composer, engineer, composer, performer, and educator with more than 20 gold or platinum records to his name. He's worked with De La Soul, A Tribe Called Quest, Common, JayDee, Run DMC, Jungle Brothers, D'Angelo, Miles Davis, Spike Lee, Erykah Badu, David Byrne, The Roots, and Pat Metheny, among others. The preceding quote was transcribed from an interview that was posted to YouTube in March, 2008 as part of a series called *Technology Today* (Magnet Media Films). Later in that same interview, Power shared his personal philosophy on the role of a producer:

"It's really about the artist and the music and not about me. I am a facilitator, I am supposed to help people. And ideally, after working with me, maybe those people won't need me anymore. And that's a good thing."

Not all record producers are cut from the same cloth as Bob Power, especially at the same level of success and accomplishment. There are many other philosophies out there, but his is one I fully resonate with. It is also consonant with the views of other notable producers who are great role models professionally and as individuals. One such example is Hank Shocklee, who is interviewed in Appendix C, "Interview with Hank Shocklee."

The term "producer" has evolved over the decades along with the changes in music, technology, and the business side of the industry. Even now, it has different implications depending on the scene and situation. Producers define their roles according to any number of criteria, such as those cited in the quote at the beginning of this section. Some are collaborators who work with talented songwriters to best help them produce their original music. Perhaps they are even a friend or member of the band. Others mold raw talents and are involved in directing every aspect of the music and production. This involvement falls on a spectrum of motivations, including genuinely wanting to help launch an original artist or band, or molding the act at the behest of the label and A&R, as exemplified in the unfortunate phenomenon of industry-created "boy bands." On the flip side, electronic music producers largely evolved outside of the major label world and do most everything themselves, as we will soon discuss.

The "Classic" Record Producer

Like everything else in our industry, record production started out as a very simple process. The first pre-recorded records were sold in 1888. Production of such records did not yet include mics or amplifiers. The process involved nothing more than having musicians play while facing the gramophone's concave-shaped horn so the acoustic sound waves could be collected and thus converted into electrical signals that controlled the mechanical etching of analogous waves on shellac (wax) disks. Ten years later, in 1898, Fred Gaisberg stopped working with Berliner in New York to become the first A&R for Berliner's partner company in the U.K., the London Gramophone Company (later to be HMV/EMI). Shortly thereafter, Gaisberg ran the company's first recording studio, arguably becoming the first ever "producer." To match the dynamics in a score, he instructed an opera singer to change his distance from the gramophone's horn.

Fast forward 60 or 70 years to the 1950s and 1960s, the decades that birthed the musical recordings we can most easily trace as the precursors of modern popular music—the explosion of rock 'n' roll, soul, R&B, funk, modern jazz, Motown, and early electronic music. By the 1960s, the archetype of the modern record producer coagulated due to the works of producers like Phil Spector, Berry Gordy, George Martin, and Tom Dowd. In many ways, and in varying degrees, producers in this mold were like some combination of a director and an executive producer of a feature film. They guided the whole process from song writing, to hiring musicians and engineers, to recording, to performance coaching, and beyond. As bands with original material became more of a norm, producers commonly resembled helpful collaborators, guiding the production process more so than mainly directing talent on how to best perform the songs handed to them. Quincy Jones, Phil Ramone, Alan Parsons, Mutt Lange, Brian Eno, Rick Rubin, Lee Scratch Perry, Steve Lillywhite, Hugh Padgham, Sylvia Robinson, Hank Shocklee, Butch Vig, Dr. Dre, Sylvia Massy, Adrian Sherwood, Jack Endino, Terry Date, Steve Albini, DJ Premier, Neil Davidge, Trina Shoemaker, Nigel Godrich, The Neptunes, Timbaland, and Missy Elliott are just a few of the significant record producers from the last 40 years. While some of these producers are also known as musicians and performing artists, when assuming the role of producer, they are not only often like a member of the band, but they are also ultimately responsible for final results.

In the great documentary *Something from Nothing: The Art of Rap* (2012), Ice-T interviews a lot of major players in hip hop, including Dr. Dre. During their discussion, they cut right to the heart of what it means to be a producer.

Ice-T: People I've talked to that have had the privilege of working with you have said the same thing....When you go in the studio with Dre it's not a game…you gonna do it until Dre thinks it's right. And they all appreciate that. There's a big difference between a beat maker and a producer.

Dr. Dre: Yeah, you know what, there's definitely a big difference between a beat maker and a producer, 'cuz once you finish the beat you have to produce the record.

So what exactly does Dr. Dre mean in this quote? He means that coming up with some good musical ideas or even solid songs is a far cry from what it takes to complete a quality production. The ideal producer understands the musical and technical aspects of production either as a musician or an audio engineer—or at least well enough to know who best to bring in to those roles. The ideal producer also knows his or her artists' strengths and weaknesses, the market and audience, how to coach performances, and if relevant, what the label wants (and how to bring the best out of the artist even if it is not exactly what the label wants). This type of producer evolved in the big-label world for a number of reasons. A producer is often necessary simply to oversee the whole process and make sure the right people are involved in the project. Also, since A&R discovers and signs artists to the label based on a variety of marketable characteristics, labels often require a producer shape the album to maximize marketability and sales. For established artists, even ones who are exceptionally skilled and talented musicians, the producer is there to help take them to the next level. So whether for business reasons or creative purposes, producers are invaluable to many artists and labels. But what if record sales are not a significant factor in guiding the creative or production process? What if there is no big label expecting a return on its investment? What if you want to be your own producer?

DIY/Independent Music/Producers

As discussed in Chapter 1, "Musica Universalis," by the early 1980s, the DIY and independent label component of the music industry was in full bloom. Without the dual pressures for large-scale commercial viability and recouping big advances that come with a big-label record deal, the need for a producer diminished, and it became more common for artists to self-produce. In these situations, the production of the record was now most commonly a collaboration between the artist or band members and a recording engineer. By the early 2000s, more and more people could afford production technology, so they tried to do it all themselves at home—usually oblivious to the historical significance and value of a producer.

The *de Facto* Producer

The vast majority of these self-productions require a skilled audio engineer at various points in the process, often for help recording vocals and other instruments, but especially for mixing and mastering. In many cases, the productions are not actually ready for mixdown, and the engineer finds himself or herself having to make significant changes to the composition, arrangement, and even instrumentation during the mixing process. Though not entirely new, it is increasingly common for audio engineers to find themselves assuming the role of *de facto* producer long after the project started—and therefore when it is too late to fully guide the process. Of course, some engineers simply refuse to do more than mix when being paid to mix. But many indie engineers want to help new talented and personable artists and want the resulting work to sound as good as possible so they can feel comfortable having their name listed in the credits.

Because this situation appears to be a new norm, audio engineers are increasingly having to clarify roles to these talented musicians who are also amateur self-producers. This trend has implications on a number of levels, most commonly pertaining to compensation, album credits, and share in publishing. One of the biggest mistakes made by a lot of engineers who work with cash-strapped new artists is simply doing work for hire without any stake in publishing. Often, the productions they engineer, but also *de facto* produce, subsequently help the artists get noticed and even land record or licensing deals. I am not talking about trying to take credit from an artist or being greedy by asking for a big percentage. It is common practice to agree on a better rate up front in exchange for a few publishing points, since it usually is a good deal for all parties. But at some point, those who regularly find themselves in the position of *de facto* producer might want to consider explicit redefinition of their job title.

Professional Independent Producer

If your goal is not only to produce your own music, or if you keep finding yourself as a *de facto* producer, then you are likely interested in pursuing opportunities as a producer in more of the classic sense. Making this happen will take a lot of work and planning, but is well worth the effort if it is what you really want to do. There is no manual anymore for such as career, as if there ever was one to begin with. As an independent producer, you need to have a DIY attitude toward everything. Don't wait for people to come to you; you have to go out there and discover artists you want to produce. So in a sense, you are also A&R. This means you should also develop relationships with some labels, too. Throughout this book, you will find information, discussion, tips, and suggestions on how to get your career moving. I also highly recommend that you read the interview with veteran producer/engineer John Jansen in the companion book to *The Music Producer's Survival Guide*.

Musician or Accidental Producer?

Are you a musician interested in certain aspects of production? Or are you a producer who also happens to be a musician? If you just want to make music, and production is a means to an end for you, then what is the difference between musician and producer? Just as many engineers find themselves in the role of *de facto* producer, many musicians might be thought of as stumbling into the role of accidental producer. An accidental producer is a musician who, through the process of figuring out how to make quality recordings of his or her own music or remixes, slowly figures out that production is a vast topic traversing a wide array of skill sets. In fact, it is very common now for people to be self-producing without realizing that is what they are trying to do. It is important to understand what is going on here for those of you who are accidental producers, or anyone who might find himself or herself in the role of *de facto* producer. We could even say that the rise of the accidental producer and *de facto* producer are like two sides of the same coin; one leads to the other. Some accidental producers decide to refocus on writing and performing music and start to work with engineers and/or skilled producers, while others realize what they have gotten themselves into and dive into the deep end head first.

Electronic Music Producer

When it comes to electronic music producers (EMPs), the story is a little different from the aforementioned cases. EMPs are the original DIY producers, dating back to the 1940s. When compared to the emergence of self-production in the classic producer sense, we are looking at a mirror image when following the trajectory of electronic music. By mirror image I mean backward; self-production in electronic music was there at the beginning rather than emerging later. Indeed, having another producer step in didn't occur until decades after electronic music's inception.

Electronic music doesn't exist without audio technology and/or computers, which are natural aptitudes and passions for electronic musicians, so self-producing is a logical extension of the music form. It was not until electronic music crossed over into pop music that professional audio engineers became integral to some of the productions, as exemplified by Kraftwerk's close working relationship with Conny Plank on its first four records in the first half of the 1970s. Even into the 1980s and 1990s, most classic EMP tracks were DIY creations by musicians at home or in a friend's studio, including most of the early classic tracks from house, techno, electro, jungle, IDM, and other popular styles. Collaboration with producers started in the 1970s, but it was not commonplace until the 1980s, when electronic music styles and audiences evolved to the point that more traditional production processes were required. The norm is still for most electronic music producers to self-produce, though they do commonly work with skilled audio engineers.

Historically, electronic music producers not only composed and recorded their own music, but they also often had to design, build, and/or customize their own tools (or work with those who could do it for them). In the 1950s, Stockhausen first had to conceive and then build the first additive synthesizer before he could synthesize sounds based on Fourier's theories. The important dynamic related to collaboration between electronic musicians and electrical engineers is famously illustrated between Wendy Carlos and Bob Moog. Moog modified the designs of his first modular synth production models in the 1960s based on Carlos' feedback; Carlos then used Moog's synths in many famous compositions. (Chapter 8 further explores this story and collaborative dynamic.) Electronic music producers still regularly design their own tools, most commonly with software like Reaktor or Max/MSP.

Like any producer, electronic music producers are responsible for the final result of the production. When compared to the wide assortment of classic record producers, electronic music producers most resemble musician/producers and engineer/producers. That said, a significant proportion of dedicated electronic music producers fully epitomize DIY. They run their own independent boutique labels, event production and promotion companies, and/or booking agencies. With a lower threshold of entry into production and the increasing popularity of electronic music, many of today's aspiring electronic musicians are basically the 21st century equivalent of indie bands trying to make records themselves in the 1990s. Because "producer" has a few definitions and implications, it makes sense that a whole new generation of musicians, electronic or otherwise, are stumbling into production before they realize it is what they are in fact getting themselves into.

What Does "Professional" Mean?

Because of significant changes in our industry, specifically related to the democratization and increasing affordability of production technology, the dominant role of expert professionals has eroded. Anyone with a laptop and a lot of software can theoretically have access to all the tools once found only in expensive studios and operated only by skilled professionals. Yet, when people say things like, "There is no such thing as professional anymore," they are overstating the situation and possibly even making a confused assertion. The transformation of the music system that kicked off in 1999 does not mean there are no professionals simply because there are fewer big studios and DIY self-production is more prevalent than ever before. When people employ the word "professional," it can imply different meanings, and often they are conflated with each other. Because one of the overarching goals of this book is to help DIY and independent music producers with their career, it necessarily follows that we are also talking about being a professional music producer. Let's make sure we are clear on what we are saying, so we can move on to the next chapter, which is all about planning your career.

The word "professional" has different meanings depending on the context. It can be a noun, adverb, or adjective, and can be defined by four distinct definitions with their own characteristics. Consider the following phrases:

   ▷ She is a consummate professional.
   ▷ He is not very professional.
   ▷ The final mix was professional quality.
   ▷ That piece of equipment was not designed for professional use.
   ▷ He was a lifelong professional.
   ▷ I would like to do that professionally.

Each of these phrases points to one of the following characteristics associated with the word "professional":

   ▷ **Skill:** Professionals are associated with developed skill sets that allow them to complete tasks that those without training cannot do. Many professionals get their training through formal education, such as the traditionally defined "professions" of medicine or law. These types of professionals spent a lot of time in school and were thoroughly tested before being granted their titles and degrees. Some musicians and engineers also have a lot of formal training, but not all. Many professionals in our industry learned on the job and developed their skills to levels recognized by their peers as being "professional." The final quality of a production is demonstrative of skill. (See the third example above.)
   ▷ **Income:** We also define professionals as people who earn their living with their skills, especially if it is a full-time career. That being said, working part-time in a given field will also apply when there is corresponding skill level. (See the last two examples above.)
   ▷ **Attitude:** A professional attitude means taking your career seriously in all aspects, especially as it pertains to working with others. High standards, reliability, punctuality, and consistency are a few things valued by those with a professional attitude. Even beginners and novices can have a professional attitude before they have the skills or income to be a professional. This attitude is very important for producers and anyone else who relies on their reputation for their income. (See the first two examples above.)
   ▷ **Industry:** Each profession, field, career, and occupation involves a variety of standards, norms, and tools. This overlaps with skill and attitude, but also points to gear and technology. For example, professional equipment is designed to meet the needs of a specific market, but does not necessarily imply higher quality than consumer products. Low-end entry-level professional gear doesn't sound nearly as nice as the high-end consumer audiophile products purchased by people who love to listen to music on insanely expensive home stereo systems. Professional audio requires a different feature and toolset to make the music than for people who want to listen to it with perfect, crystal-clear fidelity. (See the fourth example above.)

Aspiring Pro, Semi-Pro, or Serious Hobbyist

When considering all the people who are now in the production game, it can be hard to tell the difference between those who are hoping to make a living at music production, those who simply enjoy doing it for fun, and those who honestly aren't sure themselves. If we strip out the income variable, we are left considering the other three—skill, attitude, and industry—although ultimately, it comes down to attitude more than anything else.

Aspiring professionals are most commonly those at the onset of a career path. Of course, it is common for people to change careers a few times, so youth is not always the case. Regardless, "aspiring" means actively pursuing a career producing music and working with audio. They might not yet have the skills, income, or industry-standard tools, but with the right attitude, patience, and persistence, there is a good chance of meeting those goals.

Semi-professionals are people who only do music and production part-time. This might be an aspiring pro well on his or her way to going full-time. It might also be someone who for whatever reason has other work for income. This might be by choice, as is common for those who have other passions they want to simultaneously pursue. Or it might be by necessity if music production is not bringing in enough income to meet current needs. Some semi-pros are very established and have an international following and/or reputation. By all external subjective standards, these folks are professionals, even if music is not the sole source of their income. In the world of indie music, as broadly defined, it is possible to be well-known for your music and still not able to comfortably earn a living doing it. Especially in bands, where all income must be split, it can be even more difficult to go full-time. Many musicians and producers are able to juggle paying gigs along with the creative projects they are known for but don't pay so well, often even for decades.

Serious hobbyists are people who have decided, for whatever reason, that they do not want to pursue a career in music production. They might be very skilled and have all of the industry-standard tools, but they are not chasing a goal in this domain. Often, people who consider themselves aspiring professionals for more than a decade or so are actually serious hobbyists who don't want to let go of an earlier dream, but who are not taking the necessary steps to further that goal. An aspiring professional who does not reach his or her financial goals is still an aspiring pro as long as he or she has the attitude. But if the drive and attitude are not there to make the necessary moves, lifestyle decisions, and sacrifices, some people really should admit to themselves that they are passionate hobbyists. There is nothing wrong with being a hobbyist, serious or otherwise. Music, music technology, and music production are fun, fulfilling, and rewarding. Moreover, for a rare few, hobbies organically become careers in unexpected ways. Also, serious hobbyists can make great clients, and can help the rest of us to pay the bills while we help them enjoy life.

Whether you are fully committed to pursuing a career as a professional music producer or are concerned about the uncertainty in such a pursuit and might be satisfied as a serious hobbyist, the essence of a good producer's attitude is the same. In *Something from Nothing: the Art of Rap*, Dr. Dre offers this expert advice to aspiring producers: "Make sure that your word is the last word, that way you don't play the blame game or anything like that. If it comes out hot it's on you, if it doesn't come out hot it's on you. Ya know what I'm sayin', that's all there is to it."

Last Refrain

We live in exciting times at the convergence of multiple revolutions. The Internet and digital technology are transforming our civilization in front of our eyes, and the music system is evolving right along with it. The means of music production, manufacturing, and distribution are now commonly available and increasingly more affordable and powerful. The revolution in music distribution, illustrated by the jukebox's 110-year arc from coin-operated mechanical device to network-distributed digital streams of information accessed almost magically from a "celestial jukebox," is just one of the recent revolutions in the music system. The home and project studio revolution is just as significant and also equally illustrative of the spiraling thematic patterns characteristic of revolutions. These spirals might even follow patterns not unlike the harmonic ratios shown in Figure 1.1.

By the early 1950s, Les Paul was already releasing records utilizing the sound-on-sound overdubbing technique he invented with a modification to the very first Ampex Model 200A tape recorder. He and his wife Mary Ford were the only musicians, and they recorded in their home, but it sounded like a whole band was playing. No one knew what he was doing, nor could they figure it out by listening to the records. Even Tom Dowd didn't know what was going on, and he worked with the second Ampex 8-track ever made and built Ray Charles' first console with his innovation of "slide wires" (what we call faders). Les Paul is interviewed in the 2003 documentary *Tom Dowd and The Language of Music*. While answering a question about how what he was doing in the 1950s resembles today's home studio productions with computers, he stated: "I look today and where are they? The kid today is in his bathroom, he's in his bedroom. And he is making his record in his home!" Les Paul revolutionized music production when he invented sound on sound in his home studio. The digital revolution's collision with the home-studio boom brings us back full circle, yet at a higher octave.

Now that you have a better understanding of where we've been, how things have changed, and where we are, let's turn our attention to the future. More specifically, let's turn our attention to developing your plan to best take advantage of the new uncertainties present in the complexified music system—and also the new opportunities.

What Is Your Plan?

3

The danger is not to set your goal too high and fail to reach it. It's to set your goal too low and reach it.

–Georges St-Pierre

Many of life's failures are people who did not realize how close they were to success when they gave up.

–Thomas Alva Edison

If you don't have a plan, you become part of somebody else's plan.

–Terence McKenna

Did You Choose This, or Did It Choose You?

This is not a trivial question, it is an existential question. I truly love this lifestyle and what I do for a living, but occasionally I've wondered what life would be like if only an easier path could be equally fulfilling. I've had this discussion with a lot of artists over the years, mostly friends and acquaintances, usually during rough patches. Why couldn't we be satisfied with a more "normal" life? What if we could really like being an accountant, an auto mechanic, a doctor, or a math teacher? Those are all respectable jobs, right? We always come to the same conclusion and move on. Many artists and musicians, among others, will tell you that they did not "choose" to be what they are; instead, it "chose" them. It was a calling. More than dedicated, they are naturally passionate about their work. The overarching goal, then, is simply to do what you love.

In the documentary *Something from Nothing: The Art of Rap* (2012), host Ice-T asks Dr. Dre about the first lesson he'd teach a young kid who wants to be a producer like him. Dr. Dre responds:

> *First of all you have to make sure that this thing is for you, and it's who you are, and you're built for this. And then you have to give the passion that's necessary. Like I said, I don't do it for the money, the money's gonna come. I do it because of the love that I have for it, you know what I'm sayin'? If I was a plumber or something like that, I still would make hip-hop records. That's how much love I have for it. I've been in the game close to 27 years, and…I've never been out of the studio longer than two weeks in my entire career. That's how much love I have for this thing that I do. So, that's the thing, just the passion you have for it. And really, really put your all into it.*

Sense of Direction

It is not uncommon for someone to "fall into" a profession, including those who enjoy what they do. It happens without a plan. I certainly did not have a real plan for realizing the goal of being a professional musician when I felt compelled to walk away from a full grad school scholarship, with stipend, to move across the country from Michigan to San Francisco. All I knew was that I loved music and music culture, and wanted to make it the focus of my life. Enabled by a few thousand dollars of extra student loan money and a friend who had an open room waiting for me, my naïve plan was this:

1. Move 2,400 miles west to San Francisco.
2. Find a job.
3. Start a band.
4. Be creatively successful and critically acclaimed.
5. Make a living as a musician.

It took about three years to realize the first four steps, and another two years before I ran into the following reality: Critically acclaimed creative success often does not pay the bills for long, if at all. So now what? Fortunately, during those five years, I had also immersed myself in many aspects of audio engineering, electronic music production, Apple computers, and the Internet, so I had acquired skills that opened options for paying the bills in various aspects of the industry, including music production. Way too many musicians and

DIY producers get to the "now what" and have no obvious satisfactory opportunities in front of them. They've made so many sacrifices to "make it" that the risks have seemingly outweighed any rewards.

Like anyone else with a career in music production, I have worked very hard and made a lot of sacrifices, but there is no doubt that I have also been very fortunate, too. Not only fortunate to be in the right place at the right time on a number of occasions, but fortunate that key people at various points were also very generous in sharing opportunities. Although there are still many goals left to achieve, following my heart and instincts has mostly worked out so far. A number of big calculated risks over the years were largely worth it, as evidenced by the fact that the book in your hands exists. There is something to be said for just going for it and hoping for the best, but for most people, "the best" does not happen through hope alone. Everyone who hopes to become a professional musician or music producer will not be able to do it for a living, but many who did not reach their goals very possibly could have, if only they'd had a plan.

Having a certain amount of freedom is a major draw to this career and lifestyle. There are very few set paths for independent and electronic music producers. There is no boss who hires you for a job with a benefits package and clear promotion opportunities. Even after many years in the industry, having to hustle for good-paying, interesting work is normal. So with this freedom comes uncertainty, and with uncertainty comes risk and opportunity. Uncertainty is to be expected when you embrace a certain amount of chaos as integral to your goals. Going forth into the unknown is exciting, but you don't want to drift too far off course. That said, the helmsman steering a ship through water does not keep a perfectly straight path. He knows where he wants to go and continually reacts to the feedback from his environment to right the course—sometimes with little effort, sometimes persevering through storms and hardship, occasionally beached after running aground, and sometimes even capsized by a rogue wave. With the right preparation, however, recovering from most any setback is just a matter of time.

I realize that some of you are not naturally analytical and prefer to go with feel, intuition, or instinct. As much as Einstein was a logical-mathematical genius, he also relied heavily on a well-developed kinesthetic sense, often using sensations in his muscles to help guide his creative thinking while working through complex mathematical ideas. I am not asking you to give up your natural predispositions, only to add to them. At the same time, if you are naturally an analytical planner, you too will likely need to augment your natural predisposition, by honing intuition and instinct. Planning your career as an independent/electronic music producer is ultimately about big life decisions. It is about your vision of where you want to see yourself in the future. What risks and sacrifices are you willing to take and make? What do you value and how do you want to spend your time? Do you feel a calling? A combination of logic and intuition, analysis and instinct, will help you to best answer those questions.

The Butterfly Effect

M.I.T. meteorologist Edward Lorentz solidified his place in history as the preeminent pioneer in the emerging field of chaos theory in 1972, when he published a paper entitled "Predictability: Does the Flap of a Butterfly's Wings in Brazil set off a Tornado in Texas?" It refers to a central concept in chaos theory known as *sensitive dependence on initial conditions*. The complete back story behind this discovery is fascinating; in short, he accidentally discovered that the simple act of rounding off computer calculations to slightly fewer decimal amounts led to sharply diverging weather models. It was not a programming error as originally thought; thus, he discovered that long-term weather prediction is impossible (without an infinite amount of data). In other words, small changes in a complex system can unexpectedly lead to big differences in outcomes.

Figure 3.1 and Figure 3.2 are different views of the Lorentz attractor, arguably the most famous strange attractor. Its fractal structure is created by plotting data points that are measured in the convection of certain fluids such as our atmosphere onto an X,Y coordinate system. At first, it all seems random. But once enough of the points are plotted, the attractor's geometrical shape is revealed. This revolutionary discovery taught us that a system can be unpredictable and yet still deterministic. The mainstream 1998 movie *Sliding Doors* fictionally explores sensitive dependence on initial conditions by following someone's life diverging in two very different directions—when she barely catches the subway, and when she misses the same train by a few seconds. The 2004 film *The Butterfly Effect* explores this same idea with a dark, sci-fi time-travel story. Both are great illustrations of this aspect of chaos theory, one plausible and the other fantastical. The Lorentz attractor is more than a powerful visual metaphor, as its very existence is rooted in hard science relevant to understanding the natural world around us.

So what does the butterfly effect have to do with you, and this chapter? It tells you that long-term prediction in chaotic dynamical systems is impossible. You are part of numerous such systems, so you should be prepared to expect the unexpected and reevaluate your plans from time to time. It also teaches you that small initial differences can, over time, lead to very different outcomes. Yet, unlike meteorological data points, you can reorient yourself as you proceed, assuming you know where you want to go.

The inverse of the butterfly effect's stated implications lends insight into how large initial differences might also unexpectedly lead to similar results. This corollary might help explain how it is that very different paths can lead to equal success—thus, that there is no single "right" plan, and therefore why each of us must figure out our own plan. The system is not random, it is unpredictable and deterministic, there is cause and effect, and our actions do influence outcomes. Not defining goals and failing to develop a plan is like tying a message to a helium-filled balloon, letting it go up in the air, and hoping it gets to the desired destination.

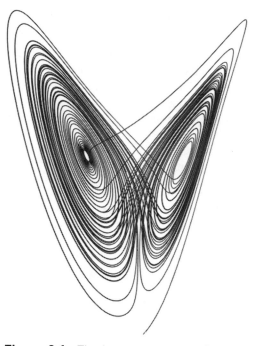

Figure 3.1 The Lorentz attractor demonstrates how small initial differences in chaotic dynamical systems can lead to drastically different outcomes (image modified by author).

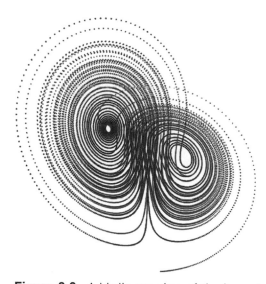

Figure 3.2 A bird's eye view of the Lorentz attractor. Many points create the pattern, resulting in a system that is not random and that is also unpredictable (image modified by author).

NOTE: The section in the introduction, "One Thing Leads to Another," is illustrative of the butterfly effect—how this book is an unexpected outcome of a small tip from a friend more than 20 years earlier.

Patience and Persistence

The importance of both patience and persistence is difficult to overstate. Ask any successful person; if they are honest, they will tell you something similar. Frustration is just a state of mind and quitting is not an option. Make it your mantra: patience, persistence, patience, persistence, patience, persistence. Before, during, and after periods of success, you will experience ups and downs. You will experience failures and setbacks. You will make mistakes. People with less talent and experience will get opportunities that you think should be yours. You may even run into a nemesis that appears to have it out for you for no good reason and tries to hold you back. But remember: Nothing worth doing is going to be easy, and pursuing a passion for music and music production is certainly worth doing.

If you want to do this with your life, a conscious commitment to patience and persistence can be the difference between reaching your goals or falling short of them. Patience does not mean complacency. It means that frustration in and of itself does not lead to resignation, envy, resentment, or a sense of hopelessness. Persistence means to keep trying, to not give up or quit, to continually try new things as required to reach your goals. One might say that I am also talking about determination, which implies persistence with drive, purpose, and heart. Do not confuse determination or persistence with stubbornness. Being stubborn will most likely just lead to more frustration. In essence, we all should know how to focus frustrated energy in constructive ways. Do your research, put in the hard work, and prepare for your highest aspirations. But also be flexible and keep an open mind.

Many successful artists, musicians, and producers do not see measureable success until after they have been at it for a long time—10 to 15 years is not unusual. Even then, fame or critical acclaim do not always lead to financial security. As discussed in Chapter 4, "Master Your Craft," you must continually develop your skills and then make use of them until your career takes off. And even after attaining degrees of success, longevity is difficult in any creative field. So these skills are very useful even after the proverbial 15 minutes of fame, and will allow you to continue to earn a living doing something that you truly enjoy. Patience teamed with persistence is crucial, but adaptability is equally important.

We can learn a lot from what Steve Jobs had to say about setbacks and persistence. He spoke about how getting fired from Apple in 1985 led to one of the most creative periods in his life. He founded NeXT and Pixar, met his wife, and then ultimately returned to Apple in 1996 to take it from the brink of doom to the company we know today. I highly recommend that you dig up the full text of his Stanford University commencement speech from June 12, 2005. Here is a small part of what he had to say that day:

> I didn't see it then, but it turned out that getting fired from Apple was the best thing that could have ever happened to me....Sometimes life hits you in the head with a brick. Don't lose faith. I'm convinced that the only thing that kept me going was that I loved what I did....Your work is going to fill a large part of your life, and the only way to be truly satisfied is to do what you believe is great work. And the only way to do great work is to love what you do. If you haven't found it yet, keep looking. Don't settle.

Luck, Talent, Preparation, Opportunity, and Success

Some people just seem destined for success. They are born with natural talents that make things easier for them. In most cases, they still had to work very hard to get where they are, even if others would have to work a lot harder for equal accomplishment. This is even more true if they are able to maintain a long, successful career.

There is also no denying that some people have better luck than most. A rare few are naturally, inexplicably, very lucky or very unlucky. Most of the time, though, what people see as luck is actually the result of planning and preparation allowing one to take advantage of opportunities. Unpredictable does not mean random. Through experience, knowledge, and skill, we can cultivate instincts for making good judgments. You have to put yourself in a position to be lucky and have the skills to take advantage of the situation. In other words, most lucky people make their own luck. They are not only prepared, but are also willing and able to adapt situations on the fly. Professional poker players perfectly represent a balanced mixture of chance, luck, flexible thinking, and skill, and it is no coincidence that the same familiar faces consistently make it to final tables at big money poker tournaments year after year.

NOTE: Make sure to check out this book's companion book, *The Music Producer's Survival Stories: Interviews with Veteran, Independent, and Electronic Music Professionals*, which is largely comprised of interviews with a variety of professionals, from big time to indie. Although those interviews cover topics found in every chapter, what they all have in common is discussion highly relevant to this chapter in particular.

"It's Normal For People To Not Like You": Chapter 5, "The Social Scene," discusses different types of people in a variety of social situations. In Chapter 9, "Lifestyle Tips," I talk about considerations for who you choose to surround yourself with as it relates to your career. When it comes to planning, if you are ambitious, you will inevitably experience all sorts of weirdness from some of the people around you. No matter how good you are at what you do, or how hard you try to be a good person, once you put yourself out there you should expect to be at the receiving end of negative criticism. Sometimes the criticism is actually a critique, which usually implies constructive feedback, even if it is harsh and hard to accept. Yet, there are times when people will dislike or even hate you for reasons that are not of your doing; it is more about them than it is about you. They might feel threatened, they might be jealous of your skills or successes, or perhaps your work is forcing them to look into a mirror they'd rather ignore. Some artists thrive on the negative reactions to their work; it means that people are not only paying attention, but also that it is having an impact. With regard to this latter point, we might be talking about nothing more than contrived "shock-value," but at its best, these negative reactions mean you are doing something right and revealing a "truth."

Dan Waldschmidt is known for interesting takes on topics related to sales, business, and entrepreneurship. As DIY/independent producers, we share many professional dynamics with his target audience even if we don't like to spend time thinking about such topics. Dan posted the following to his "Edgy Conversations" blog on January 4, 2013 (danwaldschmidt.com):

It's Normal For People To Not Like You
How do you stay focused and inspired?

1. *Be clear in your own head about why what you want to achieve is so important.*
2. *Accept responsibility for the parts of your zealotry that need to be improved.*
3. *Build a group of friends and mentors whom you can trust to be fair and honest.*
4. *Laugh off the silliest accusations and make yourself smile even though you don't feel like it.*
5. *Take time each week to review through your goals and ideas and progress.*
6. *Tune out almost everyone around you most of the time.*

It's not easy to do. Or fun.
But that's the price you pay for doing what most other people only read about in books.

Defining Your Goals

Goals are what we want to accomplish, while a plan is a way to attain goals. Especially if you are just getting started, but also if you are simply looking for ways to diversify an existing career, there are two basic steps we all need to consider. Regardless of your goals' degree of ambition, you need to spend time thinking about how to accomplish them.

It may sound obvious, but defining your goals is the crucial first step. Once you are clear about what you want to achieve, then you figure out what you need to do to make it happen. Goals and plans often display a degree of fractal self-similarity, so any step in a plan might also be a goal that is part of the larger plan to reach larger goals. Perhaps one of your goals is to be a professional remixer. As part of your plan to get your name out there, you might do free or cheap remixes. Goals and plans are different in that there will be parts of the plan that are obviously a means to the ends of realizing your goals. This might include working at a disposable job you don't like but need for now because it helps to pay the bills while in school.

Now that you understand that specific goals and specific parts of a plan might be the same, let's refocus on goals. We'll return to planning shortly.

Brainstorming

Start by writing down big goals. These might include the following:

▷ Win a Grammy.
▷ Score for your favorite movie directors.
▷ Start a new genre.
▷ Produce albums for successful artists you really like.
▷ Own a state-of-the-art studio with an A-list clientele.
▷ Be known and remembered as a true master of your craft.
▷ Travel the world with your best friends.
▷ Pay off your parents' mortgage.
▷ Help end world hunger.

The Music Producer's Survival Guide

Things like getting signed or finding more work are steps that can be part of your plan. Although you can write them down if they come to mind, think big right now. Be very honest with yourself, and don't gloss over anything. It may be significant. Like a personal diary, you don't ever have to show this list to anyone. What are your hopes and wishes? What are you passionate about? Don't be critical at this point. If this kind of process is new to you, and/or you are not satisfied with just writing a list, research common brainstorming techniques such as mind mapping. (For an example of how I used such a technique as a first step to help organize some of the historical and biographical connections research for this book, look ahead to the messy scribbled notes in Figure 3.3.) This initial list does not have to be realistic, or even probable. Visualizing the future is a creative process. As with any creative process, editing comes later.

If you need some help getting going, the following list includes a bunch of questions that should prime the pump:

▷ What are you really good at doing?
▷ Do you prefer working behind the scenes or being out in front?
▷ What do you most enjoy about music and production?
▷ Is your primary goal to produce your own music?
▷ Is this goal going to be your primary source of income?
▷ Do you want to make commercial music? Underground music? Both?
▷ Do you want to tour and perform?
▷ Do you want to work as a solo artist or with other artists?
▷ Do you like working as a musician in support of other artists?
▷ Do you want to produce other artists?
▷ Do you want to collaborate with other musicians? In a band?
▷ Do you like audio engineering? Do you like doing live sound?
▷ Do you want to do remixes for name artists?
▷ Do you want to work with companies to help them design products?
▷ Do you like computers? Do you like programming?
▷ Do you like teaching, demoing, or presenting?
▷ Do you want to run a business? Do you think of yourself as a business?
▷ Do you want to be a DJ?
▷ Do you want to be a promoter?
▷ Do you want to also do other types of art? Visual? Interactive? Written?

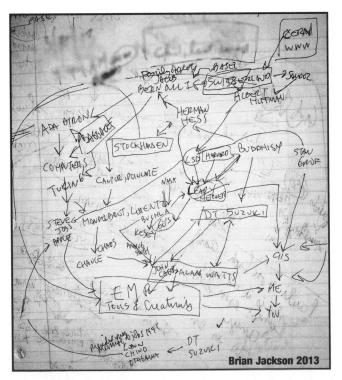

Figure 3.3 An example of what the results of a brainstorming session might look like before any editing and cleanup. Many of the ideas did not make it into the final product.

▷ Do you like community building?
▷ Are you interested in using music to help causes you care about?
▷ What are you naturally good at?
▷ What do you love about music and production?
▷ What are you sure you do not want to do?

NOTE: Using a mobile device for keeping track of ideas on the go is recommended. You can even utilize a cloud-based service that is Web accessible and syncs to all of your devices, such as Dropbox, Google Drive, or Evernote. But I highly recommend doing the brainstorming process with pen/pencil and paper, such as can been seen in Figure 3.3. Being able to quickly scribble ideas in a non-linear way, out of order as they come to mind, by drawing circles and boxes connected with lines, is more conducive to a free flow of thoughts than typing with a keyboard while staring at a computer screen. After you complete your first solid draft, scan it, digitize as text, or use diagramming software such as Omnigraffle or the Drawing feature in a Google Drive document.

Time, Energy, and Money: At a fundamental level, our experience of time shapes many of our decisions. Time flies when you are having fun, and slows to a crawl when in pain or bored. Einstein's special theory of relativity gave us the mathematical and scientific tools to prove that time is indeed relative. GPS works only because of the practical application of Einstein's equations. The fact that our perception of time seems to change in dangerous and emergency situations has been shown to have a basis in our neurochemistry in experiments such as those done by neuroscientist David Eagleman of the Baylor College of Medicine.

When you love your work, it does not feel like a job. It could be argued that part of this positive experience has to do with how we experience time when we are focused on enjoyable tasks. On the flip side, when you can't stand your job, time moves a lot slower, and people usually don't like that feeling. So you might think about your choice of career as a choice about how you would like to experience time. Yes, a career plan is ultimately about how you want to earn a living and focus your energy, but it is equally about how you spend your time in the global economy. Let's use physics and metaphysics to break down what drives a civilization's economy to the most fundamental components.

▶ **Energy:** The capacity or power to do work.
▶ **Work:** The transfer of energy from one object to another.
▶ **Labor:** Exertion of energy—physical or mental—for wages.
▶ **Money:** Socially constructed and agreed-upon medium accepted in the exchange of goods or services, often as wages. Money also directly equates to capital and assets.
▶ **Debt:** Owed money, time, or labor. Money borrowed against future earnings to be paid back with interest that accrues over time.

Einstein's most famous equation, $E=mc^2$, basically means that matter and energy are equivalent to each other. E stands for energy, m for mass, and c for the "constant," which is the speed of light in this case. Therefore, according to Einstein, energy equals mass multiplied by the speed of light multiplied by the speed of light. The speed of light is 671 million miles per hour, or 186,000 miles per second. Any way you consider it, when we talk about energy or mass, we are also talking about time either explicitly or implicitly. So just as mass and energy are not separable, the same goes for time and energy. Money is exchanged for time and energy. Therefore, in our civilization, time, energy, and money are simply different forms of the same thing. To build or develop something, you need at least two of the three. If you have a lot of any one of them, you need a lot less of the other two, and vice versa.

Let's take the example of building a professional-quality recording studio. If you have a lot of time, you do not need a lot of money or energy, as each day you can do one or two small things, pick up materials when you can, and just inch along week by week, month by month, year by year. If you have a lot of money, you don't need as much time and will not have to expend much of your own energy, as you can purchase all of the materials at once and hire a bunch of people to design and build it for you very quickly. If you have a lot of energy, you don't need to spend as much money on hiring people, and can learn what you need to do it yourself in a timely manner.

If you are still skeptical about all of this, consider the following. Time is treated as a commodity in a profit-motive economic system. Time is money. Time is running out. Budget your time. Work "over-time" and earn "time and a half." How good are you at time management? How do you want to *spend* your time? Do you have a lot of *free* time? Free time is considered to be a luxury or a reward. Paid "vacation time" is a job benefit. Are you having a hard time? Being sentenced to "hard time" in prison is a punishment. In fact, there is such a thing as debtor's prison, a place that exists solely for serving time for failure to repay debts. In the U.S. such places disappeared in the 19th century, yet even today you can be sent to jail or prison for failure to pay state-imposed fines. Moreover, it was not until 1971 that immediately converting monetary judgments to jail time for the indigent was ruled unconstitutional.

Leaving aside medieval punishments, for maximum control over how you can spend your time, you cannot ignore the implications of debt. Debt usually implies owing borrowed money plus interest. Historically, interest on loans was severely frowned upon and, when even allowed, capped at low rates. These rates would have been no higher than the average subsidized Stafford student loan. They most certainly were nothing resembling those *legally* found in our culture today, like the exorbitant 30% credit-card rates or completely insane payday loans that are as high as 1,300% for a 14-day loan!

Given the current discussion, we can think of monetary debt as borrowing time or energy, since it is essentially time shifting of energy. Sometimes, this time shifting/borrowing is not a good idea at all. Other times, it is either necessary, helpful, or just convenient, although it can be smart, shrewd, or even prudent when well managed and carefully considered. Yet, all too often, debt in our culture is like an invisible control system—one that pressures debtors to focus their time and energy on working for wages just to pay interest to the usury agent instead of focusing on the goals that motivated the debt in the first place.

Our civilization runs on a fractional reserve banking system, which at its core is based on debt. There are a lot of advantages to this system, but as we learned all too well from the global financial crisis of 2007–2008, when it goes wrong, the consequences are devastating to millions of people. A few entities and individuals made out like bandits, especially the big banks that are actually bigger than ever. I am not suggesting you memorize the powerful, educational, and well-intentioned (though metaphysically flawed) *Zeitgeist* movies, nor run to the hills for your bunker stocked with supplies. I *am* suggesting that it is worth learning and thinking about how each of us interacts with such a system—most pertinently, how it affects one's career path in a creative field. There is no question that debt is helpful in the short term, but how much will it limit future options or hamper creative freedom and artistic independence?

One of the best things anyone can do for themselves at the beginning of a career is to be very mindful of the true costs of debt, and to keep it as low as possible. Choosing a career, making a living doing what you love to do, largely is about how you want to spend your time. Therefore, all of us should take into account the interconnectedness of money, debt, energy, and time.

Developing a Plan

Chaos in the midst of chaos isn't funny, but chaos in the midst of order is.

–Steve Martin

What is Steve Martin getting at in this quote? I think his statement alludes to our thresholds for handling some amount of chaos in a given situation. Surely he was talking about the art of comedy, just as in music we consider the effectiveness of dissonance in a composition with or without some consonance. Plans are like paths cut through a jungle. If not well tended, or if poorly designed, the path is quickly reclaimed by the foliage, forcing you to pay attention or suffer the consequences of getting lost. When life happens, when the unexpected occurs, if you have a plan, you can readjust and reorient yourself—perhaps even laughing at the irony or absurdity of the situation while doing so. If you have no plan for attaining your goals, are just flowing along in whatever chaotic streams that sweep you up, then more chaos can simply be overwhelming. It will not be funny.

Plans can take many forms, depending on where you are in life and in your career. A plan can be very detailed and include moving to a new city and going to school. Or, it might be simple, including guiding principles and modest goals to help reorient and grow an existing career. All of us need to spend time learning about our options, including alternate paths and backup plans.

It is useful to break goals and plans into three phases:

▷ **Near-term:** This can include time frames from right now through the next year or two. It might be as simple as figuring out which school to attend, focusing on graduating, or perhaps even toughing it out at a crap job until you save enough money so you can move to a new city. If you are looking to expand an existing career, it might be things like writing a good business plan, upgrading your studio, putting together a PR campaign, or writing a book for indie and electronic music producers.

▷ **Medium-term:** This can range from about a year away to as much as four to six years after that. It might include developing your skills, finishing school, going on tour, setting up a commercial-quality project studio, getting high-profile gigs, or getting established in a scene. For an established professional, this could also include attracting more desired clientele or other aspects of a business plan, such as income goals or serious upgrades to your studio.

▷ **Long-term:** Where do you see yourself in five years? 10 years? 20 years? Visualize what you would like to see here. This is the part of your plan where you should not put any limits on what you think is probable or possible. If it is something you would like to achieve, it belongs somewhere in your plan. Long-term goals may change over time as you pursue unexpected avenues.

Take some time to clean up the list you generated during brainstorming. Next, take three sheets of paper and write "Near Term" on one, "Medium Term" on the second, and "Long Term" on the third. Then go through your goals list and start sorting them accordingly. You may have the same goal on all of the lists, representing different levels of success. For example, if one of your goals is to produce a full-length album, the near-term goal might be your first personal releases, the medium-term goal might be the release of an established indie artist you admire, and the long-term goal might be producing for your favorite A-list artists. I recommend that you work backward when making these sort of lists, starting with your long-term vision, since it will influence the planning of your medium-term and near-term goals.

Now that you have defined your goals, including time frames for achieving them, you can start to figure out how to realize them. What do you need in your plan to make them happen in each of the phases?

> **NOTE:** If you are new to the world of music production, you may want to read Chapter 4 before finishing the first complete draft of your plan. Having a fuller understanding of all the aspects of production may influence your decisions, especially when it comes to schooling and training.

Possible Pieces of the Planning Puzzle

Do the difficult things while they are easy and do the great things while they are small. A journey of a thousand miles must begin with a single step.

–Lao Tzu

Numerous variables outline the parameters for the realization of your plan. Generally speaking, the younger you are and the fewer responsibilities you have, the more potential paths you will have immediately in front of you, and vice versa for those who are older with more responsibilities. But all options and paths are not equal, and more options does not necessarily imply better options. There are pros and cons to both sides of the spectrum. Even if some of the sections that follow are tailored primarily toward those just getting started or those who are more established, I recommend you give equal consideration to all of it. It is likely that you will identify with aspects on both sides of the spectrum, so just modify the considerations to fit your situation.

Limiting Factors

Few people have the luxury of basing their plan solely on what their heart desires. As discussed in Chapter 7, "Creative Process," having unlimited options is not the treasure it is often assumed to be, as limitations actually play a major role in shaping productive creativity. Overcoming limitations is a powerful motivating factor, which can drive you to improve your situation. Moreover, you will gain important life experience and appreciate your successes more than those who had things handed to them. Whether the limitations are financial, geographical, physical, or based on obligations and responsibilities to others, there are options for you. Because we have no way of predicting which potential options and paths will be successful, limitations are not necessarily bad or good; they just are what they are. Overcoming limitations can easily translate into assets and opportunities.

The following list of limitations are addressed primarily in near-term planning, but also likely in some mid-term planning too.

▷ **Finances:** This is the most obvious and common limitation at the onset of a career path. If you don't have the money to do what you need to do, then figuring out how to earn income so you can save up what you need to get started will be a big part of your near-term plan. You might have to work at a few jobs that really suck for a while. You will have to make sacrifices. But if this is your passion, you will be willing to make them.

▷ **Obligations:** Are you married? Do you have kids? Do you help run a family business? Having honest discussions with significant people in your life is imperative. Figuring out how to best approach the subject might even be part of your plan. Their level of support will have huge ramifications for your plan, especially when it comes to your significant other. This limitation has the potential to be a very powerful advantage in the form of a powerful support system. Even if these significant people are skeptical at the onset, once you have a few public successes, such as being in a magazine, there is a good chance they will realize you are not just following a pipe dream.

▷ **Geography:** Even with the Internet, where you live will influence your plans. Someone in Boise has different challenges than someone in Brooklyn. It might be necessary to move from a small town to a nearby city, college town, or big city, or to move from a big city to somewhere more affordable. Moves can also be small, and might include simply moving across town so it is easier to be out and about in the scene.

▷ **Physical/psychological:** ALS didn't stop Steven Hawking from achieving greatness as a physicist, and blindness didn't stop Ray Charles or Stevie Wonder from becoming great musicians. Many great artists have persevered though struggles with various autistic spectrum disorders, depression, and alcoholism and other addictions. If you have some sort of physical or psychological limitation, you will have to tailor your plan accordingly, but there is no reason not to go for it. Focusing your energy on music production can even help in dealing with many of these challenges.

Are You Already a Pro or Skilled in Something?

Changes in the industry have forced a lot of professionals to grow and evolve. In recent years, there has been a noticeable increase in the number of accomplished musicians, DJs, and even audio engineers who have had to update and expand their skills. On numerous occasions, I've had the good fortune of being their instructor, usually for private lessons. Learning how to use a specific DAW is the most common request, mixing and mastering a close second, with vocal recording, sound design, and synthesis vying for third place. In most cases, their questions overlap multiple aspects of the production process, forcing big-picture discussions. The three most common outcomes, for beginners and professionals alike, are as follows:

▷ **No go:** After a few lessons, it dawns on them that learning how to produce their own music is a lot more involved than they assumed. They don't continue the lessons and decide to just stick with what they are doing. They often try to find new partners or collaborators who have the necessary skills. This is most common with DJs.

▷ **Modify plan:** After a few lessons, it dawns on them that learning how to produce their own music is a lot more involved than they assumed. They continue lessons, but with a better understanding of the whole process. They know what they want to do for themselves and what can be handed off to engineers. They choose to focus on the aspects of production in which they are most interested, such as recording their own vocals or MIDI sequencing virtual instruments. This is most common with "traditional" musicians and singer/songwriters.

▷ **All in:** They either already know or realize that they have a lot to learn, and are excited by it. Whether they continue lessons with me or not, they keep moving forward and leverage their existing assets as they add new skills to their arsenal. This is most common with audio engineers and tech-savvy/electronic musicians.

A lot of time, energy, and sacrifice goes into establishing a name and reputation for your skills and talents. Deciding to do something new can be a very humbling experience. It is important to realize that adult education is a growth industry for a number of macroeconomic reasons, largely related to globalization and the democratization of technology. It is much more common to find older students in all sorts of degree programs than it was just a few decades ago. Having to take a few steps back and reinvent oneself can be a scary prospect, especially if you have family responsibilities and the like. There must be good reasons for considering making these moves in the first place, so trust your instincts. The following tips are targeted at non-beginners, but are valuable considerations no matter your current level of achievement.

▷ **Have a beginner's mind:** We all develop habits and sets of assumptions. When learning something new, it is often best to forget how much you already know. Approach it like a beginner. Don't try to continually prove how much you already know, or you will hamper the process. For an accomplished professional to make this possible, you might have to find safe, ego-free zones. You can learn in an environment that allows you to stay anonymous or, ideally, from people who respect your current accomplishments and your willingness to have a beginner's mind.

▷ **Use your network:** Talk to people you already know in the industry about your desire to expand your career options. Start with your close circle of peers and associates. Pick their brains for ideas, and see what opportunities might immediately pop up. For all you know, some of them are also looking for ways to expand *their* options that might be mutually beneficial and synergistic.

▷ **Learn by teaching:** Consider trading services with other pros, with the understanding that you want to learn from each other while doing so. You might also trade training for training—for example, you teach them piano and they teach you a DAW. One of the great things about teaching is that it forces you to do a lot of learning—about new material, and also by deepening your current understanding.

Are You Just Getting Started (or Starting Over)?

If you are just getting started, a plethora of options can help to make up for your lack of experience and connections. Really think about how you want to move forward based on what you determine is best for you and your personal situation. Learning and training are going to be a fundamental part of your plan. Keep in mind that Chapter 4 discusses the learning process in addition to the four main areas of production.

School

Even if music is your sole passion, don't underestimate the value of a well-rounded education. Earning a bachelor's degree is highly recommended. While having a degree often does not directly translate into a job, *not* having one can shut you out of opportunities for years to come. Moving away to go to college is great life experience for anyone who can afford to do so. In addition to your studies, it is a great place to meet a lot of different kinds of people and to expose yourself to new ways of thinking. Even if you decide to stay local, you can reap many of the same rewards as long as you make an effort and don't treat it like a continuation of your high-school days. You don't have to attend a big university, either. There are a lot of great state and city colleges.

A common approach that can save you many thousands of dollars is to stay at home and do a one- or two-year degree at a community college, and then transfer to a bigger school for completion of the degree. Just make sure your credits will transfer to where you want to go. It is even possible to do a degree online if you don't have the time or money to attend in person. In some cases, a certificate/diploma or associate's degree might be what suits your current situation best. Let's briefly consider some common options.

Generally speaking, assuming a full-time course load, a bachelor's takes about four school years, an associate's about two school years, and a certificate/diploma one school year. The one- and two-year degrees tend to be much more focused on a specific trade craft, such as audio engineering, and/or cover general education requirements that are part of any four year degree. In addition to offerings by state and community colleges, there are numerous schools dedicated to music production and audio technology.

If you go the bachelor's degree route, here are a few combinations to consider, which might meet your needs or, if nothing else, give you some ideas:

1. **B.F.A., B.M., and/or B.A.:** This route includes majoring in music, music business, broadcast, and/or audio technology. Some may additionally choose to add a double major or minor in digital or classic visual arts, literature, or creative writing.
2. **B.A.:** This route includes majoring in the humanities or social sciences, such as cultural anthropology, psychology, sociology, or philosophy. You can then also take music or audio technology courses as a double major, a minor, or electives.
3. **B.S. or B.C.S.:** This route is for those interested in the most technical aspects of our industry, and would include majoring in electrical engineering, physics, and/or computer science. Degrees in this option are the ones most likely to lead to a good-paying job after college.

If your route closely resembles the second or third bullet, more than the first one, you will need to make best use of your extracurricular activities. Getting involved in the local music scene and the college radio station are great places to start. You are also going to have to spend free time developing your music and production skills outside of the classroom, which can be challenging if you also have to work a lot to cover the tuition. Make sure to check out the upcoming section entitled "Personalized Training."

If you already have a college degree or decide not to go that route, you may be considering one of the many state-licensed audio technology schools that offer one- or two-year degrees. It is equally important to fully research these schools as with any college. Some of them are quite good, while others are a mixed bag at best. Regardless of their quality, don't make assumptions about what you think you will learn there. In most cases, if you want to learn audio engineering, you are looking into one kind of program, while if you want to study music you are looking for another program. Over the course of the last decade, as an instructor at multiple audio-engineering schools, there has been a significant number of students under the impression that the program is designed to teach them how to write songs or make beats. In some cases, they are months into the program before they realize they are mistaken. In most cases, it was solely their fault for not paying attention, but some schools do advertise their programs in a way that might lead one to such assumptions. Just be sure you are going to get what you are signing up for, and then make the best of your time there.

Take It Seriously: Even though you are paying to go to school, you should also think of it as your first career experience. In addition to the skills obviously related to your goals, you are learning about people in general—yourself, others, and social situations. As you will read in Chapter 5, "The Social Scene," you are part of a social ecology. So school is where you can develop a network of connections, some of which might turn out to be substantial throughout your life. Whether you realize it or not, you are also starting to establish your reputation in terms of reliability, integrity, intelligence, creativity, and work ethic.

Paul White, the editor in chief of *Sound On Sound* magazine, wrote an article in the July 2004 edition entitled "Learning Difficulties." The topic of the article is students in audio-technology programs, but the main points apply to any related course of study or general interest in music and production. I recommend that everyone dig up the complete article; here, I've quoted his thoughts on what makes for a successful student in an audio engineering program:

> *The successful student will spend every possible moment in the college studio, will trade food, cash and body parts for anybody else's spare studio time and will talk about little else other than recording to the extent that all their non-musical friends will lose the will to live. The same person will walk into their friends' homes or into record stores and notice instantly if the speakers are out of phase, and regardless of their own musical interests, will absorb any information on every aspect of recording. This same person will go home from college and, barely pausing for food, will boot up his or her computer and try to put some of this new information into practice. The main bathroom reading will be* Sound On Sound, *and our candidate will know all about the technical issues associated with recording as well as the artistic ones.*

Instructors often are your first serious connections in the industry. After you graduate, they might offer you opportunities. For example, they may need an assistant for their personal work or know someone who does. Also, letters of recommendation can be very helpful, if not necessary, when applying for internships and jobs. I've written very good letters of recommendation for average-talent students who had excellent attitudes and work ethics, while talking some smarter, more naturally talented students into withdrawing their request. Why? I tell them that they won't like what I write because they often missed classes, didn't complete projects, and didn't demonstrate commitment to their education. What would I write? That they might be good if they actually show up and do their work?

NOTE: According to the U.S. Consumer Financial Protection Bureau, in 2012, student loan debt in the U.S. hit $1 trillion dollars, which exceeds total car loans and total credit-card debt. Student loan debt is obviously a serious problem in the U.S., for a lot of reasons—not the least being the rapid rise in tuition costs over the last few decades. Do what you can to keep your student loans to a minimum. In most cases, this means relying on them only for living expenses when necessary. Over the years, the interest can really add up. Even a few thousand dollars a semester earned with a part-time job can save you many times more later on. Look into work/study options or part-time positions at the school that might count more toward tuition credit than an equivalent off-campus job can earn hourly.

Personalized Training

Even after school, there is much more to learn. If you don't go to school for music production, you will be figuring out how to get all of the skills and experience you need. The fact of the matter is that most producers are self-taught to a large extent. Some people are naturals at working with technology and audio equipment and will not need much, if any, formal education. While you will likely focus on areas that most interest you, also make sure to at least familiarize yourself with a wide spectrum of topics, ranging from practical, classic, and tried and true, to experimental, novel, academic, and niche. Following are common options, even if you decide to mostly go the autodidact route.

▷ **Private lessons:** This is a great option for professionals, people who already have a good amount of knowledge, busy people, and anyone who prefers one-on-one training. The key here is to find people who are not only skilled, but who are also experienced teachers, who will work with you to develop a personalized curriculum. Keep in mind that all things being equal, private lessons cost more per hour than when taking a group class. Depending on how quickly you learn and the quality of the teacher, this comparison may not be a good way to make a decision. You may move more quickly in a private lesson than in a class, get help that would not be possible in a classroom, or simply get the personalized and customized attention only possible in one-on-one training.

▷ **Classes:** Many places offer group classes and even programs on many aspects of production. Often, they are non-profit arts organizations, or small shops owned by other musicians, producers, and DJs. Quality and cost will vary wildly in this category, so do your research. One of the advantages of classes over private lessons is the social aspect. If you need to meet people and make connections, take that variable into account.

▷ **Training centers:** There are places that offer various "official" certifications with a specific company's products, such as Pro Tools or Logic. These places basically teach a curriculum given to them by that company. Other places are certified by a company to teach their products, which is different from offering end-user certification. For example, Ableton certifies schools to teach Live, but users can only become Ableton certified directly through Ableton.

▷ **Workshops/seminars:** While you cannot build a plan around workshops, they are a great way to pick up things and meet like-minded people. Often, these are associated with a specific company's product and take place at music instrument retail stores. They might also be at some of the other places mentioned in this list.

Learning on the Job

A great way to learn about something is to see how it is done in the real world. Internships are the traditional entry-level position in our industry. Nowadays, internships are often unpaid, though they are likely to count for college credit. Some internships start as unpaid, but can evolve into paid internships, and then occasionally into a job offer. You might find an internship at a record label, a recording studio, a post production facility, or perhaps with a composer or jingle house. Due to changes in the industry, there are a lot fewer high-visibility options at the top end of the scale than in the past, but many more that are smaller, private, and therefore harder to find. Ideally, you want to look for facilities, labels, and studios known for the types of projects and music you love. This approach can greatly increase your chances of landing an internship at such a place. And, should you get the gig, it makes it more likely that the common interests with your associates will translate into an entry-level position. Should you start with an entry-level position instead of an internship, this approach then increases the odds of advancement and longevity.

Be prepared to do a lot of uninteresting grunt work at first, such as making coffee, wrapping cables, answering phones, stuffing envelopes, updating blogs, or even cleaning bathrooms. Yes, some places take advantage of interns as cheap labor. But if they are serious about your position, certainly they are watching how you handle situations. While it may seem that you are not doing anything special, they are noting how responsible you are, how dependable you are, how you interact with people, and even how aware you are of subtle aspects of a given situation. They are making sure you will be a good fit for the personalities that are already there. In essence, all of these factors are the interview if there is a potential job offer at the end of an internship. Every place is different, so don't make assumptions until you understand the culture of that environment.

If an internship is not right for you, find ways to garner the same experiences. Any chance you have to be around professionals as they work is an opportunity to jump on. I first learned about mixing just by sitting near the engineer who mixed my band's records and watching what he did and in what order. If you want to learn about mastering, sit in on the sessions with the engineer mastering your music. If you have friends who are going into the studio, see if you can tag along. In any of these scenarios, just watch and listen, stay out of the way, and pick up what you can. Pay attention to everything going on—not just the technical bits, which likely will be out of your line of sight anyway. Often, what you will learn is not what you expected.

Moving

People commonly move for school or work. Leaving those two reasons aside, deciding to move somewhere for your career when there is no specific job offer on the table can be very risky, but the rewards are often worth it. Yes, the Internet offers many opportunities that once required a move, but your location might still be a significant limiting factor. This decision is a very personal one, and the details will vary widely depending on the person, his or her goals, where he or she is in life, and the specific opportunities he or she is seeking.

There is no doubt that long-distance moves present more risks than smaller ones, yet relocating just a few hours away is still a big change to take seriously. When considering a move, I recommend doing a simple "pros versus cons" list. Take a piece of paper, draw a line down the middle, and think about each side of the issue. No matter your situation, the following list of considerations is worthy of your attention. It is up to you to determine how much weight to give to them.

▷ **Change factor:** Are you happy where you are, or do you really want to live somewhere else? How did you end up at your current location? Were you born there? Is it where you went to school? Or did you move there for a relationship? Don't move just because you are not happy with your life. That being said, there are times when a major change in environment is called for.

▷ **Support system:** Do you have a strong support system where you are? If so, is it making you complacent? Would moving involve bringing people with you? If you decide to make a big move, having some friends or solid acquaintances in the new location is highly recommended. Don't underestimate the importance of having even a minimal support system in place at the destination of a big move.

▷ **Scene:** This consideration overlaps with your support system. Is there a local scene related to what you do? Is there a specific place that a significant number of your influences come from? Is there a community of like-minded people? If not, where is your scene and community? Can you find them online? If so, will that be enough? I've had friends move from San Francisco or New York City to Austin or Denver just because the scene and community there better fit them.

▷ **Income options:** Do you have a steady source of income where you are? Is it what you like doing? If not, can you find better options without moving? If you want to find work as a recording engineer, consider places with a lot of bands and studios, such as Southern California, New York City, Austin, Chicago, Seattle, or Nashville. Depending on the specific styles and genres that interest you, you might be best suited for niche markets, such as Tampa, Miami, Atlanta, or even Las Vegas. If you want to do sound or music for video games, you are likely considering Los Angeles, San Francisco, or Seattle. Yet, I've known people who prefer to live where they like and just spend a lot of time traveling. The more established you are, the less it matters where you live. Legendary multi–Grammy winning mastering engineer Bob Ludwig moved from New York City to Maine, where he opened a world-class mastering facility in the middle of nowhere. The work comes to him.

▷ **Expenses:** Do you need to live somewhere cheaper? If you live in an expensive city, you may have to work all the time just to pay your rent. If you already have a decent job and four roommates, and are still struggling to find time to work on music, then something needs to change. In recent years, numerous bands and DJs have moved to cheap cities like Detroit or Baltimore. Because they are often traveling, they've decided to stop wasting money on rent for apartments they rarely occupy. It is also possible that you just need to find another neighborhood or an outlying area close to the city. There are a lot of musicians and producers who live just across the Hudson River from Manhattan in New Jersey, or in Oakland across the bay from San Francisco.

▷ **Adventure:** If you are in a position to do so, moving somewhere just for life experience should be considered. If the opportunity arises to go stay with a friend or relative, and you can easily return to your place of departure, the potential rewards easily outweigh the risks. You may decide to stay there, or it will simply give you a new perspective on where you would like to end up.

If you decide to make a big move, seriously consider the following tips.

▷ **Be prepared:** The Internet makes it easy to do your research, so do it. What is the average price of an apartment, house, or room share? What parts of town are ideal? What parts of town should you avoid? What is the current job market? How many months of a deposit are required and what documents will you need to rent a place? Did you send off some résumés shortly before making the move? Who do you need to know in the scene, and where do you need to go to meet the people you want to meet? Don't wait until you get there to figure out the basics. Hit the ground running.

▷ **Stick it out:** Even if you have friends in your new location, getting used to a new city can be rough. Especially if you are moving to a big city, be prepared for unexpected difficulties. After a few setbacks, many people give up and head back to where they came from. It can take two years to really get a feel for a new place, and quite a bit longer to get established. If you are a big fish in a small pond, be prepared to feel like you are starting over when you land in any talent-saturated city, especially the international hubs like New York City or London. Those places are full of people who were also big fish in small ponds, but also decided that they needed to grow past that comfortable situation. The whole reason for this move is to expand your opportunities and to step up your game. This will involve leaving your comfort zone in more ways than one. It is possible that the move was not a great decision, but you will have no way of knowing unless you really put your all into making it work first. If you get somewhere and you find things aren't going your way, realize that it will take only a great experience or two for you to realize you *did* make a good decision, and thus why it is worth struggling to make it work.

Backup Plans Versus Alternate Paths

If you have a safety device, your mindset is you're at ease, and your thought is, it's okay, we can use it.

–Nik Wallenda

What are your thoughts on a backup plan, in case you don't meet your goals in the desired timeframe? What does backup plan mean to you? Does it mean another field altogether, such as nursing, law, sales, or accounting? Does it mean using skills related to what you really want to do, such as settling into a full-time job working for a popular audio software company? Perhaps it might be something else that you also love doing? It is important to understand that keeping your options open and being flexible about readjusting goals and plans does not necessarily mean you are giving up. It is highly likely that unexpected opportunities will present completely new paths at some point in your career. Moreover, most people reevaluate their values, goals, and motivations at least a few times in their life. So, when pursuing interests you are passionate about, it is better to consider those options as alternate paths.

The notion of a backup plan has negative connotations when pursuing an artistic career, and for good reason. It has different implications than an alternate path when it comes to your career's relationship to a fulfilling life. Before we consider the differences between backup plans and alternate paths, keep the following points in mind, but don't read into them specific advice on what *you* should do:

▷ Most every single person who is successful in a creative field pursued their primary goals as if failure were not an option.

▷ Starting out with a backup plan exponentially increases the chances that it will be needed. The quote at the top of this section is by Nik Wallenda from a June 8, 2013 NPR interview. He is from the famous family known for their aerial stunts. On June 25, 2013, he successfully walked across the Grand Canyon on a 1,400 foot long tightrope, 1,500 feet above the ground, with no net or tether.

The details that differentiate an alternate path from a backup plan are very subjective. They are based solely on where you feel the line needs to be drawn. It would be disappointing if music production were just a serious hobby. Yet, I have almost equal passion for Integral theory and most of its subject matter, such as East-West psychology and philosophy, complexity studies, chaos theory, evolution of culture and consciousness, education, and the arts. If I had decided to complete my Ph.D. and go into academia, at least I would still be very passionate about my work. In that sense, this personal anecdote illustrates a difference between an alternate path and a backup plan. Personally speaking, a full-time nine-to-five job would be a backup plan, no matter the company, industry, or salary. Pursuing a career in a different part of our industry, or potentially even another field altogether, can be an alternate path, not a backup plan—as long as you find it inspiring, exciting, and fulfilling.

There is no judgment here, so if for whatever reason you feel the need to develop a backup plan while you are working on your main plan, please at least consider the following caveat. Be mindful about making a hedged bet, and therefore not really putting your all into the primary plan. Be sure that your backup plan is really only there if all else fails and you have no choice. While it is a good idea to consider many options, those due-diligence considerations can become distractions. Therefore, the biggest downside of a backup plan is that it can become a self-fulfilling prophecy. The comfort of knowing there is a cushy safety net consciously and unconsciously influences one's decision-making processes. It may seem like there is a lot to ponder here, but to simplify your musings on the topic, just ask yourself if you agree with Dr. Dre and Steve Jobs: that you have to have love for what you do.

Be Flexible

Be like water making its way through cracks. Do not be assertive, but adjust to the object, and you shall find a way round or through it. If nothing within you stays rigid, outward things will disclose themselves.

–Bruce Lee

Empty your mind, be formless, shapeless, like water. Now you put water into a cup, it becomes the cup. You put water into a bottle, it becomes the bottle. Put it into a teapot, it becomes the teapot. Now water can flow or creep or drip or crash. Be water my friend.

–Bruce Lee

Remember, a plan is like a compass to guide you to a destination, not the vehicle that gets you there. Don't confuse plans with goals. No matter how hard you work on your plan, at some point you will likely have to throw much of it out the window and come up with a new one. Stubbornly sticking to a plan in the face of new realities or unexpected opportunities can be just as problematic as having no plan. Einstein once defined insanity as "when you keep doing the same thing over and over again, and keep expecting a different result each time."

For those of you who have a tendency to freeze up when confronted by big decisions, or fear making the wrong decision, or are perfectionists and want to always make the perfect decision, consider the preceding Bruce Lee quotes. Much of Bruce Lee's philosophy was essentially Taoist. The core of Taoism's ancient wisdom reflects a deep understanding of nature, some of which science rediscovered in a way that the modern mind can understand through chaos theory. The butterfly effect was discovered while trying to predict the weather, a ubiquitous chaotic system that envelops us for our whole lives. And just as changes in the atmosphere that sustains us are unpredictable, no matter what we do there will always be some uncertainty. Hoping for total control of our future is futile. It leads to unnecessary worry, fear, and rigidity, and is not helpful. Bruce Lee was not an armchair philosopher, he was incredibly successful in multiple endeavors—master martial artist, world-famous movie star, popular culture icon, and a true pioneer in many ways.

In 1989, the L.A.-based band Bad Religion released its fourth album, *No Control*, on Epitaph Records (an indie label started by its guitar player in 1980). It is a notably catchy melodic punk classic by all accounts. Greg Graffin, Ph.D., the band's cofounder and singer, is known for some of the smartest punk lyrics of all time. The lyrics to the album's title track ponder the arc of history, culture, consciousness, and epistemology. The pre-chorus emphasizes impermanence, the cyclical nature of creation and destruction, and therefore how control is temporary even for a conquering king. Ultimately, even if you think you understand the path in front of you, believe it when Graffin repeatedly states in the sing-along chorus that we are not in control.

While still active as a musician and author, Graffin is also a professor at UCLA and Cornell University, with an academic background in geology, biology, and zoology. His dissertation project focused on the intersection of evolution, naturalism, and religion, so his thinking is also very philosophical—more big picture than day to day. Given this context, it would be a mistake to assume that having no control means hopelessness or nihilism, especially since Graffin spent another 18 years of hard work to complete his Ph.D. after writing those lyrics. On the contrary, although it may not seem like an obvious conclusion, freedom actually emerges from embracing this lack of control. French sociologist Edgar Morin is one of the premier philosophers on the implications of complexity and chaos. According to Morin, "Freedom is a development of the ability of a self-organizing being to use uncertainty and chance occurrences in a way that is itself aleatory and uncertain but leads to autonomy. Freedom therefore appears as a consequence of complexification."

> **NOTE:** Greg Graffin is a great example of a musician who not only took an alternate path, but figured out how to successfully do both careers simultaneously.

Synchronicity: No, I am not referring to the Police's final and most popular album, although Sting's inspiration for the title comes from the topic at hand. Everyone experiences coincidences at some point. Have you noticed that some of them seem more meaningful than others? Psychologist Carl Jung coined the term *synchronicity* to differentiate these meaningful coincidences from ones that are inconsequential. Jung's professional relationship with Nobel Laureate quantum physicist Wolfgang Pauli is well documented and worthy of your time, should you be interested in such things. One of the results of their mutual inquiries into chance and probability was a paper published by Jung in the early 1950s entitled "Synchronicity: An Acausal Connecting Principle," alongside a monograph published by Pauli.

Jung explains his selection of the word *synchronicity* as follows: "As its etymology shows, this term has something to do with time, or to be more accurate, with a kind of simultaneity. Instead of simultaneity, we could also use the concept of *meaningful coincidence* of two or more events, where something other than the probability of chance is involved." (p. 104) Jung passed away in 1961, so while he was influenced by the world-changing discoveries of quantum physics, he missed the breakthroughs in cybernetics, fractal geometry, and chaos theory. Jung heavily influenced Arthur Koestler, but also passed away before Koestler advanced our understanding of parts and wholes in systems, that all things are holons in a holarchy.

According to Jung, these events reveal underlying patterns. In modern terms, we could talk about these underlying patterns in systems terminology, as dynamical systems, perhaps even as strange attractors. We are all holons in this complex, interconnected network of holons, and chaos theory teaches us that unpredictability does need mean random. In other words, we can write off normal mundane coincidences to simple chance, but recognizing repeated serial patterns of themed coincidences may in fact be synchronicities. Meaning is subjective, so only you can know if a coincidence or series of them is meaningful, but you should start developing the ability to notice them. Just as we must train our ears to perceive different aspects of music and sound, so too can we hone our perceptive abilities in this more nebulous terrain.

Look for synchronicities, especially during uncertain or transitional periods of your life, whether positive or difficult. Many, many creative people have experienced intense periods of these at various points in life, including numerous friends, acquaintances, and yours truly. They will get your attention and focus your mind on certain themes. Sometimes they are just a way to help determine if you are on the right track, while at other times they may be a source of creative muse and inspiration. In all cases, they are open to interpretation. If you do learn to notice them, and they become so intense as to make you question your sanity, don't dismay. Simply find another artist, Jungian/transpersonal psychologist, or the like to talk to. In all likelihood, you are just fine, and simply experiencing cognitive dissonance as you open up to the seemingly non-rational nature of the chaos all around us.

If you are interested in the connections between Jung's psychology, chaos theory, fractal dimensionality, and other related topics, check out the 1997 book *Archetypes and Strange Attractors: The Chaotic World of Symbols* by Jung Institute graduate John R. Van Eenwyk, Ph.D., a clinical instructor at the University of Washington School of Medicine.

Some Considerations, Strategies, and Options

Once you have defined your goals and outlined a plan, it is time to figure out how you are going to make it all happen. There are many options and a few basic strategies to consider. In the next chapter, I talk about the value of leveraging your strengths when developing skills in weaker areas. The same basic concept applies equally when executing the specifics of your plan, as is succinctly stated in the well-known idiom, "Put your best foot forward." The following sections are not meant to be comprehensive, but simply to cover scenarios and options that are most likely to be necessary details that complete an outline.

Technology and the Internet

Every one of us must take into account the accelerated rate of change in our culture and industry. You don't have to be a tech geek, but no matter what you want to do, you need to be comfortable with computers and be Internet savvy. We all need a presence on the Internet, so make sure you at least have a decent website, are active on a few forums, and know your way around social media. Because this alone is a huge topic, and the specifics are rapidly evolving, make sure to do your research and include it in your plan.

Before Skills Pay the Bills

Figuring out how to pay your rent until music or production start earning sufficient income is a ubiquitous conundrum. The following topics are common options while you develop your skills and work on getting known. There are two basic categories here—disposable/semi-disposable/low responsibility and good pay/industry-related—and the route you go will depend on your current skill level and various thresholds related to income needs, work hours, and responsibilities while there. You never know what the future will hold, so don't burn your bridges as you leave a job in search of greener pastures.

Disposable, Semi-Disposable, Low Responsibility

One common approach for income while you develop your creative career is to take a job that offers flexible scheduling and low responsibility. Low responsibility is significant because it means you don't take the job home with you and can therefore focus on your creative pursuits. Many of these jobs are also low wage, but not always. With this approach, if you need to go on tour, go to an audition, play a gig, or the like, you likely can get days off and still have a job to return to. If not, you can quit and then find another similar job when you return (in theory).

This type of job is often referred to as a "disposable" job. In other words, this type of job is not related to your career goals in any direct way, other than as a means to and an end of earning a paycheck. Restaurants, bars, coffee shops, and even office temp work are common examples of disposable jobs. The other route is to go with a slightly related, semi-disposable job, such as working at a retail shop that sells musical instruments or music. In either case, try to make the best of these gigs. If possible, try to find one that is frequented by people you want to meet. If nothing else, the social aspect of being behind a counter can be meaningful.

Good Pay, Industry-Related

The other route has two basic variables. The first one is to find a good-paying job so you can save a lot of money that can be put toward your career plans. Not everyone is able to get these type of jobs, so if the opportunity arises, it can be very tempting. As long as you can maintain focus and remember why you are there, and you are suited to the environment, then there is a strong argument to see if you can make it work. The danger with some of these types of jobs is that they can accidentally turn into a backup plan and become a self-fulfilling prophecy.

The second option is to find an entry-level job working in the industry, such as for a record label, instrument manufacturer, or audio software developer. While the full-time, high-responsibility nature of this type of job can be very challenging, there are huge potential rewards. Not only can you often earn a decent salary, but you can make a lot of great contacts, learn a lot about the industry and your craft, and even get free or cheap hardware and software. I know a lot of musicians who stay with some of these companies for very long periods of time as they continue to work on their own music, especially when the workplace is an enjoyable environment. The upside to one of these jobs is that you are surrounded by people with common interests and passions, and the work is related to your interests. Sometimes, connections made while working at one of these jobs lead directly to bigger and better opportunities. The downside of these situations is that the upsides can become traps and make it easy to never fully go for it. I also know a number of people who recognized the traps, left on good terms, and took the risk of less financial stability to fully pursue their goals—for example, a former Ableton employee from NYC who is doing really, really well. Lastly, should you find yourself surrounded primarily by jaded, cynical, bitter, and/or consistently unhappy people, take that as a sign that you need to improve your situation.

Paying the Bills with Your Skills

If your primary goal is to produce music for sale as the way you make a living, you should still figure out how you can pay your bills doing production-related things until that happens. Should you be one of the fortunate few who fully achieves that goal, maintaining that level of success is also incredibly challenging. No matter where you are in a career, if you only want to pay the bills with your music-production skills, consider some of the following options. Every one of them can be exciting, fulfilling, and a lot of fun.

▷ **Start your own company:** Odds are that at some point, you will be a freelancer or contract worker, which means you are your business. Figure out how to get your name out there so people will pay you for your skills. This might include any of the following points in this list, but might also include being a promoter or starting a record label. Just be aware that those last two options often involve loss of money, at least at first, so approach those carefully. Since you are your company, your reputation is everything, as discussed in Chapter 5. As a freelancer, there will be droughts and floods, so it is highly recommended that you have at least a few months of expenses put away in savings. Two months is the bare minimum; ideally, you should work toward six to eight months' worth of savings. Also, make sure you understand your self-employment tax situation as a freelancer.

▷ **Education:** It is common to find composers who are music professors at colleges and universities, including many famous academic electronic musicians. Even without a graduate-level degree, you can often find teaching work at a trade school or as adjunct faculty at a college that offers an audio-technology program. Teaching at an audio-engineering or audio-technology school is a great way to learn a lot about the craft and to meet other professionals, namely your coworkers. Being able to spend all day talking about music and audio production with other passionate people is very cool, and you will also hear about all sorts of shows and parties going on every week. Moreover, there are often other industry-related perks, such as discounts on gear and invites to private industry events. Offering private lessons is always an option, too, and should be considered as part of a freelance career.

▷ **Scoring:** Writing music for movies, video games, and radio/TV commercials is a sought-after career in and of itself. It can be very rewarding creatively and financially. Big-name Hollywood composer Danny Elfman started out in the band he co-founded, Oingo Boingo. Mark Mothersbaugh is one of the founding members of Devo. Charlie Clouser is known by many as a former member of Nine Inch Nails, but millions of people who have never heard of him have heard his movie and television scores, with credits including the *SAW* movies and all six seasons of the CBS show *Numb3rs*. Long-time Ninja Tune artist Amon Tobin was the first big-name electronic musician to score all the music for a major video game, *Splinter Cell 3: Chaos Theory*. Now it is common for video games to have Hollywood-level productions and skilled composers on the soundtrack.

▷ **Sound design:** You can design sounds for video games, movies, or TV. You can also freelance for companies that make sample libraries.

▷ **Publishing:** If you like writing, you can accomplish two things at once: getting paid while also getting your name out here. Do reviews for magazines or blogs. Write a book, or work as a technical editor for someone else's book. Make tutorial videos for one of the popular online training companies such as macProVideo, Lynda, or Groove3. A lot of companies also need good technical writers to help with the copy for their promotional materials or on their website.

▷ **Consulting:** You can do anything here, from helping people design their studio and then put it all together to helping artists figure out the technical aspects of their live performances. There are a lot of options here.

▷ **Find a cool job:** A part-time gig in the industry that is interesting, offers degrees of flexible scheduling (so you can gig and tour without losing the job), and also pays well is a highly sought after treasure. If you can land one of these, think twice before passing it up. They don't come around that often. Even if the pay is not so hot, the tradeoff is often access to amazing contacts and a wealth of talented successful people to be around. Work for a PR company that works with artists you like. Get a gig working in artist relations for a software or instrument company. Work for an established label in your genre of interest. Work for a festival such as Mutek, Sonar, or Movement (Detroit EM Festival). Work as an assistant for a high-level composer or audio engineer. There are a lot of possibilities here, but each one will be hard to find.

Be Involved

Chapter 5 talks about personality types, scenes, communities, networking, and other related topics, so you may want to revisit this section after reading that chapter. Are you already part of a scene? Are you around a supportive community? When it comes to your plan, in most every case, there needs to be an element related to meeting people for a variety of reasons. This is a people industry, and people need to know who you are.

If you are just getting going and have yet to develop a network of peers and/or significant industry contacts, then figure out how to make that happen. You might volunteer at a non-profit or DIY art and music space or see if any of the local DIY promoters need help running their events. Find out about local user groups for the software you use or start your own. You don't have to be a scenester who knows everyone, but being a familiar face can lead to unexpected opportunities.

If you have been around a while, and are already established to some degree, it might be time to check out some new scenes. Meeting people on parallel paths in a different scene might be just what you need. While it is always nice to see familiar faces when out and about, getting out of your comfort zone is a good idea from time to time, especially when you are looking for new opportunities and inspiration.

No matter how you decide to get out there and be involved, there are a few dynamics I've noticed over the years that are noteworthy. These dynamics talk to some of the most relevant differences between younger scenes and ones that are older and more established. Consider the following points on a series of spectrums or overlapping bell curves:

> **NOTE:** While comparing generalized differences between younger and older scenes, I am not making any value judgments or using any terms in the pejorative.

▷ **Drop out effect:** The younger the average age of people in a scene, the more likely that any given person in that scene will move on to other things. Whether they are not cut out for life as a creative or creative-technical professional, they simply realize they have other interests, or they are pressured into pursuing a more conservative path by friends and family, a high percentage of these folks' future relationship to music is simply that of a fan. Yet, for an established producer looking to discover new talent, younger scenes are also the breeding ground for the musicians and music producers of the future. The right combination of youth, drive, and career focus opens a lot of doors for those who are able to stand out from their less dedicated peers.

▷ **Connectedness:** People in younger scenes are not as connected as people in older scenes. I am referring not only to the number of connections they have, but to the weight and relevance of them for your career. Scenesters and hipsters will know tons of people, but most of their connections are fool's gold. People in older scenes are more likely to have serious connections, but they are likely to be more choosy about sharing them, as their reputation is involved when doing so.

▷ **Career focus:** Younger scenes are not as career-focused as older scenes. I didn't even *think* about what I would do as a "career" until I was already in my 30s. Younger scenes are much more likely to be hipster focused, which is more about cultural cachet than career development.

Thoughts on Partnerships and Collaborations

You don't have to go this alone. The myth of the hero's journey is very compelling, but there is strength in numbers, too. It is undeniable that collaborative situations at their best produce results that define the idiom "more than the sum of its parts." Full discussion on each of the following points could easily be a book unto itself.

▷ **Bands:** Being in a good band is a great experience, although even great bands often resemble dysfunctional families. For the perfect example of the latter point, watch the 2004 Metallica documentary *Some Kind of Monster*, in which they literally hire a counseling therapist for the band. If you find other serious musicians that you work well with and like being around, then see how far you can take it. Many great producers started out in bands.

▷ **Partners:** If band life and dynamics are not for you, but you like collaborating with others, then consider developing a few solid partnerships. Electronic music producers often go the collaboration route. That way, you can work on a variety of projects, at different times and levels of intensity, while also developing productive creative relationships.

▷ **Collectives:** Collectives are groups of artists with common goals, interests, and/or aesthetic sensibilities who pool their resources. Often, they center around a label owned by one or more of the members. The cool thing about collectives is that there are many creative options available at any time, and the synergistic results can be amazing. The downside to a collective is that it is a collective, meaning they only work well if everyone involved shares common values and can balance the needs of the collective with their personal ambitions.

Planning Your Artistic Musical Identity

It is important to remember when producing your own music that when you are the artist, you may have different goals than when producing other artists. In any case, most aspiring producers have good reasons as to why they've chosen to produce a particular style of music. The obvious reasons are based on influences and inspirations. The following list of questions is designed to help make sure you are clear about your motivations and that they match your goals. A number of important decisions are based on how you answer these questions—creative, professional, and otherwise. There are no right or wrong answers, and they will likely change over time. How do you think about the music that you want to make?

▷ Is it accessible, is it challenging, is it mainstream, is it extreme?
▷ Do you have a unique vision?
▷ Do you want to make music like your influences?
▷ Are you making music for musicians, producers, consumers, or a combination?
▷ Do you want to make music for a specific type of audience or environment?
▷ Do you want your music to be in movies or video games?
▷ Do you want to be known for specific vibes and/or styles, or for being eclectic and diverse?
▷ Are you trying to get on a specific label?
▷ Do you want to keep current with trends and happening genres?
▷ Why do you make music? Is it because you feel compelled to do so, because you think it is fun, because you like getting attention, because you like the lifestyle, or some combination of all of the above?

Outro

There are no easy answers, at least when it comes to predicting the future. At the end of the day, as long as you follow your passion and are mindful of what you are trying to accomplish, then you are already heading in the right direction. This chapter will read very differently to people at different points in their lives and careers. Youth is a time to experiment and make mistakes, so not everyone needs to get serious about all of this immediately. As long as really bad decisions with lingering consequences are avoided, there is no need to worry about always making good ones. Then, at some point, you will appreciate the need to do some planning. Those of us who are a little older, with more life experience, having been there and done that, possibly even with a family to consider, will likely be more attuned to the value of a well-considered plan.

When you do decide to put together a detailed plan, never forget that it is a map to a changing terrain, so don't confuse it with the territory. Modern approaches to architecture and engineering in earthquake zones no longer attempt to design structures simply based on strength and rigidity. We've learned that such an approach does not work very well. Instead, we design buildings and bridges to dissipate the energy in a variety of ways. Skyscrapers now sit on insanely large ball bearing systems, while bridges and tunnels are flexible so they can twist, turn, rock, and roll with the seismic waves. No matter the metaphor, analogy, or simile employed to elucidate the ideal plan, we all want to do our best to balance a plan's powerful utility with any pitfalls it might also introduce.

There are those who have intricate plans and follow them religiously, sometimes to great success and sometimes not so much. Others never have a plan and just go where life takes them. Occasionally they meet their goals, but usually not. You may find that you only need to work with a plan when you are sure that something about your current situation has to change. If you are just starting out, obviously a lot needs to change. Once you've met some goals, forgetting about the plan and just going with things is not a bad way to go. Then, every so often you will realize that you're stuck or the situation changes, and you can do a new plan. Find the approach that makes the most sense for you, and then do it well.

Master Your Craft

4

The illiterate of the future will not be the person who cannot read. It will be the person who does not know how to learn.

–Alvin Toffler

The height of cultivation always runs to simplicity. Before I studied the art, a punch to me was just like a punch, a kick just like a kick. After I learned the art, a punch was no longer a punch, a kick no longer a kick. Now that I've understood the art, a punch is just like a punch, a kick just like a kick. The height of cultivation is really nothing special. It is merely simplicity; the ability to express the utmost with the minimum. It is the halfway cultivation that leads to ornamentation.

–Bruce Lee

THERE IS A LOT TO LIKE ABOUT BEING A MUSIC PRODUCER. One of the beautiful side effects of spending years learning how to make music with technology is that it forces you to use both sides of your brain simultaneously. In simplified form, brain lateralization as it is known in neuroscience states that the brain's left hemisphere processes analytical thinking while the right hemisphere processes intuitive thinking. Learning a technical skill, whether music or computers, requires left-brain analytical skill. In contrast, creative processes rely heavily on right-brain activity. Practically speaking, when you are trying to remember what buttons to push or what notes to play, and in what order, the creative process can find itself on the back burner. For most people, there is a constant tension between technical skill and creative process. The accomplished artisan, however, experiences synergy. When learning new skills, it is normal to feel less creative, especially when dealing with computers and their frustrating quirks. Once you master your craft, the technical and the creative are one and the same.

Carl Rogers, a pioneer of humanistic psychology, once stated: "The only person who is educated is the one who has learned how to learn and change." To stay relevant, the modern music producer is constantly learning. There is an endless field of pertinent knowledge, with specializations branching off in every direction. If you are just getting started, you have a lot to learn—literally. But everyone involved in a technology-centric field must always be learning. Evolve or die. Because learning how to learn is a skill unto itself, I want to discuss the learning process before I hit the music and tech topics, so you can eventually master that skill too.

Styles of Learning

Howard Gardner's 1983 book *Frames of Mind* introduced the world to the theory of multiple intelligences, which is now essential, foundational material for anyone in education. The current version of Gardner's theory posits nine basic types of intelligence:

▷ Linguistic
▷ Logical-mathematical
▷ Musical-rhythmic
▷ Bodily-kinesthetic
▷ Spatial
▷ Naturalistic
▷ Intrapersonal
▷ Interpersonal
▷ Existential

Each of us has strengths and weaknesses in each of those categories—relative to other intelligences in our own personal profile, but also in relation to other people. For example, musicians are more expressive through music than sports, and some are naturally more musically talented than other musicians. When considering geniuses, their natural gifts in one area are often at the expense of others. Brilliant mathematicians and scientists stereotypically lack interpersonal intelligence (nerds), while great professional athletes, or kinesthetic geniuses, commonly are challenged with intrapersonal and existential intelligence (jocks). In the extremes, you get "Rain Man" (an autistic savant) or O.J. Simpson.

Because of Gardner's work, good educators know that students differ in how they take in new information. Some students easily absorb spoken lectures, others must see something done, while others must physically do something to best soak in the knowledge. A combination of teaching-learning methods is ideal, and for what we do, it is necessary. You should spend a little time reflecting on your personal learning history. Take into account your learning style when developing your plan for mastering your craft. Capitalize on your natural strengths and work on your weaknesses.

Stages of Learning

Regardless of one's personal intelligence profile or natural learning style, every one of us develops skills in stages. The Bruce Lee quote at the beginning of this chapter describes a common experience as one evolves through them. It is equally useful to consider these stages as applied to individual skills and overall skill level as an artisan—what I refer to as a *workflow system*. For present purposes, then, workflow system refers to the totality of one's skills (the whole) and the relative levels of attained competence in each individual skill (the parts). The four stages of competence is an especially relevant learning model that emerged from humanistic psychology in the early 1970s (formalized by Noel Birch, popularized by Abraham Maslow). To illustrate each of the four stages, consider the example of learning to play a simple song on the piano that has the following notes: BAGABBB AAA BDD BAGABBBBAABAG.

▷ **Unconscious incompetence.** Novice. You don't know what you don't know. For example, you have never touched a piano, and you don't know anything about music theory.

▷ **Conscious incompetence.** Beginner. You know what you don't know. For example, you hear a song that you want to learn to play and find a teacher.

▷ **Conscious competence.** Intermediate. You learn how to do something, but completing the task requires attention and you need to break the process down into smaller parts to complete it. For example, after a few lessons, you can find the notes, but you have to look at the keys and still have to approach it step by step. It may take a few tries before you can play the correct notes at the right rhythm, and at a steady tempo.

▷ **Unconscious competence.** Advanced. You have internalized the skill, and it is easily accomplished, often while multi-tasking. For example, you can play the song by heart without looking at the keyboard while communicating with your drummer about the next song in the set and pumping your fist in the air.

A fifth stage of competence is now commonly discussed in education and organizational development circles. While the mainstream academics debate the details, I think British higher-education expert David Baume is right on the mark. As Baume states:

Reflective competence—a step beyond unconscious competence. Conscious of my own unconscious competence, yes, as you suggest. But additionally looking at my unconscious competence from the outside, digging to find and understand the theories and models and beliefs that clearly, based on looking at what I do, now inform what I do and how I do it. These won't be the exact same theories and models and beliefs that I learned consciously and then became unconscious of. They'll include new ones, the ones that comprise my particular expertise.

Given that, I'd like to add a fifth stage of competence to the list:

▷ **Reflective competence.** Master/expert. You are able to reflect on how you unconsciously accomplish tasks, and can competently explain or teach them to others. For example, not only can you effortlessly play the song in a variety of styles, but you can also skillfully explain to others what you are doing. If teaching, you can choose from a variety of methods that best tailor the lesson to that student, even using ones that you've modified or developed yourself. Reflective competence also opens up additional skills related to flexibility and adaptability, which is very useful when under pressure and short on time.

Even though academics have just recently identified a fifth stage of learning, something resembling reflective competence is a given for any master craftsman who successfully trains apprentices. This level of competence should be your long-term goal as a producer. In the near term, unconscious competence is the goal for the skills you most need to develop. Everyone who is just getting going needs to ask themselves a question, whether carving your niche as a specialist with very high levels of expertise in a more narrow range of skills or pursuing the maximum flexibility of a generalist with competence in many areas. Because you can't learn everything at once, how do you determine where to place your focus?

Skill Versus Energy, Attitude, and Style: Back in the 1970s and 1980s, the world was exposed to the rebellious raw energy, power, and emotion of punk, techno, house, and industrial music. Unlike some other more extreme or experimental styles, such as various branches of heavy metal, these genres did not require a high level of training. The primary skills were communicating emotion, vibe, ideas, and attitude. Many of the pioneers of these styles were naturally talented artists, and some of them did have formal music or art training, but technical skill was not at the forefront—and in some cases, was purposely circumscribed.

When I was in college, a number of my DIY punk musician friends were afraid to learn too much theory, since they thought it would limit their creativity. Their argument was that it would make them follow more rules, and therefore distract from the vibe and rawness of the music they liked. Needless to say, I don't think any of them ever went on to have any sort of career as a musician. Yet, they did have a valid point, even if they failed to see the bigger picture. Their point ultimately only refers to the conscious competence stage of learning. When learning new skills, if you have to constantly focus on the rules or steps of that skill, it is reasonable to assume that vibe and attitude are the first things to go out the window. It is very common to hear accomplished musicians and artists invoke unconscious competence when they say something to this effect: "Learn the rules, and then forget them." Of course, this does not imply that you need to learn everything before you can start to forget "the rules."

So what are the implications here if you make vibe- or attitude-based music? It means you have to be patient and keep pushing until the rules are sublimated, and you are free to break them at will. Yet, you must know them and be able to apply them should the situation require it. Confusing "pre" rules knowledge (unconscious incompetence), with "post" rules knowledge (unconscious competence) is a simplified version of what Ken Wilber calls the *pre/trans fallacy*. Refer to the Bruce Lee quote at the top of this chapter. Does it make more sense to you now?

Lines of Development

In the introduction and in Chapter 2, "Plot Point on the Space-Time Continuum," I talked about how records historically were created by a team of specialists, each playing a role in the process, all coordinated by the producer. Modern producers with a computer and software have access to the tools to do it all themselves for a tiny fraction of the cost. Yet, the various skills and roles are not reducible to technology or a set of tools. How do they differ, how do they overlap, and what does it mean for you as you strive to master your craft?

> **NOTE:** Keep in mind that there are hundreds of books and websites dedicated to all of these topics, so I can only scratch the surface of each one here.

Each specialization includes a set of skills associated with a realm of technical and creative knowledge, which can be considered lines of development. Each of these lines progresses through the stages of competence, which includes not only many individual skills that are combined to accomplish complex tasks but also the overall skill level. We all have strengths and weaknesses in differing areas, which, when considered together is another way of talking about a workflow system. For example, accomplished musicians are often familiar with audio effects and the recording process, while they struggle with computers and software. As modern independent and electronic music producers, we should not only improve on our strengths, our fortés, but we must also bolster our weaker areas whenever possible. A complete producer is well rounded, competent in all key facets, their workflow system well developed. Trent Renzor and Butch Vig are high-profile examples of successful, well-rounded music producers (regardless of whether you like their music).

Holons: Wholes, Parts, or Whole/Parts?: I briefly introduced the term holon in Chapter 2, "Plot Point on the Space-Time Continuum," in the sidebar about complexification. Arthur Koestler's 1967 book *The Ghost in the Machine* was an inspiration for The Police's 1981 pop masterpiece *Ghost in the Machine*. More importantly, in the book, Koestler coined the terms *holon* and *holarchy*. Although there is such a thing as a hierarchy of power or control, what most people think of as a structural hierarchy is better considered as a holarchy, a nested system of holons. In his 1978 book, *Janus: A Summing Up*, Koestler tells us that each member in a holarchy:

> *...is a sub-whole or "holon" in its own right—a stable, integrated structure, equipped with self-regulatory devices and enjoying a considerable degree of autonomy or self-government...[holons] are Janus-faced. The face turned upward, toward the higher levels, is that of a dependent part; the face turned downward, toward its own constituents, is that of a whole of remarkable self sufficiency.*

If you can name it, it is a holon. Holons are whole/parts, but in any given context we can choose to define something as the whole or a part. If the context changes, wholes become parts or parts become wholes. The concept of holons is very useful whenever considering a system. Systems are wholes made up of parts, and the parts are likely wholes with their own parts, just as the system is likely to be a part of a larger whole.

Since there is a natural tendency to think of holons and systems as only "things out there," leading Integral theorist Ken Wilber makes it very clear that each holon includes at least four basic dimensions: interior, exterior, individual, and group. Through an investigation into language he distilled these perspectives down to I, We, It, and Its. So anytime we talk about a holon it is from one or more of those perspectives. See Appendix B, "Integral Theory Primer," if you are interested in further discussion about holons and each of their four dimensions.

The Big Four Production Holons

Ultimately, the terms *facet, skill, tool, specialization, role, aspect, competence, system,* and *workflow* all refer to holons. As discussed in the preceding sidebar, a *holon* is a whole/part with four basic dimensions. The production holon includes at least four distinct and interrelated holons. I refer to these as the Big Four:

▷ Music
▷ Sound design
▷ Tools/DAW
▷ Audio engineer

While they are fuzzy sets, lacking definable boundaries, representing them as a Venn diagram enables you to see the various areas of isolation and overlap (see Figure 4.1). Before I discuss how the holons relate to each other, let's first consider some definitions. Although I cover a lot of ground, I am not attempting to be comprehensive.

> **NOTE:** Aesthetic sensibility, which includes artistic facets such as taste and style, is a holon unto itself that permeates all the production holons.

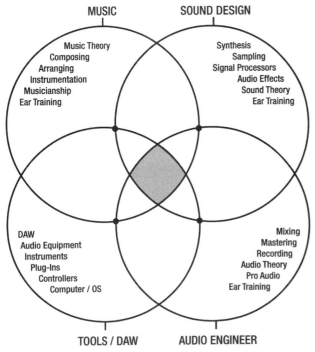

Figure 4.1 A Venn diagram of the Big Four holons encompassing most of the skills, knowledge, and tools of music production.

Music

Music is a temporal art form communicated with sound, organized with the intent of having an emotional, intellectual, and/or kinesthetic impact on a listener. Often referred to as "the universal language," music is as diverse as humanity's emotional, intellectual, and kinesthetic experiences. The following list offers key definitions from this holon of interest to music producers.

▷ **Music theory.** The formalized language of music. Including, but not limited to, rhythm, melody, harmony, timbre, form, structure, consonance, dissonance, tension, release, point, and counterpoint. Keep in mind that music systems from non-Western cultures and traditions are also worthy of your attention.

▷ **Composing.** The creation of a piece of music, song writing, and scoring.

▷ **Arranging.** Finalizing the structure of a piece of music. Sometimes referred to as orchestration.

▷ **Instrumentation.** The selection of the instruments that play the various parts in a composition. Timbre is the key word here, so any sound can be your "instrument." Also, sometimes referred to as orchestration.

▷ **Musicianship.** The skill level of a performing musician, or in applying music theory. For the most part, musicianship assumes training on a specific instrument, such as piano, vocals, or theremin, although it might also include MIDI sequencing and, at its best, turntablism.

▷ **Ear training.** The perceptual skill developed for listening to music, allowing for the precise identification of specific components of a composition. It might be simple, such as recognizing popular instruments, key, meter, or single notes in a bass line. More evolved ears can also indentify complex relationships between multiple instruments' parts as they evolve throughout a sophisticated composition.

Sound Design

Sound design has two basic meanings: 1) sound design, the creation and/or manipulation of individual sounds, and/or 2) sound design, the creation of a cohesive palate of multiple sounds. Both aspects are particularly significant for electronic musicians and those interested in audio post production for movies, TV, and video games. The following list offers key definitions from this holon of interest to music producers.

▷ **Synthesis.** Refers to synthetic sound creation, as opposed to acoustically generated and/or amplified and recorded sounds. This is accomplished primarily with either analog electronics and/or digital algorithms. This is a pretty big topic, ranging from subtractive analog synthesizers to digital granular synthesis and beyond. The basic parameters and components found on most synthesizers are necessary knowledge, since they are commonly found on many other devices.

▷ **Sampling.** The use of recorded snippets of audio, whether from original sources or sourced from existing recordings. Most samplers share numerous parameters with synths.

▷ **Signal processors.** A large category of devices that manipulate audio signals, ranging from the practical to the creative. Generally speaking, signal processors output just the modified original signal, not a mix of the processed and unprocessed. Examples include EQ, compressor/limiter, distortion, pitch-shifting, noise reduction, etc.

▷ **Audio effects.** A subset of signal processors that range from the practical to the creative. Generally speaking, they output a mix of the processed and unprocessed signal or are added to the dry signal as part of an effects loop (send/return). Examples include delay, reverb, chorus, etc.

▷ **Sound theory.** Understanding of the science and psychology of sound and audio so that desired results are easily attained. There are significant overlaps with acoustics and pro audio theory, including digital audio theory.

▷ **Ear training.** Specialized perceptual training in recognizing timbral and dynamic characteristics of sounds, especially ones that were created or modified electronically.

Tools/DAW

Any artifact, including music, is created with tools of some sort. Ideas are abstract and exist only in the mind. The artistic process requires a tool set to realize ideas, apply theory, and produce music that can be distributed. The capabilities and limitations of specific tools shape the creative process in obvious and subtle ways. In the past, analog consoles and tapes were the primary audio canvas; today, most producers rely on a DAW. The following list offers key definitions from this holon of interest to music producers.

▷ **DAW.** A digital audio workstation (DAW) is the primary canvas for your creations. It is used to record, compose, mix, master, design, and more. Most DAWs are applications installed on the personal computer of your choice, but "turn-key" systems do exist. MIDI sequencing is included here.

▷ **Audio equipment.** This category includes a wide variety of hardware tools, analog and digital. Mixers, audio interfaces, microphones, signal processors, and speakers are common examples.

▷ **Instruments.** This refers to traditional musical instruments, but also electronic devices such as synths, samplers, and any other "playable" sound makers.

▷ **Plug-ins.** Software that extends the capabilities of various applications. They are most commonly virtual instruments and signal processors, tools found in the audio equipment and instrument categories, but also include a variety of utilities. This is a huge category; there are many dozens of popular commercial options, and they number in the thousands when taking all of them into account.

▷ **Controllers.** Various hardware/software combos that increase tactile interaction with software, interface limited hardware, and other devices. Includes MIDI controllers, mixing surfaces, iPads/tablets, motion-tracking cameras, and various sensor-based systems. This is a quickly evolving area with a fast rate of innovation, both commercial and DIY (circuit benders, Maker community, etc.). Protocols such as MIDI and OSC, in general, are also included here.

▷ **Computer/OS.** Your Mac or PC, your operating system, and data storage systems. In addition to general computer, Internet, and networking literacy, professionals must constantly also do file management and system optimization. Computers are likely the foundation of most everything you do. If it dies, you are out of the race.

Audio Engineer

This refers to the technical skills and knowledge needed for working with professional audio equipment and creating quality music productions. Keep in mind, I am focusing on music production; there are additional considerations for live sound and broadcast audio. The following list offers key definitions from this holon of interest to music producers.

▷ **Recording.** Using various transducers and converters to electronically store sound on an analog or digital medium. The science involves a deep understanding of microphones, preamps, acoustics, and instruments. The art not only includes a developed aesthetic sensibility, but also interpersonal and psychological skills for getting the best performances out of artists in a studio environment.

▷ **Mixing.** The art and science of making all the elements of a composition work together to best communicate the intent of the piece of music. Mixing is ultimately about the whole, not making sure that every part sounds as good as possible in isolation (which would be considered sound design).

▷ **Mastering.** The process of mastering is arguably the most opaque sub-holon in the Big Four production holons, possibly due to the elite level of audio knowledge and skill required at the professional level. At its most basic, mastering is the final creative step before manufacturing. Technically speaking, mastering occurs at the manufacturing plant. It is the actual creation of the master object used to create all of the duplicates. What most people think of as mastering is actually pre-mastering, but for our purposes, the terms are interchangeable. Traditional pre-mastering emphasizes ensuring consistent volume and frequency balance across all of the songs on an "album," in addition to adding the final polish or sheen to each track. (World-class mastering engineer Greg Calbi, senior engineer at Sterling Sound in NYC, compares this aspect of the process to color correction in photography.) Pre-mastering also includes all the technical bits related to the final output format so that the songs are in the right order and with the desired spreads, crossfades, and metadata. In the home and project studio world, mastering commonly refers to the process of enhancing individual mixes to make them sound as good as possible for digital distribution.

▷ **Audio theory.** Includes, but is not limited to, acoustics, psychoacoustics, audio electronics (analog and digital), and signal flow. This holon is vast.

▷ **Pro audio.** This includes the audio equipment category in the tools holon, but adds a layer of professional knowledge about all the equipment used, such as large-format consoles, mixers, mics, processors, speakers, power amps, cables, connectors, patching/signal flow, and "how it works."

▷ **Ear training.** Some music ear training, some sound-design ear training, but also specialized perceptual skills related to audio signal flow, recording problems, minute changes in EQ and dynamics, reverberations, etc.

Consider the Source: Manuals, forums, blogs, magazine tutorials, online video tutorials, and other readily available sources are great guides for focused practice and experimentation. Just make sure to take into account the source of the information. Just because someone is good at doing something doesn't mean that person is good at explaining it to others. Especially with free tutorials, healthy skepticism of any statements that are not directly demonstrated or well referenced is advised. The more technical the concept, the more likely you should fact-check it yourself. Opinions about popular and/or trendy techniques, gear, DAWS, plug-ins, and such are usually worthless distractions unless you are sure they are coming from a credible source. As they say, "Opinions are like [rhymes with *has-wholes*]: Everyone has one." Learn to filter out the noise for an optimal signal.

Skills Does Not a Skill Set Make

Skill is not a precise word. Actually, it is quite vague. For learning purposes, it is useful to consider three loosely defined distinctions:

▷ **Macro skills.** Macro skills are overall capabilities, or skill sets, such as you might list on a résumé. For example, can you produce a song?

▷ **Micro skills.** To produce a song, you likely need drums. Knowing how to play or program a drum beat is a micro skill, a component skill of your skill sets.

▷ **Nano skills.** These are the fundamental techniques and theory put together in a micro skill. With the example of playing or programming a drum part, multiple nano skills seamlessly work in harmony. Minimally, they are a merger of rhythm theory, knowledge of music genres and styles, and physical skill as a drummer or technical knowledge of specific software or hardware.

Figure 4.2 shows the holarchical relationship of the skills in the preceding example, in a simplified 2D graphic. You could easily swap out "program drums" with other micro skills, such as "record vocals," with relevant nano skills in the Venn diagram at the center. Instead of digitally generating a more complex 3D image to represent all such hypothetical diagrams combined, we need only turn to nature for the perfect visual metaphor (see Figure 4.3).

> **NOTE:** Distinctions made between macro, micro, and nano skills are for learning purposes only. I am not suggesting a need to consider hierarchies of skills during the production process. Remember that skills, whether macro, micro, or nano, are holons (whole/parts), so they can be a whole or a part given the context. Moreover, skills are processes, not objects. They are not bricks, they are more akin to cooking. With the same ingredients, you can cook a wide assortment of dishes simply by altering measurements, methods, and combinations. With more ingredients and additional recipes, the possibilities are endless. Frying might be a minor step in preparing a complex dish, or you might just be making griddled cheese. Regardless, the quality of the final product rests on each step in an accumulative, additive process. Start with good ingredients, and don't mess them up as you go.

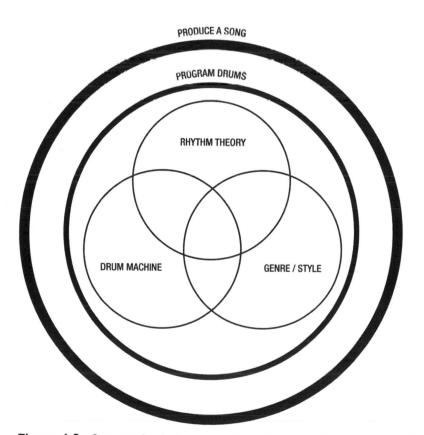

Figure 4.2 Concentric circles and a Venn diagram show interaction between macro, micro, and nano skills in a given skill set (in this case, programming drums while producing a song).

Figure 4.3 Romanesco broccoli is an oft-used example of self-similarity. The same pattern repeats throughout, as with micro and nano skills in various workflows.
Source: Public domain via pdphoto.org.

Workflow: Putting It All Together

"Why don't my tracks sound like the ones I buy?" Students ask such a question so often that I've stopped counting. Do you remember the central chaos theory tenet of sensitive dependence on initial conditions (the butterfly effect)? The quality of the studio, its equipment, and talent are surely factors, but equally important is the fact that countless decisions lead to the final result of your productions. Decisions made early in a creative process are of fundamental importance because they set an initial trajectory, necessarily limiting outcomes of later decisions. For example, if you start with weak sounds or problematic recordings, whether due to lousy talent or technical error, there is only so much you can do to improve things when mixing.

Avoid the following series of traps: "We'll sort out the arrangement in the studio when tracking." Or, "We'll fix the botched recording when mixing." Or, "We'll fix a mix problem during mastering." Frank Zappa was a perfectionist, and in characteristically sarcastic fashion famously stated: "We'll fix it in the shrink wrap." Of course, in his era, digital distribution did not yet exist, so the very last step before shipping an LP or CD to the retail shop was shrink wrapping the packaging. Extrapolating from his dig at slacker musicians, engineers, and producers, we can take away an important lesson: To get the best possible final result, appreciate the importance of every holon.

The Concretization of Potential

"Everyone who's ever taken a shower has an idea. It's the person who gets out of the shower, dries off and does something about it who makes a difference."

–Nolan Bushnell, Founder of Atari and Chuck E. Cheese's

All creative processes are essentially non-linear. Music production is art and science, intuition and analysis, so the degree of non-linearity varies depending on the nature of the project and the disposition of those involved. That said, we have to start somewhere, and there is a definite progression from one phase to the next until completion. I like to visualize the process as little circles within bigger circles—a sort of fractal epicycling arc. This trajectory traverses four amorphous yet identifiable phases:

▷ **Phase 1: Emerging.** This is the easiest phase and is the least structured. It includes your initial inspirations, intuitions, and emergences from the unconscious. Initially, you should not analyze or judge. Many experiments, brainstorming sessions, and musical sketches are narrowed down to ones you deem to be worth pursuing. Early planning and pre-production, likely including focused research and sound design, indicate you are entering phase 2.

▷ **Phase 2: Forming.** This is the development phase with the initial focused steps. Ideas are consolidated as a composition, including instrumentation, Sound Design, recording, and laying out a rough structure with a solid direction in mind. New producers often get stuck at phase 2, resulting in many unfinished ideas littering folders on their hard drives.

▷ **Phase 3: Refining.** Here you finalize your arrangement and instrumentation. Additional recording and editing covers any missing elements. Final embellishments, fills, and transitions are added and tweaked. A rough mix helps determine if any last-minute changes are necessary, and points mixing engineers in a direction. Finally, you clean up, organize, and prep the project before mixing. The common trap during phase 3 is endless tweaking and never moving on to completion. Don't let some concept of the perfect get in the way of the good.

▷ **Phase 4: Completing.** For this phase, most producers work with experienced mixing and mastering engineers. A good final mixdown ensures that the song translates as best as possible on as many common systems as possible. Mixing might also include minor arrangement changes, especially stripping back parts that distract from the most important elements. The final mix is then mastered and ready for distribution.

NOTE: Tips and strategies for maximum productivity during creative sessions are central to Chapter 6, "Producer Tips" (primarily phases 2 and 3). The sole topic of Chapter 7, "Creative Process," is creative process (primarily phase 1), which also includes discussion of common "four stages of creativity" explanations scattered around the Web. The four-phase model of the production process discussed here is not based on any of those models.

From Start to Finish

Let's spiral through an example of how one might string together various interwoven workflows to produce a single song. I am basing this example on my personal approach for self-producing a high-quality electronic music track in collaboration with a vocalist. Every producer has his or her own way of doing things. The following example is representative of approaches common to electronic music producers, but it is by no means the only way to go. The exact genre or style doesn't matter, since personal taste and aesthetic is baked into each creative decision. Although I want to capture as best I can the intermingled nature of the holons during this process, the degree of granularity is quite coarse. To mix a few metaphors, I am presenting the Cliffs Notes, and not zooming in on each step to reveal the swirling eddies peeling off of the major streams.

Ingredients

The ingredients for the following example are as follows:

▷ Producer/musician/audio engineer
▷ Vocalist/lyricist
▷ DAW
▷ Personal computer with plenty of plug-ins and sample libraries
▷ The necessary elements of a decent home/project studio

Workflow

The workflow might go as follows:

NOTE: Each of the following steps contains two numbers in parentheses. These identify the *minimum* number of significant and obvious holons in action. The first number is how many of the Big Four holons are at play and the second number is the total number of sub-holons. For example, (2, 4) means that two of the Big Four holons and four sub-holons are significantly involved.

The Music Producer's Survival Guide

1. Initial discussions with the vocalist help to determine basic parameters of the song, such as style, tempo, key, and vibe. (1, 2)
2. I like to start with drums, which is natural for a producer that started out as a bass player. I find a drum kit that is close enough to the desired sound and pencil in a few basic beats in the appropriate style. There is no need to rely on a click for the next steps. (2, 10)
3. Using a MIDI controller and a virtual instrument in the DAW, I play around with a few bass, melody, and harmony ideas. Unless there is already a specific sound ready to go, I just use a piano or basic synth sound to get the ideas recorded. (2, 10)
4. Once I feel like I am on the right track, then it is time to find better sounds for each of the parts. At this point it is common to apply a touch of EQ and possibly a bit of other processing to make sure each sound will work in the mix later. (3, 6)
5. If needed, a slight detour into sound-design land ensures each of the instruments will work. Adding some reverb and delay here and there is common at this point. (4, 10)
6. Once there is a solid sound palate in place, it is time to revisit the initial performances to refine the raw ideas, adjust voicings if needed, and create variations for different sections of the song. Not only do I want to make sure that the sounds work well together, but also that there is sufficient sonic space in the vocalist's preferred range. (4, 10)
7. With a solid sketch in place, it is time to throw together a very rough short arrangement. Export the rough arrangement and send the file to the vocalist for feedback. (2, 4)
8. Based on discussions with the vocalist, there are a few changes needed. The tempo is upped by a few BPMs, the key is lowered by a half step, and the lead synth is transposed up an octave and edited to have a shorter release time. (3, 5)
9. Now it is time to focus on the drum sounds, possibly by designing a new kit or just swapping out a few elements such as the kick, snare, or hats. (3, 7)
10. Based on discussions with the singer, the arrangement is adjusted to match the current state of the lyrics. The first rough version of the song is exported and sent to the vocalist so he or she can finalize the lyrics and vocal parts. (2, 3)
11. The vocalist records a very rough version of his or her part and sends a file for review. The singer receives the feedback and then a recording session is scheduled. (3, 3)
12. All sounds are optimized, and perhaps some of the virtual instruments are replaced with audio recordings of hardware synths or other instruments. (3, 5)
13. Next comes a thorough rough mix, including preliminary dynamics processing and EQing, messing with a few creative effects and, if not already done, setting up a few returns with reverb and delay. (2, 4)
14. The DAW session is prepped, cleaning it up and organizing it to make the recording session flow as smoothly as possible. (1, 2)
15. The physical space is prepped for the recording session, including general straightening up and cleaning. Because we are recording in a multipurpose space, not a proper recording studio, gobos are moved into place to create a makeshift vocal booth. Prep also includes setting up the mic, testing the record path, and setting up and testing the cue mix. Anything that can be done to make sure the vocalist is as comfortable as possible before he or she arrives will help that person give his or her best performance. (2, 3)
16. We spend a day recording the vocals. I do a few comps and a quick rough mix, export the song, and send it home with the vocalist to check out. (2, 4)
17. Next, comp together all the best takes, do some clean up editing, and make any adjustments as discussed. (3, 5)
18. After getting the vocals recorded, I realize that a few of the synths need some adjustment, both in terms of timbre and the performance, removing them from a few places altogether. (3, 6)
19. Make changes to the arrangement if needed, hopefully minor, such as extending a breakdown by a few bars. (2, 2)
20. Fills, subtle variations, transition sounds, and other embellishments are either added or created by editing existing parts. (4, 7)
21. We decide to record a few more vocal parts, primarily for texture and background, but also to redo one phrase on the vocalist's request. (2, 4)
22. Do a preliminary mix. We listen to it a bunch of times over the next few days, note any little issues, and then spend a few hours finalizing the track. (4, 8)
23. Spend a whole day mixing. The only arrangement changes at this point are muting some parts here and there and automation of various parts for dynamics and creative effect. (3, 6)
24. We listen to the mix the next day on a variety of systems. The following day, we make final tweaks to volume, effects, panning, etc. I export a 24-bit stereo WAV at the session's sample rate, leaving plenty of headroom for mastering. (3, 8)
25. We are happy with the mix. If we are self-releasing, I wait a few days if possible, and then master it myself, which takes less than an hour. If it is getting a proper release, having another set of ears is crucial, so I send it to one of my friends who specializes in mastering. (2, 4)
26. The mix is uploaded to the Internet for release. (1, 1)

While reading through the process, were you able to identify skills and skill sets working together? Do you notice the wave-like ebb and flow of skills needed from beginning to end? Refer to Figure 4.1 if needed. There is no answer key, as this is more a thought experiment than it is a test.

Music Production, Martial Arts, and Pop Culture: Throughout this book, I deal with a common pattern: the consequences of complexification. The knowledge, skill, and trade craft that once solely belonged to different roles or jobs often are now held by a single individual. This evolutionary pattern is not unique to music production. In fact, it is all around us. It is more obvious in pursuits directly reaping the benefits of the digital revolution, such as filmmaking or even a Web-based home business. Yet, there is a parallel that is seemingly unrelated to the digital revolution that is ripe with powerful analogies and metaphors for understanding our craft.

There is significant overlap in pop culture between electronic music/hip hop and martial arts. Think Ninja Tune, Wu Tang Clan, and Dim Mak. The following words are equally descriptive of music production and martial arts: skill, discipline, technique, art, instincts, sacrifice, creativity, master, teacher, student. To test their skills, martial artists face off against each other, but there are also turntablist, emcee, MPC beat, and break-dance battles. Beat- and bass-driven styles (DnB, hip-hop), along with music common in animé culture and video games, seem most likely to include these references, but the overlap is more diverse.

In the movie world, we find another parallel. Electronic music and sci-fi movies have always gone together, but the rise of "electronica" and electronic dance music (EDM) in the late 1990s transformed soundtracks into great compilations of current artists, especially in sci-fi action movies. Check out the amazing soundtrack to Darren Aronofsky's first movie *Pi* (1998). Also in the 1990s, American action movies began to prominently feature influences from Hong Kong action cinema and its elaborate kung fu choreography. *The Matrix* (1999) is a notably good example of this dual emergence. Nearly every song on the original soundtrack (OST) is some form of electronic music, and mixed into other scenes we find source music by the likes of Massive Attack and Richie Hawtin. The prominent kung fu fight sequences throughout *The Matrix* trilogy (1999, 2003, 2003) were choreographed by Hong Kong action cinema legend Yuen Woo-ping. Yuen Woo-ping also worked on Quentin Tarantino's *Kill Bill Vol. 2*, as did RZA. All the *Blade* films feature electronic music, including works by Massive Attack and RZA, with the fight scenes from *Blade II* being choreographed by Hong Kong martial arts star Donnie Yen. Those are just a few examples; there are many more.

Martial arts itself experienced a major evolution in the 1990s. Prior to November 12, 1993, most martial artists practiced just one or two styles. They were specialists. Was Tae Kwon Do better than wrestling? Was sumo better than Savate? Was boxing better than Brazilian jiu-jitsu? These questions were answered on the date in question in Denver, CO at Ultimate Fighting Championship (UFC 1: The Beginning), the birth of mixed martial arts in its modern form. Now, to compete and win, martial artists have to know about all these styles and be very good at at least a few of them. The emerging generation is well-rounded in all areas, and only the elite of the old guard are able to stay competitive in the new game. Unfortunately, in its early years, the UFC was marketed as a tough-man blood sport to sell pay-per-views. Almost two decades later, it is the fastest-growing sport in the world, attracting elite athletes from around the globe—male and female—including numerous Olympians and professionals from other sports.

> *Actually, the father of mixed martial arts, if you will, was Bruce Lee. If you look at the way Bruce Lee trained, the way he fought, and many of the things he wrote, he said the perfect style was no style. You take a little something from everything. You take the good things from every different discipline, use what works, and you throw the rest away.*
>
> –Dana White, President of UFC

Swap out a few words here and there, and Dana White's quote about Bruce Lee could easily describe a lot of modern music or the modern music producer. To stay relevant in mixed martial arts (MMA), you must always be honing your skills, learning, evolving, and finding ways to stay ahead of the competition. To stay relevant as a music producer, you must always be honing your skills, learning, evolving, and finding ways to stay ahead of the competition.

Learning Strategies

Considering all that there is to learn is intimidating to most people. Generally speaking, it takes about one to three years of dedicated, concerted effort, practice, study, and experience to achieve a basic, intermediate competence as a music producer. I am speaking globally here, about the Big Four holons collectively. This is not to say that it takes that long to get to a point where you can get your stuff out there, especially if you are already a competent musician, sound designer, or audio engineer. Experienced graphic designers, video editors, and computer programmers, as well as skilled DJs also have a solid foundation from which to build. The best way to learn is by doing, but just blindly doing is not the fastest way. Let's consider some approaches that I have found very useful over the years.

Identifying Strengths

What comes easiest to you? What is the most fun? What has helped you get where you are today? What is your "bread and butter"? Identify your strengths and use them to shore up your weaknesses. If you are particularly talented or skilled at something, use it as your foundation and build on it. Fight the urge to always use it as a crutch, since it will be there as a safety net. Over time, as weaknesses become strengths, you should notice an exponential leap in your workflow system's overall capabilities. The more you *do* know, the more you *can* know.

Identifying Weaknesses

Identify what is most limiting execution of your current ideas. What do you find most frustrating? What do you commonly avoid? Are you getting consistent feedback about what you could be doing better? What is limiting your income? What causes procrastination? There is a famous saying, "Hard work pays off in the long run, but procrastination pays off now." Unless you are just plain lazy, you likely don't procrastinate when it comes to things you truly enjoy doing.

When you are just getting started, significant areas of weakness are more likely to be one or more of the Big Four holons. Eventually, if you continue to evolve, only sub-holons will need work. No one, given a normal lifetime, will achieve true mastery of every holon and sub-holon, so there is always something to learn at any stage of your career. Ideally, you should focus on your weaknesses whenever possible, but sometimes you just need to get something done—or more importantly, just have fun and enjoy doing what you are already good at doing.

Order Out of Chaos: Ilya Prigogine was awarded the Nobel Prize in Chemistry in 1977 for showing how disorder can lead to order, and in 1982 published a book entitled *Order Out of Chaos*. Central to his discoveries are what he calls *dissipative structures*. You've seen one in action if you've ever witnessed a tornado or hurricane or watched a whirlpool in an emptying bathtub. Basically, any system that continually moves energy through it but maintains a stable shape is a dissipative structure. The most flexible and adaptive dissipative structures are self-organizing systems that exist at "the edge of chaos." Prigogine discovered that if a dissipative structure is perturbed, it will either break down or restructure at a higher level of organization. It may seem counterintuitive, but a balanced amount of chaos is necessary for successful restructuring, as the opposite of chaos is a steady state, which in biological terms equates to death. His ideas inspire great artists and are applied in various fields, from computer science to psychology. Therefore it makes sense for us to use this knowledge when considering how best to improve our workflow system.

Learning Sessions

Learning while you work on projects is necessary and important. But you really should also set aside time for focused learning sessions. These sessions should include the following:

▷ Reading articles and books on theory and technique
▷ Watching good instructional videos
▷ Watching, reading, and listening to interviews with established artists and pros
▷ Discussing these topics with interested friends, peers, and pros
▷ Getting your hands on the gear

I take the "quanta" approach when I do one of these sessions. That means I like to focus on a small, narrowly defined topic. Then, once I am comfortable with my new knowledge, I integrate it into existing workflows. For example, if I want to learn some new chord progressions, I don't worry about sound design or drum patterns. After I am comfortable with the new progressions, I might set up a practice project and see how they work with sounds I might actually use in a current project. On the flip side, if I am learning a new synth plug-in, I start with musical phrases that I already know and let them loop while I mess with the synth. During these hands-on sessions, all you need to care about is picking up new skills and deepening your understanding of concepts. You never need to play the results for anyone, so don't ever judge outcomes when experimenting.

Regardless of your competence in three of the Big Four, you will always need to be learning about updates, changes, and new releases in the tools holon. I recommend mastering one DAW as soon as possible because it is the centerpiece of your studio and foundational for most of your learning sessions. Especially when it comes to the endless features and plug-ins found in software, you need to make sure you don't get lost and distracted by all the options. To maximize productivity and minimize incessant tinkering with new virtual toys, I recommend developing your own system based on the following phases:

1. **Equilibrium.** Stabilize your workflow system, with conscious competence in most of the tools and skill sets you've focused on. You are satisfied with what you have and are not planning on acquiring new software or hardware at the moment. Here you just get things done with minimal distractions.

2. **Praxis.** Focus on further developing competence in that system by applying all the theory and techniques you've already studied. See how far you can get with current limitations, as your options are still more or less infinite. Deepen your knowledge of your current tool set by using what you already have for new ideas and projects. The goal here is unconscious or even reflective competence.

3. **Stasis.** Whether a music producer or an athlete, plateaus are inevitable. When you fall into creative ruts or need new tools for paid gigs, you will need to shake things up a bit to get to the next level. But don't assume every creative block or frustrating moment implies stasis, and don't use this as an excuse to install a bunch of new plug-ins that will distract you from finishing projects. Experienced producers know when they have actually hit a plateau.

4. **Destabilize.** Perturb and deconstruct your workflow system by experimenting with new tools, techniques, and ideas. Pick topics and tools most interesting to you or most needed for a gig, and increase your learning sessions. Experienced producers know how to approach what they already own in new ways. This often happens by revisiting an instrument, plug-in, or effect they've not used in a while, since recently acquired knowledge places that tool in a new context.

5. **Iterate.** Return to phase 1.

Outro

One thing I've realized teaching music and recording is that you have to think of it as music first. I often get asked, "Wow, I love your kick drum sound. How do you record it?" But music is a moving target, and people forget about that. So when people get into electronics and physics, they forget that every day is something different. A C9 [chord] is never the same twice.

–Bob Powers

Because there is so much to learn, we all need to pick areas of emphasis. An analogy might be majors and minors with college degrees. Perhaps you are a double major, music and audio engineering, with a minor in sound design. Over time, you can continue to accumulate more "degrees" and "certificates" in various aspects of production. While we all want to be well rounded, most people have a specialty or two. Regardless, if you are serious about your art, then you will want to be constantly improving. There is always someone to learn from, no matter your level of accomplishment. Experts share their skills with each other. Even black belts have teachers.

John Cage: Some Rules for Students and Teachers: John Cage popularized the following list, so it is commonly attributed to him even though he is the author of just one of the rules. In fact his friend Corita Kent is its original author. (Thanks to writer Maria Popova for this clarification.) The context was Merce Cunningham's Dance Company in Manhattan's West Village, but you can easily apply these rules to any creative field.

- ▶ **Rule One:** Find a place you trust, and then try trusting it for a while.
- ▶ **Rule Two:** General duties of a student: Pull everything out of your teacher; pull everything out of your fellow students.
- ▶ **Rule Three:** General duties of a teacher: Pull everything out of your students.
- ▶ **Rule Four:** Consider everything an experiment.
- ▶ **Rule Five:** Be self-disciplined. This means finding someone wise or smart and choosing to follow them. To be disciplined is to follow in a good way. To be self-disciplined is to follow in a better way.
- ▶ **Rule Six:** Nothing is a mistake. There's no win and no fail, there's only make.
- ▶ **Rule Seven:** The only rule is work. If you work, it will lead to something. It's the people who do all of the work all of the time who eventually catch on to things.
- ▶ **Rule Eight:** Don't try to create and analyze at the same time. They're different processes.
- ▶ **Rule Nine:** Be happy whenever you can manage it. Enjoy yourself. It's lighter than you think.
- ▶ **Rule Ten:** "We're breaking all the rules. Even our own rules. And how do we do that? By leaving plenty of room for *X* quantities." (John Cage)
- ▶ **Hints:** Always be around. Come or go to everything. Always go to classes. Read anything you can get your hands on....Save everything—it might come in handy later.

5

The Social Scene

Keep away from people who try to belittle your ambitions. Small people always do that, but the really great ones make you feel that you too can become great.

–Mark Twain

Be nice to those you meet on the way up, because you will meet them on the way down.

–Walter Winchell

If Pac-Man *had affected us as kids, we'd all be running around in dark rooms, munching pills and listening to repetitive electronic music.*

–Marcus Brigstocke

THERE ARE MANY CLICHÉS ABOUT SUCCESS IN THE MUSIC INDUSTRY BEING DEPENDENT ON WHOM YOU KNOW. The fact of the matter is that humans are social creatures, so who you know is very important. As we will discuss, simply knowing a lot of people is insufficient for success. It is equally important to consider how we each interact with groups and individuals. Furthermore, some people are more important than others in the context of a career. We tend to use connections that already exist for numerous reasons, but convenience and familiarity are the most obvious ones. During the course of any given project, it is always easier and faster to first reach out to qualified friends, peers, or acquaintances when in need of certain skills. Given a tight deadline, it is not uncommon to first consider an established contact who is less than perfect. Even though you would rather search for a potentially better fit, in some cases it is more important to minimize unknown variables and find consolation in the fact that you are at least working with a known quantity. There are risks and rewards on both sides of that equation. Yet, as the saying goes, "Better the devil you know than the devil you don't." That colloquialism explains an oft-unfortunate outcome of a natural human inclination: It is rare for the virtuoso bedroom musician to get recognition, while untalented hacks can find their 15 minutes of fame. In other words, a balance of talent with cultivated social connections is ideal. When one is predominant and the other is lacking, the most likely outcomes are obscurity or, at best, short lived success.

For a lot of musicians and other creative people, spending significant time alone working is natural (and of course necessary). Your passion is producing tracks, making beats, or songwriting, so going out late at night to clubs, bars, parties, and other social events may seem like a distraction and a waste of time when you aren't thrilled about the performers, crowd, or venue. For others, being out all of the time is exciting and a natural drive—if this is you, other chapters in this book will present tips to make sure you get work done, too. Regardless of whether you are a natural introvert or extravert, this chapter is designed to help you successfully explore the fun and chaotic netherworlds of music scenes.

Chaos theory (as discussed in the preface and in Chapter 3, "What Is Your Plan?") and its parent field systems theory (as introduced in Chapter 2, "Plot Point on the Space-Time Continuum") offer a number of valuable insights relevant to the dynamic, unpredictable nature of social scenes. It is useful to think of music communities as ecosystems—dynamic, constantly evolving, and full of complex relationships. At any given time, some are thriving and have more energy moving through them than others. There is a lot of structure in a jungle, but it is impossible to define an exact border, and determining precisely where the trees end and the roots begin is a fruitless exercise. There are cute friendly creatures and apex predators, dense bustling areas and spots that are relatively quiet, and tasty fruit and poisonous plants (some that can kill you, others with more "interesting" effects). On the Discovery Channel's *Survivorman*, Les Stroud shows us how to survive in the wild, where the stakes are life or death. Surviving and thriving in social ecologies isn't as serious, but your success as an artist and music producer can hinge on how well you learn to avoid dangers and exploit opportunities.

Scenes and Communities

Scenes are associations of people that congregate in public or online around common cultural interests. The electronic and indie music worlds are full of numerous overlapping scenes, varying in size, duration, and intensity from year to year, city to city. Each has its own topography and texture. Some scenes are basically local, others are more international or "jet set," and most of them are actually sub-scenes of larger ones. If you would like a visual metaphorical, refer to Figure 1.6, the screenshot of the Techno page from *Ishkur's Guide to Electronic Music v2.5*. These days, scenes often don't directly equate to musical genres and their subgenres, yet you can see how they might relate to each other. Regardless of their scope, understanding the basic dynamics of scenes can make or break your career.

The Music Producer's Survival Guide

Most independent and electronic music scenes are anchored by established, often tight-knit, communities. Communities are the major components of scenes. They are built on personal relationships, based on shared history developed over years or even decades. Although always evolving, the indie and electronic music scenes of the early 21st century have roots going back as far as the late 1970s and 1980s (as discussed in Chapter 1, "Musica Universalis"), so some relationships are more than 30 years old! Older established communities may even display family-like dynamics, from supportive and synergetic to co-dependent and dysfunctional.

Having been around numerous music scenes since 1987, I've come to the conclusion that a few loosely defined core values most commonly inform and inspire the passions, careers, and lifestyles. The first and foremost value is commitment to the integrity of the music we love. When that music is somehow undermined, we aren't happy. So the other key values relate to a suspicion of mainstream commercialism and, more significantly, to a distrust of entertainment corporations (that is, major labels) and their minions, because they often treat artists as disposable products. Personally, I don't equate success with mainstream commercialism. You can be very successful, creatively and financially, and still have the respect of your peers and fans.

Because big trends regularly emerge from smaller scenes, scenesters and veterans are often suspicious of people looking to exploit their talents or cultural cachet—in other words, steal their styles and ideas. This is not paranoia, because as the famous saying goes, "Good artists borrow, great artists steal." By definition, new ideas have to start somewhere before they can go everywhere. So it is the norm, and even a natural evolutionary process, for underground styles and ideas to eventually leak their way into the mainstream, albeit in diluted form. I see this dynamic as an outgrowth of complexification, the natural ongoing ubiquitous process discussed in the preface and in Chapter 2, so I don't take it as personally as many of my peers and acquaintances. Today's mainstream is yesterday's *avant-garde*, which is future generations' quaint history. Digest that fact and learn to live with it.

Talent, creative and technical skill, breadth and depth of knowledge, honed artistic instincts, and good taste are very important. But, unless you are that super-rare genius, virtuoso, or artistic savant, they are insufficient. Why? They are traits of an individual. In *The Evolving Self* (1982), Harvard developmental psychologist Robert Kegan points out that not only are we an individual, but that we are also an "embeddual." In other words, interpersonal interactions and social relations define us at least as much as we think we define ourselves. As Alan Watts once stated, "Trying to define yourself is like trying to bite your own teeth."

To understand how embeddedness affects our success, consider the following questions that people might ask themselves about you. (You should also be asking yourself the same questions about them.) These answers will determine whether you are someone they want to work with in the future.

▷ Can you be trusted?
▷ Are you reliable?
▷ Do you have a good reputation?
▷ Are you worth the investment of their time, money, and/or energy?
▷ Do they know people who can vouch for you?

No matter how good you think you are, if they answer no to but one of those questions, let alone a few of them, then you're going nowhere fast. You can always hope to go viral on YouTube.

Personality Types: The terms "introvert" and "extravert" were coined by Swiss psychiatrist and psychologist Carl Jung (1875–1961). Jung is truly one of the 20th century's intellectual giants and places in any top-10 Most Influential Psychologists of All Time list worth its salt. Musicians and artists regularly find inspiration from the more esoteric and mystical side of his ideas and writings—for example, alchemy, synchronicity, the collective unconscious, mandalas, and archetypes. Earlier in his career he developed some of the first personality typologies relevant to the modern world.

Today, the most popular version of his typology is found in the Myers-Briggs Type Indicator (MBTI; see myersbriggs.org). There are 16 basic types, each based on four sets of preferences in a dichotomy: Extraversion/Introversion, Sensing/Intuition, Thinking/Feeling, and Judging/Perception. Typologies such as the MBTI do not make value judgments. While some types are more suited to certain career paths and lifestyles than others, no type is better or worse; they are just different.

If you are interested in knowing more about how your personality influences your perception of the world—and therefore your decision-making style—you should consider taking a few personality tests. Although taking an official MBTI isn't free, since it can be given and interpreted only by a certified professional, you can easily find unofficial versions online for free. Like the MBTI itself, the best free versions will be fairly long, and if well designed can offer insights into your strengths and weaknesses in the social sphere. Though such insights are valuable in general, they are that much more so if you struggle with making and maintaining good industry connections. With regard to free online tests, no one of them should be taken too seriously, and averaging the results from a few of them is a good idea.

If you are curious, I test as INFJ (Introversion, Intuition, Feeling, Judging), which is a perfect fit. While I've always been social and good at making friends, being a natural introvert explains why I was such a late bloomer in deciphering the social ecology around me. An "epic fail" story that is recounted in the "D'oh!" sidebar later in this chapter illustrates how easily you can miss opportunities, even those emerging from relationships developed over years while prominent in various scenes. All things being equal, it simply requires more effort and experience for introverts to develop savvy social-scene skills than it does for extraverts.

Networking 101

Like most aspects of life, networking is about balance. It is as much art as it is science. Introverts and extraverts have natural tendencies and need to find the "sweet spot" that works for them. Introvert doesn't necessarily mean "shy" or "antisocial," and extravert doesn't necessarily mean "outgoing" or "social." The terms refer to the primary mode by which you relate to the world and make meaning of your experiences. That said, it is generally easier for extraverts to be natural networkers, but more effort is required for introverts.

I define networking as a focused social activity with the intention of making professional connections. In simplistic terms, you could think this implies just going out and meeting new people that have something to offer you with the expectation that you have something to offer in return. I would call that approach the "trade show/exchange business cards" model, which is but a tiny piece of the puzzle. In reality, it is fundamentally about developing and maintaining a variety of constructive relationships, and there is nothing simple about it.

Hopefully, you already agree with me that networking is important. If you're just getting started, it is absolutely crucial; it is less vital the more established you are as an artist and producer. Either way, never lose perspective and forget that it is a means to an end. Especially when your career is also your lifestyle, it can be difficult to know when to "leave it at the office." If you are always "on," you might miss hidden, unexpected opportunities. If you're always in networking mode, you might start to think of everyone as an asset, always wondering who they know, what they can do for you, and how they can help further your goals and ambitions. Unless you are a covert CIA operative, people are not assets with only extrinsic value. In the extreme, pathological networkers can come off like salesmen at a trade show—not exactly a good persona for a creative person.

Even when you're in full-on networking mode, you will meet amazing, interesting people who aren't in the scene or industry and won't help further your career in any obvious way. A diverse assortment of friends and acquaintances is always a good thing. Pathological networkers ignore the fact that every person also has intrinsic value, and they will quickly move on in their search for more useful connections. With experience, you will learn to quickly discern when you are actually wasting your time. Also, depending on the social context, networking should be toned down and more informal (for example, in a chill room), whereas in other places it is very formal (for example, at trade shows, conferences, and so on). Modulating this intensity is also a skill you will develop with practice.

The Cast of Characters

The entertainment industry is truly a people industry. It is also somewhat unusual in that regard, given its mix of intense creative types with equally intense business types. Networking is not just about meeting people and exchanging contact information. People need to know who you are, and you must maintain a good reputation. Developing meaningful relationships with like-minded people in your field is a salient ingredient of professional longevity, as is avoiding those who just want to step on your head to move up in the world.

Unlike many other fields, careers in entertainment involve working in environments full of people who are there just to be entertained. From potential fans to the "bridge and tunnel" crowd simply out for a good time on a Friday night, you are going to meet a literal potpourri of characters: important professional contacts, peers, icons, pioneers, like-minded enthusiasts, drunken idiots, wannabes, pathological networkers, jaded hipsters, scenesters, journalists, bloggers, and random venue employees, to name a few. Navigating this jungle takes practice, persistence, confidence, humility, and a good sense of humor. Have fun and remember to always enjoy the music, which is the point of it all in the first place.

Movers and Shakers

In a given process or system, some people matter more than others.

–Malcolm Gladwell

I know I'm stating the obvious, but some people are more worth knowing than others. When it comes to friends and acquaintances, to each his own. If you're just out for a good time, whatever works. But when you're engaging people with your career in mind, then you really need strong criteria for making good decisions as to who you should seek out and who to avoid. People who have been around for a while have surely figured out a lot of this for themselves—often by trial and error, or perhaps with the help of a mentor, or possibly also by reading books.

In chaos theory, perturbation refers to the "pushing" of a stable system away from the balanced tension between order and chaos towards a more chaotic state (as briefly discussed when talking about Prigogine in Chapter 4, "Master Your Craft"). Consider the following very simplified example. If you spin a top with perfect vertical and horizontal balance on a smooth, level, hard surface, it will continue to spin until friction converts enough inertial energy into heat for gravity to win out (not counting the final scene from Christopher Nolan's 2010 film *Inception*). If you blow on the top, its movement becomes chaotic until it topples over in an unpredictable direction. A new behavior emerged from your small push, the perturbation. In more complex systems, the cause of the tipping point is harder to discern, and what emerges more unexpected.

There is a significant amount of research on what pushes stable systems into chaos. This phenomenon is commonly referred to as a *tipping point*. Journalist Malcolm Gladwell's 2002 best seller *The Tipping Point: How Little Things Can Make a Big Difference* is a fascinating exploration of epidemics, with a title that also invokes the butterfly effect. Specifically, Gladwell is most interested in what he refers to as "word-of-mouth epidemics"—that is, how information travels, catches on, and results in unexpected social phenomena. This book is a bible of sorts to viral marketers and ad agencies for its revelations about promotion. I have a feeling that you may be interested in promotion too. Gladwell writes:

> *Epidemics are a function of the people who transmit infectious agents, the infectious agent itself, and the environment in which the infectious agent is operating. And when an epidemic tips, when it is jolted out of equilibrium, it tips because something has happened, some change has occurred in one (or two or three) of those areas. These three agents of change I call the Law of the Few, the Stickiness Factor, and the Power of Context.*

> **NOTE:** Of Gladwell's three "agents of change," only the Law of the Few is discussed in this chapter. The Power of Context refers to the influence of the environment, social and otherwise, on human behavior. We discuss related social psychology topics in Chapter 6, "Producer Tips," though not based on Gladwell's book. Stickiness is fascinating, but not covered at all, so I offer a very brief descriptions here to quell any distracting curiosity. In music, the Stickiness Factor is exemplified in a catchy hook that you can't get out of your head, often referred to as an "earworm."

According to Gladwell, social epidemics are "driven by the efforts of a handful of exceptional people…. It's things like how sociable they are, or how energetic or knowledgeable or influential among their peers." In sociology and economics, a variety of scenarios follow the 80/20 principle. Basically, this principle states that 80 percent of *X* is caused by 20 percent of a given group. Gladwell's Law of the Few is a form of the 80/20 principle, except a significantly smaller percentage of people are responsible for causing a tipping point. There are three roles people fulfill when they are part of this rare group: Connectors, Mavens, and Salesmen.

Connectors

Connectors don't just know a lot of people; they also know the right people. Gladwell cites the work of social psychologist Stanley Milgram to make his point. Milgram was a brilliant researcher. His curiosity about how we're all connected motivated one of his most famous experiments, which studied what is commonly referred to as the *Small World Problem*. You likely know the results of this study as "six degrees of separation" (or of Kevin Bacon). The key insight is not just that we're all connected to each other by only six degrees. The most useful discovery was that some people are nodes or hubs, connecting a lot of people, whereas most people in the network connect to fewer people. Connectors are those nodes. It is not just that they are extraverted and very social; they are also especially gifted at connecting people to each other.

According to Gladwell, acquaintances can actually be more important for new opportunities than people you already know well. Sociologist Mark Granovetter coined the phrase "the strength of weak ties" in the results of his 1974 study "Getting a Job." As Gladwell states, "It isn't just the case that the closer someone is to a Connector, the more powerful or the wealthier or the more opportunities he or she gets. It's also the case that the closer an idea or a product comes to a Connector, the more power and opportunity it has as well."

Unlike most individuals, their social terrain crosses many scenes, communities, and beyond. In my experience, Connectors enjoy introducing people to each other, notably when they think it catalyzes mutually beneficial relationships. They like to help people help each other, and they relish seeing new relationships develop because of their introductions. This is where your reputation comes into play, big time. Befriending a Connector or two is highly recommended if you want to meet new, interesting, successful people. The sidebar that follows this section illustrates the value of knowing connectors, and also identifying the ones you already know.

Mavens

If Connectors form the infrastructure of the network, then Mavens control the information that flows through that network. In short, Mavens are the people who know what's up. They tell you about new music, new clubs, new software, and new ideas, but they don't necessarily try to convince you to like it. These are the people consistently into new artists, labels, genres, or styles before they blow up, regardless of whether they thought they might even do so. As Gladwell writes, "to be a Maven is to be a teacher. But it is also, even more emphatically, to be a student. Mavens are really information brokers, sharing and trading what they know." In my experience, Mavens like to share what they know and enjoy garnering new and obscure knowledge that others may find useful. As the Connector enjoys introducing people to each other, the Maven enjoys introducing people to new knowledge.

Salesmen

If Connectors are the infrastructure and Mavens the information, then Salesmen convince you that something is worthy of your attention. Salesmen are charismatic people with natural powers of persuasion. Gladwell describes a person he considers to be an especially great salesman as follows: "He seems to have some kind of indefinable trait, something powerful and contagious and irresistible that goes beyond what comes out of his mouth, that makes people who meet him want to agree with him. It's energy. It's enthusiasm. It's charm. It's likability. It's all those things and yet something more." They convince us that something is important and that attention should be paid to it. They persuade you to obtain what they convince you is cool—information obtained by way of the Maven. For obvious reasons, Salesmen in the music world are often journalists, bloggers, promoters, and other industry people, but any tastemaker is in essence a Salesman.

D'oh!: The following story transpired almost two decades ago. I have a very good memory, but to be honest, exact details of conversations are a little foggy. Therefore, I've paraphrased them rather than quoted them. I am, however, completely sure of the key elements.

When I moved to San Francisco from Michigan in December of 1994, I was 22 years old. I was able to make the move thanks to some extra student-loan money and the help of two more established Michigan expats. In fact, one of them helped the other two of us, as he had already been there for a few years and was a well-known character from the Midwest and Bay Area DIY punk scenes. At the time, his public persona was Smelly Mustafa, founder/frontman of the band Plainfield (which at times included members of the Melvins).

Unbeknownst to me, Smelly was a legit Connector. He knew everyone and was very generous with his contacts. Sometime in 1995, after a show at the out-of-the-way venue Bottom of the Hill, he gave me and another person a lift to get some food at a taqueria on Mission Street and then head for home. The other person was one of my teenage idols: Jello Biafra of Dead Kennedys fame and owner of Alternative Tentacles Records. That should have been hint number one.

By early 1996, I had been in and out of bands that hadn't really gone anywhere, and I was just getting started with digital audio on my home computer. Smelly knew I was still looking for other musicians. One day I got a phone call from a guitar player named Richard. He was looking for a bass player, and Smelly gave him my number. He was super friendly and humble, and we talked for a while about what he was looking to do. He said it would be guitar- and vocal-focused and would have a pop element to it. By this time my interests had already started to evolve away from projects without an electronic or experimental component, but I would have been open to the right project. He never mentioned his previous bands, and for some unknown reason that befuddles me to this day, I didn't ask. The project didn't sound like something I was looking for, so we both said good luck, and that was it.

A few months later, Smelly asked me what happened when Richard called. Why did I tell him I wasn't interested? I said it sounded too pop-oriented. He looked at me like I was insane (and for good reason). My response: What? Why? Who was he? It turns out that he had just left one of my favorite NYC bands, the legendary Alice Donut (Alternative Tentacles), and was looking to form a new band in SF. Alice Donut did have a substantial pop influence, but it was filtered through deranged, psychedelic, noisy, brilliant sonic insanity. In *Freaks In Love*, a 2011 documentary commemorating the band's 25th year, Jello Biafra described them as "the missing link between R.E.M. and the Butthole Surfers." For a good example of his stylistic guitar and background-vocal work, dig up their song "Magdalene" from 1992. To make things even worse, we likely would have clicked musically, since I really loved their bass lines!

If I knew then what I know now, I would've taken into account that Richard called me on recommendation from Smelly, and I would've asked a few more questions. I would've at least met with him in person and jammed once or twice. Who knows, it may not have worked out anyway. I went on to start I Am Spoonbender with the other Michigander (1997–2000), which was creatively successful by all accounts, but I missed a potentially life-altering opportunity nonetheless.

Moral of the story: Pay attention to how you meet someone. Was the connection made by a Connector? Don't make assumptions; ask thoughtful questions.

True Connectors, Mavens, and Salesmen are rare. Surround yourself with as many of Gladwell's "agents of change" as possible. Various characteristics of the three roles show up in different people on a spectrum of intensity, but legit Connectors, Mavens, and Salesmen are easy to identify for one reason: Their impact on a scene, a community, or even a large-scale commercial market is significant. Together, they create tipping points. Looking for someone who is all three is akin to searching for Bigfoot, although there are a scarce few who are some combination of two—such as Connector-Maven, Maven-Salesman, or Connector-Salesman.

Vampires, Werewolves, and Zombies

We can make important connections in a variety of social settings, but nightlife/party environments are often ideal networking opportunities. Because we might want to be there in the first place, mixing work and play is perk of our career. Inevitably we run across a few particularly problematic characters, commonly when combining our personal social life with professional networking into a cloudy mixture.

The mythological archetypes of the vampire, werewolf, and zombie represent extreme manifestations of common human traits, though sometimes we run across a real person that seems to embody aspects of one of those fictional characters. These are the people on the social scene that we need to be careful around, especially when it comes to your creativity and career. Caution and distance are the key words here. Each of these archetypal creatures comes in many forms, and looks can be deceiving.

I am presenting caricatures—ideal types—and people are complex, so be mindful about labeling them. It is possible that they might also be a Connector, Maven, or Salesman. People do change, sometimes for the better and sometimes for the worse, so you need to continually reevaluate your relationships as the years go by. Also, different people relate and interact with each other in diverse ways. So, one person's vampire or zombie is another person's friend, relative, or partner. You must always take into account people's relationships to other people when making decisions, especially as far as your creative career is concerned. At some point, everyone has experienced this dynamic in daily life and asked himself or herself, "How can this good friend of mine be friends with *that* person?"

Vampires

Vampires require your attention more than the other two creatures. Unlike werewolves and zombies, vampires are just as likely to appear in any industry related context as another. Although fairly rare, you will certainly run across at least a few of them. They want something that you have and may even seduce you in some way to get it. They are commonly charming, charismatic, powerful, and perhaps influential, so sometimes you may just have to deal with them. Not all vampires are even aware that they are users or energy suckers, especially when they're younger. But professionals survive in the world with honed manipulation skills, perhaps even Machiavellian in character. Because a vampire can be a Connector, Maven, or a Salesman, it is not always obvious what he or she might be seeking from you. It might be obvious, such as wanting your money or to financially exploit your creative works, but it's commonly something more ephemeral, such as popularity, social acceptance, or cultural cachet. So how can you tell when you're dealing with a crafty, sophisticated vampire?

Williams S. Burroughs (1914–1997), one of the great creative intellectuals of the 20th century, said it best:

If after having been exposed to someone's presence you feel as if you've lost a quart of plasma, avoid that presence. You need it like you need pernicious anemia. We don't like to hear the word vampire here...trying to improve our PR. Interdependence is the key word, enlightened interdependence. Life in all its rich variety, take a little, leave a little. However, by the inexorable logistics of the vampiric process they always take more than they leave.

> **TIP:** Do yourself a favor and look up "William Burroughs's Advice for Young People" on YouTube. Hearing Burroughs speak his own words is essential to full appreciation of his brilliance.

Werewolves

Werewolves are shape shifters who live two very different lives: normal by day, animal at night. Unlike a vampire, werewolves are usually harmless and aren't scheming to use you in some way. They are also somewhat rare, but everyone runs across one eventually. Most of the time, werewolves are no different from anyone else you might meet, but when they change, look out. Their uncontrolled actions can cause a scene or are at the center of incidents.

In my experience, there are two basic types of werewolves. One type consists of musicians, artists, or other industry types who are part of your community and potentially worth helping out. The other type is commonly personified in the random nightlife partygoer or possibly a peripheral acquaintance (for example, the cousin of a friend of a friend). Regardless, alcohol is by far the most common trigger for werewolves, although other drugs could be involved, too. Have you ever known a binge alcoholic? Unlike most alcoholics, they can go for a long period of time without drinking. But once they start they cannot stop, and they totally lose control. Often they black out and are unable to remember the night before. Not all binge alcoholics become violent or cause trouble, but the ones that do are good examples of a werewolf. The most dangerous werewolves are the ones that suck you into their troubles by proximity. Serious damage to your reputation is at stake. In the extremes, their behavior might even get you kicked out of a venue, drawn into a fight, or worse, into trouble with the law. What a disaster if you were hoping to get a gig at that venue!

If the werewolf is a Connector or Salesman, that person probably won't be as successful or established as he or she should be due to reputation damage from said incidents. If the werewolf is especially smart or talented, that person might also be a successful Maven, because he or she can probably get away with more eccentric behavior. It is possible to be friends with a werewolf as long as you limit your interactions to safe times and environments. Keep werewolves sober or make sure they at least find a safe alternative to their triggers.

Zombies

Zombies are the most common of the music-culture creatures, but they are also the easiest to avoid and the least likely to be important connections. As in the movies, zombies can look like anyone, can be of any background, and are most dangerous in hordes. They are followers, the mindless masses, victims of circumstance, or even perhaps "cracked out" members of an entourage. They unwittingly want to turn you into one of them.

The danger with zombies is that they will distract you from your goals, lull you into a stupor, encourage conformity, and inhibit creativity. The key characteristic of zombies is lack—lack of curiosity, lack of engagement, and lack of vibrancy. Many of these people have just done too much partying over the years. Sadly, you might also find once-aspiring artists and producers who have given up or, more tragically, a real talent who has crashed and burned. In the unlikely event that they might be a Connector, Maven, or Salesman, odds are their best days are in the past or they never reached their potential in the first place.

On the upside, there is a cure for those who want to get their act together. Joining the horde can be a temporary phase, so if you wake up one day and realize that you've been infected, don't lose hope. Change your environment and associations. Look for people and scenes that are healthier, more optimistic, and most importantly, inspired.

Implications

When it comes to our professional and creative successes, we should always keep in mind the major role played by the people we meet. Sometimes their influence is obvious, though often times it is subtle and no less significant. At the same time, it is important that we don't rush to judgment about people because first impressions often result in flawed assumptions. Paying attention to gut feelings and instincts is valuable, but we should also first collect a nice list of evidence before we stick a label on someone. Learning to avoid werewolves and zombies, or at least minimize their negative impacts on our creativity and career, comes easy with experience. Vampires, on the other hand, are a lot trickier to manage because they are often unavoidable in the professional world. As we gain life experience, each of us figures out how best to navigate the more challenging elements to be found in any social scene.

The Laws of Power: Beware of the Dark Side: Working in Hollywood inspired Robert Greene to write his 2000 bestseller, *The 48 Laws of Power*. So it is no surprise that it is highly acclaimed by numerous movie and pop stars. I've learned many of the lessons in this book the hard way and have found it essential in helping me navigate certain situations and people. An understanding of these laws is not only personally empowering, but it can also help you develop good leadership skills, cultivate your public professional persona, and avoid a variety of unproductive expenditures of time and energy by helping you better adapt to any variety of social situations. If your primary motivation for using the knowledge in this book is to manipulate others and gain power, and not to protect yourself from the power-hungry, please consider the following wisdom.

> *But beware of the dark side. Anger, fear, aggression; the dark side of the Force are they. Easily they flow, quick to join you in a fight. If once you start down the dark path, forever will it dominate your destiny.*
>
> –Yoda, *The Empire Strikes Back* (1980)

Following are a few of the laws that I most appreciate and utilize as much as possible, though all 48 laws are worthy of your attention. The name of the law I've taken directly from the book, while I've offered my own abbreviated summaries and examples relevant to the topic at hand.

- ▶ **Law 1: Never outshine the master.** There are people in positions of power over your survival and success. Impressing them with your talents is important, but if they are threatened by you and if they are insecure, they can block your progress.
- ▶ **Law 5: So much depends on reputation; guard it with your life.** Don't let others tarnish your reputation. A good reputation is a key that opens many doors. Regaining trust is harder than gaining trust in the first place, and it might not even be possible. Avoid drama and don't be petty.
- ▶ **Law 10: Infection: Avoid the unhappy and unlucky.** Their negativity can rub off on you and bring you down with them. If you determine that someone is hopelessly insecure, make sure to keep your distance and avoid collaborations if at all possible.
- ▶ **Law 19: Know who you're dealing with; do not offend the wrong person.** You can't always tell who someone is by how he or she looks or acts. Many successful veterans don't seek attention in public. Label owners and publicists often dress fairly conservatively compared to musicians and producers. Do your research and avoid insulting someone out of your ignorance. (See personal anecdote below.)
- ▶ **Law 35: Master the art of timing.** Wait for the right moment to approach someone you want to meet. Get your music out there before the trend emerges, or you may seem like a train jumper—but not too early, or people may not understand what you're trying to do. The party gets going at different times depending on the city and scene, so don't assume that 1 a.m. is either late or early.
- ▶ **Law 48: Assume formlessness.** Be flexible and ready to adapt to the unexpected. Trends come and go. The only certainty is change. David Bowie and Brian Eno are quintessential examples of this law applied to successful, long-lasting music careers.

I broke at least a few of the Laws of Power when I got back to NYC in 2007, which cost me potential opportunities garnered through years of network-building. This story evolved over a few years, so I think it's a good anecdote demonstrating the unpredictable nature of the social scene. I'm leaving all third parties' names out of this tale to protect the innocent and the guilty.

Memory Systems was an electro/synth pop/techno/IDM/live video collaboration between me and video artist/musician Phoenix Perry. An independent promoter in Miami booked us to play one of their semi-regular nights at a club in the Miami Design district during WMC 2003. Our pay was round-trip plane tickets from New York City and five nights in a downtown Miami hotel—which was awesome, but we still incurred substantial expenses. The expenses were worth it to us because we were booked as the only opening act for a really happening electro duo at the forefront of our scene. The packed crowd was to be full of sophisticated music fans and high-profile players in the indie electronic music world.

An influential promoter for an über-hip hotel in Manhattan heard that the other act was playing too small of a show for WMC and decided to have one of his friends in Miami book them for a big venue, just a few weeks before the gig. So we ended up headlining the event. Sounds great, except that we were the only act, and there were only about 20 people there, mostly locals. It was a great show, and the crowd liked us, but the whole trip turned out to be more of a fancy vacation than a career-changing trip. The promoter in Miami was really cool about it, didn't cancel the show, and at a loss for their generosity. Needless to say, no one was happy with that fancy-pants hotel promoter in Manhattan—who, by the way, just a few months earlier lavished us with obsequious flattery, telling us he'd heard we were the next big thing coming out of Williamsburg and that we just *had* to play his venue soon (even mentioning the act we were to share the bill with).

Fast-forward from 2003 to 2007. I was thinking about getting back into throwing parties. While looking for venues, I ran into a solid acquaintance. He just happened to be in the process of opening a new medium-sized venue with a seriously world-class sound system in lower Manhattan. I went there to meet him and see the space, which was still a raw, empty, concrete warehouse (more or less), upstairs and down.

Everything was going well; he was into what I wanted to do and sounded serious about giving me a night or two each month. It sounded as if I had an in at an upcoming hotspot in Manhattan. On the way out, he mentioned that he might be doing some collaborations with the promoter from the hotel. Without thinking, I said a few negative words about the promoter screwing me a few years back. It turned out they were good friends. We said goodbye, talk soon, and so on. And I never heard back—no returned emails or phone calls. Shut out. Done.

The club didn't open for another two years, and by then I had decided to focus on production and stay out of promoting and DJing. But it opened as a popular venue with great sound and solid booking. Fortunately, I had decided to focus on audio engineering and studio production, and ultimately it didn't mess me up. But it could have.

Moral of the story: Know who you're dealing with, and don't offend the wrong person.

Finally, as Abraham Maslow famously stated, "If all you have is a hammer, everything looks like a nail." Most people you meet aren't Connectors, Mavens, or Salesmen, or vampires, werewolves, or zombies. It is common for many people to exhibit traits or tendencies of these character types, positive and negative. Like any aspect of personality, there is a spectrum of behaviors, skills, and dispositions, with very few people measuring at the extremes.

Final Thoughts, Tips, and Strategies

The last few topics in this chapter are most relevant to those who are just getting started, as they primarily address knowledge that is gained from life experience. Most people who have been around for a while likely have figured some or all of this out for themselves. That being said, I think there is something for everyone in the next few pages.

Scarcity Is Often an Illusion, Especially in the Realms of Cultural Currency

There is always more than enough credit to go around. The ideal is for everyone to get what he or she wants. If your goal is to be creatively successful, let those who want the glory have the glory—not the credit, the glory. Glory is fleeting and often forgotten. If you're in this for the "long game," someone less talented than you will inevitably find a few minutes of success. Jealousy and envy can cloud your thinking and stifle your creativity. Just work harder and smarter. That said, don't ever let others take credit for your creative work; always get credited for your talents.

Respect Others Dedicated to Their Craft—Especially Veterans and Even Has-Beens

Choosing a creative life and doing it for a long time is not easy. Respect doesn't mean that you have to like their music or creative work or even pretend to. Mutual respect based on the recognition that the sacrifice required for dedication to your craft is a beautiful thing.

I've been a serious mixed martial arts geek for almost a decade. Most of those fighters have a ton of mutual respect for each other, even if they don't like each other. They literally beat each other up to make their living. Yet, many will go get a beer afterward. Some even travel around the globe to train with someone who defeated them, to continually improve their art. We are in a collaborative craft, so if prizefighters can respect each other after trying to cause bodily injury, we should be able to as well. Bruised egos can heal much faster than broken bones, if so desired.

What If You Really Don't Like Networking but You Know You Need to Do It?

How do you approach this problem? It depends on your plan. If part of your plan is also to DJ and promote your own events, then you need to either revise your plan or figure out how to start enjoying that aspect. When I was actively promoting an electronic-music party in San Francisco, I was out three to five nights a week, often at multiple venues each night. I didn't always stay very long; sometimes I just handed out a few flyers and said hi to fellow promoters (not unusual for a promoter, by the way). Many of those nights I really just wanted to stay home and chill.

If you are in a band or have creative partners, you can divvy up the networking. Each of you can pick events that most interest you, or at least lighten the load if you go together. Just as each of you has strengths in different aspects of music and production, also make use of your relative strengths when it comes to making new connections in different aspects of the social scene. List events in order of importance and at least hit the ones you think are most worth your time. Even if you don't have the time or don't want to go out, you should at least make an appearance if it's an important event in your scene.

The Internet is important, and you can make a lot of headway via social networking and over email, but in-person meetings are still the most powerful. Whenever possible, try to get to events where you can meet up with Internet friends in person. With a little bit of planning, trade shows, conventions, expos, and festivals are awesome opportunities to strengthen cyber-relationships and make a slew of new contacts in just a few days or hours.

Tips for Newbies on Interacting with Successful Artists

When you're new to the artist/production side of the music world, it can be difficult to stop thinking like a fan. But you need to shift your mindset from one of a consumer to one of a producer. When you start to associate with your heroes, idols, and inspirations, it can be awkward. What do you say? Remember, they often want a break from their work, so just treat them like normal people. If possible, try to find a common interest outside of the genre or scene, such as obscure music, books, movies, sports, martial arts, comedians, food, or even cities and other countries you've visited. They might want to geek out about gear and music, but not always. Successful artists and producers are constantly bombarded by people who want something from them, even if it's just attention or knowledge. It's all about trust and comfort.

Outro

No matter where you are in your career, there is value in making new social connections. Sometimes these contacts are strictly business, but just as often they are also something more. The fact that successful people tend to know other successful people should not be misinterpreted in a cynical fashion. Yes, there is nepotism and the like, but is it only natural that we gravitate toward people, communities, and scenes based on common interests. So, another interpretation is that we should choose our associations based on not only their levels of success, but also on what we have in common. There is value in an address book full of very successful contacts that you don't know very well. Yet, significantly more valuable is a few dozen closer (even though perhaps not quite as successful) professional connections composed of friends, peers, and acquaintances.

Producer Tips

I've learned that people will forget what you said, people will forget what you did, but people will never forget how you made them feel.

–Maya Angelou

If something can go wrong, eventually it will.

–Murphy's Law

And if you want something to be unclear, then you have to be clear that you want it to be unclear.

–Bob Power

Here, we are not talking about tips as in tips and tricks. The tips in this chapter are more along the lines of those from a friend you are visiting in New York City, such as where to find the best slice of pizza at 2 a.m., and making sure your wallet is never in your back pocket, especially in crowds and on the subway. This chapter essentially weaves together topics from the previous two chapters with topics from the two that follow, so we are going to oscillate our focus to and from very different domains. This oscillation toggles from one end of interaction to the other, from social situations to spending quality time with your data, computer, and other production tools—topics that overlap with Chapter 4, "Master Your Craft," Chapter 5, "The Social Scene," and Chapter 8, "Selecting Your Tools." We are also going to cover some gear and software history to elucidate relevant issues, and preview a few topics from Chapter 7, "Creative Process," specifically related to planning, deadlines, and pressure. No matter your level of accomplishment, there is something in here for you.

> **NOTE:** Jargon alert: If you are totally new to all of this, you may want to reference Chapter 8 while reading this one, or perhaps even read it first. Chapter 8 gets into all of the equipment and software used in production, as well as clarifying otherwise vague terms like "sound quality."

Keys to Success

There are many keys to success. Positive attitude, persistence, hard work, instinct, experience, natural talent, honed skills, connections, and a bit of luck are a few of those keys. One of the big differences between a skilled amateur and a true professional is how they approach all the details that support a consistently successful production process. To be a successful producer, one must also know how to run successful production sessions. To maximize productivity and creativity during those sessions, it is best to think about them as having at least three phases: before, during, and after. As a producer, the session starts before anyone shows up and continues after they are all gone. If self-producing, this basic concept does not change. It is actually useful to feign split personality disorder and consider yourself as multiple people, since you are filling the roles of at least producer, performer, and engineer.

Plan and Prepare

Nothing says "survival guide" more than an emphasis on preparedness. As the saying goes, "Hope for the best but prepare for the worst." Unlike "doomsday preppers," you don't need to build a bunker or stock up on food, water, and ammo, but you do need to be prepared for the unexpected. There are differences in scale and intensity if you are producing your own music in a home studio or another artist's tracks in a commercial studio, but the considerations are the same either way. As a producer, you are responsible. The buck stops with you. It is not only your responsibility to work on music and recording, but also to figure out what needs to be scheduled, organized, set up, purchased, rented, or otherwise. If relevant or appropriate, you might delegate some of these responsibilities. So you don't have to keep all of this in your head, become a huge fan of making checklists and using calendar software for scheduling and task tracking.

Time Management

You can't just turn on creativity like a faucet. You have to be in the right mood. What mood is that? Last-minute panic.

–Bill Watterson

Most everything in the production process takes longer than you think it will, even assuming nothing goes wrong. Deadlines, limitations, and pressure are actually good for productivity and creativity (as discussed in the next chapter). That said, you needn't always feel like you're under the gun and should book sufficient time for each part of a project whenever possible. But, always be on the lookout for procrastination. We all do it, for as American humorist Sam Levenson once said, "I'm going to stop putting things off, starting tomorrow!" Projects with seemingly distant deadlines all too often insinuate an insufficient sense of urgency at their onset. As the approaching deadline exponentially multiplies pressure, anxiety, and stress, most everyone wishes they had worked just a little harder each day when there was a lot more time to go. Legendary IBM computer scientist Fred Brooks once asked and answered, "How does a project get to be a year behind schedule? One day at a time." Brooks is an authority on issues related to planning and scheduling long complex projects, having published the seminal book of note on the topic for software developers in 1975, *The Mythical Man-Month* (reprinted in 1995).

Booking enough time and not procrastinating early in a project grow in importance as the number of people involved increases. The more people's schedules there are to accommodate, the more likely there will be unexpected delays. If you are working with people who are notoriously late or flaky, take that into account and make sure to schedule extra days. Perhaps even tell them that the meeting times are a bit earlier than when you actually need to get to work, so when they are late, they are on time. No matter the case, always assume you will need more time than you think you'll need. You'll probably need it. At all phases of the process, it is important to prioritize, leaving the least important elements to last, in case you run out of time and need to cut something out. More often than not, you will need to cut something out. As William James once said, "The art of being wise is knowing what to overlook."

It is always a good idea to create a schedule with milestones, but their value exponentially increases as a project's scope, duration, and complexity increases. In addition to other general factors, there are at least two key considerations that make milestones vital in any professional situation. The following considerations often occur together but they might be isolated.

▷ **Deadlines:** Don't end up with way more work than is possible as time gets short and the deadline approaches. If you track your progress with the milestones, you will always know when you are falling behind.

▷ **Compensation:** Don't get yourself into a project that earns you significantly less than it should or leads to cost overruns that understandably upset a client. If you quoted a project rate, you can't just decide to charge more at the last minute to complete it because of your lack of project-management skills. The client needs to know what will add to a quote, where they are in a project so they can prioritize what they want to get done, and thus also if they want to pay more than initially discussed. Another option is to give a quote based on an hourly rate, which has its pros and cons. Hourly rates motivate most clients to be better organized and minimize impulsive or frivolous requests for additional work without expectation of additional payment. Yet, it is equally important to avoid unnecessary time overruns that may seem suspicious to a new client.

Time management is a skill a lot of us need to develop. When well done, it is a key component of "work smart," which makes things easier and more efficient when we "work hard." There is a lot of software available worth looking into, and some of it is already on your computer or phone, including iCal, Google Calendar, or similar. You might also want to look into solutions designed for freelancers and contractors, such as OmniPlan (Mac) or MS Project (PC), or do a Web search for "time tracking" or "project management" software. Some solutions even offer billing and invoicing features.

When figuring out how much to charge, there is no standard beyond market rates or what someone is willing to pay you. Many of us vary our "standard" rates depending on the client, how interested we are in the gig, and/or how busy or idle we might be at that time. For example, it is common to lower the rate for an interesting, friendly artist when you are between gigs, just as it is to raise the rate for an established artist with a label budget or an ad agency. Find out the going rate in your area for someone with your skills and/or facility. Talk to established professionals who might be willing to help you figure out what works best for them, and therefore what might work well for you. You might also check out the freely downloadable music industry salary guide published by Berklee College of Music, "Music Careers in Dollars and Cents."

Separate Sessions

Minimizing distractions and unnecessary tangents is a top priority when it comes time to be productive and creative. There are so many aspects to what we do that keeping focused and on track is regularly a challenge, so there is no need to make it more of an issue than it needs to be. One of the biggest mistakes made by new producers is a failure to set aside dedicated time for focusing on different aspects of production. Just as in a restaurant there are prep cooks and dishwashers who support the chef before and after the dinner rush, we need to prep, clean, and organize before and after the main session. In fact, there are at least four basic types of sessions, each emphasizing different tasks and types of mental focus. In addition to the primary creative/productive sessions, there are three others that happen before and/or after them:

▷ **Creative/productive:** These sessions are what most people would call "a session." During these, you want to focus on creative process, running a recording session, and/or otherwise effectively getting things done. To best ensure successful outcomes during these sessions, you need to also set aside time for other types of sessions.

▷ **Sound design:** Nothing bogs down creative flow or the composition process like sifting through thousands of sounds and presets. Set aside time for sessions dedicated solely to making your own sounds, saving and organizing your favorite presets, sifting through sample libraries, and creating templates. When it comes time to work on new music or capture a new idea, you are much less likely to get lost in tasks that drain inspiration, since you will already know what you want to use or at least have a much smaller list to audition. I will talk more about presets in a bit.

▷ **Maintenance:** Between sessions, take the time to back up all your important files. Organize hard drives, folders, files, templates, cables, adapters, and anything else that needs to be in the right place at the right time when inspiration strikes or deadlines approach. Sometimes, you just need to keep a session moving; this is the time to address the small details that you had to ignore at that time, such as cleaning up session files and addressing bad or incorrect filenames. In addition to making backups, this is the time to run your hard-drive maintenance utilities, which should be done regularly. There is always something to do in this category for those times that you are not feeling creative but want to be productive. I will return to topics relevant to maintenance sessions in a bit.

▷ **Learning:** Learning on the job and/or in real-world scenarios is valuable, but only with regard to a limited sort of knowledge. In addition to gaining practical, experiential knowledge, there is always something to learn about what we do, namely of the technical or creative variety. Although there are times when busting out a manual in the middle of a session is appropriate (if not necessary), it should be a fairly rare occurrence. All of us should set aside times for sessions dedicated solely to learning new features and tools and experimenting with new techniques. Figuring out a new feature for the first time when you have a vocalist in the booth is a bad idea. It is okay to combine learning sessions with sound-design sessions, just not every time.

While there are times when we are not feeling creative and productive, it is always valuable to put our energy into any one of these types of sessions instead of doing nothing. That said, there is a fine line between busy work and procrastination. Prolific horror fiction writer Stephen King once said, "The scholar's greatest weakness: calling procrastination research." We can easily translate this to music production; just replace "scholar" with "producer" and "research" with any of the aforementioned tasks outside of creative/productive sessions.

Keep Things Moving Forward

It's all about understanding the part of the process you're in at any given moment. When I'm writing, I have to force myself not to perfect my parts. I do a lot of programming and sequencing, and not perfecting is a very conscious decision. It reminds me of what I have to do with someone who's in creative mode. I keep things moving forward.

–Bob Power (sonicscoop.com, 2011)

What is the priority of the moment? Musicians and engineers focus on their focus (tautology intended). For example, drummers pay attention to their performances and the sound of their drums. Vocalists' attention is on their lyrics, phrasing, pitch, and performance. The engineer makes sure mics are well placed, levels are good, sessions are organized, and performers are comfortable and can hear everything in their cue mix. As the producer, you may also be in one or more (or all) of these roles. Regardless, the producer needs to pay attention to all those details and the big picture. Don't let the session get hung up on small details when vibe and momentum are key. If the singer is really warmed up and hitting all his parts, it is not time to search for the perfect reverb for the drums. Don't worry about style and vibe when small technical details are the focus of attention. If the engineer is troubleshooting a problem with the headphone mix, just give him a signal when he asks, don't worry about a perfect performance. The Bob Power quote at the top of this section is a perfectly concise summary of prioritization guidelines. I'll talk about some of these issues in more detail in Chapter 7, when we consider how stages of the creative process interweave throughout the four phases of the production process, as discussed in Chapter 4.

Bugs, crashes, software authorization snags, lost adapters, and missing files are just a few of the setbacks that can pop up in the middle of a session and derail the flow. Being prepared means that when you *do* run into problems, you already have ideas for workarounds and backup plans so you do not get bogged down. If it is necessary, yes, stop and take the time to address the issue, but sometimes it is better to just get it done. Especially during recording sessions, it is usually better to capture an inspired performance in a less-than-ideal manner than to perfectly capture one that is not so good. Always be ready and able to record. There are many instances of improvisational genius and brilliance that ended up on records because engineers were smart enough to capture those moments. When you are with talented artists who are ready to go with a fresh exciting idea but there is some sort of problem, the philosophy needs to be "whatever works." Once you capture the inspiration, find an opportune time to take a break and do some troubleshooting, cleaning up, refining, or otherwise. Like much of what we do, it is only through experience that we develop good judgment to make the best calls at the right times.

Working with Others

Hell is other people.

–Jean-Paul Sartre

Everything that irritates us about others can lead us to an understanding of ourselves.

–Carl Jung

We are not self-made. We are dependent on one another. Admitting this to ourselves isn't an embrace of mediocrity and derivativeness, it's a liberation from our misconceptions.

–Kirby Ferguson

Do you strongly relate to any of the preceding three quotes more than the others? Do you not relate to any of them at all? If you only relate to the Sartre quote, then odds are you are self-producing your own material or going through one of life's rough patches. Talented artists can be antisocial and successful, but not producers. Don't get me wrong, Sartre brilliantly captured aspects of the human experience, and there are times in life when we all feel like there is "no exit." Sometimes, other people are a real bummer. But if you want to be a successful producer, then other people must also be a source of inspiration, motivation, and joy. A producer's role includes figuring out how to bring out the best in everyone involved, including the producer.

When collaborating with other artists, find out what you can about how they work so you can develop a game plan for getting the best out of them. To minimize common sources of tension during projects, make sure to get all of the business out of the way before starting. Take the time to work through implicit assumptions so everyone is clear about their role and how they are going to be compensated. If you can't work out the details before people are emotionally and financially invested, then it is safe to assume that it will only be worse once the project is underway.

Some people are simply a pleasure to work with for any number of reasons. Some people are a challenging, frustrating hassle, but are worth the effort due to their unique talents, brilliant ideas, exceptional skills, or deep pockets. In some cases, no matter their skill level or natural gifts, it is simply not worth the hassle even when you are very well paid. In any case, otherwise seemingly normal people can get weird in intense creative environments, in particular when they are inexperienced and/or insecure, and especially when there is also pressure. Learning how to best deal with people in challenging situations is a life skill that some of us are more naturally suited to than others. As with any skill, this one can also be developed with a little learning and effort. Don't assume that a crash course on pop psychology is sufficient. There is more going on here than just individuals and their personalities. In some cases, the situation itself is what most requires your attention.

(Social) Psychology

Producers are not just musicians, engineers, and project managers. We are also often coaches, mentors, and *de facto* psychologists. In many cases, there is no producer, so a good recording engineer assumes those responsibilities in the studio. This reality is such a part of our industry that some audio technology schools include a psychology course in their curriculum, which makes a lot of sense for any profession that is largely about working with people. There are a lot of good articles online on the topic of studio psychology that are worth reading. I am going to hit a few points here, but also make sure to check out this book's companion website, www.iempsg.com, for links. Studio psychology ultimately is about getting the best performances possible out of the artists when in the studio. Therefore, studio psychology is a psychology of the moment. It is about what makes us tick and how best to relate with everyone's idiosyncrasies—brilliant, quirky, funny, bizarre, beautiful, challenging, endearing, and otherwise. I already talked about a psychology 101 topic, personality types, in the previous chapter, and in the next one we will explore the unconscious as it relates to creative process. Both of those subjects emphasize individual psychology, but the studio environment is equally about how social interaction and the environment shapes behavior.

Social psychology is the study of how social situations influence individual behavior. You can think of this field as the opposite end of the psychology spectrum from personal therapy. Sociologist Erving Goffman's 1959 book, *The Presentation of Self in Everyday Life*, is widely considered one of the most important and influential sociological works of the last 100 years. In that book, he extensively uses theater metaphors as he makes the case that much of our behavior is like that of an actor playing a role. Of greatest relevance to producers is that two of his main points explain people's behaviors in social situations. The term "power of the situation" is a central notion in social psychology, and an understanding of this concept is necessary for fully making sense of how people's social environment influences their behavior. Goffman pointed out that most people present themselves in public largely so as to avoid uncomfortable situations, namely embarrassing others or oneself. This point alone is a crucial understanding when working with performing artists in general, and particularly in recording sessions with inexperienced or insecure musicians. The second major point is about the different "roles" people play in different situations. In simplified form, when in the role of parent or child, we act differently than when in the role of boss or employee, or in the role of performer or audience member.

Power of the Situation

You probably know at least a few people who behave very differently when you are with them one on one compared to when they are in public. All "normal" people change their behavior to some extent depending on the social environment and the role they are playing at that time. Given the same situation, some artists and musicians will thrive while others will crack under the pressure. Some are so influenced by their surroundings that the situation determines their level of performance. A related dynamic is found in the well-studied phenomena of crowd behavior—how some people more readily give in to a "mob" mentality, while others keep their wits about them, refusing to lower their moral standards to that of the mob. This "anonymity of the crowd," as it is known, is clearly illustrated in riots, as it weakens individuals' sense of responsibility and obedience to authority and power structures.

You are not working in anonymous situations, however. When it comes to how people behave in more intimate settings, we turn to two groundbreaking experiments that elicited such shocking revelations on the power of the situation that they forced changes in ethical guidelines for research in the U.S. They revealed how both explicit and perceived roles can be the single most dominant influence on behavior. Both studies are taught in most every university, often in multiple departments, most commonly sociology, psychology, and/or philosophy (ethics).

MILGRAM EXPERIMENT (1961), YALE UNIVERSITY

Stanley Milgram, professor of psychology at Yale University, conducted his landmark "obedience to authority" experiment just a year after famous trials of Nazi war criminals. A flier posted on campus offered students a chance to make $4.50 for an hour of their time to help with a memory study, which was paid up front. Accounting for inflation, $4.50 in 1961 was roughly $30 in 2012 money, which is a nice chunk of change for a college student.

When students arrived at the lab, they found what they thought was another volunteer there, as well as the person running the experiment, known as the "experimenter." Both volunteers blindly selected a piece of paper that determined who was going to be the "teacher" and who was going to be the "student." The student was then taken into the other room, where, according to the experimenter, he or she was hooked up to electrodes. The teacher was given a list of word-association questions. Every time the student answered incorrectly, the teacher was to administer a shock. Inevitably, the student would get a lot of the questions wrong. The machine started out at a low 15v, which was not a big deal. But with each wrong answer, the teacher was to step up the voltage another 15v. The machine had 30 switches, and it went all the way up to 450v, which is way past dangerous and life threatening. As the voltage stepped up, the student started making audible sounds of pain and discomfort. If the teacher told the experimenter that he or she didn't want to continue, the experimenter would prod the teacher on by saying, "Please continue." If the teacher still resisted, the experimenter would then say, "The experiment requires you to continue," and, if need be, "It is absolutely essential that you continue," and finally, if the teacher still refused, "You have no other choice but to continue." If the teacher refused after the fourth prod, the experiment ended. Otherwise, it kept going until the teacher had administered three 450v shocks.

Here's the catch: It was not a memory study, and there were no shocks at all, since only the teacher was the subject of the experiment. The "student" was an actor who was part of the research team. Both pieces of paper said "teacher" on it, so no matter what, the volunteer would be in that role. The biggest shock was that 26 out of the 40 participants went all the way, even though most of them showed symptoms of stress, anxiety, and cognitive dissonance. The combination of deference to authority, guilt from having already been paid for the work, and other factors led to most every participant continuing after being prodded by the experimenter, with all of them making it to 300v. The most detailed description of his findings weren't published outside of academic journals until his 1974 book, *Obedience to Authority: An Experimental View*. Examples from this experiment are commonly used to illustrate Lawrence Kohlberg's (1927–1987) equally important and influential theory of stages of moral development (which is central to Integral theory's understanding of the moral line of development; see Figure B.1 in Appendix B, "Integral Theory Primer").

ZIMBARDO EXPERIMENT (1971), STANFORD UNIVERSITY

About 10 years after Milgram's experiment, Stanford psychologist Philip Zimbardo carried out the now infamous Stanford prison experiment. This study was largely funded by the U.S. Navy to help determine the cause of conflicts between guards and prisoners at military facilities. Zimbardo and his team set up a fake prison on the campus that had actual cells and a prison yard. After narrowing down the participants to 24 male students, the researchers randomly assigned some of them as "guards" and others as "prisoners." The prisoners were even "arrested" at home and "booked" before being put in a cell. The predominantly white, middle-class participants were prescreened to make sure they were psychologically healthy and without a criminal history. They were to be paid $15 per day for a two-week study (accounting for inflation, $15 in 1971 was about $84 in 2012). The results were so unexpected that they had to stop the experiment after just six days. Some of guards became sadistic, abusing their authority and punishing prisoners for not following their commands—even psychologically torturing some of them. Prisoners acted out, displayed all sorts of negative emotional and psychological conditions, and essentially began to act like real prisoners. Some of them even offered to go without any pay if they could get out early (be paroled). While not all of Zimbardo's conclusions are universally accepted, other peer-reviewed studies have confirmed the central point: Most people's behavior is shaped by the environment and their perceived role in that environment, as much if not more so than their personality.

Knowledge Is Power

These famous experiments revealed how hierarchies of power structures influence people's behavior, largely based on the role they are playing and where that role sits in that actual or perceived hierarchy. So how do these findings help a music producer? Whether the people involved are conscious of it or not, there is always some sort of hierarchy of power in professional situations. Sometimes it is formal or informal, sometimes it changes or even reverses in different contexts and situations. Once extremes are clearly illustrated, it is easier to perceive subtleties. Just as we exaggerate sonic problems while sweeping boosted frequencies with an EQ to make it easier to identify unwanted frequencies we want to cut, it is always easier to recognize something when there is a lot more of it than we need. These studies, and many others, tend to point out the dark side of human behavior. Yet, the power of the situation, and the roles people play, can just as easily be a positive influence and conducive to elevated behaviors and desirable outcomes.

In our industry, power structures can be all too clear on the business side of things—when there is a boss/employee relationship, or when it is obvious that someone's career is in someone else's hands. When it comes to collaborations and creative work during the production process, the structures are not always so obvious—or important, for that matter—even in a client/contractor or mentor/protégé situation. When roles are unclear, behavior is no less influenced by the power of the situation, as assumptions and perceptions fill in the blanks. As the producer, it is always a good idea to be aware of the stated structure, and equally, the assumed or unstated assumptions about roles and power over decisions and outcomes. When everything is flowing smoothly, everyone is happy, and there are no mysterious tensions, then there is no need to worry about such things. If things do get weird or people suddenly, unexpectedly change their attitude for the worse, then you have one more tool to help figure out how to get things back on track. More often than not, a little communication can clear up most issues, assuming you are dealing with "honest brokers."

In a healthy situation, with trust between players, the power of authority is not that of "the man keeping us down." Instead, people are authorities on a subject, respected experts in a community, with valuable opinions and constructive feedback. Chapter 9, "Lifestyle Tips," addresses considerations when deciding with whom to surround ourselves in the context of our career and creative lifestyle. These social psychological dynamics are powerful, but they are not the whole story. We can learn to consciously create environments that better guide us and our collaborators in creative and productive directions. As discussed in the next chapter, free will is always a factor in influencing outcomes.

Communication

Good communication with artists and collaborators is crucial, and can make or break a project. It is an ongoing part of the process. As producer, it is up to you to ensure there are no breakdowns, and if there are, to fix them as best as possible. Before any project gets going, always take the time to discuss goals, expectations, time frame, and budget. Find out people's level of experience and comfort in the studio, even if they are good musicians. Singers are known to need time for adjusting to studio environments, but it can be a scary, intimidating, or uncomfortable situation for any musician. Scheduling and compensation are best determined after all of these discussions have occurred.

If the situation involves a studio and a separate control room, the talkback button should be on between every take, just so the artists know what is happening. If you have to fix something, tell them you need a minute. Never leave them guessing, especially when working with inexperienced or insecure artists. In the latter case, it is often recommended that you clear the control room to help the performer focus. If people in the control room are joking around and laughing with other band members, make sure the artist in the booth is in on the joke so he or she doesn't mistakenly conclude you are laughing at his or her last performance. In general, it is better to err on the side of more open talkback mic than less.

When it comes to giving feedback on a performance, you need to know your artist so you best phrase the feedback for him or her. Generally speaking, feedback should begin by pointing out what the person is doing well before getting into what is not working. We want the artist to feel comfortable and confident. Some artists need to be pushed, others need to be humored or even pampered a little, while still others need to be indulged until they figure things out for themselves. Sometimes they are stubborn, although often, some sort of misunderstanding is the culprit. When dealing with tense situations and/or overly sensitive and insecure artists, giving feedback is challenging. Sometimes it is useful to ask questions instead of making statements. For example, if the previous take was not so good, don't tell them it was not good. Instead, ask them how *they* felt about it. Often, they will want to do it again anyway, and then you can agree to go along with another take, or two, or three, or 10 (but hopefully not so many). In some challenging situations, artists will insist they are right about something when it is obvious they are incorrect. In such a situation, to keep the session moving, don't get sidetracked in debating what is not working. Figure out how to offer feedback that points to what is working.

Thoughtful, accurate, useful feedback and communication in the studio should be the norm, but honesty is not always the best policy. This point is best illustrated in stories told by Butch Vig about recording Kurt Cobain. "Recording Nirvana: Drain You (Butch Vig Breaks It Down In The Studio)" was Posted on YouTube in 2009. In this interview, Vig sits in front of a large console with the original raw tracks from that session routed to individual channels. He explains how he obtained that song's full guitar mix by telling Cobain that he had to redo performances because of technical problems with the previous takes. Cobain otherwise would not have agreed to do so many overdubs. The resulting 1991 album, *Nevermind*, is widely considered one of the most important rock records of all time.

Pre-Presets: Patches, Programs, and the Prophet: Why are presets often called *patches* or *programs*? Modular synthesizers required patch cables to connect modules to each other, so a "patch" was a configuration that was often hand drawn on a template to make recall possible at a later time. When electronic musical instruments gained the ability to digitally store settings, they were referred to as being "programmable," so a "program" is essentially a snapshot of the configuration of all the knobs, buttons, and sliders that is stored with a specific program number to make recall possible at a later time.

Presets as we know them are dependent on digital technology—memory and microprocessors—and those didn't appear until the late 1970s. It makes sense that presets first appeared in completely digital systems, such as the New England Digital Synclavier (1977), Fairlight CMI (1979), and PPG Wave Computer (1979), all of which were multi-function computer workstations affordable only for rock stars and big studios.

Sequential Circuits was founded by Dave Smith and John Bowen in 1974, in San Jose, California (Silicon Valley). Originally, they made analog (CV/gate) sequencers for other company's synths, but got into using microprocessors with their Model 800 in 1976 so they could store sequences in banks. At that time, Smith had the idea to put the same microprocessor technology in an analog synth so it, too, could store settings, but he was sure that such an obvious idea was being pursued by the "big" U.S. companies at that time, Moog and ARP. A year later, when no one had done it, he decided to use Zilog's Z80 chip (another San Jose company), and in 1977 they demonstrated the Prophet-5 (See Figure 6.1).

Figure 6.1 Sequential Circuits' Prophet-5 (1977), the first all-analog synth with presets.
© Brad Berry (perfectcircuitaudio.com). All Rights Reserved.

This landmark all-analog signal path synth not only sounded amazing, but it was polyphonic (five voices, a luxury in those days), and was the very first electronic music instrument designed around a microprocessor. It was also, therefore, the very first "programmable" analog synth, and could store 40 programs. (Shortly thereafter, in 1978, appeared Roland's 4 voice Jupiter 4 and Oberheim's monophonic OB-1, each of which could store eight programs.) Yamaha bought Sequential in 1987, and Smith went on to work for a number of different companies, including a few of his own. The resurgent popularity of analog synths in the late 1990s found the Prophet a perennial favorite with accompanied vintage pricing on the used market. In 2002, Germany's Native Instruments released its Pro-53 plug-in, the same year that Smith started Dave Smith Instruments, which finally resurrected the all-analog Prophet in 2008 (the Prophet '08). See Figure 6.6 at the end of the chapter for other significant historical connections involving Dave Smith and NI.

In 2007, the great British website sonicstate.com produced a series called the *Top 20 Greatest Synths* (sonicstate.com/top20). Found about 20 minutes into the episode "Top 20 Synths 3–5" is an interview with Dave Smith. While discussing the development of the Prophet-5, he said:

> You have to remember that back then, the concept of creating patches didn't exist, 'cuz there were no programmable synthesizers out there. So the idea that you have to come up with x number of patches for your new instrument, well, ya know, we were the first ones to do it. We did it in house…and we came up with the first set of 40 patches, which was of course a huge number back then, but a tiny number now.

Presets: Data Mining or Time-Saving Sound Designing?

We are literally surrounded by presets, and continually inundated with more of them. Their abundant, ubiquitous presence is a taken-for-granted fact of life in the modern production environment. All of us deal with them, but they are such a common source of confusion and distraction, especially for newcomers to the world of modern music production, and even more so for software-centric electronic music producers, that I am devoting more than a few pages to the topic. The following discussion is both philosophical and practical, and is intended to bring clarity to an otherwise nebulous and messy topic.

Not counting the equally endless supply of MIDI sequences, loops, and audio samples, we routinely find presets for synths, samplers, drum machines, effects, channel strips, and beyond, for both software and hardware. Native Instrument's Komplete 9 Ultimate software bundle advertises that it includes 65 different products, a 370 GB sample library, and 16,000 sounds. The Eventide H8000FW digital effects processor ships with 1,600 presets. The Access Virus TI2 synthesizer ships with 3,840 presets stored in RAM or ROM, and Access touts that there are more than 7,000 available. So with only those three products, there are more than 24,600 presets. If you spent only 10 seconds with each one, it would take you more than 68 hours to get through them all. Put another way, if you turned this tedious task into a full-time job for a week straight, it would take you almost 10 hours a day with no breaks to simply audition all of them, let alone use any of them. It is safe to say that you will never need or use more than 99% of the presets that exist in the world, so why are there so many of them, and what influences their propagation and design?

Before we go deeper into this topic, let's first consider some definitions and distinctions. The word "preset" literally breaks down into "pre," meaning "before," and "set," meaning "arranged." Presets then are simply a snapshot of some combination of parameters and files that take some time to develop. Therefore, in theory, they are a timesaver because they are *arranged before* they are needed. The fact that Wendy Carlos created the hugely successful *Switched-On Bach* (1968) record with nothing more than Moog's new monophonic modular analog synthesizer, and an analog 8-track tape recorder custom built by Carlos, is nothing short of astonishing. Not only did she masterfully perform complex Bach pieces without any multitrack editing capabilities, but she also did all of the sound design on a synth that was monophonic and required dozens of patch cables for each instrument's sound. If you ever have the urge to blame creative blocks on "bad presets," just listen to any good music made prior to 1977 and ask yourself why you care so much about presets in the first place.

Although all presets are pre-set, there are at least three basic types.

▷ **User:** These are custom presets you make. As discussed, writing down all of the settings was the only way to save a synthesizer patch prior to 1977. As Wendy Carlos could certainly attest to, writing down every knob's setting and patch cable's routing was a very time-consuming process. Given that recalling settings with these devices is a long, tedious process, wanting the ability to quickly store and recall these settings is an obvious no brainer. In that sense, we would call such presets "user presets." User presets are the best kind of presets, because we chose to save them and therefore they must be valuable to us. We like our own presets, and should make them, organize them, and set them up as our *default* settings when possible. (In recent years the boutique modular synthesizer market has blown up, surely in part as a reaction to preset overload. So it is not correct to speak only about vintage synths and the need to write down settings.)

▷ **Factory:** These are the presets made "at the factory" that ship with software or hardware. Most of these are worthless to most people most of the time, especially ones that come with a DAW or keyboard workstation. Leaving aside good implementations of practical presets that cover perennially useful instruments such as pianos and organs (for example Clavia's Nord Electro or Stage), many factory presets exist to meet the expectations of hobbyist, amateur, and beginner demographics. Given that more must be better, libraries grow over the years as more presets are developed to ship with new versions, which explains why so many presets are either very old or not inspired. That said, some companies are known for higher-quality factory presets, usually when they are bundled with a third-party product or created by a well-known sound designer. In a few scenarios factory presets can actually assist in the creative process, such as when dealing with a creative block.

▷ **Third-party:** A third-party product is one designed for use with another product. Common examples include plug-ins for your DAW or presets and libraries for plug-ins. These are often like factory presets in that someone else makes them, but they are more likely to be sorted by style and genre, so you can pick the product with ones most likely to be useful to you. The companies that specialize in sound design are also most likely to offer current, relevant presets. Third-party presets are more likely to be an improvement over standard factory presets, but they are often still plagued with the same issues, just not to the same extent of uselessness. Also, many third-party libraries and presets are put on the market to take advantage of current trends, so they are often as trite and cliché as they are current.

If you were born after 1990 or so, it might be hard to believe that some of the best records of all time were made without using one single instrument preset. As mentioned, there were no presets other than hand-written notes until the late 1970s. The first digital reverb was the EMT 250 in 1976 for $20,000, and the first with a microprocessor was the Lexicon 224 in 1978 for $7,900. The EMT did not have any presets in the conventional sense, but it could store five sets of values for the "soft" sliders (a precursor to today's "soft" knobs with "pickup" behavior). The Lexicon 224 had four programs. As discussed, at this time, programmable synths also started to hit the market. It was not until the early 1980s that presets became commonplace, in large part due to the dropping costs of microprocessors. Not only did these new chips make it possible to put multiple audio effects in one single unit, but synths and drum machines were also quickly growing in popularity, which created the need for MIDI (Music Instrument Digital Interface).

In 1981, Dave Smith proposed a new specification, the Universal Synthesizer Interface, at the 70th AES convention, based on discussions with Tom Oberheim and Roland's founder Ikutaro Kakehashi. Keep in mind that even in 1982, synths such as Roland's new Juno-60 not only had to back up their programs via ¼-inch cable to compact cassette tape, but also couldn't "talk" to other companies' synths. To solve this increasingly common state of affairs, Dave Smith, Roland, and Yamaha together developed the MIDI 1.0 specification, which was first demonstrated to the public at the 1983 Winter NAMM show. With the increasing popularity of microprocessors, accelerated by and coupled with the industry's acceptance of the new MIDI protocol, the stage was now set for uncontrolled preset proliferation. When it comes to the initial genesis of synth preset overload, the premier precedent was set by Yamaha's DX7.

When the Name Says It All...: A lot of presets are designed to match well-known characteristics of classic devices. When it comes to synths, some companies do a pretty good job of naming presets so you can easily tell what it will sound like even before auditioning it. Following are a few names found in the factory presets of a few popular products. Do you know what they will sound like based on the name alone? Which classic instruments are they based on? (Hint: They are all from the same era from the same company, as discussed in Chapter 1, "Musica Universalis").

- ▶ Ableton's Operator, synth, preset: Acid Bass
- ▶ Pro Tools' Structure, sampler, preset: 1980s Drums
- ▶ Logic's Ultrabeat, drum machine, preset: Vintage 09 Kit
- ▶ NI Reaktor, ensemble, preset: Junatik

The Yamaha DX7, Suspect Zero

The DX7 is featured in sonicstate.com's *Top 20 Greatest Synths* series from 2007, coming in at #4 (right after the Prophet-5, discussed earlier). As the "sound of the 80s," Yamaha's DX7 is one of most popular synths ever (see Figure 6.2). Released in 1983, it was one of the first synths with MIDI functionality. More importantly, it was the first commercially successful keyboard synthesizer to use FM synthesis. FM synthesis was invented by Stanford's John Chowning in 1967. Also an electronic musician and computer-savvy inventor, Chowning had recently set up one of the first computer music programs with the help of undergraduate math whiz David Poole, along with Max Matthews, the father of computer music. Stanford licensed FM to Yamaha in 1973 (which brought in $20 million before expiring in 1994). This success likely helped pave the way for Chowning's founding of Stanford's now legendary Center for Computer Research in Music and Acoustics (CCRMA) in 1975.

Figure 6.2 Yamaha DX-7 (1983), one of the most popular and best-selling synths of all time. Despite its great sound, it was so hard to program that users relied on presets.

The DX7 offered exciting new timbral capabilities, but was incredibly difficult to program, for a few reasons. First off, competent programming of an FM synth requires a good amount of technical knowledge, and therefore is not an intuitive process that reaps many rewards through simple knob twiddling as with subtractive synths. Second, the DX7 has a terrible user interface, comprised of a tiny LCD screen, a lot of buttons, just two sliders, and no knobs. Sonicstate.com's own Nick Batt described the experience of trying to program with this interface as being similar to "painting the hall through a letterbox." Since it was portable, relatively affordable, and sounded great but was basically impossible for most musicians to program, it resulted in the first notable case of widespread "preset hoarding." Musicians collected as many presets as possible, swapping them in and out of the 32 RAM memory locations via 32 program RAM cartridges, and later other MIDI devices and librarians. It is not uncommon to find people selling DX7 preset libraries online containing more than 10,000 presets for about $20 or so. Brian Eno is often cited as one of the few musicians who was good at programming the DX7 back in the day, but what is often left out of that story is that he had one of only 25 Jellinghaus DX programmers—huge, custom-built devices that offered a knob for every parameter.

Sonicstate.com interviewed Roger O'Donnell of The Cure about his thoughts on the DX7 and its place in synthesizer history. O'Donnell said, "I think it did irreparable harm to keyboards and keyboard players for a whole generation of keyboard players, and to programmability, and it led to a generation of keyboard players that didn't know how to program a synth. In fact, even now, I think it is still guilty." Fortunately for us, the power of FM synthesis now exists with more user-friendly software interfaces such as NI's emulation of the DX7, the FM7 and its current successor FM8, Ableton's Operator, and Logic's EFM1.

> **NOTE:** Figure 6.6, found at the very end of this chapter, shows significant connections between the people and topics just discussed with other parts of this chapter and the one that follows.

Presets, Complexification, and Proliferation

Synth presets really took off in 1983 with the DX7, but effect presets turned a corner a few years later in 1986. That year, the market was introduced to landmark multi-effect rackmount units like the legendary Eventide H3000, with its raw power and breakthroughs in pitch-shifting, and the first multi-effect box under $1,000, the Alesis MIDIverb. Due to the sheer volume and complexity of parameter combinations in these new multi-effect units, presets were as much a necessity as a convenience. We can consider this evolution of presets in the context of the technological advances of the last 40 years, and the simultaneous L-system branchings of evolving genres (as illustrated in Figure 1.6, and on the cover). As you may recall from the sidebar in the introduction, *complexification* refers to the increasing complexity of evolving systems as they include other systems as their component parts, which results in an overall simplification of system function but with a more complex structure. Does this not perfectly explain how presets started small, few, and simple to become what they are today? For example, many more people can easily use expertly programmed multi-effect configurations through a few simple commands, even though most of them have no idea how to reconstruct the settings if needed.

An increasing profusion of musical genres and styles became notable in the 1970s, but it was not really until the late 1980s that electronic music's penchant for incessant micro differentiation emerged as one of its defining characteristics (as discussed in Chapter 1). These persistent, continual, unrelenting bifurcations finally made it untenable to keep track of every genre and sub-genre by the late 1990s. Most new genres are essentially a novel mixture of elements from all of those classic genres. Then and now, producers desire the sounds from each of those genres, which are often possible only with specific pieces of equipment—unless you know how to analyze and mimic sounds or collect presets created by sound designers with those skills. By the late 1990s, not only were effect and synth presets everywhere, but there was also a similar proliferation of complete pattern sequences and demo songs. In 1996, two notable products hit the market: Roland's MC-303 Groovebox and Propellerhead's first product with its name on it, ReBirth-338 (as a public *alpha* version). Whole preset sequences from these products were even used in released club tracks with no more than very minor changes to them.

As we will discuss in Chapter 8, there is a feedback loop between producers and musicians and the companies that make products for that market. The increasing sophistication and complexity visible in the evolution of equipment, productions, sound design, genres, and styles are demonstrative of this positive feedback loop. Sounding like contemporary influences is a much more complex undertaking that it was a few decades ago. In addition to musical ideas and styles, the explosion of production techniques and timbral options means that it takes longer to learn how to do everything. Given this growing popularity and availability of increasingly sophisticated and technical music-production tools, it is no surprise that the influx of novice users demanded help with the learning curves in the form of presets—and the market obliged. Companies learned to add a lot of presets to satisfy a wide range of tastes. For many products, the wide variety of presets is intended to cover numerous situations, styles, genres, and aesthetics, so there is no way that any one person would find most of them useful. Occasionally, presets are added as a quickly thrown together afterthought, so users feel like they are getting their money's worth. Often, presets are created specifically to demo the capabilities of the devices, but just as likely to show off every bell and whistle in the hope that it will grab your attention in a crowded, cacophonous room of other potential customers at a gear shop or tradeshow.

In 2006, Native Instruments released Kore, which it touted as "the next step in the evolution of music production." Although the hardware component of that product was discontinued in 2011, the system it introduced for tagging and finding presets according to a number of useful criteria is now a standard feature on most every one of their virtual instrument products. Why did NI put so much effort into developing a feature set for finding presets in its products? The simple fact is, it often takes too much time to find useful presets, which are supposed to save time, because there are just too many of them. It appears that this explosion of presets was a natural process, and is therefore no one's fault. That said, most developers and manufacturers have certainly not helped the matter, nor have lazy, uninformed, or benignly novice musicians and producers who demand them in the first place. There must be some value in presets or we wouldn't have so many of them. Like many complex aspects of modern life, presets are not simply good or bad, so the goal is to mindfully and skillfully approach and utilize them.

Presets being so ubiquitous and of such variety are a complex topic. They can be your best friend or your worst enemy. They are your best friend when you take the time to develop your own libraries and favorites lists. Because factory presets are largely generic, uninspired, and/ or out of date, they are generally useless, a source of distractions, and a waste of time to deal with in the middle of a creative or productive session. There are a few exceptions to the latter, especially when they are by companies that specialize in sound design. Either way, there are often diamonds in the rough, so it is worth taking the time every so often to figure which ones you might actually like. During sound-design sessions, pre-sorted factory presets can serve as starting points for your user presets, and can be valuable learning tools, too. On that last point, it is important to realize that learning how to competently and quickly modify factory presets is a valuable skill, which is also the precursor to getting to a point where you can make your own from scratch if you so desire. Let's get specific and talk about issues related to a few common categories.

Presets: Synths and Sample-Based Instruments

Synth presets are most useful when they are yours, ones you've modified, or factory presets that you've singled out from the pack and saved to a favorites list. Factory presets are also useful when you want a specific sound in the style of a specific artist or other classic synth, assuming you can find them quickly. Some presets are equally great time-saving starting points that need only a few tweaks to work in your current session. When auditioning synth presets, hardware or software, the first rule is always to turn off all added effects so you can hear the sound dry, and therefore actually hear just the synthesis and its timbre. Sometimes the synth's built-in effects are integral to a preset's personality, but often they are just added to make the preset more exciting in isolation. Once added to a composition, there is no need for such embellishments. After hearing how the program really sounds, you can add the effects back to taste. Instead of using the synth's built-in effects, many producers actually prefer using higher quality plug-ins, especially those most fundamental to the mixing process: reverb, EQ, and compression.

Well-designed sampler presets are arguably the most useful of all presets. For starters, it is incredibly time-consuming to record, edit, and then map all of the samples needed for high-quality sample-based instruments. Moreover, they also allow you to access sounds from around the globe and equipment you can't find, afford, or fit in your studio. Often, sample instruments ship with a DAW as factory presets, and are functional at best. Usually, the best sample libraries are purchased from third-party sample specialists like SonArte, Soniccouture, East West, Detunized, and Puremagnetik, or bundled with the top sampler plug-ins like NI's Kontakt and Maschine, MOTU's MachFive, and Steinberg's Halion. There are prime examples of both DAW and plug-in makers licensing samples from specialist companies, such as many of Ableton's Live Packs that are bundled with the company's Suite option, or even the Vienna Symphonic Strings licensed by NI for Kontakt's factory library.

Presets: Effect and Signal Processors

Beyond your custom library, the most useful presets in this category are ones with very common uses, such as reverbs, de-essers, amp modelers, rhythmic delays, and specialty processors that remove hum, buzz, and other noises. They are also very useful to give you ideas on what is possible with complex multi-effect combinations or as starting points for your own ideas. It is amazing when you consider that the list of effects in every DAW represents more than 40 years of history. Many of us learned how to use them one at a time in the form of guitar pedals or rack gear before such lists became commonplace. Because it takes a long time to learn about all of the effects, trying them out with various presets on all sorts of audio material is a valuable learning experience.

The least useful factory presets are the ones related to essential aspects of mixing and mastering. In fact, the notion of a "mastering preset" is a perfect example of an oxymoron. Presets for EQ and compression are ballpark starting points at best, because every performer and recording is different. You will have to know how to adjust them in each case regardless, so unless most of them are your user presets, they are essentially worthless unless used for purely creative exploration. The one exception is when the preset is intended to mimic a specific piece of vintage or classic equipment, which implies you already know what you are going for in the first place.

Presets: Super Presets

Super presets are like Russian dolls. They are presets that are comprised of multiple nested smaller elements, each of which can usually have its own preset. Here I am referring to any number of features found in today's DAWs that group together numerous components, such as multiple plug-ins or devices, track mixer settings, complex routings, and possibly even sequences or recorded performances too. Reason's Combinator, Logic's Channel Strips, and Ableton's Racks and Live Clips are common examples of super presets. These features geometrically increase all the characteristics of presets we've discussed. They are that much more powerful and useful when they are of your own creation, and equally that much more of a time-sucking black hole when they are factory presets. As with all presets, if you are so inclined to explore these beasts, take the time to sift through them during your sound-design sessions so you can learn how they work. By far the best use of super presets is to take advantage of these powerful features as you create your own.

Good File Management = Saved from Destruction

Attention to detail: It only takes an extra minute to get it done right, but it takes hours to fix a mistake.

–Bob Katz

Computer and file maintenance is the least sexy part of what we do, but if you own a sports car and you never change the oil, your sports car will eventually stop working. One of the things that separates a true professional from a skilled amateur is how prepared that person is for unexpected problems. The computer is the nerve center of modern production systems, and the hard drives that store your files are the component most likely to fail. If you have not yet experienced a loss of data from a hard-drive problem, then you probably haven't been at this for very long (or you are so lucky that you should also be playing the lottery on a regular basis). With just a little bit of care, when a drive does crash, any data loss is minimal if not negligible. Because storage is now incredibly cheap, or even free in some cases, there is absolutely no excuse not to do regular backups, a topic we will return to in a few paragraphs.

> **NOTE:** A cautionary tale: I once knew an aspiring producer who lost a whole album's worth of unreleased material when a hard drive crashed because he never backed it up. He was convinced that this hard-drive crash, and corresponding loss of a few years of work, destroyed his career. He became very bitter and never recovered personally or professionally. Don't let this happen to you.

Hard-drive crashes are not the only source of data loss, at least when it comes to losing or misplacing files. Here, I am referring to how organized you are with files on your computer. I have lost count of how many times students or novice producers have handed me projects that were either an older incomplete version and/or missing files. In many cases, people save their projects to whatever random directory is presented to them, without taking the time to make sure it is the ideal location. The Documents folder in the user directory on your boot drive is not for Pro Tools sessions. The desktop is the most convenient place to save files for easy access, assuming that it is not completely covered and therefore essentially unusable, but you should use dedicated drives and folders for your projects. To keep the desktop useful, it should be cleaned up on a regular basis, and when it comes to active projects, on a daily basis. If project-related files end up on the desktop, be careful about manually moving around audio files used in sessions; it is best to have your audio apps manage them for you in most cases. For files unrelated to production, at least create a few folders on your desktop and put them there so the desktop is useable for keeping creative-productive sessions flowing. There is no one right way; just take the time and develop a system that works for you.

To give you some ideas, check out Figure 6.3, which is a screenshot from my Mac Pro tower. I like to keep different types of files on different drives and partitions. Not counting external drives, the Mac Pro has four drives installed, all of which have been partitioned except the one

Figure 6.3 Four hard drives, totaling 10 volumes. Each horizontal row is one physical drive. Only the one named "Time" has not been partitioned.

Source: Apple, Inc.

dedicated for Apple's Time Machine auto backup. With this setup, I am able to easily back up or recover different types of files. This system evolved over a few decades, so there is no need to go to the same extreme, but some of the basic concepts are relevant to anyone.

In Figure 6.3, Macintosh HD is the startup disk with the OS, which is for documents such as emails, Web bookmarks, or PDF manuals, any files that need to go in the system's folders such as plug-ins and drivers, and of course apps in the Applications folder. If another drive or partition crashes, it does not take down the OS. Also, on a different drive, I have another OS installed on one of the partitions (Stuff) so I can run repair and recovery apps like Alsoft's DiskWarrior, and also so I can test out a new OS before committing to an upgrade. When it comes time to upgrade the operating system, a clean install is much easier, because there is much less to back up before doing so. iTunes' library has its own partition. The libraries partition is for large factory libraries, such as for NI Komplete, NI Maschine, Ableton Live, or any other sizeable sample libraries. My personal projects get their own partition (Verity), as do all of the miscellaneous loop and sound-effects libraries (DSP), and another partition is dedicated to any variety of temp or cache folders used by audio apps (Media). Client projects are on yet another partition (XZ) until they are archived (as discussed momentarily).

In addition, installers, manuals, and other documentation related to production software each get their own place somewhere in that mix. I also recommend using an app that keeps a catalog of your drive's contents. After a crash, you will know what was on the drive and be able to determine if you have backups of those files, and whether or not it is worth paying for data recovery. Less than three days after taking the screenshot for Figure 6.3, the drive with three partitions (DSP, Media, Stuff) crashed, and it was not backed up using Time Machine (though most of the files were backed up manually). Because I use DiskTracker, I was easily able to determine what was lost and what I could recover from backups. Fortunately, that drive contained the least important files, most of which were recoverable, and if not, no more than a minor disappointment or inconvenience.

Partitioning drives is a good idea in general, but especially on laptops because they usually have just one internal drive and it is not always practical to have your external drives connected. Keeping projects and audio files separate from the OS has numerous advantages. Ideally, you should partition the drive before installing anything on it. With a PC, this is a bit more complicated, because many of them do not include a system restore disk. With any Mac, just boot from the system restore disk, restart, launch Disk Utility, partition the drive, and then reinstall the OS. If you already have a ton of stuff on the drive, you need to properly back everything up before partitioning; and so you don't have to reinstall the OS, use solutions that do cloning, such as Bombich's Carbon Copy Cloner on OS X or Acronis' True Image on PC.

Figure 6.4 shows the partition scheme on my Mac Book Pro. Notice that the Mac HD with the OS is not the top partition. The outside of the drive is faster than the inner sectors, so I created a small Fast partition for performance purposes. (With solid-state drives, partitions

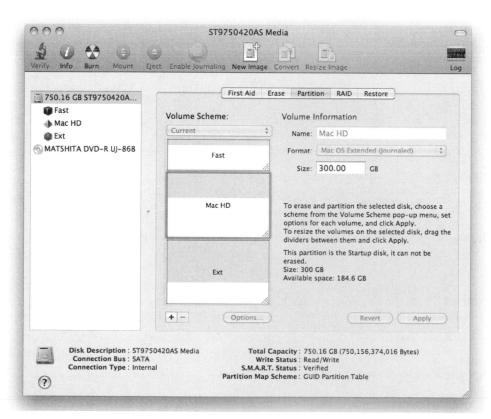

Figure 6.4 Apple's Disk Utility Partition tab. Notice that the top-most partition is labeled "Fast," since it will be a bit faster than the others. On Windows, use Disk Management.

Source: Apple, Inc.

generally are not necessary for speed, only organizational purposes.) If you have a laptop, you can set up automatic backup over WiFi with Time Machine or another network attached storage (NAS) solution. For my laptop, which is not my primary work computer, I just plug in a cheap USB drive every few days and let Time Machine do its thing. (When I upgraded from the factory 250 GB 5,400 RPM drive to a 750 GB 7,200 RPM drive, I just popped the old drive in an external USB enclosure to use for backup.)

Do You Know Your Bits from Your Bytes?

Computers are digital, and they use binary code, which means all calculations are based on strings of ones and zeros. With 1 bit, there are two options: 2^1, 1 or 0. With 2 bits, or 2^2, there are four options: 00, 01, 10, and 11. Once you have 8 bits, or 2^8, there are 256 possible combinations, which is why old 8-bit video-game systems have only 256 possible colors for generating images. Someone decades ago determined that 8 bits offered enough options to make it the basis of another important functional measurement, the byte. So a byte is comprised of 8 bits. Leaving aside video games and audio files for now, bits and bytes are used in different specifications. When specifying data-transfer rates, we use bits, which are given in powers of 10. When talking about maximum capacity, whether hard drives, RAM, or DVD-ROMs, we use bytes, which are given in powers of 2. So don't confuse your bits with your bytes, as is commonly done even by novice bloggers reporting new technologies.

- ▶ K (kilo) = thousand
- ▶ Kb (kilobit), 10^3 = 1,000 bits
- ▶ KB (kilobyte), 2^{10} = 1,024 bytes
- ▶ M (mega) = million
- ▶ Mb (megabit), 10^6 = 1,000,000 bits
- ▶ MB (megabyte), 2^{20} = 1,048,576 bytes
- ▶ G (giga) = billion
- ▶ Gb (gigabit), 10^9 = 1,000,000,000 bits
- ▶ GB (gigabyte), 2^{30} = 1,073,741,824 bytes
- ▶ T (tera) = trillion
- ▶ Tb (terabit), 10^{12} = 1,000,000,000,000 bits
- ▶ TB (terabyte), 2^{40} = 1,099,511,627,776 bytes

So if you mistake 1 Gb (1,000,000,000 bits) to mean 1 GB (8,589,934,592 bits), then you are either over- or underestimating by 7,589,934,592 bits.

Do You Know Your RAM from Your ROM?

The IT Crowd is a brilliant BBC 4–produced sitcom that ran from 2006 to 2010. In an episode from the second season called "Dinner Party," a scene with the three main characters went as follows:

Jen (Katherine Parkinson) tells the two IT guys at her party:

> *If this evening is going to work in any way, you need to pretend to be normal people...yeah? Keep the conversation about things that would interest everybody. You know, nothing about memory, or RAM.*

The IT guys, Moss (Richard Ayoade) and Roy (Chris O'Dowd), snort and chuckle, and then Moss condescendingly proclaims:

> *Memory is RAM!*

You don't have to be a total nerd to find this bit funny, not only because the actors themselves are hilarious, but mainly because anyone who is highly computer literate has had a similar discussion with their non–tech savvy family members or friends at some point.

- ▶ **RAM:** RAM is random access memory, also known as volatile memory. It is the temporary workspace for active processes such as your OS and open applications. When you shut off the computer, the data in RAM is cleared out.
- ▶ **Storage:** Your hard drive is electromagnetic storage, not memory. Writable CD-R or DVD-R are optical storage, not memory. The hard drive stores all the files that contain your data or commands that are loaded into RAM when you boot up or launch an app.
- ▶ **ROM:** ROM is read-only memory, also known as non-volatile memory. The simplest example of ROM is a DVD or CD. You can play it back, but not change its contents. Your computer's motherboard has a ROM chip on it

(often known as a "BIOS"), so when you power up it has permanent instructions that tell it to load the OS into RAM. ROM chips are also employed for "permanent" presets and other factory files in hardware instruments, which you cannot swap out. The term "firmware" refers to non-volatile memory that can be updated by the manufacturer or with files they supply, most commonly some form of ROM or what is known as "flash memory."

As flash drives (USB "thumb drives"), solid-state drives, fusion drives, and hybrid drives become more and more common, and new technologies like holographic storage hit the market, the physical differences between RAM, ROM, and storage will blur and change, but for now the basic concepts are still good.

Saving, Backing Up, and Archiving

Developing good organizational habits and following best practices at every step in the production process might seem like a waste of time, especially at the very beginning. While it is not necessary to be as strict about your methods as an archiver working at the Library of Congress, making sure to consistently do those few extra steps will ultimately save you time, increase productivity, and help you avoid frustration, confusion, and possible disaster. Let's start at the beginning.

What's in a Name?

Computer files have a lot of attributes, and the single most obvious one that they all share is name. How else do we know which ones we need to open, back up, copy, delete, find, upload, email, or otherwise? So from the start, always think about how you name new files or any elements within your files that need a name. It is okay to develop your own system of naming conventions, as long as they are logical and make sense. A name given to a project containing just a few cool ideas, with its inception taking place at 4 a.m., might make sense at that time, but in a folder of many such projects, will it make sense in a few days, weeks, or even months? If you are interested, there are various industry-recommended naming conventions, such as guidelines for producers and engineers as found in the Recording Academy section of www.grammy.org.

Always name the tracks in your DAW. Not only do clips and regions get their name from the track, but more importantly, so do new audio files. When searching for a missing audio recording, it is not very useful to have to sift through multiple files with names like Audio 1_01.wav or 0001 11-Audio.wav. If you do forget to name a track, no biggie. You can sort out the names as soon as it makes sense. Just be sure to do the renaming from within that session in your DAW, not the Finder or Explorer. Otherwise, the next time you open that session, you will be greeted with some sort of dialog box asking you to locate Audio 1_01.wav. In addition to proliferate naming habits, it is also recommended that you keep notes, whether using native features such as Pro Tools' Comments, Live's Info Text, Logic's Notes, and/or a text doc in the folder with the project.

Saving, Exporting, Rendering

When you launch an application, it loads into RAM. When you open a document in that app, it loads into RAM. When you make changes to a document, those changes are not written from RAM to the hard disk until you save them. Most audio apps can automatically save backup versions for you or have a way to recover unsaved changes from a crash, but it is not a good idea to rely on those features. Every time you've done so much work that having to redo it would either be impossible or highly undesirable, it is time to save. Make hitting Command+S (Mac) or Ctrl+S (PC) an unconscious habit.

There are times when a simple save is insufficient. It is also a really good idea to regularly take advantage of the equally ubiquitous Save As command. There are a number of reasons to have a version history in the form of multiple files:

▷ In case you ever need to retrace your steps, which is common.
▷ If you deleted or modified something, you can import it from an older version.
▷ If a session file somehow gets corrupted, you don't lose a lot of work, if any.

Figure 6.5 shows the structure of a few folders and sessions that illustrate this technique.

Whenever you are bouncing, exporting, or rendering a finished mix, stems, or just pieces of a project, take the time to think through where everything should go. Creating folders in the main project folder is always a good idea, or you can set up one central folder for all of your mixes. Either way, take the same care as when first saving new projects when outputting files from them. Figure 6.5 is also an example of how you might approach organizing folders and files for different types of projects.

Backing Up

Backing up means that there are recent copies of all important files on another hard drive. While a DAW's auto backup or File menu Save As features are important and useful, they are worthless if the whole hard drive crashes. The hope is that you never need to use your backups, but if and when you do, you will be really happy that they are there and current. Apple's built-in Time Machine feature is a great way to easily back up your files. As discussed, and as visible in Figure 6.3, there is a 1 TB drive in my Mac Pro dedicated to this feature.

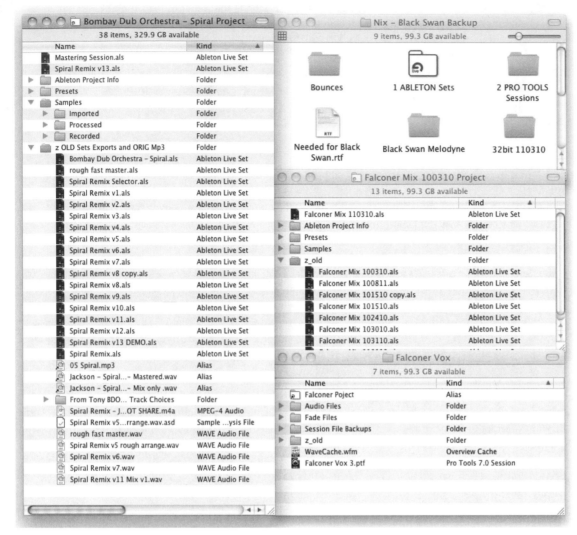

Figure 6.5 Here you can see a few examples of how one might organize a few different types of projects, including a remix and an album produced for another artist.

Source: Apple, Inc.

I don't wait for it to run automatically; I tell it to run as soon as there are enough new files or changes to existing ones to make one reel at the idea of having to redo them. Another advantage of Time Machine is that it can restore your whole boot drive should there be a hard-drive crash. You will want to also have a bootable clone of your startup drive, so if you are on a PC or don't want to use Time Machine, there are a number of other products that can handle automatic backups for you.

In addition to backups on additional drives in your studio, online file storage is an increasingly popular and robust option. It was not that long ago that online backup meant having an FTP server and dealing with very slow upload speeds. It is also worth looking into options such as Gobbler, Dropbox, and Google Drive, since you use them not only for backing up important files, but also for exchanging files with collaborators and clients. Even in the early years of the last decade, it was either impossible or extremely expensive to have Internet speeds up to the task of backing up many gigabytes of data on a daily basis. It is now common for residential Internet to offer download speeds up to 50 Mbps and upload speeds of 15 Mbps. As of 2011, Internet 2.0 is running at speeds of 186 Gbps, but is only available to research institutions, such as select universities and places like CERN (as was the original ARPAnet before becoming the Internet). The driving force behind this advancement is CERN's LHC project, which regularly generates many terabytes of data that needs to be shared with other scientists spread around the globe. To put that in perspective, in 2013, the fastest consumer internal SATA interfaces ran at 6 Gbps, with the fastest hard drives themselves reading at about 4 Gbps. In other words, they move data around the globe faster than you copy files from one hard drive to another in your personal computer. It is only a matter of time before we have cheap access to such systems, finally making online backup commonplace for large projects.

Don't forget about your hardware. Back up your presets on those devices, too. Many new ones that connect to your computer with USB have plug-ins or editors/librarians that make it easy to place files on your hard drive. With most any MIDI device, including those without some sort of editor software or ones with old school 5-pin DIN connections, you have to learn how to save them as a SysEx MIDI file. Although it sounds more like the result of too much fiber in your diet, this is commonly accomplished by recording a "bulk dump" onto a MIDI track in your DAW. If you have two of the same devices, make sure to give them each a unique System Exclusive ID, usually found in global settings. This way, you won't accidentally write over presets. Hardware settings are also considerations when it comes to archiving completed projects.

Archiving

Archiving means long-term storage. This is a career unto itself at places like the Library of Congress, the Smithsonian, Pixar, and Lucasfilm. When a project is completed, there is no need to keep it on your work drives. Yet, simply moving all of the files to another drive is not archiving for a number of reasons. You need to take into account what needs to be done so that you will be able to access the project years in the future. Will you still have Pro Tools, Cubase, Sonar, Reaper, or Logic in five, 10, or 20 years? Will you have all of the same plug-ins or hardware synths central to the production? Will the lubricant in the drive dry out and freeze up the moving parts?

In short, to properly archive projects, even minimally at the home-studio level, it is necessary to have simple audio files for all external MIDI instruments, virtual instruments, and any other plug-in–dependent sounds. For even longer-term considerations, every individual track should end up as a WAV file, all of which start at the same time so they can be easily lined up and reconstructed in a different DAW. Some studios even keep old devices and computers around in an archiving room so they can access old projects and software if need be. When it comes to storing the archived files, you can't just throw a hard drive in a closet and then forget about it. It must be stored at the right temperature and humidity, and will have to be checked and migrated every so often. If you want to minimize temperature and humidity considerations, optical storage can be a good home-studio archiving system. Name-brand DVD-R discs, if stored properly, standing upright in their own case, supposedly have a shelf life of 50 years. If you are serious about it, look into "archival grade" disks that are rated for up to 200 years! Utilities like Toast (Mac) and Nero (PC) can span projects across multiple disks so you don't have to figure that out for yourself. Just make sure to write the correct names on the media, with a Sharpie or other soft-tip marker.

Transferring

Moving projects from one computer to another requires attention to detail. Make sure you have properly copied all of the files to the new drive. Often, when you open up projects on your computer, everything will be fine because your DAW is able to play files from different drives, but when you get to the other studio, you are greeted with any variety of missing file dialog boxes. Figure out how to double-check that all files are copied into the right folders before you learn the hard way. Most software has features to do this for you, but you have to know to take advantage of such options.

Figure 6.5 shows how all the files and folders used in a project are located in central folders, so it is very easy to transfer individual songs or whole projects from one drive to another. The window on the left shows the contents of a folder dedicated to one remix. The three windows on the right show contents from different parts of a whole project. The top-right folder contains all of the folders for the multi-song project, the middle-right is for one of the songs, and the bottom-right is for the Pro Tools session that was used just for recording and comping vocals before flying them back into the Ableton set with the rest of the composition.

Upgrades and Updates

We regularly have to deal with upgrades and updates to operating systems, security patches, OS extensions/libraries, applications, plug-ins, drivers, and even firmware (rewritable ROM in some hardware). For a functioning, stable production environment, all of these components need to be compatible with each other. It is not fun when there are bugs or incompatibilities between components. Sometimes, updates or upgrades address these problems, and sometimes they offer new features and improved functionality. Yet, it is a mistake to assume that upgrading or updating always yields improvements. Before discussing important issues on this topic, let's first make sure that everyone is clear on the difference between an upgrade and an update.

To understand the basic difference between an upgrade and an update, let's talk about version numbers (but leave aside issues related to free or paid). Generally speaking, for example, it is an up*grade* to go from App X 1.0 to App X 2.0. It is an up*date* to go from App X 2.0 to App X 2.0.1 or App X 2.1. The term "point release" generally refers to an incremental update from version X.0 to X.1, while a "bug-fix release" generally refers to an incremental update from X.0 to X.0.1. So-called point releases usually include bug fixes but often also include other minor changes or enhancements, while the bug-fix releases are usually just to fix bugs or address minor feature improvements.

Not all updates and upgrades are created equal. There are hierarchies of importance that have a cascading effect on other components. Let's consider them from most fundamental to the least.

▷ **Operating system:** Your operating system determines compatibility more than any other component of your system. This includes your desktop and laptop computers, but also other hardware such as MIDI controllers, synthesizers, and tablets. Any change in the OS means that developers need to update their products to ensure compatibility. Even a simple point-release update can have big implications that cascade through your system.

▷ **Drivers and firmware:** From MIDI controllers to audio interfaces, the drivers need to be compatible with your OS. Sometimes, before you can use one of these devices with an OS, you need to update the device's OS, which might also first require a firmware update. Do not update or upgrade your hardware's OS or firmware unless the manufacturer requires it so their drivers will work with your OS. Firmware upgrades and updates are not to be taken lightly. Read all instructions very carefully.

▷ **Applications:** Your audio apps have basic system requirements, which include compatible operating systems. Make sure your DAW and other crucial production apps will work with your OS. Before updating or upgrading the OS, check with each developer to see if they support the latest and (supposedly) greatest versions. Apps and drivers can more or less be considered of equal importance in terms of updates and upgrades.

▷ **Plug-ins:** Just like your apps, plug-ins and other utilities are dependent on certain versions of the app and OS. Always check the release notes before updating or upgrading your plug-ins.

Backward compatibility is an important consideration, especially for compatibility with collaborators and clients, or if you are ever forced to do a downgrade (reverting to an older version of an app, plug-in, or OS). Developers approach their file formats in different ways. Some apps are designed so that even older versions can open files created on new versions of the software. For example, Pro Tools has features specifically designed to make sure that most any version can open documents created on any other version. In other words, Pro Tools 7 can open sessions created with Pro Tools 9, without any extra steps. If you are using Pro Tools 10, then all you have to do is change the session format to the appropriate older format from the Save Copy In command, accessible from the File menu. Logic is also quite good at backward compatibility, as are many other DAWs. On the flipside, some apps can only open docs created with current or older versions, such as Live and Reason. For example, a document created with Live 9 cannot be opened in Live 8, nor can a document created with Reason 6 be opened in Reason 5. File-format compatibility was the single biggest source of outrage when Apple released Final Cut X, which cannot even open projects created with older versions of Final Cut Pro! With such apps, it is a good idea to keep previous versions of the app on your HD if possible, and then take care to open projects in the appropriate version so you and your collaborators can keep going with minimal version-related snags.

Never Upgrade in the Middle of a Project!

I repeat, never upgrade in the middle of a project. There are a few rare occasions that it is absolutely necessary, such as when your computer dies and you procure a replacement that is running a newer OS. Seriously, a simple point release can wreak havoc, so even when it comes to seemingly minor updates, unless they address a specific bug that is causing you significant issues, avoid updates in the middle of a project. It is normal, and even recommended, that you skip updates until they've been out for a while and are known to be stable and compatible with your current setup. Always read the release notes and check the chatter on forums. If relevant, turn off automatic updates so you can decide on a case-by-case basis.

There is a big difference between keeping up on the latest and greatest in your industry and actually trying to always have all of it installed on your primary workstation. It is very common for studios and other professionals to be a few months, or even years, behind. When everything is working and stable, try to keep it that way as long as possible, and plan ahead for periods of downtime before making major changes. If you want to keep up on the all the latest stuff, simply create another boot drive, and install software that needs to be tested for compatibility with a new OS on that drive.

To make life easier, develop a system to keep track of all your software account logins, serial numbers, and installers. Keep everything in one folder, or even in a text doc that you sync with a cloud service so it is accessible from any computer or mobile device. Before performing a major upgrade, start collecting all the necessary updates and upgrades so you don't have to track everything down all at once. For example, create a folder for drivers and utilities that are OS specific, including your current one.

Synths, Samplers, and Sound Modules/ROMplers

Can you easily explain the difference between these three types of electronic instruments? In many cases, they have so much in common with each other that there is no obvious difference. Yet, it is very important to understand the differences for file-management purposes, which minimally includes issues pertaining to backing up, archiving, and transferring files. Generally speaking, the difference is in how the initial sound is generated and therefore how presets and linked files are managed. Keep in mind that some devices and plug-ins utilize combinations of synthesis, sampling, and ROM-based sample playback.

▷ **Synthesizers:** Synths use oscillators to generate audio signals with either analog circuits or digital algorithms. Synth presets, then, are simply snapshots of the settings, which means there are no audio files to manage. There are a few exceptions to the latter point if the oscillators are capable of resynthesis, most commonly granular or spectral resynthesis, such as found in NI's Absynth or Camel Audio's Alchemy.

▷ **Samplers:** Samplers use audio files that are loaded into RAM as their sound source. In the case of most software samplers, just a small percentage at the beginning of each sample is loaded into RAM, and the rest is streamed from the hard drive, making it possible to play back enormous sample libraries not possible in hardware. These samples might come from the manufacturer, a third-party library, or your very own recordings. Sampler presets are basically a mapping file and also the audio files with their directory paths, much like a DAW project includes the session file that maps to the audio files on the hard drives. So when you save a sampler preset, you additionally have to make sure that all of the audio files are also managed. Most software samplers give you options for collecting samples along with the setting file. Just make sure to read up on this topic in your sampler's manual, and also possibly your DAW's manual if the sampler is built-in, such as Logic's EXS24 or Live's Sampler. Just as you want to copy project folders from one drive to another, not just the session file (e.g., PTX, RSN, ALS, etc.), you need to do the same with your sampler's project files (e.g., NKI, ADG, MPRJ, EXS, etc.).

▷ **Sound modules and ROMplers:** These are the hardware and software versions of the same sort of instrument. Sound modules store manufacturer-recorded audio files in ROM chips, and ROMplers are plug-ins that come with a fixed sound library. In other words, they are like samplers in that they play back pre-recorded audio files, but they are different in that they can only play back files provided by the manufacturer or third party in the appropriate format. Sound modules peaked in popularity in the 1990s, when there were dozens of them to choose from, such as the very popular Roland XV series or ones from E-mu and Ensoniq, most of which now sell for no more than 10 percent of their original cost. To add more sounds, you either purchased an expansion board from the manufacturer or bought another module. Hardware-based ROM playback is now most commonly found in hybrid devices such as drum machines or in workstations like the Korg Triton, Yamaha Motif, or Roland Fantom. ROMplers are often third-party sample libraries that run in popular software samplers, but commonly ship with their own plug-in interface, such as Vienna Symphonic Library's Vienna Dimension Strings or East West's Fab Four.

Opcode, Max, OMS, AMS, Apple, and Cycling '74.: Nowadays, the choice of Mac or PC for music production largely comes down to subjective preferences. In the 1990s, there were many significant, objective criteria that put Macs far in the lead. The perfect illustration is exemplified in a Mac application known as OMS (1990–1999). OMS was included in a list of the top technological achievements in our industry from 1975–2000 in *Keyboard* magazine's 25th anniversary edition (2000).

By the 1990s, Silicon Valley's Opcode Systems had established itself as a major player in the emerging personal computer–based music-production software market. Opcode was known for its powerful and innovative sequencing software and patch editor/librarian duo, Vision and Galaxy. Galaxy started out as a DX7 programmer licensed from David Zicarelli (future founder of Cycling '74) in 1986. In 1989, Opcode licensed the relatively new software MIDI patching environment Max from IRCAM. In 1990, Vision became Studio Vision, and in tandem with hardware from Digidesign, was the first personal computer system to combine Audio and MIDI recording and editing in one app. Opcode also made arguably the best MIDI interfaces.

Prior to Mac OS 10.2 (2002), no consumer operating system included native features for handling MIDI, specifically in regard to how different pieces of software could interact with MIDI interfaces and connected devices, let alone talk to each other internally. That meant if you had a MIDI interface with five different devices connected, you would have to go through a setup process with every piece of software that you wanted to use with that hardware. Moreover, if you wanted to send MIDI from one piece of software to another, you had to go out of the interface to MIDI cables and then back in another port on the interface. To address this shortcoming, Opcode, a Mac-only developer, created OMS, which originally stood for Opcode Music System and then Open Music System. OMS was an application that recognized the MIDI interface and allowed you to graphically specify which devices were connected to which ports, and moreover, any relevant settings. If an app was OMS compatible, it would find your setup there and save you a bunch of steps and time. It also included virtual MIDI ports that allowed one app to send data to another app directly, which was called the IAC (inter-application communication) bus. By the mid-1990s, OMS was essentially industry-standard freeware on the Mac. Nearly every major commercial software title with MIDI functionality was OMS compatible.

In 1998, Gibson Guitar Corporation bought Opcode. At first, there was a lot of optimism and excitement in the community, as users hoped this would equate to more resources for Opcode products. The exact opposite occurred. Gibson shelved everything. By 1999, all development on Opcode products ended, never to see the light of day again. Public pressure mounted for Gibson to make OMS open source, which even included a letter to Gibson's CEO from OMS's creator at Opcode, Doug Wyatt. By the 2000 Winter NAMM show in Los Angeles, Gibson's intent to do nothing with its new assets was clear, and the "Save OMS" buttons handed out there by SaveOMS.org would become no more than historical mementos. Not one of Opcode's product's continued past the Gibson purchase, with one exception. Because Max was just licensed by Opcode from IRCAM, and MSP creator David Zicarelli had actually been maintaining and releasing Max since the late 1980s, he was able to eventually take over full control of Max, culminating with the first Cycling '74–branded version in 2000.

At the time OMS ceased development (1998), Apple was in the midst of transitioning to its new UNIX-based OS X. For a few years, most of us stayed on the final version of OS 9, until OS X's new Core Audio and Core MIDI functionality matured sufficiently (circa 2002–2003). The Audio MIDI Setup (AMS) utility that is on every OS X–era Mac is how we access this Core Audio and Core MIDI functionality. If you are thinking that AMS seems similar to how I described OMS, you are correct. While working at Opcode, Doug Wyatt created OMS. After Opcode's demise, Apple hired him to architect these new core-level features in OS X. In short, the same person who programmed OMS at Opcode in 1990 was one of the key developers for Apple's AMS a decade later.

Figure 6.6 shows how these topics connect and relate to other topics in this chapter and book.

Things You Should Know

There are many things we all need to know, but here are a few that will step up your knowledge and results really fast. Much of this section overlaps with topics covered in Chapter 4 and Chapter 8. The following topics could easily be their own chapter, and there are many more things you should know that are not covered. That said, these are key issues relevant computer-centric music production.

Listen

One of the big advantages of producing music with a computer is that you have a lot of visual information at your disposal, whether editing audio or MIDI, looking for files and sounds, or quickly accessing a huge variety of tools on a whim. When it comes time to sit back and give your work a listen, however, it is easy to keep staring at the screen. The assortment of visual information, such as metering, grid lines, or any geometric patterns made by a variety of software objects will color your perceptions. It is best to not see any of your work or edits, and at most to have a counter visible so you can make notes. Many producers and engineers come up with ways to do this. It can be as simple as setting up a sleep corner for your displays, enabling a blank screen saver, or using an empty text document as the front-most app. Often, you will want to take notes, so having some sort of min:sec or bar:beat counter is all you want to see. Most DAWs have customizable floating counter windows, and there is also an assortment of freeware plug-ins floating around for such purposes.

If you use Pro Tools, check out the free, unsupported Massey Tools by Steve Massey (Massey Plug-ins), which includes Listen. Steve describes this utility as "the opposite of a meter plug-in. Will dramatically improve your mixes!!" If you use Max For Live, check out Monolake's free Black device, which Robert Henke describes as follows: "It displays songtime in hours:minutes:seconds…. And it allows you to black out the computer screen while listening to the music, which I find sometimes very important." Both of these are easily found with a simple Web search.

Avoid Distractions When Working

It is really important that you and your collaborators give your full attention to the production process, whether in full-on creative mode, tracking well-rehearsed songs, or organizing session files. Unless you are working in a busy commercial studio, or have questionable Internet habits, it is not necessary to stress about having a "clean" audio computer that is not connected to the Internet. That said, your computer should be configured so it does not interrupt or distract you. Quit any apps and background processes that are not needed for making music or otherwise working on the project. Because phones are basically computers these days, make sure to put yours out of sight, and turn off all notification sounds. Only look at your phone when taking a break or when you are expecting a call or message related to the session. Figure out a way for people to get a hold of you in case of emergencies so you know when it is a call you have to take, perhaps with a dedicated VOIP line that is just for such occasions. Nothing says unprofessional like a cell-phone ringer bleeding into a recording.

Having a home studio is very convenient, but there are a lot of distractions. Make sure you figure out a way to either physically or psychologically isolate your workspace from the rest of your place. Some people find that they need to move their studio to a dedicated space to ensure focus. For a lot of us, avoiding distractions is nearly impossible on certain days and at certain times, which is why a lot of creative people like to work either very early in the morning or very late at night. I find that I am most productive during the day, but most creative late at night when the city is quiet, the phone and doorbell are not ringing, and there are no emails coming in that require my attention. It is no surprise that a lot of musicians and artists are late-night people, but it is not uncommon to find mixing and mastering engineers who are get-up-at-the-crack-of-dawn types. Each of us has different thresholds and abilities to maintain focus in different environments, so just figure out what works best for you and your clients and collaborators.

If It's Not Broken...

This topic includes the discussion found earlier in the section on updates and upgrades. If everything is working fine, then think twice about trying to improve something that doesn't need to be improved. But the idea here goes even further and gets at the all-too-common desire for more gear, plug-ins, samples, and the like. Chapter 8 spends a good amount of time talking about selecting a DAW and other tools, and how modern production software is incredibly powerful and full-featured. The steep learning curves combined with Internet buzz can lead one to think that frustrations are solved with another app or plug-in. Sometimes this is the case, but often it is a matter of patience and practice, so don't keep switching or adding tools unless there is a good reason. If you are productive with your current setup, think twice about making a major change until you have some downtime.

Less Is More

One of the most common characteristics of new producers is a tendency to compensate for lack of skill or experience by adding more parts, tracks, layers, or effects. If a song lacks emotional or sonic impact, adding more of any of the above should not be your first instinct. Yes, sometimes you need another part or sound to take a song to the next level, but if the core essence of the composition is weak, usually the effort should go into improving that core. The concept here scales relatively to the genre and style, such that whether the goal is a dense, textural, layered composition or one that is sparse and minimal, odds are that there is something already there that can be improved without the need to add more.

In the case of weak samples or recordings, instead of layering more sounds or going to town with EQ and compression, learn how to select better quality sounds and improve your recordings. When you have no option but to use what you have, learn to use less compression and more subtractive EQing. In other words, cut out what you don't want to hear as much of before you turn up what you want to hear more of. If you are concerned with loud and competitive yet dynamically rich and punchy masters, then the idea of "less is more" is not just a philosophical approach, but an actual technical necessity. In digital audio, the highest encodable level is always, without exception, 0 dB FS.

Bass

Bass is tricky for a number of reasons: acoustic, psychoacoustic, and headroom limitations in electronic devices. When compared to mid-range and most higher frequencies, low frequencies require more power and headroom to be as loud. The fine line between too much and not enough bass is only consistently drawn by experienced producers and engineers with suitable rooms and equipment. That said, there are a few considerations that will help everyone get closer to their goal. Imagine your production playing back on a giant system. What sounds are primarily driving the subwoofers? To get the best results, it should either be primarily the kick or primarily the bass line, not both equally. Think *focus*, *punch*, or *impact*, not just "more bass." Too much bass in the lowest frequencies (below 50 Hz or so) is rarely needed, as it just overworks the woofers and eats up headroom. This situation results in a muddier mix and/or masters that are not as naturally loud or overly limited to compensate. This is another example of less being more.

> **NOTE:** For a more detailed technical discussion on loudness and other issues pertaining to hearing, make sure to check out the "Protect Your Hearing" section in Chapter 9, including Figure 9.4.

Sound Selection and Voicing

One of the upsides of composing with electronic music-production tools is that we have most every sound and instrument available to us in an instant. One of the downsides of composing with electronic music production tools is that we have most every sound and instrument available to us in an instant. Experienced composers understand not only how to select their instruments but also what octaves are best for each part's performances. Consider the standard instrumentation of a professional rock band. The guitar and the bass guitar each sit in different ranges. Each of the components in the drum set also work in well-thought-out frequency ranges. It is much easier for each of these musicians to play parts that complement each other and fit well together in a mix than when an amateur composer arbitrarily picks sounds based their individual characteristics. To make your mixes easier and more clear, punchy, and impactful, make sure to consider the instrumentation and their voicings. Also, remember to leave room for the vocals! I highly recommend that you do a Web image search for "orchestra frequency chart" and also "future music frequency map," especially if these concepts are new to you.

Watch Your Levels

While there is no need to be all OCD at every stage of the creative process, watching levels is important throughout the production process, especially when recording audio. Even if working solely in the box with virtual instruments, it is important long before getting to mixing and mastering. There are numerous places for setting gain and volume in any signal path, essentially whenever you are dealing with electronic devices, whether analog or digital, hardware or software. For example, let's consider recording electric guitar. There is a volume knob on the guitar, a gain knob at the input of the amp, a volume knob at the output of the amp, often a pad switch on the mic, a gain knob at the input of the preamp, a volume knob at the output of the preamp, and likely also settings for the converters in the audio interface. With less-than-optimal settings, you either record a lot of amplified noise or unwanted clipping and distortion. While recording, there is the actual recording path, but also the monitoring path for the control room and the performer's headphone mix. Assuming a good recording, not only is there a volume control for every track, but also at the input and/or output of each plug-in, send, return, and more. Learn to keep an eye on things as you build up a project so you don't have a total mess on your hands when it comes time to mix. Finally, learn to turn down tracks and master faders, and then turn up the volume control on your interface or monitor controller for your speakers and headphones. All of these concepts take time to master as you build up your audio-engineering skills, but the basic idea is simple and can be applied immediately. If your compositions are already pretty strong, this tip alone can instantly help you step up your game.

The Art of Analysis

What do you like? Why do you like it? If you refer to Figure 4.1 in Chapter 4, you will see that ear training is in three of the "big four" production holons. One of the best things that all of us can do to keep current is to spend time analyzing music and sounds as part of our learning sessions. Import songs, stems, or even loops into your DAW. Matching the global tempo to that of the material's is very useful. Use your DAW's playback, tempo change, marker, editing, phase and spectrum analyzers, and processing features to help you isolate the parts you want to analyze. Do your best to copy melodies, harmonies, drum rhythms, and synth timbres. Put markers or locators at each place in a song when there is a change so you can learn about song structure and arranging. Bust out a pen and paper and write down what instruments you hear at those different sections, what effects are audible on them, where they are placed in the stereo field, and anything else you notice. Perhaps even create a couple of spreadsheets to help you keep track of all these elements. The more you do this, the easier it becomes to compose what you hear in your head, find sounds, and realize your ideas in general.

Tips and Tricks on the Internet

The Internet is an amazing resource that is a great benefit to us all. And just like anything on the Internet, there is a huge variance in accuracy and quality. Many people think tips and tricks are shortcuts to developing real skill. Sometimes these tips are useful, but sometimes they cause more confusion. A lot of people simply don't know what they are talking about or are not good at explaining what they are good at doing. Many of these problematic ideas, tips, or tutorials go through the Internet's meme-replicating echo chamber, and thus propagate to an extent that they become the source of common myths or outright falsehoods. Even if the information is accurate and well described, it is easy for a beginner to assume that it therefore must be important and something he or she needs to know right away. With regard to examples of the latter point, I refer you to the parody tutorials created by YEAHDubz on YouTube, such as the classic "LETS LERN how to MASTER!!" Through comedic satire, these faux-tutorials make fun of everything that is wrong with electronic music production tips and tricks on the Internet. There are a lot of good sources, so look for those with a consistent track record or better yet, people you know and trust. You might start by checking out www.groove3.com, www.macprovideo.com, www.music-production-guide.com, www.sonicacademy.com, and www.pensadosplace.tv/.

Regular Practice and Maintenance

Do something every day related to your craft, even if you are super busy with other work or obligations. You don't have to wait until you can find a few hours of dedicated time. Even just 15 minutes here and 20 minutes there is valuable and will add up. This point is even more important when learning something new that requires a lot of practice. Learning is not just about attention and retention; it also includes repetition, which is required for every major aspect of music production. All habits are hard to break, including the good ones. So it is in everyone's best interest to develop good habits pertaining to file management, gain structure, ear training, and anything else that is of daily importance to any aspect of music production.

Outro

Each of the topics covered in this chapter require attention and practice, whether interacting with groups of people in the studio or sitting by yourself in front of your computer. Navigating the preset jungle should also be a lot easier for you. Learning about file management, hard drives, and such may not be fun, but it is of fundamental importance. No matter how creative or talented you are, if you lose all of your files, you might as well just stick with performance and leave the production to others. Everything covered here is fundamental to being a skilled music producer, and will also help ensure smooth sailing when applying topics discussed in the next chapter.

NOTE: Figure 6.6 is referenced in multiple places throughout this chapter. All the connections represent direct, significant relationships. There are two exceptions, marked by arrows, which indicate a significant influence that was publicly stated by Stockhausen in his creation of Kontakte, and Stephan Schmitt in his creation of Reaktor. The few nodes that were not discussed in this chapter are covered in Chapter 7.

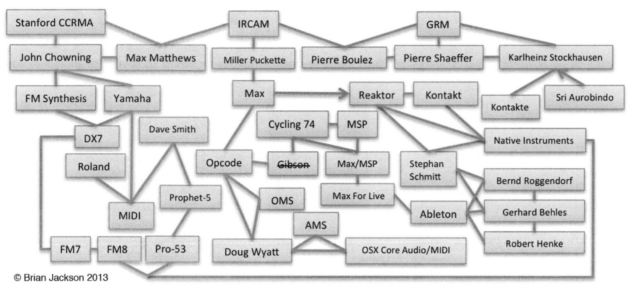

© Brian Jackson 2013

Figure 6.6 This chart shows significant connections between major players and products discussed in this chapter, with a few discussed in Chapter 7.

Creative Process

7

CREATIVITY AND CREATIVE PROCESS ARE AN INTEGRATION POINT FOR MANY OF THE TOPICS DISCUSSED THROUGHOUT THIS BOOK. A wide variety of subjects in this chapter approach creative process from many angles, with ideas and methods well suited to the naturally intuitive and analytically inclined. Philosophy, techniques, historical thinking, modern music production scenarios, nonsense, chance, dreams, gravity, granular synthesis, and LSD are just a few of our jump-off points. There is something in here for everyone.

A lot of the approaches to creative process are relevant to everyone, while others need to be framed within the context of a specific craft such as music and music production. With regard to the latter, a variety of situations and scenarios commonly emerge during each phase of the music-production process. Just as the last century gave us countless new technologies, techniques, and methodologies, so too did it create a parallel stream of creative philosophies, approaches, and techniques. Whether you are a solo electronic music producer or are working with other artists, it is highly likely that you are not the first one to bump into any given creative challenge. As discussed in Chapter 1, "Musica Universalis," one of electronic music's most significant innovations is creative process itself. Although all of the ideas and techniques are valuable to everyone, most of them emerged out of historically important *avant-garde* movements, so they are best suited to electronic musicians and adventurous producers.

I start this chapter with a general discussion on the nature of creativity before moving on to the section called "Being Creative." If you are not concerned with philosophical understandings of creativity, you might want to jump to the "20th Century Innovations" section, which gets into techniques and approaches pioneered by master artists. If that material is still too esoteric for you and you just want some practical ideas for music production, feel free to jump way ahead to "Practical Techniques." That being said, you will not find the following combination of material in any music production book, so starting from the top is highly recommended.

There Is Nothing That Is Not Creative

I can honestly say that creativity is not mysterious at all. I can equally honestly say that creativity is completely mysterious. You may think I am contradicting myself, such as to say that A is B and not B. The analytical mind ruled by the brain's left hemisphere is telling you that it is impossible, or at best it is a paradox, like M.C. Escher's famous drawing, *Drawing Hands* (1948), of two hands drawing each other. Surely if I expressed this notion in a Venn diagram, as found elsewhere in this book, I would see that something is illogical.

Charles Lutwidge Dodgson was an accomplished mathematician and logician before earning fame as the author of *Alice's Adventures in Wonderland* (1865) and *Through the Looking Glass* (1871), using the pseudonym Lewis Carroll. One of his many great characters is The Hatter. Back in his day, hatters were known to be a little kooky, or even outright insane. Later, it was learned this was caused by poisoning from the mercury that was used during the hat-making process. This is the origin of the colloquialism "mad as a hatter," which is why his character is commonly known as The Mad Hatter.

> *The Hatter: If I had a world of my own, everything would be nonsense. Nothing would be what it is, because everything would be what it isn't. And contrary wise, what is, it wouldn't be. And what it wouldn't be, it would. You see?*
>
> –Lewis Carroll

Dodgson was not only a very entertaining writer, he was also an exceptionally brilliant philosophical thinker. No matter how ridiculous a conclusion, technically speaking it is "logical" if it follows from the premise. Usually we can weigh the validity of an argument based on the truth of the premises, but Lewis Carroll created his own universe, so there is no measurement of objective truth to be had. When pushing against the boundaries of the logical, we often find the irrational staring back at us. Upon further scrutiny, one is confronted with the realization that we create our own mental boundaries as we use language to define our world. If you have a bit of training in the formal logic of philosophy, you might not be surprised to hear that Lewis Carroll may just have been proposing that everything and nothing are actually the same thing.

Those who are "mad" are not constrained by the construction of reality inherited by the socialization processes of one's culture. In fact, it is the dissolution of the perceived boundary between everything and nothing that may in fact lead to insanity…or creativity, or enlightenment. The relationships between social constructions of reality, insanity, creativity, non-ordinary states of consciousness, and spiritual experience are part of a long discourse dating back thousands of years, spanning many cultures, and filling up countless pages of text. As much as I would love to, I cannot go deeply into this rich terrain, but I will cover a few related topics in this chapter.

Before moving on, let me just leave you with one tidbit about insanity and enlightenment. During a transpersonal psychology course I took with Stan Grof in grad school, he shared a joke on the topic, which I paraphrase for you as follows:

Q: What is the difference between a psychotic and a mystic?

A: The mystic knows who not to talk to.

Dr. Stanislav Grof, PhD, M.D.: In 1955, Stan Grof was still a graduate student in psychiatry when he became one of the first people to receive LSD from Sandoz Labs, for early research on its potential uses for understanding schizophrenia and other psychological conditions. He is also one of the very first humans to experience a massive dose. After originally working in his home country of Czechoslovakia, he relocated to the U.S. in 1967 to become a professor of psychiatry at Johns Hopkins University, and later chief of psychiatric research at the Maryland Psychiatric Research Center. In 1973 he moved to Big Sur, California, where he was a scholar-in-residence at Esalen Institute until 1987. He co-founded the field of transpersonal psychology with Abraham Maslow in 1969, and founded the International Transpersonal Association (ITA) in 1977. He continues to write, teach, and train in the field of transpersonal psychology.

Unlimited Creativity, Limited Relevance

Most anyone can be productive or creative. Creativity is easy; it is the natural way of things. As you will see in the next section, an examination of our physical universe clearly shows that everything is part of a creative process. Creativity is usually associated with products that are judged by a consuming public. As such, it is to an artist's creativity that we pay the most attention, especially when it communicates something meaningful. It is relevant when that communication is a truth that captivates, resonates, inspires, affects, or connects to someone. Relevance to a person, or a few people, is not the same as relevance in the larger cultural context, which implies connecting to many people at the same time. Let's consider common definitions:

▷ **Creative:** Originative, imaginative, having the power to create or produce
▷ **Relevant:** Pertinent, applicable to the matter at hand, current
▷ **Innovative:** To introduce something new, using or showing novel ideas or methods, advanced, groundbreaking, inventive
▷ **Productive:** To produce, to generate, to make, to create, yielding results

If creativity is easy and relevance is challenging, then what about innovation? Innovation is closely connected with our common understanding of creativity, since it implies making something new. Novelty—in its truest meaning, not the pejorative—simply means new or original. And just as creativity is easy, so is novelty—thus the reason that word so often suggests cheapness. So innovation by itself is not necessarily special. Artists who are both creatively and critically successful are both innovative and relevant. Additionally, to make a career out of creativity, it is necessary to also be productive. Productivity is the most significant difference between being creative and being a creative professional.

Integration of Art and Science

Music production is both an art and a science. As 21st century music producers, we are technical-creative professionals. It is not uncommon to simultaneously be considering multiple decibel measurements or calculating delay times between microphones to avoid phase problems as we work out rhythms and melodies or choose from a variety of effects best suited to a particular singer during the second chorus. Unlike a painter, dancer, or traditional musician, our creative process is inexorably blended with sophisticated hi-tech tools. For the technical-creative professional, art and science go hand in hand. They are not separate.

Former NASA astronaut Mae Jemison is not only the first African-American woman to go into space, she is also a physician, a dancer, and an art collector with nine honorary doctorate degrees and an appearance on *Star Trek: The Next Generation*. Her February 2002 Technology, Entertainment, Design (TED) talk was about the importance of teaching arts and sciences together, the importance of intuition and logic, and a need to reintegrate science and the arts. Every bit of her 20-minute talk is worth quoting, but here is the central point:

> *The difference between science and the arts is not that they are different sides of the same coin...or even different parts of the same continuum, but rather, they are manifestations of the same thing....Let me say it again another way: Science provides an understanding of a universal experience, and arts provides a universal understanding of a personal experience.*

> –Mae Jemison

Mae Jemison is not alone in her thinking. More so than any other living thinker, Integral philosopher Ken Wilber goes much further and deeper into this terrain, as originally spelled out in his books *Eye to Eye* (1984/2001) and *Sex, Ecology, Spirituality* (1995/2001). He employs the term *validity claim* to discuss the three basic spheres of knowledge. In very simplified form, for present purposes, we can think of these domains as values (morals, ethics), science (empiricism), and art (subjective/interpretation). Each of these ways of knowing have their own forms of inquiry and endeavors and their own validity claims. Therefore, it is a category error when one domain attempts to apply its criteria to the others.

Notice that Jemison doesn't say that there are no differences between science and art. We are not trying to force them together as some sort of thesis-antithesis-synthesis/dialectical triad. To transcend notions of synthesis, in the 1940s seminal Integral thinker Jean Gebser coined the term *synairesis*, which means something along the lines of "mind grasping from all sides." Gebser was not only friends with Picasso, but points to the post-Cubist explorations of a fourth dimension in his paintings (e.g., *Femme en Pleurs*) as illustrative of a consciousness able to perceive from multiple perspectives simultaneously, which he referred to as *aperspectival* consciousness. Simply stated, it is possible to consider what we perceived as the differences between art and science as like looking at a mirror through a prism from slightly different angles. So it makes sense when Wilber tells us that each validity claim by itself is partial and incomplete.

Paradoxes often seem to arise when comparing the knowledge garnered from art and science. These paradoxes are not necessarily problems to be solved. We can allow them to co-exist. In fact, an evolved creative process accepts paradoxical relationships as complementary. This approach is not to be confused with irrationality (pre-rational); it is actually transrational (post-rational). In other words, we are capable of rationality, can choose to be irrational, or can even transcend rationality's limited validity claims altogether. Many of the mind-boggling implications from discoveries in relativity, quantum physics, cosmology, and chaos theory are not rational, nor are they irrational. These implications are transrational and point to creativity at its most fundamental level.

In the Beginning...

> *The universe is not only stranger than we imagine, it's stranger than we can imagine.*

> –Arthur C. Clarke

The single most creative event known to humans is the birth of our universe. Through art, science, and exploration of consciousness, we have learned a lot about creativity—about its nebulous, intangible, intuitive processes, parallels to the forces of nature, and unpredictable but deterministic rules. This body of knowledge points to the characteristics of creativity that we think we understand. But no matter how much we think we know about these processes, what is completely mysterious is how it all got started, and further, why. The Big Bang theory attempts to explain the how—how everything around us came from nothing, how space itself came into being, how billions of galaxies, each containing billions of stars, started out as an infinitely small, infinitely dense point. We still have no idea of how, even when considering any of the various multiverse theories that are gaining traction in the scientific community. As for the why, we don't know that either, although every culture and religion has a story to tell.

It is not only artists who are creative in a significant way. Innovators in any field are creative in the truest sense. Scientists are very creative thinkers. (They are not to be confused with technicians, or people who simply happen to work in a scientific field.) It is no surprise that theoretical astrophysicist Janna Levin is married to a musician when one considers her presentation at TED Talks March 2011, "The Sound the Universe Makes."

> *I'd like to convince you that the universe has a soundtrack and that soundtrack is played on space itself, because space can wobble like a drum. It can ring out a kind of recording throughout the universe of some of the most dramatic events as they unfold....So in this ambition to capture songs from the universe, we turn our focus to black holes and the promise they have, because black holes can bang on space-time like mallets on a drum and have a very characteristic song, which I'd like to play for you, some of our predictions for what that song will be like.*

> –Janna Levin

We do not actually have recordings of sounds made by black hole–induced gravity waves…yet. Instead, Levin plays sounds for the audience based on simulations of these waves made visible through the state-of-the-art animated CGI simulations from NASA. Figure 7.1 is a single frame image from one of these animations, which are based on more than 30 years of research. Leaving aside the fact based tagline from 1979's *Alien*, "In space no one can hear you scream," you are correct to wonder how such long wavelength vibrations are made audible. It is accomplished with a relatively simple process known as *sonification*. Just as transposing musical performances up a few octaves from bass to tenor maintains musical pitches, sonification transposes infrasonic (below) or ultrasonic (above) frequencies into sonic (audible) range. For example, the fundamental frequency of the note C1 is 130.81 Hz. If you double it three times, you get 523.24 Hz, which is the note C5. All you have to do is keep doubling infrasonic signals until above 20 Hz, or halving ultrasonic signals until below 20 kHz, and then run the information into a system that converts the vibrations into sound waves.

Figure 7.1 NASA simulation of gravity waves created by a smaller black hole orbiting a larger black hole. The orbit more resembles an electron and nucleus than a planet and star.
Source: public domain via NASA Goddard Space Flight Center, NASA.gov.

Gravity, Stars, Supernovae, and Black Holes

This is the greatest discovery of the scientific enterprise: You take hydrogen gas, and you leave it alone, and it turns into rosebushes, giraffes, and humans.

–Brian Swimme

We now know enough to confidently say that the universe is inherently creative, that self organization is baked into the cake. Just a few minutes after the Big Bang, hydrogen forms. From this, the simplest of all elements, all matter is created. It is only a matter of time before gravity creates clouds of hydrogen. As these clouds grow in density, gravity causes incredible pressure and heat. The hydrogen atoms start to fuse together, creating helium and giving off an enormous amount of energy, a process known as nuclear fusion. This is the birth of a star, a gigantic ball of gas trying to blow itself up but held together by gravity. Over time, the heat and pressure continues to fuse atoms together, creating heavier elements, such as helium, carbon, oxygen, sodium, climbing up through the periodic table of the elements until the fusion process creates iron. Iron sucks up energy from the fusion process. Within a fraction of a second, gravity overcomes the balance of power, causing the star to collapse in on itself, which then causes a gigantic explosion known as a supernova.

Before the chaotic maelstrom shoots matter light years across space, the energy from the inconceivably powerful explosion induces more fusion, creating all of the naturally occurring elements heavier than iron, such as copper, gold, zinc, and the heaviest, uranium. As elements stick together, they form molecules, which continue to complexify. This process repeats countless times, even now. Eventually, there is enough matter spewed across space for gravity to start pulling together clumps of molecules into huge dust clouds. Stars serve as a gravitational anchor for these swirling clouds of dust that gravity forms into clumps, then rocks, then asteroids, and finally planets and moons. If the star is massive enough, the supernova leaves behind a core that is so dense that it becomes a black hole. And just as stars anchor solar systems, super massive black holes stabilize galaxies (their mass is usually about 0.5% of the galaxy's total mass). Without galaxies, there would be no stable solar systems, which support planets able to provide for the evolution of intelligent life (as far as we know). It is not just poetry when you hear someone say that we are made of stardust; it is pretty literal. All of these processes continue to this day. The universe is in a state of constant creation. All of these forces created us, so we are part of this constant creation as our universe continues to evolve. The Alan Watts quote at the beginning of this chapter, too, is more than just poetry. Our creativity is the universe's creativity. They are one and the same.

The Creative Power of Chaos, from Simplicity to Everything: *The Secret Life of Chaos* (2010) is an hour-long BBC Four–produced documentary about chaos theory, hosted by Professor Jim Al-Khalili, a British theoretical physicist. During the last five minutes, the program talks to Torsten Reil, CEO and cofounder of Natural Motion, a leading video-game technology and development company. Rockstar, Ubisoft, Activision, Bioware, and THQ are some of the companies that use Natural Motion's algorithms. In explaining the development of the company's industry-standard AI algorithms, Reil says, "One thing that we found, particularly in our original research, is how powerful evolution is as a system, as an algorithm to create something that is very complex, and to create something that is very adaptive."

Natural Motion used computerized evolution to create a "virtual brain" to control "virtual bodies." They started by randomly generating 100 two-legged "brain/bodies," which were not able to do much more than fall over. They then programmed the software to select the brains that showed a slightly better ability at controlling bipedal locomotion and had them breed to create new virtual offspring. They then kept reiterating the process. After 10 generations, the figures were able to walk. After many more iterations, they had generated an algorithm that mimics human motion so well—including reacting to unexpected events—that it is beyond the capability of conventional programming. They are now part of many game engines used in popular video games.

Reil stated, "Eventually, miraculously, you actually end up with something that works. The scary thing is you don't know why it works and how it works. You look at that brain and you actually have no idea actually what is going on, because evolution has optimized it automatically.…Even though we programmed these algorithms, what actually then happens when it unfolds live we don't control anymore, and things happen that we never expected. It's quite a funny feeling that you create these algorithms and they do their own thing." All it takes is a few simple rules and feedback for amazingly complex systems to emerge. Self organization is a basic characteristic of our universe.

Being Creative

There is no right or wrong way to be creative. There are as many styles and approaches as there are people. What works for one person might not work for another. Some artists never formalize their creative process; they just follow their instincts and do what works. Others develop very sophisticated methods and utilize them at all times. Most producers are somewhere in the middle. There are many factors that influence any given producer's process such as style, taste, genre, skill level, experience level, personality type, tool set, collaborators, deadlines, and degree of commerciality. Regardless of these varying factors, the nature of creativity is equally relevant to all of us.

Questions surrounding the nature of chance are central to classical inquiries into creativity—often centered around philosophical debates on the nature of free will dating back at least to Aristotle. The age-old question here points to classical arguments in philosophy on *determinism* versus *indeterminism*. Is everything that happens determined in advance? Do we have free will? Are we choosing our creative actions? William James (1842–1910) is the preeminent pioneer in modern Western psychology, and his thinking on the nature of free will and creativity is based on a belief that we choose from any number of possible futures. Chance is involved, but we can direct outcomes. A hundred years ago, James came to a conclusion that is now commonly understood in our era, but based on only 100 years of understanding garnered from the fastest expansion of new knowledge in human history.

Henri Poincaré is best known for his pioneering work in mathematics that laid the foundation for chaos theory and fractal geometry, but he also worked in psychology and philosophy. Like William James, Poincaré's investigations into chance and free will were incredibly prescient and forward thinking, although in his own way, he too believed that chance is not the ultimate cause of our actions. Not only can we direct outcomes with conscious action, but Poincaré was also onto something about the nature of our unconscious as a major factor in creative process. His ponderings in *Science and Method* (1914) are relevant 100 years later to our current topic:

> *It is certain that the combinations which present themselves to the mind in a kind of sudden illumination after a somewhat prolonged period of unconscious work are generally useful and fruitful combinations, which appear to be the result of a preliminary sifting. Does it follow from this that the subliminal ego, having divined by a delicate intuition that these combinations could be useful, has formed none but these, or has it formed a great many others which were devoid of interest, and remained unconscious?*

> *Under this second aspect, all the combinations are formed as a result of the automatic action of the subliminal ego, but those only which are interesting find their way into the field of consciousness. This, too, is most mysterious. How can we explain the fact that, of the thousand products of our unconscious activity, some are invited to cross the threshold, while others remain outside? Is it mere chance that gives them this privilege? Evidently not. For instance, of all the excitements of our senses, it is only the most intense that retain our attention, unless it has been directed upon them by other causes.*

NOTE: Poincaré's use of the term *subliminal ego* more or less equates to what today we might call the *personal unconscious.*

So for at least 100 years, we've known that personal creativity is a combination of chance, unconscious processes, and conscious action. After a few thousand years of experience and knowledge in the arts and sciences, there is strong evidence to back up the assertion that practically speaking, creativity is limitless and infinite. At the same time, this is not what most people personally experience when it comes to artistic expression. For some reason, except for a rare few, being creative is not as easy as it should be given its ubiquitous pervasive nature.

There is an explanation for this odd status quo: We place limitations on our own creative potential consciously, unconsciously, and instinctively. We focus our creative potential toward specific activities forced upon us by our environment. This impulse surely helped our species to survive and evolve. If you are a hunter/gatherer, then your creative energy is focused on finding food, shelter, and protecting your family from the elements and predators. As recently as 11,000 years ago, 500-pound saber-toothed tigers with foot-long incisors still roamed this planet. Except for a rare few humans, those who expended too much energy on arts and crafts, not essential to daily life, were much less likely to last long enough to pass on their genes or traditions.

Unlike other survival guides, if you are reading this one, it is safe to assume that immediate survival is not an issue. Chapter 9, "Lifestyle Tips," discusses Abraham Maslow's hierarchy of needs. In his five-stage model, creativity sits at the top of the pyramid, with physiological and safety needs at the bottom of it. In our post-industrial information society, it is safe to refocus our creative potential toward art and music. The same instincts that kept us from being eaten now work to ensure we can pay the rent. We do still have survival concerns, but for the most part, not really when compared to our ancestors. That means with a little practice, you can choose to remove survival instinct–induced limitations most anytime you want to. It is simply a matter of free will to put the processes into motion.

Influences and Originality

Those who do not want to imitate anything, produce nothing.

–Salvador Dalí

You are likely familiar with the idiom "imitation is the sincerest form of flattery." Creativity does not happen in a vacuum; it is a combinatory process. Artistic works result from conscious and unconscious influences, personal life experience, internal subjective processes, one's emotional life, and influences from other artists. Music largely advances incrementally as artists work in existing styles with musical ideas of their influences. Often, influences are obvious to attentive music fans, but not always. And when an artist's work has very obvious influences, sometimes it's no less original or distinctive. On the flip side, there are many technically skilled artists whose work is not only influenced by others, but is derivative to the point of being unoriginal, if not essentially a rip off. So what is the difference between having influences and being derivative? There are many factors, but the single biggest one associated with true originality is authentic expression of what that artist brings to the table.

Let's continue with the understanding that, technically speaking, all music is creative, although much of it is not relevant or innovative. There are many classic artists who exemplify originality and creativity. A few who come to mind are The Beatles, Pink Floyd, Frank Zappa, King Crimson, Kraftwerk, Einsturzende Neubauten, Oingo Boingo, Public Enemy, Radiohead, Sonic Youth, Björk, Massive Attack, and Aphex Twin. The same could be said about countless records, singles, and tracks by producers who had their moments. When you consider acts that followed in the footsteps of the aforementioned, are they necessarily any less creative than their influences? Pink Floyd got their name from American blues musicians who influenced them. Kraftwerk studied with Stockhausen, but their appreciation for James Brown helped drive their transition from *avant-garde* jam band to the slightly funky robots we all know and love. Radiohead is obviously in the lineage of Pink Floyd, but yet still has a distinctive, influential sound. Sonic Youth developed as unique and distinctive a sound as any rock band; they regularly cite influence by the Velvet Underground and The Stooges/Iggy Pop, among others. More recently, a glance at Empire of the Sun's videos and stage shows reveals imaginative, creative minds at work. If you listen to their 2008 release, *Walking on a Dream*, every song seems familiar. It is saturated with influences. Yet at the same time, the band successfully created a very distinctive sound that is unique and original. Obvious influences, therefore, are not mutually exclusive with originality.

Like many of the topics in this book, we are in seriously subjective territory, discussing relationships that are highly simplified even when considered on a spectrum. The listener decides if a song or artist is authentic, unique, pretentious, original, contemporary, retro, reminiscent, contrived, or just plain derivative. In fact, many listeners don't care as long as they like it. They may not even know enough to make a judgment even if they did care to do so. There are also times when an artist is simply so good at what he or she does that even educated listeners are willing to give the artist a pass on the originality front. The most important factor, then, is the audience, and this varies wildly from genre to genre, style to style, and scene to scene. What is considered original or derivative by an informed and serious music fan is not the same as for a casual Top 40 listener.

The skill level and aesthetic sensibility of the artists and producers obviously play a major role in the success of any music, no matter the artistic goals and intended audience. There are of course many counterexamples to any generalizations, but assuming good production value, generally speaking the following holds true:

▷ The more commercial and mainstream the intended audience, the more likely the audience will enjoy music that is largely derivative and unoriginal. Examples include most music aimed at a Top 40 market, and an established act like Kid Rock, as his fans actually like that he sounds just like their favorite classic rock artists.

▷ The more commercial and mainstream the intended audience, the less likely the audience will enjoy music that is too original and unique. No example needed here.

▷ The more current and trendy the influences, the more likely the sound will be derivative and less original. Examples include the majority of music played in big dance clubs or on Top 40 radio.

▷ The more obscure the influences to the audience, the less derivative and more original it will sound. Examples include anyone influenced by The Residents, widely considered the weirdest band ever. You can hear their influence in the idiosyncratic vocal style of Primus' Les Claypool (also composer and performer of South Park's opening theme song). He cites them as one of his favorite bands.

▷ The more unique and/or diverse the combination of influences, the less derivative and more original it will sound. Examples include highly skilled and respected acts like Mastodon, Goldfrapp, and Phoenix.

The importance of this line of thinking varies widely depending on the goal of any given project. In some cases, it may even be an overarching consideration for a career. The priorities of these aspects significantly shifts in one direction or the other if your primary goal is expression of original ideas than if it is to make hits and get rich. Those two goals are not necessarily mutually exclusive, by the way. No matter where you fall on the spectrum, there are many fine lines that can be skillfully balanced if your creative impulses and desires for commercial success seem at odds with each other.

If you are chasing success by trying to jump on bandwagons, you'd better be insanely talented and well connected. Otherwise, trend jumping is largely a quixotic enterprise. And when someone does successfully jump a trend, that success is usually short lived in terms of a career. It is a rare few that naturally possess an intangible ability to consistently stay current with popular trends for more than a few years. In fact, those same people are just as likely to be trendsetters at some point in their career. On the other hand, staying current and relevant does not necessarily imply trendy, as with skillful execution of ideas it is possible simultaneously to express your unique vision and give wider audiences something to relate to. Just as the meteorologists tracking weather systems developing off the West coast of Africa have no way of knowing which ones will blow up into hurricanes before they cross the Atlantic, there is equal unpredictability and uncertainty when it comes to knowing which songs or artists will catch on and blow up until it is already happening. Given this reality, as long as you do what is authentic to you, and do it as well as possible, then you are maximizing your chances of finding success as you define it.

Berlin-based DJ and electronic music producer Ellen Allien, founder of the BPitch Control label, was interviewed on the theransomnote.co.uk in June 2010. During the interview, Allien was asked a question pertinent to our current discussion, about the effect of the digital revolution on creativity. She replied:

> I am sure creativity has changed for some artists, always checking which tracks are number one...but this is the wrong approach I believe. It is better to adopt some individuality and uniqueness in music, that is more exciting for me. Creativity comes from the inside, not from the outside. Every artist has to figure out how their own creativity can grow, and some artists need to withdraw while others need movement.

Stages of Creative Process

Strewn all over the Internet are various multistage models of creativity. Almost all of them can be traced back to a four-stage model first popularized by Graham Wallas in his 1926 book *The Art of Thought*. Wallas based his model on a four-stage model put forth by Henri Poincaré, who himself added a fourth stage to Hermann von Helmholtz's three-stage model. (Helmholz's influence is widespread throughout science, including most everything we do with sound and audio.) Let's briefly consider them before contextualizing them in the production process.

1. **Preparation:** Idea collecting, research, brainstorming
2. **Incubation:** Informal consideration of ideas, often subconsciously or even in dreams
3. **Illumination:** "Light bulb" or "eureka" moment, sudden clarity of idea to pursue
4. **Verification:** First concrete steps taken to produce or realize the idea, to verify that it will work, that is in fact a good idea
   (This step is now commonly referred to as "implementation.")

In Chapter 4, "Master Your Craft," I put forth a simple four-phase model of the production process: emerging, forming, refining, and completing. The first three stages of creative process are most prominent in the emerging phase of production, and the verification stage of the creative process is certainly significant in the forming phase of production, but the phases and stages do not directly map to each other. Both the production process and creative process are non-linear, but not in the same way and not to the same degree. The production process has an arc resulting in completion of a project. It is a mistake to consider the four stages of creativity only for a whole project. These creative stages exhibit fractal properties, as they appear throughout the production process, varying only in scope and intensity at different phases.

Defining Boundaries and Priorities

We are always defining boundaries for ourselves through the simple act of making decisions. Deciding to make Detroit techno defines different boundaries than if making Norwegian black metal. Once we decide on a style or genre, we still have infinite options and directions to pursue. Given the multitude of creative decisions in front of us at any given time, it is very useful to be mindful of the goal of any given creative session. As a project develops, the priorities develop, too. So what is most important at any given moment, in any given process, of any given project?

Boundaries are largely defined by the nature of a project and its current production phase. It is very important to understand this basic concept. Sometimes you are dealing with specific parameters such as instrumentation, key, meter, tempo, and duration. You might be working with an artist who already has a well-defined sound and who wants to keep it that way. Other times, the parameters are wide open. There is no client, no other artist, no deadline. You are able to pursue any idea that comes to mind, even messy, nonsensical, stream-of-consciousness sketches.

The previous section discussed stages of the creative process, and that they have a fractal relationship to the production process. Let's consider two hypothetical situations to illustrate how all these stages and processes might play out in the real world:

> **Example 1:** There is an impending deadline and you want to meet your client's expectations. The project is well into production phase three, refining, and you are close to moving on to completion. In this scenario, it is rarely productive to fully dive back into the preparation stage of the creative process. Doing so would not only be an inefficient use of time, but any new ideas would most likely require major changes, causing the project to go over budget and miss the deadline. Even when troubleshooting or problem solving, the early stages of creative process need to be as short as possible. Your goal is to quickly get to the verification stage, either solving the problem or finding a workaround so you can get back on track and meet the deadline.

> **Example 2:** There are no externally applied expectations or deadlines to meet. You are just starting to think about your next personal project and are fully immersed in the preparation stage. It is counterproductive to analytically judge everything that comes to mind. You should be playing and experimenting, brainstorming, collecting thoughts, and creating sketches. There will be plenty of time for analysis at the verification stage.

Most situations are not so clear as these hypothetical examples. Chapter 4 discussed the five stages of learning. All of this becomes more clear and more effortless as you develop your skills to unconscious and reflective competence (the fourth and fifth learning stages). Any boundary in a natural process is fractal, self-similar at multiple scales, so there are no definitive borders when applying these concepts. Over time, through trial and error, the skilled producer develops good judgment for modulating limitations and boundaries at any given moment, in any given process, of any given project. More often than not, such judgments are essentially invisible, unconscious, and immediate due to cultivated skill, instinct, and intuition.

Salvador Dalí: Madness, Einstein, Cheese, and LSD? If you are interested in pure creativity and uniqueness, but don't know much about Spanish Surrealist artist Salvador Dalí (1904–1989), then you are in for a treat. He was the first artist to attain rock-star status in the modern era. No fine artist alive today is as famous as he was at his peak. Over the course of 50 years, he produced more than 1,500 paintings. Dalí also worked in film, having co-created the landmark silent film *Un Chien Andalou* with Luis Buñuel in 1929, collaborated with Disney on *Destino* (1945/2003), and having designed the dream sequence in Alfred Hitchcock's *Spellbound* (1945). He was cast as the emperor for $100,000 a day in Alejandro Jodorowsky's never-completed 1971 production of *Dune* (also involved: Mick Jagger, Orson Welles, and H.R. Giger, with original music by either Stockhausen or Pink Floyd.) Dalí was brilliantly creative, highly innovative, outlandishly eccentric, and masterfully skilled. In Dalí we have a case study of the fine line between genius and insanity. His personality and behavior was far outside the lines by all standard measurements of normalcy, yet he was as in control of himself as any "normal" person. He famously stated in *The American Magazine* in 1956: "There is only one difference between a madman and me. I am not mad."

Found in the New York Museum of Modern Art's permanent collection is Dalí's most famous painting, *The Persistence of Memory* (1931). What suggests relativity and LSD more than images of melting clocks? Believe it or not, neither of them inspired that painting. Decades later, Dalí was influenced by the work of scientist Ilya Prigogine (discussed in Chapter 4). Once, Prigogine asked him if Einstein was an inspiration for the "soft" dripping clocks in *Persistence of Memory*. Dalí insisted that his inspiration was a Surrealist perception of cheese melting in the sun, not the theory of relativity. Which is actually true, according to the official story on dali.com, home of The Salvador Dalí Society. They tell us that after waking from an afternoon nap "he looked at the clock and felt that time was somehow 'moving slowly,' he next noticed the cheese that was left on the table had melted. What happened next gave birth to one of the most ingenious images ever created. Dalí took his observations about the clock and the cheese and came to the conclusion that time was doing the same thing that the cheese was, in a sense, time was melting."

Given the nature of his art, many people assume that Dalí used LSD. When asked if he ever used drugs, his response was pure Dalí, as quoted in Ramona Fotiade's *André Breton: The Power Of Language* (1999): "I have never taken drugs, since I am a drug. I don't talk about my hallucinations. I evoke them. Take me, I am the drug, take me, I am hallucinogenic." Timothy Leary once commented that Dalí was the only artist on LSD who never actually took LSD. Of course, many of his works historically predate LSD, which was not even synthesized until 1938, and was never used until Albert Hofmann's legendary accidental "Bicycle Day" in 1943.

One of the single most talented, creative, innovative, original, successful, and famous artists of the 20th century, if not since the Renaissance, did not use drugs as part of his creative process.

Intentions and Mis-takes

Mistakes are almost always of a sacred nature. Never try to correct them. On the contrary: rationalize them, understand them thoroughly. After that, it will be possible for you to sublimate them.

–Salvador Dalí

Are mistakes bad? James Brown famously fined band members when they made mistakes on stage. It is a mistake when accidentally sending an email to the wrong person. It is a mistake when you miss Brian Eno talk because you thought the date printed on the ticket as "May13" meant May 13th, when it was actually "06 May13," a week earlier, on the 6th of May, 2013. Given the previous examples, it is reasonable to conclude that mistakes are certainly not good. But what about a mistake in the context of creative process? I suggest that there is actually no such thing as a mistake. It is only through subjective criteria that we make an arbitrary judgment about actions and outcomes. Let us consider some common definitions:

▷ **Plan:** To decide on something in advance, or an organized series of actions intended to produce a desired result
▷ **Intent:** The reason, goal, purpose, or aim for an action
▷ **Decision:** A conclusion reached after considering options, often unconsciously, usually followed by an action

▷ **Accident:** An unexpected or unintended incident, often considered negative
▷ **Mistake:** An error produced by inadequate knowledge, judgment, skill, or attention to action
▷ **Error:** An action or outcome judged to be undesirable, wrong, or incorrect

Accident, mistake, and error are all related, but are different when considering the previous definitions. In the context of creative process, however, we can ignore these differences. We should not ignore when a plan, intent, or decision results in unexpected outcomes. Most of the time, we will want to fix the mistake or correct the error. But occasionally we create something special, commonly known as a "happy accident." In these rare moments, we exceed our normal planning and decision-making abilities, whether through our own unconscious action or the malfunction of our tools. If the first instinct is to always fix the mistake or correct the error, then it will be all too easy to miss the unexpected opportunity when presented to us. Often, the result of the accident appears as a strange coincidence of aesthetic, theme, or concept. As discussed in Chapter 3, "What Is Your Plan?," a meaningful coincidence is also known as a synchronicity, which is always worthy of closer attention. If you are on a tight deadline, figure out how to save the happy accident so you can revisit it in the future.

Before moving on, let me leave you with a little further food for thought on this topic. One person's noise is another person's signal. Error in one context is usable material in another. In 1913, Luigi Russolo published his manifesto, *The Art of Noises*, declaring that any sound can be musical. Riots broke out when he put his revolutionary ideas into action in Milan in 1914, during the first performance on his cacophonous creation, the Intonarumori. Glitch art emphasizes technological errors and "glitches" as component media for music and visuals. Germany's *Oval* is one of the pioneers of such music. Starting in 1991, they began creating beautiful abstract music with sounds of damaged and skipping CDs. As with beauty, so too are noise, error, mistake, and accident in the eye of the beholder.

Methods, Practices, and Techniques

I've spent plenty of time talking about creativity and related topics in general terms, philosophically, and in the abstract. From here on out, I am going to consider creative process in terms of tried and true methods, specific practices, and techniques for music production. It really doesn't matter what kind of music you produce or how commercial or *avant-garde* your sensibility. All music producers share at least two commonalities: developing ideas and then making them happen. Therefore, there is something here for everyone. Intensity of interest and application is only a matter of degrees.

There are many 20th century art movements worthy of our attention when it comes to creative process, such as Dada, Surrealism, Bauhaus, Situationism, Pop Art, Op Art, and Fluxus. Many of those movements directly influenced or closely paralleled 20th century music innovations, such as experimental music, microtonal music, Minimalism, Serialism, *musique concrète*, Indeterminism, and seminal electronic music in general. Beyond aesthetic and conceptual characteristics, all of these movements are associated with a variety of methods, practices, and techniques employed by the artists. Many of these approaches are still widely in use today. In many cases, they were influenced by their historical precursors' relevant techniques, as might be found in various forms of contemplative practice, parapsychology, or shamanism. Even though I am just scratching the surface here, the following topics still represent an array of tools at our disposal, with something here for most any producer in a variety of situations.

Let Your Subconscious Do the Work

Freud's model of the mind as being like an iceberg was truly revolutionary in its day, and although it is now technically obsolete, the power of the metaphor has not diminished a bit. Our conscious mind is much like the tip of the iceberg; we are unaware of most of our mind, just as most of an iceberg is submerged under water, out of view. At any given time, we are aware of but a tiny fraction of what our brain is controlling, processing, or storing. There are many variables involved, including but not limited to sensory input, thoughts, emotions, desires, and memories.

During normal waking consciousness, our ego governs our conscious awareness. Leaving aside popular pejorative associations with the word, depending on the particular school of psychology, there are a few different definitions of *ego*. For our purposes, we can think of it in two ways:

▷ As our sense of identity and self
▷ As the psychological mechanism through which we define our relationship of self to other

Given our chaotic, dangerous world, our ego is really busy managing all of our needs. To do this, by definition, it must limit our conscious awareness. Otherwise, navigating daily life becomes difficult if not impossible. But that means our brain and mind are capable of so much more. Learning how to tap into the power of our unconscious processes is invaluable for creativity. As we will soon discuss, many great artists rely on this wellspring of ideas and inspiration. Some of them even consider the conscious mind, the ego, to be the inferior force in the realization of their works. In *Science and Method* (1914), Henri Poincaré put forth his thoughts on the matter:

> *The subliminal ego is in no way inferior to the conscious ego; it is not purely automatic; it is capable of discernment; it has tact and a lightness of touch; it can select and it can divine. More than that, it can divine better than the conscious ego, since it succeeds where the latter fails. In a word, is it not superior to the conscious ego?*

For more than 100 years, we find the unconscious as a common thread in discussions on creative process. I will cover numerous techniques shortly. Before doing so, we cannot overlook the most obvious ways we all interact with our unconscious on a daily basis, in sleep and dreams:

▷ **Sleep on it:** Most people intuitively utilize this very common technique when faced with big decisions. Our mind continues to process our concerns, wishes, desires, dilemmas, and aspirations when we are asleep. Without effort, we wake up with a clearer sense of what we should do. Often, answers and ideas come to us when we are just about to fall asleep or as we begin to wake up. To capitalize on this, keep a voice recorder or notebook next to your bed. This is easy to do if you have a smartphone.

▷ **Dreams:** Many artists use their dreams for inspiration if not as the actual source of their work's content. Start keeping a dream journal. A voice recorder is good if you need to store musical ideas or quickly get out a story that requires dramatic flair, but handwritting is the ideal method for logging your dreams. Keep a notebook and pen right next to your bed so you can write them down immediately upon waking up. Dreams fade quickly, so don't wait. If done consistently, over time most people start to better remember their dreams and often notice themes and patterns if not blatant synchronicities. Whether through natural ability or practice, some people do not wake up when they become aware they are dreaming and are able to interact with their dreams to varying degrees. This is known as lucid dreaming. Richard D. James and Coil are notable examples of influential electronic musicians that have cited lucid dreaming as significant to their creative process.

Brain Waves and Mental States: It is a mistake to reduce the mind to the brain, but it is also undeniable that brain function is fundamental to mind function. Our brain is an astoundingly complex chemical-electrical biological system. The roughly 100-billion neurons in our brain are the primary components of our nervous system and communicate with each other by sending electrical signals that are easily measured via an electroencephalogram (EEG).

We've known for decades that our basic brain states correspond to five basic types of brain waves: gamma, beta, alpha, theta, and delta. According to the established literature on the topic, we can say a few things about each of them.

- ▶ Delta waves oscillate at < 4 Hz and correspond to deep dreamless sleep.
- ▶ Theta waves oscillate at 4–7 Hz and correspond to sleep, dreaming, deep relaxation, intuition, and meditation.
- ▶ Alpha waves oscillate at 8–13 Hz and correspond to relaxation, visions, inspirations, creativity.
- ▶ Beta waves oscillate at 13–30 Hz and correspond to alertness, active thinking, and cognitive functions. This is your daily "getting things done" brain state, most conducive to productivity. Beta is when the ego is most able to limit our conscious awareness.
- ▶ Gamma waves oscillate at 25–100Hz and correspond to extremely high-level mental activity. People with far above average levels of these waves seem to exhibit enhanced memory, intelligence, and compassion. Some researchers believe that these waves link all parts of our brains together when at their most common oscillation of 40 Hz.

Don't conflate the five brain states with states of consciousness, commonly understood as wakefulness, sleep, and deep dreamless sleep. The states of consciousness generally correspond to certain brain states, but with practice, it is possible to experience all of them while awake. The most common methods of learning to control brain states are biofeedback and meditation.

Isolation, Quiet, Focus, Clarity

Do interesting ideas regularly emerge when you're in the bathroom, taking a shower, driving on the freeway, or exercising? Many people would answer yes to that question. We are more likely to spontaneously have interesting ideas when we are focused on one task that does not require a lot of mental concentration; when we are isolated and relaxed; and when there is a reduction in stimuli. Fortunately, however, you don't have to wait until it's time to take a shower or go for a jog to get your mind to easily generate ideas.

The Sounds of Silence

The quieter you become the more you can hear.

–Georges St-Pierre

What is the difference between hearing and listening? Hearing is automatic and unconscious, while listening is an active, conscious process. The quieter the environment, the easier it is to really understand what it means to listen.

An anechoic chamber is as quiet as any place on Earth. It is a specially designed room that is perfectly soundproofed so no sound goes in or out, and also treated in such as way that there are no reflections. They are primarily used for testing and research purposes, though occasionally there are artistic applications, such as the 176-speaker Audium in San Francisco. The first one in North America was built at Harvard in 1943 for acoustic research to develop new communications technologies for the war effort. (Its designer Dr. Leo Beranek, later was instrumental in the development of the ARPANET.)

In 1951, at Harvard, John Cage went into this new type of environment expecting to hear no sound at all, but that was not his experience. As time passed, the more intently he listened, the more he noticed subtler and subtler sounds, including that of his blood circulating and other physiological functions. The realization he had there led to his most famous, or infamous, composition, known as *4'33"*. Cage considered *4'33"* as his most important piece. It was first performed by pianist David Tudor at Woodstock, New York in 1952. Tudor sat in front of a score full of blank measures and used a stop watch to know when he should raise or lower the piano lid, which marked the different movements. Over the course of four minutes and thirty-three seconds, he did not play a single note. The audience was not impressed, though, unlike with Tristan Tzara and Luigi Russolo (one of Cage's stated influences) more than three decades earlier, they did not riot. Because Cage so often spoke or wrote about silence, it is a common mistake to describe *4'33"* as silence. This piece makes the most sense when performed in front of an audience, when there is a significant amount of ambient noise in the room, since the point is those very sounds. *4'33"* is not about hearing music, but instead about learning to listen. According to Cage, "There is no such thing as an empty space or an empty time. There is always something to see, something to hear. In fact, try as we may to make a silence, we cannot."

The quote at the top of this section was posted, in quotes, to Twitter on November 4th, 2011, by Georges St-Pierre. Born in Quebec in 1981, GSP is one of the great athletes of our current era—the most dominant UFC welterweight champion ever and unanimously considered one of the top-five "pound for pound" fighters alive today. If there is any way to determine whether something is worthy of one's attention, we would be hard-pressed to find a better example than this: Seemingly opposite types of people—in this case, John Cage and GSP—are in agreement on the value of something—in this case, quiet/silence.

NOTE: The aforementioned GSP quote is generally thought to have originated with Ram Dass a few decades ago. Ram Dass, who was known as Richard Alpert until 1967, was a professor at Harvard with Timothy Leary and Ralph Metzner. Together, they collaborated on legal, though controversial, LSD and psilocybin research and co-authored one of the most important books of the 1960s "hippie" counter-culture: *The Psychedelic Experience: A Manual Based on The Tibetan Book of the Dead* (1964).

Meditation

Meditation might be the simplest thing you can do. In its most basic form, you just sit, follow your breath, and watch your thoughts come and go as if they were passing clouds or weather. Meditation approaches are as diverse as dance styles. There are many popular formal techniques stemming from Asian spiritual traditions, though the ones from Yoga, Vedanta, and Buddhism are best known in the West. Meditation usually involves sitting or lying down, though occasionally walking. It is practiced solo or with a group, which may or may not be guided. Like any practice, meditation builds and deepens over time. Doing it every day is a good habit to develop, but there is value in it at any time. In addition to numerous free online resources, including multiple podcasts, it is common to find free group options in most any city. To gain many of the same benefits from formal meditation practices, you can also just simply give in to deep relaxation, whether during a massage, lying down and listening to music, or experiencing nature. The latter was more than sufficient for Ralph Waldo Emerson and Henry David Thoreau, the highly influential 19th century American transcendentalists.

Another amazing and unprecedented aspect of the last 100 years is that we now readily have access to much of the world's accumulated knowledge from the last 2,500 years. If you are not interested in Asian techniques, there are a lot of options to be found in the aboriginal traditions from Africa, the Americas, and Australia, as well as the three big Western religions, Judaism, Christianity, and Islam. These three religions have always included mystical and contemplative traditions found alongside the dogmatic and orthodox structures. In Judaism are three branches of Kaballah, one of which is meditative. In Islam, the Sufi tradition includes meditation practices, and the writings of Sufism's most famous poet Rumi. In the Christian traditions, we find a popular form of meditation in labyrinth walking, as well as ideas and practices espoused by 20th century notables such as Thomas Merton and Rudolf Steiner and/or historical figures like Meister Eckhart and St. Theresa of Ávila.

Believe it or not, there is even a formalized contemporary, technologically forward-thinking method centered around music and listening. Deep Listening is an integrated practice, including meditation, developed by electronic music pioneer Pauline Oliveros, a founding member of the San Francisco Tape Music Center. "Silence is a friend" is the heading on the Deep Listening Institute's website (www.deeplistening.org). In 2005, she finally published a book on the topic, consolidating decades of thoughts, approaches, and techniques in *Deep Listening: A Composers' Sound Practice.*

In short, there is something for everyone.

Non-Ordinary States of Consciousness (NOSC)

Hello, Department of Redundancy Department. There is nothing ordinary about consciousness, which might be why the synonymous term "altered states" is commonly employed. Non-ordinary states of consciousness (NOSC) come in many varieties and are induced by numerous means, some fairly common and easy to experience, others more rare and extreme, falling on a wide spectrum of risk factors. Whether induced naturally, with technology, or with chemistry, they can be great sources of inspiration and ideas. They can allow us to see things differently, from a fresh perspective, and with a renewed sense of direction, focus, or clarity. Productive creativity is often not possible in a NOSC. More commonly, flashes of inspiration, profound insights, or raw sketched ideas are put into motion later. There are two basic categories of NOSC—exogenous (externally induced) and endogenous (self induced)—though for our purposes, I am presenting them in terms of risk.

Many of the following topics overlap with more in-depth discussions on health and lifestyle decisions in Chapter 9. There is no intended implication here as to what anyone should or should not do, only discussion on a topic relevant to creative process, music culture, and visible aspects of our industry. When it comes to some of the methods for inducing NOSC, I am not avoiding potentially controversial topics. A failure to at least minimally address the idiomatic elephant in the room would be irresponsible for someone with my education and training on the subject.

It should go without saying, but anything mentioned here related to your health is something for you to discuss with your health professional. Make sure you do your research before trying any new methods, which includes reading Chapter 9. Yes, with risk often comes reward, but this ratio widely various across NOSC when it comes to creative process or artistic growth. In addition to important health and legality considerations, professionally speaking, different approaches are more or less appropriate depending on the time, place, and situation. An artist working by himself or herself has different responsibilities than a producer/engineer running a recording session.

Low to Moderate Risk

Consider the following list if you are looking for safe, natural, and legal methods for altering your consciousness.

▷ **Modulation of natural function.** Three of the most natural ways to induce a NOSC are meditation, sleep deprivation, and fasting/cleansing. Meditation has been discussed. Sleep deprivation is generally safe as long as you are in a comfortable environment and don't try to do anything that might be dangerous under normal conditions, such as driving, or operating machinery or tools with warning stickers on them. Fasting is not eating. Cleanses usually involve some fasting, but also include eating or drinking specific things to rid the body of undesirables such as toxins or parasites. Safe, effective fasts and cleanses can really clear the mind and even induce a variety of NOSC, but they have to be done with care, especially if you plan on doing them for more than a few days. Always check with your health professional if you have any health issues and never skimp on drinking enough water.

▷ **Physical activity.** This might include running, walking, swimming, dancing, or yoga. Physical activity is great for the mind. The word "yoga" actually comes from the Sanskrit for "yoke" or "union," and refers to the connection between mind and body. Any focused repetitive exercise has the potential to put you in "the zone" and/or release endorphins. The latter is commonly experienced as a "runner's high."

▷ **Entrainment.** There are ways of utilizing light and sound so that your brain waves sync to another frequency. You can have experiences associated with alpha, theta, and delta waves. Creating simple beat pulses (binaural beats) with sine waves is the easiest method, but there are more sophisticated audio recordings such as the *Hemi-Sync* series developed by The Monroe Institute. There are also methods that use varied pulsing patterns of light, usually with closed eyes, such as various stroboscopic light therapies, a random assortment of weird goggles promising psychedelic-like experiences, and relatively simple devices based on rhythmic "flicker," such as Brion Gysin's notorious invention, the Dream Machine. (Any flicker or stroboscopic methods are not a good idea if you have ever had an epileptic seizure of any sort.)

▷ **Sensory deprivation.** As the Zen koan goes, "Blot out sense and sound, what do you hear?" Anechoic chambers, earplugs and a sleep mask, or a variety of esoteric yogic techniques can free your mind from having to process basic sensory information, allowing it to wander in new directions. But the ultimate safe form of sensory deprivation is an isolation tank, also known as a floatation tank. In these tanks, you lie down in very shallow water that is the exact temperature of your body and contains a high ratio of dissolved Epsom salt, enabling you to float. They are soundproof and lightproof. You can sit up and get out at any time. At first, it is just you and your thoughts. It is common to have very deep realizations or even full-blown psychedelic-like experiences after just and hour in the tank. When you sit up and get out of the tank, you are still sober and immediately back to reality. Many spas offer just the floatation aspect of these tanks, taking advantage of the relaxation and therapeutic benefits of taking pressure off of all your joints. If you ever have a chance to do this, I highly recommend it. Unlike in the 1980 cult classic *Altered States*, you will not regress into a Neanderthal. In addition to a well-known tank on Venice Beach in California, there are many others spread out here and there, and there might be one near you.

▷ **Holotropic Breathwork.** After LSD was criminalized in the U.S. (1966), Stan Grof developed this system of safely inducing psychedelic-like experiences so he could continue his research and therapeutic practice without risk of incarceration. His method involves skillful use of setting along with evocative music and controlled rapid-breathing techniques. There are no substances or any sort of equipment utilized, just breathing and loud music. If you are interested in learning more about this technique check out www.holotropic.com.

> **NOTE:** Many people have experienced spontaneous NOSC with no obvious cause or method of inducement. In extreme cases, after one seeks out professional assistance, the mainstream medical establishment will often misdiagnose these experiences as a form of psychosis or schizophrenia. In 1980, Stan Grof and his wife Christina founded the Spiritual Emergency Network (SEN, www.spiritualemergence.info) for those seeking professionals able to properly diagnose what they call "spiritual emergencies." For those interested in this topic, Grof posted an article in 2008 to his realitysandwich.com blog, "Spiritual Emergencies: Understanding and Treatment of Psychospiritual Crises."

Moderate to High Risk

The methods in the following list involve more risk and should not be taken lightly. As already stated, there is no intended implication here as to what anyone should or should not do.

▷ **Extreme modulation of natural function/activity.** Going further with some of the points from the preceding list can induce a powerful NOSC. Native American sweat lodges, marathon running, mountain climbing, long-term fasts and cleanses, and any other activities that weaken and exhaust the body are not to be taken lightly. These activities should be done only with proper training, while supervised by experienced practitioners, and/or in consultation with health professionals.

▷ **Drugs.** This topic is almost as broad as "food." Here, it is getting cursory attention at best, even including the few paragraphs that follow and the additional discussion found in Chapter 9. That said, there is no denying that many musicians, artists, and even whole generations or genres are associated with drugs, whether legal, illegal, natural, or synthetic. One could further sift drugs into categories like soft or hard, street or prescription, but for our purposes, we only need to know what is right for us and what should be avoided. If you do choose to experiment in this territory, make sure you do your research and know what you are getting yourself into. The full gamut of human experience is found here in intensified form, from mountain-peak crystalline clarity, personal breakthroughs of self understanding, and expansion of consciousness, to the odd, bizarre, or confusing, to depression, anxiety, terror, fear, tragedy, and in the worst cases, even death or insanity. It must be pointed out that there are many ways to have some of the same experiences without the same risks, such as many of the methods listed earlier. Many NOSC effects regularly associated with certain drug experiences are also induced by sleep deprivation or lack of food and water. If you stay up all night totally sober, things get weird and spacey, so don't confuse or conflate causes.

Drugs

Every individual reacts differently to every chemical. Know your body. Know your mind. Know your substance. Know your source.

–www.erowid.org

This topic requires a little bit more discussion than afforded in a bullet point, especially when talking about artists, musicians, and notions of creativity. Generally speaking, the drugs that are most physically addictive or most toxic (and therefore most risky in terms of overdose) tend to be the ones that offer the most immediate boosts of energy/euphoria or dulling of the senses, such as cocaine, speed, meth, alcohol, or heroin (and any variety of pharmaceuticals). In contrast, the drugs that are least physically addictive with the lowest toxicity levels or risk of overdose tend to be more mind opening and therefore more psychologically challenging in nature, such as LSD, psilocybin, or marijuana, all of which also have medicinal applications. If you are wondering, MDMA (ecstasy) is somewhere in the middle of those two generalizations, offering enough benefits as to be part of recently FDA approved trials, but also associated with potentially dangerous physiological effects.

Of all the drugs in the world, the ones most associated with creative thinking are marijuana and psychedelics, namely LSD and psilocybin. Even though these substances, in pure unadulterated form, have such low toxicity that it is almost impossible to physically overdose, when misused they can present equal risk. Even assuming a safe environment, it is possible to experience "bad trips," which for some people can result in long-term psychological and emotional problems, especially if not around people who have substantial experience with these situations. For advanced practitioners, there is no such thing as a "bad trip" as long as they are in a safe environment and the difficult experiences are internal. For insights into this attitude, check out *Dark Night, Early Dawn: Steps to a Deep Ecology of Mind* (2000) by Christopher Bache, Ph.D. (with a foreword by Stan Grof). The positive LSD experiences cited by countless musicians, artists, and other influential people from Eric Clapton to Francis Crick (DNA) to Steve Jobs (Apple) to Matt Groening (*The Simpsons*) are common knowledge. If you decide to follow in their footsteps, you can best avoid negative outcomes by understanding one point if nothing else: Psychedelics are not party drugs.

Beyond the obvious health, safety, and legality issues, there are a few considerations relevant to musicians and music producers. The following points address common myths or misconceptions and are primarily aimed toward those who are younger and just getting started.

▷ **Drugs do not add something to you; they can only alter something that is already there.** If you are not an artistically creative person, don't assume that drugs alone can make you creative. If you are dealing with a creative block, depending on what's going on in your life, what is causing the blocks, and what substance you are using, there is equal likelihood it will help, not help, or make matters worse. There are no shortcuts.

▷ **Don't assume that what works for others will work for you.** Realize that one person's medicine is another person's poison. Beware of accidentally forming a habit that does the opposite of your intention. Marijuana in particular can be a double-edged sword. Pot is not only the safest and most common "illegal" drug, it is actually legal in a growing number of places, not only in terms of medicinal use but even for recreational use. This is true in Colorado and Washington as of 2013. A lot of creative people make effective use of pot, but as is also common knowledge, stoners are known for their laid-back, easygoing, attitudes. That means getting high too often can just as easily limit creativity and stifle productivity. Plus, you need to be sober long enough to figure out if all those amazing ideas are actually amazing ideas.

▷ **Don't look to famous success stories of those addicted to dangerous drugs; they are outliers.** There are many famous artists who were hard-core substance abusers and even serious addicts. Just remember, it says something more about them as talented artists than it does about addiction. Most people with serious addictions are not successful artists. You have never heard of them. As George Carlin once noted, "I'll bet there aren't too many people hooked on crack who can play the bagpipes." And how many of those great musicians died too early? With outliers like Iggy Pop, Ozzy Osbourne, and Keith Richards, their longevity with artistic success came in spite of their substance issues. Moreover, they not only have access to a special tier of private doctors but likely also have the genetics to match their lifestyle.

20th Century Innovations

While we all must evolve our own techniques, there is no need to reinvent the wheel. In the process of developing methods suited to your style, it is virtually guaranteed you will rediscover methods utilized by artists who influence you or by ones who influenced them. Building on the inventions and ideas that emerged at the end of the 19th century, the 20th century's unprecedented rate of technological expansion and social change also included an explosion of breakthroughs in art, music, and the creative process. What follows is a cursory introduction to an assortment of substantial topics, from which I am cherry picking a few that I think are most relevant to indie and electronic music producers.

Avant-garde movements and ideas form the basis for most of the discussion, but don't let that scare you off if you are primarily interested in popular styles or commercial markets. As I stated in Chapter 5, "The Social Scene," today's mainstream is yesterday's *avant-garde*, which is future generations' quaint history. Many of these once vanguard ideas are so commonplace now, they are as taken for granted as the electric bass guitar or stereophonic audio. We can utilize any combination of these innovations at different times and for different reasons, commonly for collecting initial ideas, sometimes as source material, even for whole pieces, or when dealing with creative blocks. As I will discuss in the next section, digital technology allows us to quickly and easily apply these ideas.

Producing finished products is a lot of hard work, but it is crucial to always maintain an element of fun and games in the creative process. The word *serious* has a few different meanings, and one of them is an antonym to *fun*. In that sense of the word, unlike many serious 20th century intellectual artistic giants like Stockhausen or movie director Stanley Kubrick, John Cage evolved an outlook and attitude on his artistic works at the opposite end of the spectrum. As he wrote in 1957:

> *What is the purpose of writing music? One is, of course, not dealing with purposes but dealing with sounds. Or the answer must take the form of a paradox: a purposeful purposeless or a purposeless play. This play, however, is an affirmation of life—not an attempt to bring order out of chaos nor to suggest improvements in creation, but simply a way of waking up to the very life we're living, which is so excellent once one gets one's mind and one's desires out of its way and lets it act of its own accord.*

Cage in his own way was extreme in his methods. Though an extreme creative philosophy is practical for an *avant-garde* composer, it is not always consonant with every artist's vision or *raison d'être*. That said, Cage's elevation of play is always inspirational and eminently pertinent at the onset of our creative process. An innate sense of play is a key characteristic of creative people in general. Games and play are more than just entertainment to a creative individual.

Dada and the "Cut-Up"

> *I play off sense against nonsense. I prefer nonsense but that is a purely personal matter. I feel sorry for nonsense, because up to now it has so seldom been artistically molded....*

> –Kurt Schwitters

With beginnings circa 1915 in Zurich, New York City, and Berlin, Dada is ground zero for a preponderance of the intellectual and artistic innovations of the 20th century. It was the first "punk" art movement and the laid foundations for Surrealism, Situationism, Pop Art, the New York "Downtown" scene, and significant aspects of Post-Modernism in general. If one had to assign Dada a founder, it would have to be Tristan Tzara (1896–1963). In *Seven Dada Manifestos and Lampisteries* (1918), he tells us, "I'm writing this manifesto to show that you can perform contrary actions at the same time, in one single, fresh breath; I'm against action; as for continual contradiction, and affirmation too, I am neither for nor against them, and I won't explain myself because I hate common sense."

Of the many seminal 20th century art movements, Dada is number one for influence on music and sound. While there are many methods and techniques utilized by Dada artists in numerous art forms, the most central innovation is the use of chance. In 1920, Tzara caused a riot when demonstrating his new method for writing poetry. He cut up a newspaper article so each word was on its own piece. He then mixed the pieces together, randomly selected them, and put them in sequence, claiming it to be his poem. The crowd was not impressed. As he wrote just a few years earlier: "The poem will resemble you. And there you are—an infinitely original author of charming sensibility, even though unappreciated by the vulgar herd."

Of the many notable artists associated with Dada, Kurt Schwitters (1887–1948) is the one most singled out as an influence by musicians, including the likes of Brian Eno, Krautrock pioneers Faust, and Japan's preeminent Noise artist Merzbow (from Schwitters' *Merzbau*). The fact that Schwitters made numerous audio recordings of his fascinatingly eccentric "sound poems" undoubtedly is largely responsible. (His most famous piece, *Ursonate*, is easy to hear online.) Schwitters' influence also extends to Hollywood filmmaker Steven Soderbergh. Before directing big theater releases like *Solaris*, *Ocean's Eleven*, and *Haywire*, he wrote, starred in, and directed the highly entertaining indie film *Schizopolis* (1996). Not only is the dialog neo-Dada at its finest, but the main character's name is Theodore Azimuth Schwitters. One of the characters played by Soderbergh is named Fletcher Munson, which should sound familiar to any audio engineer.

The influence of Dada is ubiquitous in the techniques discussed next.

Surrealism and the Unconscious

Surrealism emerged equally from Dadaist ideas and Freud's psychology of the unconscious and dream interpretation. The movement's founder, André Breton (1896–1966), published the *Surrealist Manifesto* in 1924 and defined Surrealism as "pure psychic automatism." Breton regularly expelled artists who disagreed with him from the movement, most notably Tristan Tzara in 1920, Salvador Dalí in 1934, and Brion Gysin in 1935. These artists were quite okay with this break from Breton's dogmatism, for as Dalí stated at that time, "I myself am Surrealism."

They used a great many techniques, which are well-documented in their own works and that of numerous others on the topic:

▷ **Dreams:** Dreams are considered the gateway to the unconscious, so most of the Surrealists based significant portions of their works on dreams. As discussed previously, keep a dream journal.

▷ **Altered states of consciousness:** Breton and his core group placed a lot of emphasis on hypnotic, trance, or dreamlike states in their process. At the time, Spiritualism was prevalent, so they mimicked methods from séances, speaking in tongues, and other exotic rituals thought to produce telepathy or other visions.

▷ **Automatism:** This is the most central technique in Surrealism. Most commonly, it is known as "automatic writing" or "automatic drawing." In the 1920s, Breton and others were known to spend more than eight hours a day writing and/or sketching without any editing or guiding of the process, which often resulted in experiences of altered and even euphoric states. More than just a way to generate material for later use, it was part of their daily practice and Surrealist lifestyle. Get into a relaxed state and just start writing, drawing, or even singing (into a recorder) whatever comes to mind. Complete gibberish and nonsense is expected. Do not stop to edit, just keep going. Once you sufficiently give in to the process, interesting things start to emerge, which you may not even notice until you consider the results at a later date.

▷ **Games:** The Surrealists did a lot of collaboration as part of their creative process, and games were a big part of that. The most famous one is commonly known as an "exquisite corpse." Without anyone else looking, someone would start by drawing part of a body, then fold over the paper so only a tiny bit was showing. The next person would continue drawing the next body part, fold over the paper, and hand it to the next person. When completed, they would unfold the paper and see the whole image for the first time. This was more than just a highly entertaining way to pass time in the pre-TV era. It was common to notice themes and coincidences that seemed to appear "automatically." There was a text version of this game, which many decades later would evolve a popular relative, Mad Libs.

Third Mind, Post-Dada/Surrealism for the Multimedia Age: Brion Gysin (1916–1986) might be the most influential 20th century artist that you have never heard of. Early on, he was associated with the Surrealists, and even displayed his works alongside the likes of Picasso, Ernst, Duchamp, Magritte, and Tanguy, among others. As with many early Surrealists, the movement's founder, André Breton had issues with Gysin's work and ideas, so he was expelled in 1935 (as was Salvador Dalí in 1934). His influence starts with the Beat Generation and W.S. Burroughs and extends through notables like The Rolling Stones, Brian Eno, Throbbing Gristle, Keith Haring, Laurie Anderson, Bill Laswell, Beck, and Kurt Cobain.

In 1959, Gysin accidentally rediscovered Dada's use of cut-up text as the material for new works. This resulted in his first "cut-up," *Minutes to Go*, first broadcast by the BBC in 1960. Figure 7.2 shows an example of his process applied to printouts of rough drafts from this book. Shortly after showing this technique to his friend W.S. Burroughs, they collaborated on numerous projects that are considered landmark works by many artists. Permutation is an oft-used theme in this process, as exemplified in Burroughs' audio recording cut-up of Gysin's voice, *Recalling All Active Agents*, which was produced at the BBC studios in 1960. Permutation, which is a sequential repetition of slight variations of the elements in a defined set, is so central to electronic music that Amon Tobin used it for the title of his 1998 Ninja Tune release.

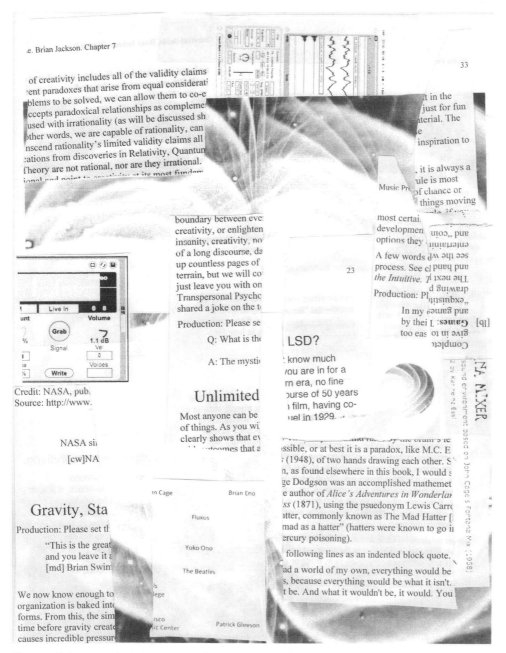

Figure 7.2 An example of Gysin's cut-up technique as done by this author.

Gysin and Burroughs both expanded and distilled many of Dada's and Surrealism's creative process innovations, for which they developed a series of techniques known as "the third mind." Originally published in 1978, *The Third Mind* is a collection of essays and interviews about their collaborative works, which is highly recommended. In one of the essays by Burroughs, "The Cut-Up Method of Brion Gysin," he tells us, "Cut-ups are for everyone. Anybody can make cut-ups. It is experimental in the sense of being *something to do*. Right here write now. Not something to talk and argue about. Greek philosophers assumed logically that an object twice as heavy as another object would fall twice as fast. It did not occur to them to push the two objects off the table and see how they fall. Cut the words and see how they fall." Whether used for lyric writing like Kurt Cobain, or a method applied to audio recordings like Coil, all of us can have fun with this approach.

On March 1, 2012, Terry Wilson posted to realitysandwich.com an excerpt from his "manual" for third mind techniques, *Perilous Passage: The Nervous System & the Universe in other Words* (2004):

> "Drawing upon esoteric and scientific sources, this 'project for disastrous success' deconstructed sound and image and computer technology, sabotaging systems of ideological transmission and reproduction, dismantling and erasing the human image repertoire *in the process*. Gysin and Burroughs asserted the absolute validity of their own psychic and mystical experiences, treating cybernetic information technologies as magical instruments for the shamanic invocation of spirits, challenging the 'known laws' of space and time."

Assemblage and Bricolage

The terms *assemblage* and *bricolage* refer to visual art created with found objects. Though there are technical differences in the academic art world, we can think of them more broadly in ways relevant to electronic music and music production, taking a cue from Amon Tobin's 1997 album entitled *Bricolage*. The most commonly known term related to assemblage is *collage*, once used by the Surrealists. For decades, this technique has been so ubiquitous as to be found in elementary school art classes. If we really break it down, the essence of this approach is the foundation for sample-heavy music styles and DJ culture in general, whether consciously or through rediscovery. Before Frankie Knuckles, Kool Herc, Public Enemy, The Prodigy, Amon Tobin, 2 Many DJs, or latecomers like Girl Talk, there was electroacoustic music. Two of the earliest forms of electroacoustic music are *musique concrète* and tape music.

Before explaining the differences between these two seminal electronic music forms, let's talk about how they are similar. Both emerged around the same time, made use of audio recordings as sources in compositions, and utilized similar production and composing techniques. At the time, turntables and vinyl records were the primary source, and as the name suggests, analog audio tape. Most of the techniques for sound manipulation developed by artists working in these forms are so commonplace now that they are completely taken for granted.

Musique Concrète

Musique concrète is widely considered the birth of sampling. It officially started in 1948 with Pierre Shaeffer (1910–1995) in France, though he was developing ideas in the early 1940s. Picking up where Luigi Russolo left off, Shaeffer added to the sound palate with electronic recording technology. He composed "symphonies" using recorded sounds collected from pre-existing sources. In 1950, Shaeffer's first public performance used just multiple turntables, a mixer, and a PA system. Understandably, he is often considered the first proto-DJ. Shortly after meeting his primary collaborator, composer Pierre Henry, in 1949, he founded Groupe de Recherches Musicales Concrète (GRMC) in 1951, now known as INA-GRM (source of GRM Tools plug-ins). There, Shaeffer worked with notables such as Stockhausen, Xennakis, Varèse, and Boulez (founder of IRCAM).

> **NOTE:** In addition to Figure 7.7, found in the sidebar on Brian Eno, Figure 6.6 (found at the end of Chapter 6, "Producer Tips") shows numerous connections between key players in this section and other significant elements in electronic music.

Tape Music

Tape music is essentially a more open-format version of *musique concrète*, additionally allowing for acoustic instruments, self-made recordings, and other sound sources. A prime example of proto-tape music is John Cage's *Imaginary Landscape No.1* from 1939, which utilized prepared piano, tone recordings, and a vari-speed turntable. In 1953, he completed *Williams Mix*, the first octophonic composition, using eight separate ¼-inch tape machines. Tape music proper didn't really get going until the 1950s, centered around the Columbia-Princeton Electronic Music Center in NYC, GRM in France, Stockhausen at the NWDR studio in Cologne, Germany, and a bit later at the San Francisco Tape Music Center starting in 1962. Tape music went further than *musique concrète* in evolving sophisticated methods and techniques for making decisions about sound selection. Many of these techniques involved some element of randomness or chance. In particular, the ideas and techniques developed by John Cage for utilizing chance in the composition process are now legendary. Not only are they still relevant, but a lot of popular techniques and software features used today exhibit his influence.

So, what largely differentiates modern electronic pop, electronic dance music, and hip hop from *musique concrète* and tape music? It is the process by which assembled selections find their way into the final product. Are they consciously selected and carefully placed, or is the element of chance significantly involved? Chance implies odds, and odds bring to mind dice games.

Aleatory Processes

The word *aleatory* comes from the Latin *alea* for *dice*, as in a roll of the dice. Aleatory techniques therefore involve some aspect of chance or probability in determining the outcome. We might be talking about cut-up techniques, tape music, or even computer-driven algorithmic composition, cellular automata, and generative music. Let's consider some definitions before moving on:

▷ **Chance:** Involving possibilities with unpredictable outcomes, results occurring without obvious mechanism
▷ **Probability:** Likelihood, the extent that something is probable
▷ **Random:** Outcomes determined by chance, without conscious intent, with all possible outcomes equally probable (The notion of "random" is a subjective one. Random also means no discernible pattern. When we figure out the pattern, we no longer consider something random, no matter how complex. Chaos theory taught us this much.)
▷ **Stochastic:** Random within finite parameters or sets (Technically speaking, when we use the term random, we usually mean stochastic.)

There are many ways to utilize chance and randomness, ranging from pure synthetic microsound granular synthesis, modulations of synthesizer parameters, MIDI drum programming, arrangement of completed sections within a composition, to ordering of whole songs in an environmental "DJ" set. You can choose to apply them at any time, at any level, or at any stage of the process. I will discuss some specific examples of techniques for you to try in a few pages.

John Cage (1912–1992): How did the Beatles transition from their early *I Want To Hold Your Hand* era in 1963 to *Revolution 9* in 1968? Surely, George Martin, pot, LSD, and transcendental meditation played a major role in their legendary transformation. In terms of *Revolution 9*, Lennon and McCartney specifically cited the influence of Stockhausen and Cage. Yoko Ono worked alongside Lennon in the creation of that milestone crossover moment of the *avant-garde* into mainstream pop music. Stockhausen is one of the many figures on the cover of *Sgt. Pepper's*, but John Cage was Fluxus artist Yoko Ono's mentor at the onset of her career in NYC, years before she even met Lennon.

John Cage first moved from California to New York in 1933 at the suggestion of American composer Henry Cowell (1897–1965), and studied with him as a student at The New School. Cowell deserves more attention than afforded in this book, but in short, he developed some of the most important and fundamental ideas foundational to electronic music in terms of composition, theory, and technology. With the help of Theremin creator Leon Termen, he invented the first rhythm sequencer (drum machine) in 1930, the Rhythmicon. Cage returned to California for a few years to study with Viennese master Arnold Schoenberg (1874–1951). Schoenberg invented the proto-Serialist "12 tone technique" and formally established *variation* (permutation) as a compositional technique in the 1920s. Though they never met, Cage was also heavily influenced by Erik Satie (1866–1925), a pioneer in minimal and repetitive composition styles (also a friend of Tristan Tzara). After two years with Schoenberg, Cage taught at UCLA and Mills College (future home of SF Tape Music Center) until finally returning to New York in 1942, where he lived for the rest of his life as a powerful influence on multiple scenes of influential performers, artists, and musicians.

Cage would still be considered an important composer if his career had only extended to 1950. In addition to his many beautiful piano pieces and forays into experimentation with electronics as early as 1939, he is also responsible for what is known as "prepared piano." Beyond his musical influences of Cowell, Schoenberg, and Satie, Cage transformed the composition process by developing techniques that flipped decision-making processes on their head. In the late 1940s, he began to study Buddhism with D.T. Suzuki, who was largely responsible for popularizing Zen in the U.S. along with Alan Watts. It was through their mutual connection to Suzuki that Watts and Cage met. (In *A Year From Monday*, Cage recounts an amazing synchronicity that occurred in 1950 between himself, Joseph Campbell, and Jean Erdman at a dinner party hosted by Alan Watts, who had just moved to New York.) Zen transformed Cage's relationship to the self (for lack of a better term), reinforced his aesthetic sensibilities, and collided in a geometrical synergy with his insights into the nature of silence.

Cage also studied other Asian philosophies, most notably the Chinese "book of changes," the *I Ching*, which one of his students introduced to him in 1951. More than anything else, the *I Ching* laid the foundation for the actual techniques utilized in his creative process. A system of divination dating back more than 4,000 years, the *I Ching* is essentially a 6-bit binary system that, through chance operations, can yield 64 different results known as hexagrams. Each hexagram's symbol has a name and is interpreted to have meaning at that time. Cage used this binary method to make his compositional selections for him. Whether flipping coins or dropping pencils on paper, he relinquished control to chance in 1951.

Though he fully utilized some form of his *I Ching*–based method from 1951 onward, it fully came to fruition with his landmark *Williams Mix* in 1953. He used the *I Ching* to generate a 193-page score, with chance determining sounds selected from six categories ranging from urban and rural field recordings to electronics, to proto-granular snippets. (The sounds were recorded by Louis and Bebe Barron, future composers of the all-electronic soundtrack for the seminal 1956 sci-fi classic *Forbidden Planet*.) The scores themselves were elaborate designs and often visually resembled modern art. As an example, Figure 7.3 shows a freeware app based on his 1958 *Fontana Mix*. The background image shows one of the 22 pages from its innovative score.

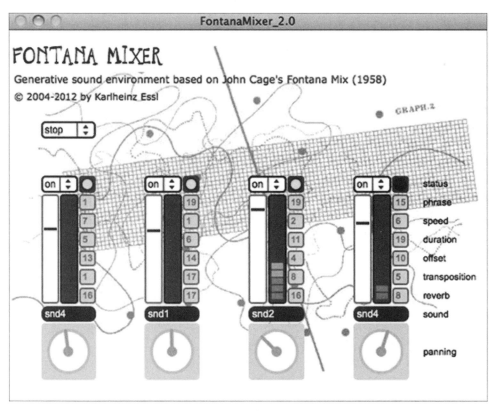

Figure 7.3 Karlheinz Essl's freeware Max/MSP app based on Cage's famous *Fontana Mix*. The background image is one page of Cage's score for the 1958 tape music landmark.
Source: Fontana Mixer by Karlheinz Essl.

Cage's chance techniques represented a severe break from one of the most significant aspects of Dada and Surrealism—a reliance on the unconscious. Although there are "cut-up" elements in tape music, Cage's compositional technique is a conscious removal of personal taste and unconscious decisions. As such, he also was not a fan of improvisation. For Cage, *indeterminacy* in performance simply meant that a piece can be played in a number of ways determined by chance, not improvised by the musicians. In a 1957 talk in Chicago, he used the following simile: "The composer resembles the maker of a camera who allows someone else to take the picture."

You may have heard that Cage was into mushrooms. He was an avid mycologist, and almost died a few times from accidentally eating wild mushrooms he gathered himself, but he never used the "magic" variety or any other mind-altering drugs commonly employed by many of his contemporaries—unless you include his beloved coffee and cigarettes.

DUB, DUb, Dub, dub...

Jamaican dub must be mentioned in any discussion of approaches relevant to contemporary electronic music. The aesthetics and techniques pioneered by the likes of King Tubby and Lee "Scratch" Perry in the 1960s and 1970s are indispensible. Growing out of the legendary Jamaican "sound systems" that would later have an incalculable influence on the birth of hip hop and B-boy/DJ culture in New York City, King Tubby turned sound-engineering science into the vehicle for creative process itself. Widely considered the first remixers, these dub pioneers turned the mixing desk, echo, reverb, EQ, and filtering into playable instruments. Along with reggae-influenced bass sounds and drum rhythms, creatively using excessive amounts of spring reverb and tape delay (commonly with the Roland RE-201 Space Echo, first released in 1974) are central to classic dub approaches.

Though traditional dub is based on reggae, its techniques are commonly heard on nearly all electronic music now, regardless of the underlying vibe. To find inspiration for new techniques, simply listen to any classic dub record, such as anything on the Wackies label. There is also a lot to garner from modern hybrid productions such as those found on numerous releases involving legendary British dub/EDM specialist Adrian Sherwood, any of the *High Fidelity Dub* compilations, dub's German techno offspring labels Basic Channel and Rhythm & Sound, and Montreal electronic musician Deadbeat. For some artists or projects, dub can suffice for all needed creative inspiration.

Practical Techniques

When you start to apply any of the techniques or methods discussed in this chapter at the early stages of creative process, it is highly recommended that you keep in mind the following guidelines.

▷ **First rule of creativity:** Have a sense of "purposeless play."
▷ **Second rule of creativity:** Create, then edit.
▷ **Third rule of creativity:** Avoid tedium.

The following techniques are useful in a variety of scenarios, at most any point in the creative process, and with any number of goals in mind. You might use them just for fun and experimentation, to help unlock a creative block, or to generate usable material. The generated material might represent the basis of a whole composition, a single instrument's part, original sound effects and transition sounds, or simply inspiration to guide any of the above or beyond. For popular styles of music, it is most likely that you will find short sections worthy of looping or using at opportune moments when that little something special is needed to take a track to the next level.

Unless you have a specific musical idea in mind for a specific composition, it is always a good idea to remember the second rule of creativity. This rule is most important early on in the creative process or any time you are making use of chance or unconscious processes. To avoid getting distracted or sidetracked and keep things moving forward, make use of placeholders, scratch tracks, and temp tracks. For example, if you are trying to generate melodic parts, don't start tweaking on drum sounds; just use something good enough for that moment. Once you've generated the desired material, then move on to the verification stage to make sure all the parts will work together. Potentially great moments and ideas never happen in the first place if you jump ahead in the process.

With our matured audio technology—namely computers and software—we can easily and quickly apply techniques that once were time-consuming. Computers quickly help us record and edit audio, select from an infinite library of sounds, and generate chance selections or random patterns. There is no need to physically cut tape or dub from one reel to another, with associated fast forward and rewind required. Every DAW, and even the most modest freeware file editor, offers capabilities only dreamed about by the most visionary minds of 50 years ago. Beyond the countless plug-ins and small apps, features and capabilities in Max/MSP, Reaktor, and Ableton Live represent prime examples of the culmination and integration of ideas and techniques from the last 100 years.

Generate, Sift, Edit

This approach is quite simple in concept: Generate a bunch of material and then pick out the parts that you like. There are a few important fine points crucial to success:

▷ The material should be generated with some sort of aleatory process or through improvisation.
▷ Let the process happen, and don't think too much about what is happening.
▷ Try not to generate too much material.
▷ If you do generate too much material, don't sift through all of it right away, per the third rule of creativity. Don't worry about missing something; you can revisit it later for other projects. Over time, you will develop instincts for when you are generating too much or not enough.

Jam Sessions

Can, one of Krautrock's preeminent bands, is known for splicing together their favorite parts from various jam sessions. Two of the founding members were students of Stockhausen in Cologne, and were heavily influenced by key figures in the New York City *avant-garde* scene, but their sonic aesthetic is equally reminiscent of American funk meets late 1960s psychedelic freakout. Because their drummer had such amazing timing, that they were able to do old school–style tape edits without the noticeable sudden tempo shifts common in that era with such techniques. Fittingly, his last name is Liebezeit, which translates to "love time" in English. Can is a cited or obvious influence on the likes of PiL, Bowie, Eno, and Stereolab. Their compositional approach was one of the biggest influences in the production of the first two albums by one of my old bands, I Am Spoonbender: *Sender/Receiver* (GSL, 1998) and *Teletwin* (GSL/Mint, 1999).

Knob Twiddling

Jam sessions are not the only way to generate material through improvisation. You can also go dub style and play the faders and knobs, or any of the new unique and abstract interfaces commonly found in multi-touch apps on tablets or other mobile devices (such as TouchOSC, Beatsurfing, or Lemur). Using recorded audio or MIDI performances, simply improv the recording of automation or CC data. This can be as simple as mapping a few MIDI controller knobs to effect parameters or FX sends and then just recording a few passes of improvised knob or fader movements. With either hardware synthesizers or controller-mapped soft synths, focus on just a few key parameters and do the same, such as the filter cutoff, envelope, LFO, or arpeggiator values. Setting an arpeggiator to hold is an easy way to generate patterns without the need for prerecorded parts. Many hardware instruments also offer onboard recording of parameter changes, especially drum machines and grooveboxes, but also devices like DSI's Evolver. To get the most out of this approach, you will want to be comfortable with your DAW's methods of handling automation and MIDI CCs. It is not a bad idea to make an audio recording of your twiddling improvs in case you don't have a need or desire to mess with all of the new data.

Generative Approach

This approach is the most aleatory of them all. It ranges from pure algorithmic methods to common features found in popular software. Algorithmic composition usually involves making use of computer software that utilizes various mathematical models to generate scores and compositions, such as those based on fractals, cellular automata, or evolutionary mutation. Generally speaking, algorithmic composition rarely results in complete pieces that are musically interesting outside of academic environments, but when used as part of a larger creative process there is a lot of value here. Max/MSP, Pure Data, Csound, SuperCollider, and Symbolic Composer offer unlimited options in this terrain but require some level of programming and steep learning curves. Fortunately for those of us who prefer not to go that deeply into tool creation, those who do regularly give away their creations. Other than countless Reaktor ensembles available in NI's user library (for registered users of course), no other environment is responsible for more apps and utilities than Max/MSP, and therefore also Max for Live. Ableton Live's basic functionality also offers numerous options for generative processes, namely their Follow Actions feature, which allows you to specify probabilities for clips launching each other.

In any DAW, it is also a lot of fun to record MIDI performances that are randomly generated on other tracks or external hardware, usually with arpeggiators or other MIDI processors. Collaboration also offers a lot of fun options. Perhaps have one person control MIDI performances that are sent out to some hardware controlled by someone else. You can hear an example of the latter in the 1998 song by I Am Spoonbender, "Mr. Knife, Miss Fork," about 6 minutes into the track. (That song, and the album as a whole, *Sender/Receiver*, utilized some aspect of most every technique discussed in this chapter.)

Audio Processing

There are many ways to generate parts or ideas with extreme audio processing. I am not talking about using effects for sound design of instruments or to spice up a part. Rather, I am talking about processes for generating ideas, parts, or even whole compositions. Electronic musicians commonly use the results in their pieces, but they can also serve solely as inspiration for ideas of new compositions. By the early 2000s, computing power reached a point that allowed developers to implement most everything in real time, usually as a plug-in or track-based feature in a DAW. Offline and rendered processes are usually considered to have limited usefulness these days, but they do offer additional possibilities and can lead to different results than their real-time counterparts.

Time Stretching

Time stretching is a feature in most every DAW, whether called Warping, Elastic Audio, or Flex Time. Set up a session in your DAW just for these experiments. Push the feature's capabilities to its limits, use the "wrong" algorithms, and possibly even draw in tempo changes. Use a variety of material ranging from your own voice, to whole songs, to single drum hits, and all sorts of melodic and harmonic performances. When happy, render out your results. Then you can sift through the results to find useful loops, samples, or even foundations of a composition.

For creative processes, offline time stretching is useful for more than just saving CPU. Check out the available options in your DAW or file-processing apps like DSP Quattro and Wavelab. For example, SoundHack's Phase Vocoder feature (see Figure 7.4) allows you to specify any length of time as the desired output from a file (not to be confused with the robot voice-type vocoder). This means you can take a one-second sound and stretch it to be one minute long, or take a 10-minute file and make it one second long. I thought I was really smart when, in the late 1990s, while experimenting with this feature, I (re-)discovered that timbre and rhythm were interchangeable. Kick drums became vibrating rhythms and whole songs turned into timbrally rich one-shot percussion samples. A few years later, I discovered that this way of thinking about sound was central to Stockhausen's process dating back to the 1950s, and even the topic of a few of his famous journal articles.

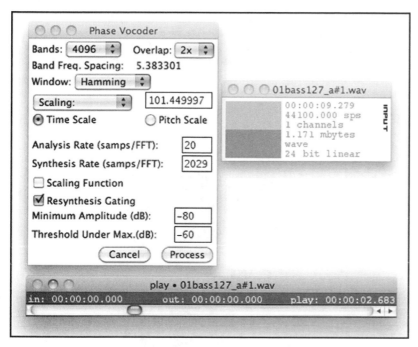

Figure 7.4 The Phase Vocoder "hack" in Tom Erbe's freeware SoundHack, which has been used for offline time compression and expansion since the early 1990s.
Source: SoundHack by Tom Erbe.

TIP: SoundHack also features an Open Any file menu command. After using it, you can add the necessary audio file header information to a non-audio file and save it as an audio file. Most of the information in non-audio files simply represents loud, distorted noise or silence, but occasionally there are useful rhythms or textures to chop out and then process further. Just watch your ears and speakers if you try this experiment.

Granular Synthesis and Resynthesis

Granular construction of audio was first theorized by Dennis Gabor in the 1940s, first applied by Iannis Xennakis in the late 1950s using analog tape, and brought into the digital age by Curtis Roads in the 1970s. We all have easy access to this technique now: Live's Warping engine, Max for Live devices such as Monolake's Granulator (see Figure 7.5), numerous Reaktor ensembles such as GrainStates, AudioMulch's granulator, Absynth, Csound, and a plethora of commercial and free plug-ins as might be found at www.granularsynthesis. com. Most commonly, we employ *resynthesis*, which means that we start with a digital audio file or stream and then apply granular processing to it. Instead of using FFT and phase analysis, this method approaches sound processing by grouping samples into grains and then sequentially processes each grain (samples as in 44,100 samples per second). Either way, granular synthesis is perfectly suited any time textural or atmospheric sounds are desired.

Granular resynthesis is an alternative method to phase vocoding for time stretching. When well implemented, it can offer more natural sounding results. When utilized in the extreme, this approach leads to completely different sonic outcomes. Ableton Live offers the quickest and easiest workflow for realizing usable results with this approach. If you don't have Live, just download the demo from their website. Import any relatively short audio file, set the Warp Mode to Texture, click the Double Original Tempo (*2) button as many times as it will let you, set the Global Tempo as low as possible, launch the clip, and then mess with the Grain Size and Flux parameters (see Figure 7.6).

Figure 7.5 Robert Henke's (Monolake) Granulator II free Max For Live device, which resynthesizes any audio file into brand new textures, in real time.
Source: Granulator II by Robert Henke.

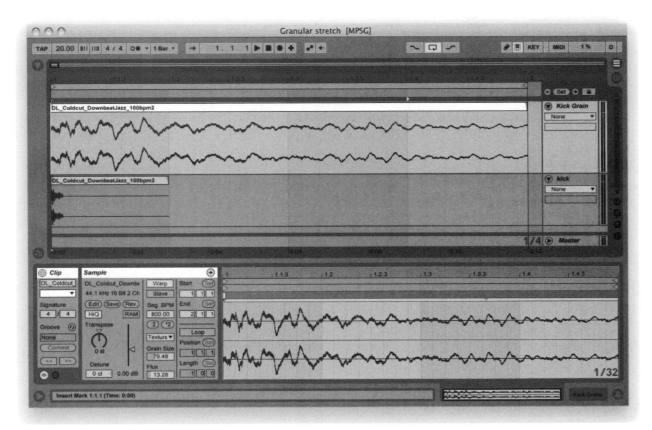

Figure 7.6 What started as a kick drum, the first ⅛ note in a factory drum loop is now an oscillating, 12-second texture due to extreme misuse of Live's Warping Engine.
Source: Ableton Live.

It Slices, It Dices...

Another approach that can yield interesting and unexpected results is to take advantage of another common software feature. When we had slow computers, before real-time time stretching algorithms were commonplace, companies used methods based on slicing. Essentially, through some sort of transient detection method, metadata is added to the audio file that specifies events. When the tempo is sped up or slowed down, the software spaces out the slices instead of reprocessing all of the digital audio. Propellerhead's Recycle and (now) Sony's Acid were the first commercial programs to offer these options. In addition to these REX and Acidized WAV files, and similarly created Apple Loops, we also have a slew of other options. Kontakt's Beat Machine mode, Reason's Bounce Clip to REX Loop, Ableton Live's Slice to New MIDI Track, and Logic's Convert Regions to New Sampler Track are common features to misuse by applying them to non-rhythmic material, possibly even generated with one of the aforementioned techniques. You might also then use arpeggiators or other aleatory MIDI performances to trigger your newly sliced up audio. Or, you might skip slicing and go right to real-time shuffling with a plug-in like iZotope's Stutter Edit or a Max for Live device such as Buffer Shuffler. Record the output of these processes and sift through the results for any number of possible gems, or as material for further processing.

Brian Eno (1948–): When it comes to simultaneous creative and commercial success in music and music production, U.K.-born Brian Eno is in a league of his own. No one has straddled the *avant-garde* and the commercial big label worlds to the same extent. Eno's practical philosophy to creative process is an integration of the best insights from key 20th century art movements into approaches perfectly suited to electronic music, the recording studio, and music production in general. In his 1995 book, *Brian Eno: His Music and the Vertical Color of Sound*, Eric Tamm states:

> If Eno's approach to music can be summed up here, it is in terms of inventing systems and setting them in motion, vigilantly maintaining an open mind and child-like curiosity with regard to the infinite play of musical possibilities, taking command of technology's array of music-making equipment from tape recorders to synthesizers to mixing consoles, generally working within a relatively narrow range of expressive possibilities for any given piece, and accepting happy accidents at any stage of the creative process.

Eno coined the term "ambient" music, and in collaborations with Robert Fripp, Jon Hassell, and Cluster laid the foundation for a whole genre. As a producer he's worked with the likes of John Cale (Velvet Underground), David Bowie, Devo, The Talking Heads, U2, and Coldplay. He is the connecting thread between influential musical aesthetics, ideas, and techniques that emerged in the 1970s from the New York downtown scene, Germany's Krautrock movement, and elements of arty, sonically textural British glam and post-punk. His affiliation with the Fluxus movement in NYC included collaborations with one of that scene's prominent mentors, John Cage. Eno decided to produce Devo's first album after hearing their demo in 1977. At this time, he was working with Bowie in Berlin, so he brought them to Germany, where they worked at Connie Plank's studio in Cologne. Plank was the preeminent engineer in the Krautrock scene, most notably as a close collaborator with Kraftwerk for their first four albums. Figure 7.7 shows some of Eno's connections to other significant players in the evolution of electronic music and various art scenes.

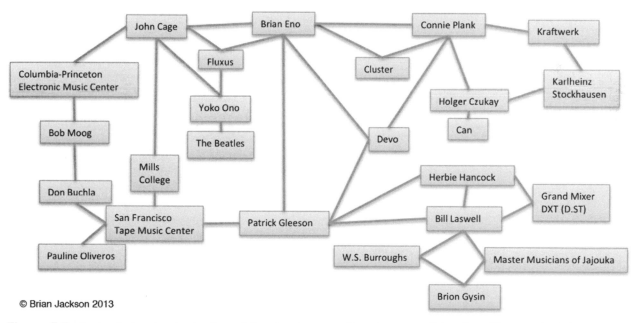

Figure 7.7 A chart showing just a few of the direct connections between Brian Eno, Krautrock, John Cage, Brion Gysin, and other topics in this chapter and elsewhere in this book.

Though Eno cites Stockhausen as an influence, he is more so the true successor to John Cage. Eno is widely considered as the artist who introduced Cage's ideas of chance to popular music. A prime example of this influence is found in a deck of cards he created with Peter Schmidt known as *Oblique Strategies*. In use now for more than 30 years, they were employed on all of the records he co-produced for Bowie—the Berlin Trilogy of *Low* (1977), *Heroes* (1977), and *Lodger* (1979)—and as recently as 2008 while producing Coldplay's *Viva La Vida*. Each of the cards has a phrase on it that could be useful in any variety of music production situations, especially when stuck, in need of a fresh idea, of just for fun. Following are a few examples of what you might find in the *Oblique Strategies*:

- ▶ "Honor thy mistake as a hidden intention."
- ▶ "Do something boring."
- ▶ "Try faking it."
- ▶ "How would someone else do it?"

While having a deck of the sought-after cards is really nice, you will also find a variety of paid and freeware applications for your computer and mobile device.

Not So Random...

Aleatory methods are not for everyone. Sometimes, we just need a guidepost or some set parameters to get us going and get something done. Here are a few fun ways to jump start the creative process when productivity is at the forefront of your priority list or you simply prefer less computer-centric approaches.

Define Limitations

Earlier, this chapter discussed how creativity is infinite, and that we need to learn how to remove our self-imposed limitations on being creative. Once we are in the production process, and have already opened up to all the options, that limitlessness of creative possibilities can easily stifle productivity. More is not always better. As a successful commercial producer used to high-pressure projects and big-label deadlines, Brian Eno's emphasis on the power of preset limits during the creative process most certainly makes sense. Yet, deadlines are not the primary motivation in the development of this technique. The modern production environment offers so many options, they can easily sidetrack intuitive creative process. The January 1999 edition of *Wired Magazine* included an article by Brian Eno titled "The Revenge of the Intuitive: Turn Off the Options, and Turn Up the Intimacy." He stresses the importance of known limitations for developing an intimate relationship with our tools and instruments. He argues that having too many options limits intuitive creative processes, and points out that beloved classic instruments have limited options, in his experience, because: "Intuitive actions confine the detail work to a dedicated part of the brain, leaving the rest of one's mind free to respond with attention and sensitivity to the changing texture of the moment. With tools, we crave intimacy."

> **NOTE:** The preceding Brian Eno quote also appears at the beginning of Nate Harrison's highly recommended 2005 video essay, "Bassline Baseline," which is a fascinating exploration of how Roland's TB-303 went from commercial failure to electronic music classic.

Due to the sheer volume of options sitting in front of us every time we boot up our computer, defining limitations is more important than ever. Severely limit the parameters available to you at any given stage in the production process and work with them. If you need to write a melody, pick one sound or instrument and use it until the melody is complete. If you want to use a synth, pick one synth. As discussed in Chapter 6, make use of presets and sounds that you organized during sessions dedicated to such tasks. Pick a tempo, pick a key, choose the duration of the song, even define the exact song structure in advance. Anyone who understands the nature of creativity realizes that there are still infinite possibilities.

"Bad" Cover Version

Create something totally new and unique by poorly doing a cover song. The idea is to use an existing song as a guide, but to purposely do a terrible job replicating the original. Change the tempo, key, chord structure, melody, and/or instrumentation. Perhaps find a song that is the exact opposite of something you would want to write and invert everything about it. If it is upbeat and happy (major), make it slower and more somber or serious (minor). If it is very complex, simplify it or vice versa. Another similar approach is to generate your guide track with some of the audio-processing techniques mentioned above, or by randomly chopping up and rearranging parts of different songs together. Slow down or speed up a song by double or half, pitch-shift it up or down, possibly all at once by using a vari-speed mode in your DAW or DJ software. Since you've created a heavily processed "bad" version of the guide track, you might then decide to do a not-so-bad cover of it.

The flip side of this method is to do a "brilliant" cover. In other words, do an extreme reinterpretation of a song that you like. There are many great examples, but one is hard pressed to cite a better one than that found in Uwe Schmidt's Señor Coconut project. You have never heard Kraftwerk, Michael Jackson, Laid Back, Deep Purple, or Daft Punk sound like this before.

Fake Score

This technique is not only useful in creative process, but can also help develop some skill and experience if you ever want to get into scoring for real. *Dark Side of The Rainbow* is a cult phenomenon of playing Pink Floyd's *Dark Side of The Moon* while watching *The Wizard of Oz*. People swear that it is as though the 1973 album works perfectly as the soundtrack for the 1939 film. Pink Floyd insists this is just a case of apparent synchronicity.

Why not do it on purpose? You don't have to score a whole film, just find a scene or two from a movie, video game, or TV show; mute the sound; and compose away. You might also create an imaginary scenario or use scenes from your dreams as the inspiration for your fake score. Or, take a cue from the hilarious "Bad Lip Reading" videos (find them on YouTube or Tumblr), but instead of imaging what people are saying, watch concert footage and write what you think they might be playing.

Play the Fool

The fool doth think he is wise, but the wise man knows himself to be a fool.

–William Shakespeare

The fool who persists in his folly will become wise.

–William Blake

The archetype of "the fool" is not just found on the tarot deck; it pervades mythology, fables, literature, modern popular fiction, and movies. The fool will do what others will not. Without concern for convention, the fool's words and actions reveal truths or insights in comedic, profane, and/or unexpected ways. The fool is not inhibited by fear of what others will think of him or her. The fool often stumbles into success, personifying what is commonly known as "beginner's luck." The fool therefore is a paradoxical character, simultaneously a silly novice and a wise master.

To make creative use of the fool's seemingly crazy wisdom is not always easy, but can be very rewarding. Ironically, with more mastery of your skills and craft it becomes easier. Chapter 4 discussed unconscious and reflective competence as relating to skills you know so well that you are able to forget about rules or steps to perform tasks. Creative process experts who have attained high levels of reflective competence know how to use the power of the fool to break up dull routines, escape habitual patterns, deal with creative blocks, or just to have fun. There is no need to be an expert or master to make playing the fool worth your while; it is called *beginner's* luck for a reason. Just don't make a beginner's mistakes and attempt these when short on time or at inappropriate points during productively flowing sessions.

Following are a few ideas to help get you started. There is no need to always record your foolish activities, but it is generally recommended in case you create something that you will not be able to easily reproduce. Even if the result itself is not directly usable in a production, there will be ideas worthy of reconstructing or using as an inspiration.

▷ **Do something you are not good at doing.** If you can't play guitar or drums, see what you can do with your current novice level of ability. That means your goal is not to care if you are playing correctly or generating parts like someone trained on that instrument; just do the most interesting thing you can with it. If you don't sing, record yourself singing whatever comes to mind, perhaps in the tradition of automatism. Keep it simple and avoid tools with steep technical learning curves.

▷ **Feign ignorance.** Find ways to approach parts of the process as if you knew nothing about them and see what happens. Combine this with self-imposed limitations as discussed previously. Pick a few of your personal rules and habits with regard to software and hardware and break them as if you didn't have good reasons for coming to such conclusions. For example, use too much reverb, place mics backward, or tune your guitar incorrectly.

▷ **Make a game of it with collaborators.** Swap instruments. Do an audio "exquisite corpse," as discussed earlier, in the section "Surrealism and the Unconscious." Be creative in figuring out ways to have fun playing the fool, perhaps combined with some NOSC.

The fool is a common form of the trickster archetype. Although the trickster often playfully reveals truths and insights, it is better known for pranks, deception, and mischief. Both the fool and the trickster also represent what is known as "crazy wisdom," which is not only commonly found in many stories and myths from indigenous and wisdom traditions, but also in kung fu movies and classic fictional characters such as Radagast the Brown in Tolkien's *The Hobbit* (and Peter Jackson's 2013 film). The term "crazy wisdom" in English was popularized by Chögyam Trungpa Rinpoche, founder of the first accredited Buddhist university in the U.S. in 1974, Naropa University in Boulder, Colorado. Trungpa Rinpoche was also a major influence on the Beat Generation, especially Allen Ginsberg, but also W.S. Burroughs, John Cage, Philip Glass, and Patti Smith, among many others. Burroughs, Ginsberg, and Cage even taught at Naropa in its early years. I first learned about the crazy wisdom teaching method in grad school in the late 1990s. My professor, Tibetan Buddhist scholar Steven Goodman, and I regularly discussed art and music outside of the classroom. (Brian Eno was a common topic.) While researching this section, I ran across a 2005 interview with Steven Goodman on www.inquiringmind.com. When asked about teaching crazy wisdom in his workshop on the trickster in Tibetan Buddhism, part of his answer was as follows:

> *"In fact, all of the wild depictions that you find in Vajrayana—of devas and devis and extraordinary beings doing extraordinary things—are all tropes, sort of archetypal outtakes that represent how things can be when you're living beyond yes and no, when you're no longer hiding behind the barricade of hope and fear. From that space you can use con-tradition, trick of the eye, double entendre, parody, ridicule and jokes all as ways of alchemically transforming the lingering resistance to waking up into pristine play."*

Daily Practice

Arguably the best practice for your creativity simply is to do something every day. Whether you are in the studio all of the time producing or experimenting, field recording here and there, practicing an instrument, or just messing around with a fun music or sound app on your phone on the train on your way to work, just do *something*. If you are a lyricist, write every day, even random thoughts and rhymes or automatic writing. Just as painters and sculptors keep a sketch book around for practice, doodles, and other random ideas, we should also just have fun creating musical sketches and performing sonic experiments. There are so many options here, both in terms of activities and ways to easily perform or capture them. The audio and music applications available for smartphones, iPods, and tablets offer options equal in portability to what visual artists have had for centuries. Daily practice will not only help maintain your chops and keep your skills relevant, but for years to come the material you generate can serve as starting points of inspiration for full scale productions.

Time Limits, Deadlines, Pressure

> *I am one of those people who thrive on deadlines. Nothing brings on inspiration more readily than desperation.*
>
> –Harry Shearer

That cliché analogy about coal and diamonds perfectly sums up this section. As discussed earlier in this chapter, gravity, time, and pressure play a fundamental role in forming our physical universe. One of the biggest misconceptions about creativity is that limitless time, options, and freedom are always ideal. That notion is true only in the earliest stages of the creative process, when you are facilitating emerging ideas. It is not true when you are producing those ideas, transforming infinite potential and ephemeral concepts into something specific that exists in the material world.

Adam Savage is best known as a co-host on the Discovery Channel's popular show *MythBusters*. Adam is also a professional movie special-effects fabricator and sculptor with more than 20 years of experience. In the March 2013 edition of *Wired Magazine*, he shared his thoughts on deadlines, and how they actually assist in the problem-solving process by refining one's mind. He admits that this perspective seems counterintuitive, because everyone complains about deadlines. Savage explains deadlines' usefulness as such: "They remove variables…The closer the deadline, the more likely you'll start thinking waaay outside the box."

When we have unlimited time, it is easy to overthink our options and second guess our decisions. Pressure and limitations necessitate creative problem solving. In the moment, we will always wish for more time, but as is often the case, once we get some distance from the project, those little details that seemed so big will have faded into the background. In Chapter 5, I mentioned Abraham Maslow's famous quote: "If all you have is a hammer, everything looks like a nail." That quote is to remind us to keep our options open and not to have a narrow view of things. When not dealing with nails, use another tool more appropriate to the task at hand. Let's flip Maslow's quote on its head. What if you need everything to look like a nail? Then get a hammer. When you are short on time and need to narrow down options, go out of your way to do so.

Creative Blocks

> *When you start working, everybody is in your studio—the past, your friends, enemies, the art world, and above all, your own ideas—all are there. But as you continue painting, they start leaving, one by one, and you are left completely alone. Then, if you are lucky, even you leave.*
>
> –John Cage

At some point, even the most talented, skilled, and experienced artist will have periods of not feeling creative. I am talking about extended periods of time, not about a few days here or there. There are many causes for creative blocks, and they can be different for everyone. Some common reasons are related to things like unrealistic expectations, stress, worry, fear, distractions, or health issues.

Commonly, what gets in the way is our "ego ideal," which is a psychological term that points to the combined conscious and unconscious vision of what we aspire to become. Often, we base this ideal on role models, or those we look up to or idolize in some manner. Unconsciously, we tell ourselves that we can't be as good as that ideal, especially when it also involves any notions of perfection. Perfection is a subjective, slippery, moving target that has a habit of blocking productive creativity. As Salvador Dalí famously told us, "Have no fear of perfection—you'll never reach it."

Another common reason for creative blocks is other people in our lives. This is a tricky topic that is discussed in Julia Cameron's very popular *The Artist's Way: A Spiritual Path to Higher Creativity* (2002). Although I've not personally done more than flip through it, I know a lot of talented musicians and artists who swear by it as a major factor in helping them grow past significant blocks at various points in their creative evolution. In addition to some discussion of philosophical, psychological, and "spiritual" aspects she deems pertinent to "creative recovery," it is equally known for practical techniques and suggested practices to help deal with creative blocks.

Change it up, use totally new tools, learn a new instrument, or consider new collaborators. Take up another form of expression or energy outlet. Try drawing, painting, or photography. Learn how to play chess or go. Study a martial art. Many ideas and techniques presented throughout this chapter are also useful for dealing with blocks.

When you are blocked creatively, it is best to continue to work through it. Just have fun with your daily practice and don't worry about the final product unless you really must. Stop thinking about what others will think about it. Just *make*. You never need to share these works with anyone. Simply working through blocks is known to help you get to a point where you can again feel good about working on projects for a consuming public. Painters have sketchbooks, musicians have recorders. For every song or project that I've completed, there are many dozen times more folders filling my hard drives that are no more than single ideas, sonic experiments, or musical sketches.

The only wrong way to approach this situation is to accept it and do nothing about it.

When the Thrill Is Gone: Completing Ideas

Genius is one percent inspiration, ninety-nine percent perspiration.

–Thomas Edison

To me, ideas are worth nothing unless executed. They are just a multiplier. Execution is worth millions.

–Steve Jobs

It is very exciting when you first come across an idea for a song or track, and even after the first few hours of hearing it come together. There is a rush of energy, a sort of high, likely even with a release of some adrenaline or endorphins. After working on this new creation for another few days or week, however, suddenly it seems flatter, not as exciting, as though something is now missing. The thought of tedious editing or arranging adds more to the sense of fading thrill. You think, maybe the idea was not so hot after all. Maybe it's time for a new idea. Once you get that new idea going, there is that feeling again, that rush, that high. But again, after a while, it seems to have lost something.

Eventually you have dozens of projects in various states of completion and not much, if anything, completed. Guess what? This dynamic of not getting further than the emerging or forming phases of the production process is a very common experience for new producers. Yes, in some cases, the excitement experienced at the moment of creation does make us think the idea is better that it really is. When you realize that the raw energy felt at those moments is a sort of peak experience, then you will understand that the hard work necessary to take those ideas to fruition is like integrating a peak experience into daily life. By metaphysical necessity, because we are dipping into unlimited potential and infinite creativity as these raw ideas first emerge, they will almost always seem more exciting before we begin to refine them on the way to a finished product, shaped to meet requirements and expectations. To be a producer, you must finish projects, which is a lot of hard work. The trick is to learn how to focus that raw excitement into energy that drives your creative-technical realization of that idea's essence throughout the production process.

Whether with great effort or natural ease you progress through the emerging and forming phases of production, getting stuck at the refining phase is also a common phenomenon. Regardless of the level of skill and accomplishment, nearly every producer always wants the project to be better. There is always something that can be tweaked, added, or improved. It never seems quite done. Unless we go the John Cage route and fully remove ourselves from the decision-making process, we will always feel like there is something more we can do. If it were not for hard deadlines created by a client, label, or studio, some of us would never finish anything. In a 2011 interview on www.ohdratdigital.com, Hank Shocklee said it as follows: "You know, you'll never really be finished with something, you're always working on stuff until you just have to surrender it!"

Outro

Creativity and creative process are endless subjects. As with much of the discussion in this book, there are many layers to the topics covered, which will reveal themselves to different people at different times, for years to come—myself included. There is always something new to learn, and new ways to approach what you already know. If you are more analytical and science-minded, you now have some ideas on how to set systems in motion to create intuitive, unexpected results. If you are more naturally intuitive and experience-centric, you now have some ideas on how to more logically guide your process. The ideal situation is for everyone to develop equal comfort with the whole spectrum of approaches, not only for your own projects, but even more so to expand your professional capabilities in general.

Finally, creative process is relevant to many aspects of our lives, not just to art and music production. Learning to use our unconscious can also help us figure out next steps in our career or give us hints about things we need to change in our lives. Just as apparent mistakes in creative process often lead to unexpected musical ideas, they can also reveal unexpected opportunities for new relationships and career directions. Many of the techniques used to help with creative blocks or idea generation have the positive side effect of also helping us grow as individuals and improve our lives overall, setting in motion a positive feedback loop that favorably influences all aspects consequential to being a successful independent electronic music producer in the 21st century.

If you have had enough deep thinking for a while, then you are in luck. Chapter 8, "Selecting Your Tools," is all about gear, gear, and more gear. Tools are an integral part of the creative process in music production, and there are a lot of options to consider. As technical-creative professionals, we rely heavily on our tools, and they influence and shape our decisions and outcomes. So it is time to switch gears and geek out for a while!

8

Selecting Your Tools

We become what we behold. We shape our tools, and thereafter our tools shape us.

–Marshall McLuhan

When you use familiar tools, you draw upon a long cultural conversation—a whole shared history of usage—as your backdrop, as the canvas to juxtapose your work. The deeper and more widely shared the conversation, the more subtle its inflections can be.

–Brian Eno

I fear not the man who has practiced 10,000 kicks once, but I fear the man who has practiced one kick 10,000 times.

–Bruce Lee

Tools

Given that it is as familiar as it is a funny-looking and -sounding word, it is easy to take for granted *tool*. From the Old English *tol*, meaning instrument or implement, tools enable us to get things done we couldn't do without them. Although other animals do use rudimentary tools, humans have taken their use to such an extent that not only have we become the dominant species on the planet, but we've even been able to leave its atmosphere and return safely.

There are two basic types of tools:

▷ **Material tools.** These are instruments or implements that extend or enhance the physical body, such as a phone, guitar, or computer (and software). When it comes to making music, the only "instrument" that is not technically a material tool is the human voice—which might help explain why way too many people think they could be professional singers.
▷ **Mental tools.** These are intellectual and social constructions, such as language, music, math, or mnemonic devices (memory tricks).

> **NOTE:** Mental tools are often used in tandem with material tools, so the lines can get blurry at times. As our digital technology continues to get smaller and smaller, enabling us to instantly access information stored on a network as if it were in our own heads, it is easy to imagine a time in the near future when we will have to rethink these distinctions.

Whether referred to as gear, equipment, kit, rig, or setup, tool selection is determined by the task at hand, sometimes categorically, sometimes specifically. In other words, you will commonly have to sift through a variety of options in the same category before you decide which one is the one you want to use (or can afford). Productivity and creativity go hand in hand, so even when confronted by seemingly similar options in the same category, some are better than others at enabling you to easily get things done. In many cases, these differences are subjective and based on the taste and work style of the user.

On that topic, there are objective and subjective differences between tools. These differences can influence productivity and shape the creative process. They present the available options, whether perceived or actual, and therefore limit possible outcomes. So how does one make good decisions about what tools to use? To answer that question, I am going to explore a number of issues in this chapter.

> **NOTE:** This chapter overlaps with topics in a few other chapters in very significant ways. To start, I highly recommend that you refer to Figure 4.1 before going any further. This chapter most directly addresses the lower two of the Big Four production holons, especially the lower-left holon, Tools/DAW. Chapter 4, "Master Your Craft," is not the only other chapter with numerous obviously related topics, however. If you have already read Chapter 7, "Creative Process," you may recall that I point you to this chapter for further discussion on some of the topics. Conversely, I point you to Chapter 7 at times in this chapter. The sections on protecting your hearing and ergonomics in Chapter 9, "Lifestyle Tips," are also highly relevant.

Creativity and Tools

The most interesting thing about a system is the set of things it does that it was not intended to do.

–Brian Eno

The technical definition of a hacker is someone who explores the true capacity of a system. In our case, the system is the artist and their tools. There is a direct relationship between an artist's skill with his or her tools and that person's ability to realize creative ideas. You can consider this relationship from two completely different angles. The most obvious one is high levels of competence using them in ways and for tasks intended by the designers. But intended functionality does not equate to capability because in reality, a tool can be used for whatever the user is able to do with it. The second aspect, then, is how an artisan employs a tool in unexpected ways and exploits unintended capabilities. Given any isolated example, a casual observer could easily confuse a fool with a master. As discussed in Chapter 7, the difference is that the fool stumbles into his or her results, while the master may get similar results through purposeful action. Moreover, unlike the master, the fool may not be able to replicate his or her results, and likely has no idea of the implications of his or her process for later steps in the production. The master is able to act like a fool, but the opposite is not true.

> **TIP:** Check out www.lifehacker.com for many fun, practical, and creative uses of everyday objects to solve everyday problems.

D.T. Suzuki's influence on John Cage was briefly discussed in Chapter 7. That his influence extends much further to many pioneers of electronic music, related creative process, electronic instruments, and even personal computers is undeniably significant. Don Buchla publicly stated that John Cage directly influenced some of the signature features of his modular synths. Zen master Kobun Chino Otogawa, who was D.T. Suzuki's assistant until Suzuki's death in 1971 (after which he took over his position as head of the Haiku Zen Center in Los Altos, CA, just north of Apple's home base Cupertino), presided over Steve Jobs' wedding in 1991. Alan Watts was also influenced by Suzuki early in his career, in the 1930s. In 1950 Watts moved to upstate New York, and it was through D.T. Suzuki that he and John Cage finally met, subsequently became friends, and as a result further extended Cage's social circles to include the likes of Joseph Campbell (Lucas' primary influence for the Star Wars saga's storyline).

Looking into this particular branching system and set of feedback loops can help you understand how tools and creativity intersect for the skilled producer working in the lineage of the 20th century pioneers. Beyond Cage's aleatory methods, the following transcription from an Alan Watts lecture points to a perspective on the tools we use. Even though it is from the 1960s and on the topic of Buddhism, if you swap out a few words here and there, it could easily be a Brian Eno quote from the 1990s about production with electronic musical instruments and audio technology.

> *Buddhism is not interested in concepts. It is interested in direct experience, and direct experience only. So from the Buddhist standpoint, all concepts are wrong. Just in the same way that nothing is really what you say it is. Is this a stool? [turns it over] It isn't now, it's a wastebasket. [uses hands to bang out a rhythm on it] It's now a drum. What is this thing? See…it is what it does. It's this, see…. Anything you can use it for is what it is. So if you have a rigid idea that it is a stool and you can only sit on it, you're kinda stuck, but if it's all these other things as well, then you suddenly see that anything can be everything.*

–Alan Watts

> **NOTE:** This quote was transcribed by this author from the audio book version of the 1960s lecture series *Buddhism, The Religion of No-Religion* (CD 1, 16:00–16:43). There are print books that include transcriptions of these lectures, but I highly recommend the audio books for accuracy and for the simple fact that listening to Alan Watts talk is a very enjoyable and entertaining experience. Based in Jersey City, NJ, right across the Hudson from Manhattan, is WFMU (wfmu.org). As the longest-running freeform radio station in the U.S., WFMU is widely considered to be its best radio station. For years they've treated their local and online listeners to countless hours of Alan Watts' lectures.

Users and Designers

The vast majority of the tools we use are not designed in a vacuum. They evolve with a community of users. For anyone who cares to look, there is a fairly obvious, complex, dynamic system of fractal feedback loops between tools, individuals, communities, genres, developers, and manufacturers. We have a direct relationship with our tools, sometimes even developing strong emotional associations with them as we put them to use in our own ways.

Some producers and musicians use their tools in such unusual ways that they influence the world around them. Peers, scenes, and large groups of musician and producers evolve shared meaning of these tools and their uses, sometime in obvious ways, but also often buried deep in socio-cultural norms and traditions. Designers rely on these groups for their income, but also as inspiration for their next creations based on perceived demand, direct user feedback, and feature requests. Some of these tools even become associated with specific genres and styles—to the point that they become widely recognized symbols of various music subcultures. As tools are used for genre-specific purposes, developers then develop new tools targeted at those functional or aesthetic elements. The feedback then starts over.

Users Influencing Designers That Influence Users That...

Link Wray's (1929–2005) "discovery" of distorted guitar and "invention" of power chords in the 1950s changed popular music forever. Bob Moog's (1934–2005) development of the Minimoog based on feedback from musicians led to the most influential analog synth of all time. Bob Moog very publicly credited Wendy Carlos for invaluable feedback in its development prior to its release in 1970. There are many other examples out there. Smaller, more recent, and more obvious examples are perfectly illustrated by a variety of plug-ins based on techniques made popular by specific artists or styles of music. Bouncy is a freeware delay plug-in by Bram @ Smart Electronix. It enables you to quickly emulate a specific rhythm featured prominently in Aphex Twin's classic 1997 track, "Bucephelous Bouncing Ball." Electronic Musician BT worked with iZotope to develop Stutter Edit, a deep and powerful plug-in effect processor than offers a tool set to speed up a variety of effects normally accomplished only with hours of tedious editing. Sonivox Wobble is a plug-in synth designed to simplify the complex modulations made popular in the Dubstep genre. "New York compression" refers to a decades-old technique associated with the NYC big recording studio sound. Reason 7 added a right-click menu command that instantly sets up the mixer for you to do New York compression.

Moog

Creative, brilliant, talented people make and design our tools. A master instrument designer deeply understands what his or her users need and want. This designer's skill and craft is certainly grounded in science, but also in conscious and intuitive understandings of shared cultural meaning. In a 2000 interview, Bob Moog stated, "I'm an engineer. I see myself as a toolmaker and the musicians are my customers. They use my tools." Hans Fjellestad's 2004 documentary *Moog* features a number of interviews with the man himself. One of them took place at the Ashville, NC Moog factory, and focused specifically on instrument design. About 14 minutes in, Bob explains how a Minimoog generates sound with analog electronics while holding one of the main circuit boards (transcribed by this author):

> When I think of this circuit, I have a feeling for what's happening with the electricity as it goes through these parts. I don't imagine resistors being stretched out on a row like this because that has nothing to do with the sound. What it has to do with is all these little tracers on the board here that connect them together and cause the current to change as it goes from one part to the other. So I have a feeling, which is really similar to how I imagine how a violin maker feels just getting the right amount of wood in one surface of the violin. There are a lot of people who begin to feel what the circuits do in a way that's similar to the way I feel them. Now, I have technical training, so I visualize things more in terms of voltages and current, but you can also visualize them in terms of how the sound is changing. And I know for a fact that musicians make contact with this board inside the instrument. Not physical contact; it's not like they have it under their arm. There's something going around here [circles hand around his head] that connects what's going here [points to circuit board] with what's going inside here [points at his head]. It's not spiritual in the sense that its religious, but its spiritual in the sense that it uses some way of connecting with things that are in the universe by ways other than directly with our senses [pauses] that we can see with our senses.

–Bob Moog

Roll Your Own

Designing or customizing your own tools can be a rewarding experience. Most commonly, this means graphical object–based software such as Reaktor, Synth Maker, or Max/MSP. Many academically trained electronic musicians go deeper and learn more traditional programming languages for powerful environments such as Csound or SuperCollider. Learning about audio electronics can also open many options. You need some training, but you don't need a degree in electrical engineering—just a few junior college–level courses or equivalent. With some fundamentals under your belt, you can get somewhere with circuit-bending, breadboard/microcontroller kits, or even high-end DIY kits for synths, preamps, or compressors.

Pros:

> ▷ Can realize ideas not possible without custom tools.
> ▷ Can save you money, you just have to put in the time.
> ▷ Can be a lot of fun and very educational.
> ▷ Can develop into income stream doing something you enjoy.

Cons

> ▷ Is time consuming.
> ▷ Involves a lot of steep learning curves.

▷ Can become a distraction or excuse for procrastination.
▷ Solder burns and fumes are not fun.
▷ Electricity can be very dangerous.

Tools of the Trade

It may seem like I am stating the obvious, but there is a tool for every task. What may not be so obvious is that the pairing of tool and task is not the same for everyone. We all have different needs depending on where we are in our career and what we need to do. Most aspiring producers do not have the experience, skill, or budget to adequately address the audio-engineering aspects of setting up their personal project studio. It is common for producers to rely on other studios for many recording scenarios, such as tracking drums or amplified electric guitar, for final mixdown, and especially for mastering. So as you go through this chapter, try to remember that there is a difference between what you need to understand and what you need to purchase. The vast majority of engineers who know how to use a $500,000 AMS Neve or SSL console do not own them, just as commercial airline pilots don't own the jets they fly for a living.

There are a few basic considerations for figuring out what you purchase for your studio:

▷ **Need.** Although need is somewhat subjective, making it easy to confuse with want, there are many objective aspects to this consideration. What do you actually need to meet your goals? What do you need to do in your own space versus what can be done elsewhere? What is needed to take on clients? What is needed to work with collaborators? What is needed to help you earn income? When it comes to making your own music and realizing creative ideas, whatever works for you is fine. When you start to do work for clients, the needs take on externally applied requirements.

▷ **Budget.** This is the most objective and measureable of the considerations. What can you afford now without going into debt? What might you be able to afford in the future? If it costs too much, then you simply need to find another way to meet your goals. Going into debt is something to consider very carefully in this age of "buy now/pay later" deals. When you have a steady income stream, carefully managed debt can be very useful when needed. Revolving credit is usually the most problematic because it is designed to keep you paying off your creditors for as long as possible while the compound interest lines their coffers. Fixed-term small-business loans and leases can be better ways to expand your business.

▷ **Creativity.** This highly subjective consideration overlaps the gray areas between need and want. Some tools are more conducive to the creative process than others. The more high level your knowledge, skill, and experience, the more options you have to see something as creative. These ideas are covered later in this chapter and were discussed in Chapter 7.

▷ **Space/travel.** How much physical space do you have for the instruments, computers, and racks of gear? What size venues are you playing? Will you have time for a real sound check? How often do you travel, and what needs to come with you on the plane or in the van?

▷ **Compatibility.** Make sure it will work with your existing setup. Some of us like to piece everything together ourselves and are comfortable keeping track of all the little "techie" details. On the flipside, it is not uncommon for PC users to purchase turnkey systems from a PC audio specialist such as Open Labs, Muse Research, Carillon, PCAudioLabs, or Sweetwater. Not only is the computer custom built to spec for pro audio, but they also install all the necessary drivers and software for you, which they've already compatibility tested. Some turnkey systems are literally all-in-one solutions for professional-quality digital audio recording, mixing, editing, and mastering, such as the SADiE PCM-H8 Digital Audio Workstation.

If you are new to this, don't just spend a lot of money. Avoid super-cheap, entry-level junk, but recognize that you need to grow into most of the higher-end stuff to even appreciate it. If someone has never tasted wine before, that person will not appreciate the subtleties of a very good wine compared to a merely good wine that costs a fraction of the price. This developed sophistication is acquired through experience with audio gear, too. Make sure to check out buying guides or visit your local pro audio shop (not to be confused with music-instrument retailers that have a pro audio section). If you have a budget, it may be worthwhile to find a consultant to help you make the best selections.

Analog and Digital, Hardware and Software

Why is it called *analog*? Simply stated, analog audio uses electrical signals and magnetic fields that are *analogous* to pressure waves moving through the air. Sound waves have continuously variable amplitude and frequency, as does analog audio. The key words here are *continuously variable*. By definition, if it is analog, then it is hardware.

How is digital different? The key word for digital is *discrete*, which means separate or noncontinuous. Though it also uses electrical signals and magnetic fields, digital information is stored, processed, and transmitted as a binary code, which is nothing more than sequences of ones and zeroes. With this binary code, digital audio is made up of values that represent a given number of quantized measurements per second. We call this the sample rate, such as 44,100 samples per second, or 44.1 kHz. According to the Nyquist-Shannon theorem, the sample rate corresponds to the highest frequency that can accurately be represented.

So if the sample rate corresponds to frequencies, then what corresponds to amplitude? All of these ones and zeroes are lumped together into "binary words." Each possible one or zero is known as a bit. Binary words are represented in a given number of bits, such as 8 bit, 16 bit, 24 bit, etc. So, the word length corresponds to amplitude and dynamic range (6 dB per bit). As such, the synonymous terms word length, wordlength, and bit depth might be thought of as the resolution available for each sample—for example, 24 bits offers 16,777,216 possibilities for each sample to be quantized, while 8 bits offer just 256. (Bit rate is about data-transfer rates, and is a related but different concept.) If this is a bit too technical for you at the moment just remember that analog audio is analogous to acoustic waves and digital audio is a series of ones and zeros.

Digital audio does at times use optical technology with photons to transfer information at the speed of light. Most commonly, digital audio is transmitted much like analog audio, using electrical current flowing through a conductive metal (at close to the speed of light) or manipulating the spin state of electrons using magnetic fields. The key difference is that with digital, a one corresponds to values above a given voltage and a zero to a value less than that voltage. Hard drives, RAM, and many other components of your computer and other equipment work using the same basic principles, but at a much higher level of sophistication and precision.

Digital always implies that software is involved somewhere, but often it is built into hardware. So while analog always refers to a "real" physical device, digital can refer to tools that are real or virtual. Virtual simply refers to software tools interfaced via a GUI on a computer screen. Often, these are simulations of hardware tools, such as mixers, compressors, or pianos—the one exception being that some digital hardware synths model analog circuits with algorithms and are known as virtual analog synthesizers. When I say "virtual instrument," I mean digital and software. When I say "analog synth," I mean analog hardware. When I say "virtual analog," I mean software, although occasionally running on propriety digital hardware. When I say "in-the-box" (ITB), I am talking about virtual, usually mixing. Make sense?

Expensive, high-end digital audio equipment started to appear in the 1970s, including the now legendary EMT250 reverb and the Fairlight CMI. Yet, many misconceptions linger from the early days of relatively affordable digital audio in the early 1990s, mostly related to recording practices and sound-quality issues. Digital is a mature technology now, and is continuing to improve. Even cheap digital is pretty decent now. So even though digital audio can sound very good, there are still reasons that many people prefer good quality analog. This is a huge discussion with opinions all over the place, but I can simplify it for our purposes. It is commonly said that analog is not as accurate as digital, and that some of these inaccuracies are pleasing to the ears. Although that generalization is not perfect, it does help to explain common trends in software development. The advantages of digital technology are undeniable, so it is no surprise that there is a massive collective effort to perfect software that emulates the endearing quirks and pleasing sonic characteristics of analog audio. This last point is illustrated in Figure 8.1 and Figure 8.2, which show a few different companies' software products that emulate classic analog gear. We're not far from a time when only the most discerning ears will be able to tell the difference—and even when they do, they will be happy regardless.

Hardware

Hardware is getting smaller, and less of it is needed, but you will require at least some hardware for the foreseeable future. Generally speaking, when compared to software, hardware takes up more space, is more expensive, consumes more power, generates more heat, and can require repair from time to time. On the upside, hardware worth having offers tactile immediacy and/or sonic advantages not available in software, and rarely becomes obsolete as it can outlast even the company that created it. Each of the following is a big topic, and everyone has different needs; my goal here is to point you in the right direction. Just make sure to do your research.

Computer

The computer revolution has made all this possible. Since you will use a lot of software that runs on your computer, it might just be your most important piece of hardware. Nowadays, pretty much every new computer is powerful enough to handle all but the most intensive music-production tasks. You just want to make sure you get a machine that is intended for professional use. Apple's computers are a favorite amongst music producers for a variety of reasons, but stability and easy troubleshooting are the big ones. If you choose to go the PC route, go with one from a company that specializes in setting them up for audio. Don't assume that just because a PC can run your software, it is really up to par for professional use.

The other major consideration is whether to go with a laptop or desktop setup. Generally speaking, laptops cost more for less performance. If you need to be portable, then you need a laptop. If you need maximum power and flexibility, then you need a desktop. The performance gap between the two for audio is closing, so many are able to do what they need with a high-end laptop. Many professionals have one of each.

NOTE: What about tablets? At the moment, they are useful as sketchpads, controllers, sound generators, and field recorders. In the foreseeable future, given the right assortment of peripherals and accessories, they will be on par with today's laptop, and even desktop, computers.

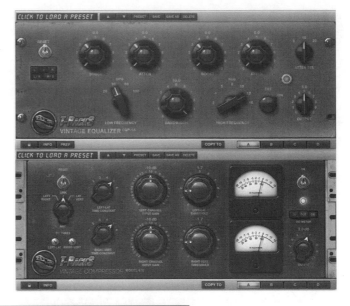

Figure 8.1 Plug-ins by URS, IK Multimedia, and Slate Digital. All do a good job emulating desirable qualities of specific vintage analog audio devices.

Sources: Unique Recording Software, Inc.; IK Multimedia; and Slate Digital.

Before buying a new computer, make sure that it is supported by your software of choice. It is a real bummer to find out that you have to wait a few months (or longer) for your software to catch up to your new fancy computer and OS. It is also worth noting that the newest, fastest models usually cost a good amount more than the one just below it. Consider buying an older model on closeout, manufacturer refurbished, or even used from a reputable vendor that offers returns and/or a warranty. If you know how to avoid scammers, and are very knowledgeable about computers, you might consider buying from a private seller to find something in your price range. You'll need to plan on reformatting the drive and reinstalling everything, so make sure it comes with an OS installer, and consider any additional software included in the deal as useless unless installers and authorizations are also provided. Be extra cautious about used laptops, as they often get banged around and dropped, are harder to repair yourself, and are more expensive to get repaired.

Audio Interface

If you are using a computer to produce music, you need an audio interface. It is literally the connection between the virtual world and the real world. At its most basic, an audio interface is a device to get audio in and out of your computer by converting analog to digital (ADC) and digital to analog (DAC). Although there are still sound cards that can be installed inside a machine with PCI slots, most people use boxes that connect via USB, FireWire, or Thunderbolt. Leaving aside entry-level "hobbyist" options, most interfaces these days are pretty decent. For quality results, plan on spending no less than $250 for the most affordable options and upward of $2,000 or more for very good, feature-laden devices spec'd for the demanding professional. Also keep in mind that the stability, reliability, and performance of software drivers vary from company to company and OS to OS. The following list hits most of the key features to consider when contemplating audio interfaces.

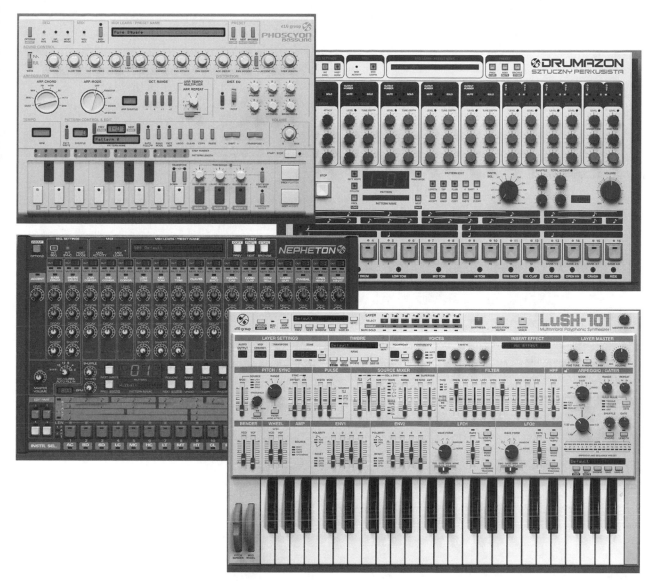

Figure 8.2 Plug-in emulations by d16 Group of some Roland analog classics from the early 1980s: TB-303, TR-909, TR-808, and SH-101.

Source: d16 Group Audio Software.

▷ **I/O (input/output).** How many in and outs do you need, analog and digital? Multi-track recording, performance, and integrating hardware devices are the key considerations.

▷ **Converters (ADC/DAC).** This is the most basic function of an interface, and its quality plays a major role in both recording and monitoring. (Stand-alone high-end converters used by mastering engineers can cost thousands of dollars for a single stereo ADC or DAC; see products by Benchmark, Lynx, Lavry, and Weiss.)

▷ **Preamps/DI.** The preamps on cheap interfaces are decent at best. High-end interfaces can include good preamps and DI (direct-injection), but often it makes sense to look into separate devices for these options.

▷ **Mixer.** Most interfaces include some sort of internal mixing, often just for direct-monitoring options (to avoid latency). Although it is common now for full-blown digital mixers to be built into interfaces, even with insert effects and full monitor control along with the included software GUI. Many people do not need hardware mixers anymore because of the advances in this territory. Products by RME, TC Electronic, MOTU, and UAD come to mind here.

Figuring out the ideal interface can be challenging even for experienced musicians and composers, because it is audio-engineering knowledge that helps one make sense of all the options. If you are still unclear about the difference between balanced and unbalanced or XLR and S/PDIF, then I recommend doing a lot of research before buying anything. Talk to an audio engineer or experienced producer known for his or her technical prowess.

Is It Live, or Is It Memorex? On September 20, 2012, SonicScoop.com posted a podcast featuring highly experienced professionals doing a comparison of the new UA Apollo (see Figure 8.3), with its Neve and tape-emulation plug-ins, against a real Neve 8068 console and Studer 827 tape machine in a high-end NYC record studio (Stratosphere Sound). To do the comparisons "blindly," they had to add a lot of noise to the digital emulations. They did notice differences, but questioned whether they were significant enough to warrant the huge differences in cost, as well as technical issues working with real-world tape machines. You can listen to them doing the tests and download the comparison recording files. To find the page on SonicScoop.com, with included links to podcast and A/B test files, just do a Web search for "Input/Output Audio Review: UA Apollo vs. World-Class Recording Studio."

Figure 8.3 Universal Audio's Apollo audio interface with UAD plug-ins and the software interface that controls its built-in full featured mixing console.

Instruments

Traditional instruments are always hardware, so here we are primarily concerned with options that are also available as software.

▷ **Synthesizer.** Plug-ins have improved significantly in this area, but nothing sounds like a high-quality analog synthesizer. The cost of analog devices may not be worth the sonic differences to the undeveloped ear, but those who can afford it have at least one analog synthesizer in their arsenal. Digital hardware synthesizers can also sound noticeably fuller and richer than their plug-in counterparts (not to be confused with ROM-based "sample and synthesis" devices). This is surprising to the many people who mistakenly assume that "digital is digital." Significant sonic advantages are possible when a company can write and optimize its algorithms for specific DSP chips in custom-designed hardware, and not to a generic plug-in container that must work on all personal computers. Companies like Waldorf, Access, Radikal, and Elektron come to mind here.

▷ **Drum machine.** Even though plug-ins are very good at the role of drum machine, sometimes it is just nice to have a box in front of you that does just one thing and does it well. Vintage drum machines have their quirks, but assuming they are in decent working order, they also sound better than samples or their virtual clones. The newer ones tend to be relatively inexpensive and can be a lot of fun (Korg Electribe series); are fairly high-end, catering to a niche market (Elektron Machinedrum); or are actually software with a dedicated hardware controller (NI Maschine, Arturia Spark).

▷ **Sampler.** Most older hardware samplers are basically worthless these days, unless you like long load times from floppy disks and limited sampling time dependent on tiny amounts of RAM. That said, there are two common reasons to use a hardware sampler, and neither of them include the old-school rack mount variety. One reason to use a hardware sampler is that it is one of the classic vintage units and you like the sound of it enough to deal with its limitations, such as the MPC 60 or SP1200. The other reason is that it is one of the new generation of modern spec'd portable samplers that is well suited for travel or taking on stage. For a great example, check out comedian/musician Reggie Watts' one man show using just an Elektron Octatrack and Line 6 DL 4. There is amazing video of him performing on *Totally Biased* on February 1, 2013.

▷ **Exotic.** Every producer has a few secret weapons, and often they come in the form of a weird, rare, or unusual instrument, device, or object. The infamous theremin, circuit-bent game consoles, acoustic instruments from other cultures, or kids' toys are just a few examples from this category, which is limited only by your imagination.

1960s Innovation: East Coast Versus West Coast Style: Bob Moog (1934–2005) and Don Buchla (1937–) exemplify brilliance, creativity, and innovation. They simultaneously invented the modular subtractive analog synthesizer. This is an example of what is known as "multiple independent discovery." Moog released his products first, but it is widely believed Buchla was actually first with a completed product. Although competitors in some ways, they became friends and developed a very close professional relationship, even working together on some Moog products. Their inventions had much of the same functionality, but one thing they always approached differently was how one interacts with their instruments.

Bob Moog was born and educated in New York City, where the Moog synthesizer was created, developed, and sold until 1978. The Computer Music Center at Columbia University is the oldest electronic music research facility in U.S. While there in the early 1950s, he developed numerous components that are standard in subtractive synths, such as ADSR envelope generators (to solve a problem for composer Herb Deutsch). The evolution of his instruments was largely based on feedback from musicians using the new timbral options available in synths for traditional musical scores. Wendy Carlos was one of the composers using his modules, and he credited her for feedback that led to many of the improvements that made his first production model possible, the 900 Series in 1967. Moog created instruments that could be immediately integrated into popular music, whether the 1960s TV commercial and radio jingles of Eric Siday, Carlos' *Switched on Bach* in 1968, or Kraftwerk's drift from their *avant-garde* jam band into electronic pop pioneers in 1973. Groundbreaking popular music, mind you. At the same time, he also knew many ruthlessly *avant-garde* artists, such as the enigmatic genius Sun Ra, to whom he gave a prototype Minimoog. Although NYC is a center for intense innovation and creativity, as a densely populated center of commerce it is more about the practical. For most musicians and composers, having to learn new ways to play notes is not very practical. To address his customer's needs Moog decided to use a traditional piano-style keyboard. He showed this to the public at the 1964 AES Convention, making him the first person to attach one to a voltage-controlled subtractive analog synth. Bob Moog was not a musician.

Don Buchla was born and educated in California. At the age of 25, he started his first company in Berkeley, just across the bay from San Francisco. Unlike Moog, Buchla is a musician and was a major part of the 1960s psychedelic counter-culture. Ken Kesey's famous acid tests used Buchla's electronic sound makers, and he designed the sound system used on the bus for the infamous Merry Prankster's 1964 road trip (as can be seen in the 2011 documentary *Magic Trip*). Buchla developed his ideas working with pioneering experimental electronic musicians such as Pauline Oliveros, Ramon Sender, and Morton Subotnick at the seminal San Francisco Tape Music Center (1960s). Free from the influence of commercial musicians, Buchla was more interested in unique and innovative interfaces than was Moog, having never added a piano-style keyboard to trigger his instruments. He instead created new types of interfaces, such as the tactile Multi-Dimensional Kinesthetic Input Port (Model 222e). When compared to Moog's synths, Buchla's instruments have a reputation for being difficult to replicate results, but this is largely by design. Influenced by the likes of John Cage, randomness and uncertainty are parameters built into some of his modules, and even have names like "Uncertainty Source" and "Arbitrary Function Generator." It is interesting to note that Buchla did not have to rely on selling synthesizers to make a living; for that, he worked for NASA and Lawrence Livermore Labs.

In terms of personality and approach, Moog and Buchla seem quite different. In reality, they are more like two sides of the same coin. Together, their simultaneous invention of the modular subtractive analog synthesizer resulted in a more complete realization of those influential tools.

Refer to Figure 7.7 for connections between Moog, Buchla, and other key players in seminal electronic music.

Speakers and Headphones

Speakers are the voice of your system, so selecting them is personal and important. Be prepared to do a good amount of research, because there are a lot of considerations to weigh against each other. There are many aspects to professional monitors, but I've distilled the basic considerations down to three:

▷ **Size.** Near-fields help minimize interaction with room acoustics and are what you need as your primary set of speakers. Anything bigger than an eight-inch woofer is getting into mid-field territory, and will likely be too powerful for a small room. Mains are basically PA-sized monitors used as the second or even fourth set of monitors in big mix rooms, for music and film, or in high-end mastering suites.

▷ **Bandwidth.** How low does it go? Hitting 20 kHz is no problem, but getting down below 30 Hz with near-fields usually requires a sub woofer. Fortunately, most producers don't need to go that low, even those making "bass" music.

▷ **Accuracy.** How neutral and accurate are the monitors? How is their stereo imaging and sense of depth? Are any frequency ranges "hyped"? Most consumer speakers are designed to sound "good," not to be accurate. You want to make good decisions based on the best information possible.

How do these three basic considerations play out for you? I find it useful to break down needs into three basic categories:

▷ **Composing.** By composing, I mean songwriting, arranging, beat making, basic recording, and the like. For these tasks, your monitors just need to be good enough to make good musical decisions. Smaller entry-level near-fields can be sufficient for this task, which at a minimum should have five-inch woofers. If you are composing music with a lot of bass, you probably want seven-inch or eight-inch woofers, and will be looking at about $300 for the cheapest pair worth even considering. If you are concerned only with composing at your studio, $1,200 for a pair of nice near-fields would be at the high end of the range unless you are earning income with your skills and want to treat yourself. Here, you may consider products from M-Audio, KRK, Yamaha, Mackie, Alesis, or JBL, among others.

▷ **Mixing.** Mixing requires more accuracy and bandwidth than composing, so be prepared to spend at least $1,000 for something up to par for professional results. If you also do a lot of detailed sound design, then your needs are the same as mixing when it comes to monitors. Having a cheap second set of monitors is good for reference to check your work, but you need one high-quality pair of monitors that you get to know intimately. If you have a big, well-treated room and a nice budget, you may also consider a pair of mid-fields. Of course, anything good enough for mixing is good enough for composing. Here, you may consider higher-range products from some of the companies mentioned for composing, plus also Dynaudio, Adam, Event, Focal, Genelec, or Barefoot.

▷ **Mastering.** This need has the highest requirements for bandwidth and accuracy. I would not worry about this unless you have been at production engineering for a number of years. Even for project-studio needs, $2,000 would be the minimum for a pair of monitors useable for good mastering results, assuming the room and ears are up to it. Dedicated mastering suites use mains for monitoring, which not only need a proper room and usually a separate high-quality power amp, but can start at more than $4,000 per speaker and go easily upward to $20,000+ for a pair. At the lower end, some of the products from Dynaudio, Event, or Adam can work in the project studio, as can Klein & Hummel or Genelec if you have a few more bucks. If you are serious about getting into mastering, check out B&W, PMC, Focal, Tyler Acoustics, or Dynaudio's audiophile range, for starters.

Figure 8.4 is a photo of Shawn Hatfield's mastering suite, which features a pair of Tyler Acoustics Decade D1. Figure 8.5 is a photo of the Critical Listening Room at Vintage King LA's showroom, which is full of high-end options from companies such as Focal and Barefoot. Figure 8.6 shows you the minimalist setup in Erik Magrini's mastering and mixing room. (Note: You will find interviews with Shawn and Erik in the companion book to *The Music Producer's Survival Guide*, titled *The Music Producer's Survival Stories: Interviews with Veteran, Independent, and Electronic Music Professionals*.

Headphones are useful for a few different reasons. You need them when recording with mics, because obviously you don't want the speakers on in the same room. You may need to work at night without waking your neighbors, or check the bass if your monitors don't go as low as needed. Often, I like to check my mixes on different headphones just for reference. I have four sets, none of them costing more than $125: Sony MDR-V700 (DJ), Sony MDR-7506 (versatile), AKG K240 (super flat), and M-Audio IE-30 (earbuds). As with speakers,

Figure 8.4 Shawn Hatfield's AudibleOddities Mastering in Oakland, CA. Tyler Acoustics D1 monitors with a nice assortment of analog gear.

Figure 8.5 The Critical Listening Room at Vintage King's Los Angeles showroom. An ideal place for accurate assessments of high-end monitors.

they vary widely in quality. If you don't have monitors you can rely on, or you can never turn them up, then investing in a good set of pro audio headphones is worth considering ($200–$350). Generally speaking, open-back headphones are better for mixing, while closed-back headphones are better for recording, especially in the field.

CAUTION: Be sure to check out the "Protect Your Hearing" section in Chapter 9.

Figure 8.6 Tarekith's minimalist Inner Portal Mastering in Seattle, WA. Lynx Hilo DAC, Event Opal Monitors, custom GIK Acoustics panels.

Acoustics

Since the size, dimensions, and acoustic treatment of your room determines the maximum size and power appropriate for monitors, let's briefly talk about that topic. Make no mistake: A well-designed room is an important tool. No matter how good the equipment, if the room is too small, shaped weirdly, or not properly treated, then you cannot trust what is going into your ears. Keep in mind that there are different needs for control rooms, vocal booths, and recording studios. This is a huge topic that you will want to research, though I will give a few tips here.

The minimum size for optimal acoustic behavior given a well-treated control room is 1,500 cubic feet, which assumes that no one dimension is much bigger or smaller than the others. This also assumes that you can set up the speakers away from corners and at least a foot from the walls. Everyone needs to treat for bass resonances, some more than others. You don't want the room to be too dead (absorptive) or too live (reflective). Finally, don't confuse treating a room with sound proofing, a related but separate concept. Sound proofing is about stopping sound from entering or leaving the room, which can be much trickier and often involves some construction. That said, with a well-treated room, there will be less sound bouncing around to leak out.

If you do go the budget route and make your own acoustic materials, just make sure to pay attention to fire codes and other related safety issues. Other than the obvious, another reason that professional acoustic foam costs more than standard packing foam is that it is fire rated. Putting flammable toxic materials all over your studio is not only dangerous, it can void your insurance coverage should there be a fire.

Microphones

Mics are to recording engineers what paintbrushes are to painters, which explains the showroom shown in Figure 8.7. Unlike recording engineers, different types of producers have hugely different needs when it comes to mics. Even if you primarily compose with plug-ins or electronic instruments, at some point you will want to record something with a mic. For vocals, you want at least one decent large diaphragm condenser, which would usually be a minimum of about $300, such as the AT-4040. Condensers commonly used on vocals in big studios regularly cost $3,500+ (for example, Neumann U-87), but nowadays for about $1,000 you can get ones that sound amazing (for example, Mojave MA-200). You might also consider a really good dynamic microphone if you don't need a slick pop sound, such as the RE-20 ($450), which is popular in broadcast but can be a workhorse in a project studio, too. If you intend to set up a proper room for recording bands, then you will need an assortment of dynamic and condenser mics suited to a variety of tasks, and likely even a matched pair or two for stereo recording techniques. Regardless, I find that everyone should at least have an ubiquitous Shure SM57 around ($99), because it can be used for just about anything not requiring the crystal clear even frequency response of a condenser. In fact, a lot of vocalists actually prefer dynamic mics in the studio when they are going for a "warmer" sound. For adding extra texture to your productions, cheap, weird, or beat-up old mics of any sort can be useful creative tools.

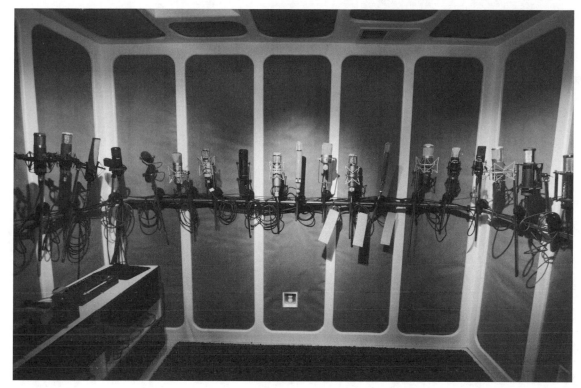

Figure 8.7 The Mic Locker at Vintage King LA. An ideal place for checking out mics with a wide variety of preamps.

Preamps, Channel Strips, and Other Outboard Gear

Microphones create very low-level signals that require amplification and impedance matching to get them up to line level. The preamps that come with entry-level mixers and audio interfaces are functional, but rarely any good. Better interfaces can include nice clean preamps, and may be all you need. With regard to the latter, most of the best ones are not bus powered; they have their own power supply to ensure optimal dynamic range. If you plan to do a lot of recording with mics, then you will want to look into getting at least one really nice preamp for vocals or a pair for stereo uses. Preamps have a huge effect on the tonal characteristics of microphones, and experienced engineers learn how to mix and match mics and pres for different types of sounds and results. If you plan to invest in some nice mics, make sure you have pres that are up to the task so you actually can hear why you spent so much in the first place.

A DI replaces a mic in the recording signal path. This is very useful when you either can't or don't want to mic an amp/speaker cabinet. Many pres include a DI so you don't need a separate device. They are needed for direct recording of guitar and bass, because instrument level is very low and very high impedance. Many electronic instruments will sound a lot better when run into a DI and not just directly to the line ins on your interface.

Even if you plan to use many of the great software options for mixing and sound design, there is no substitute for getting a good-quality recording to begin with. Many producers now use a nice analog front end for recording and then rely on plug-ins after everything is ITB. Channel strips include a preamp and a combination of other features found on a mixing console, such as EQ and compression. You may even consider looking into the very popular modular 500 Series system that enables you to build up your front end over time with modules from many different companies. With the 500 series system, you first purchase a powered chassis, which range in capacity from one to 10 slots, and then fill it with your choice of modules from a variety of companies (see Figure 8.8). You likely won't even need a lot of analog outboard gear, but having a few key pieces can serve you well in many different scenarios. One really nice stereo EQ or compressor can be awesome not only for recording or mastering, but also for reprocessing plug-in synths and other software sources. Before I reluctantly parted with my Crane Song STC-8, VST synth basses never sounded so huge.

Mixer, Monitoring, Control Room

Not that many years ago, a mixer such as the Amek Media 51 would be at the top of the list (see Figure 8.9). Now, however, so many audio interfaces offer the same features, you may not need one. Even for those who mix ITB, there are features in hardware mixers that

Figure 8.8 The Amek Neve Media 51 integrated with Apple's Logic DAW via Apogee converters at the Wave Lab NYC in Williamsburg, Brooklyn.

you may still need, even if you piece them together using a few different products. The one rack space Dangerous D-Box is a good example of a high-quality option that combines most of the features mentioned here:

▷ **Analog sound.** No high-quality analog mixer is cheap, but with the explosion of the project studio, many companies, such as Allen and Heath, Soundcraft, Toft, and Midas, are making quite good-sounding mixers at lower price points. For many producers, a summing mixer is more than sufficient to add good analog character to otherwise mostly digital productions, such as those made by Dangerous, Tonelux, Neve, and SPL. Another option is to go with a small vintage mixer like the one shown in Figure 8.10, a Quantum Audio Labs QM12b from 1980.

Figure 8.9 An Amek Neve Media 51 integrated with Apple's Logic DAW via Apogee converters at A.J. Tissian's Wave Lab NYC in Williamsburg, Brooklyn.

Figure 8.10 Tree Laboratory in Williamsburg, Brooklyn, the home studio of full-time producer, musician, and audio engineer Eric Hoegemeyer.

▷ **Preamp/DI.** If you are planning to record bands and use a lot of mics, a mixer with good preamps can be a very cost-effective front end for your DAW.

▷ **Direct monitoring.** Although many audio interfaces offer direct-monitoring features, having a hardware mixer can also be very useful in this respect.

▷ **Routing and patching.** If you have a lot of outboard gear or instruments, having everything plugged into a decent hardware mixer can make it easy to work out an idea without having to even turn on your computer. When producing, a mixer with four or more buses makes it easy to have everything plugged in and then choose which instrument gets routed to your interface.

▷ **Monitor management.** The master out fader on your DAW is not meant to be the monitor level controller for your speakers. Having dedicated hardware for controlling monitor and headphone levels is a must for any serious producer. You may also need to easily choose between a few sets of speakers. Also common on the monitor section of any decent mixer are other features, such as mono and dim. Because so many people have ditched their consoles for a DAW, many companies make dedicated monitor controllers. Check out options by SM Pro, Samson, Focusrite, Mackie, Presonus, TC Electronic, JBL, Coleman, Dangerous, and Crane Song. (The TC Electronic BMC-2 is shown in the center of Figure 8.11, in the next section.)

▷ **Cue and talkback.** If you record other artists who are in another room, you need a way to communicate. How do you send them a headphone mix and how do you talk to each other? Larger mixers include features for talkback (with auto dim) such as built-in mics and other I/O for listen mics and headphone mixes. Many of the products making monitor controllers (listed previously) also include these functions.

MIDI Controllers and Control Surfaces

In the late 1990s, there was an explosion of powerful software able to replace more expensive hardware for many producers. Native Instruments' Reaktor, Propellerhead's Re-Birth, and Cycling 74's MSP extensions to Max are standouts from that era (and even today). Even before the novelty and initial excitement of these new, affordable tools wore off, pretty much everyone began to experience the frustration of having to operate them with a computer mouse. It didn't take long for companies to release a variety of products aimed at adding tactile immediacy back into the equation. There was a similar, parallel trend related to DAWs and their mixing capabilities, especially as Pro Tools emerged as the industry standard in the recording-studio world. No longer did you need a huge, expensive console to mix down large track-count projects, but using a computer mouse was no replacement for the hundreds of knobs and sliders that were now virtualized behind a computer screen.

There are three basic needs for working with computer software, which may be separate pieces of equipment or available together in some combination. You can see a variety of MIDI controllers in Figure 8.11, after the list that follows. There are now even apps for your phone or tablet that can handle each of these tasks.

▷ **Note input.** Whether through a standard MIDI keyboard controller, drum pads, guitar-to-MIDI converter, or breath controller, you will want a way to play in notes to trigger virtual instruments. If you have a hardware synth or other digital instrument, you can likely use that for MIDI sequencing, too. Many MIDI controllers also include this functionality. There are many options in this category, but if you are looking for keys with a piano-like feel, research keyboard controller options from the likes of Roland, Yamaha, and Fatar.

▷ **MIDI controller.** These devices are multi-purpose and often include a combination of features. The defining characteristic of a MIDI controller is the ability to program its knobs, sliders, or other interface elements to various MIDI messages. Although usually lacking motorized faders, these can often be programmed to act like control surfaces (see the next bullet). For popular MIDI controllers, with and without keys or pads, check out devices by M-Audio, Akai, Novation, Korg, Livid, and Keith McMillen.

▷ **Control surface.** These devices are meant to control things that have been virtualized in software. They may or may not use MIDI at all. Many of these devices are intended to control specific software and therefore are not programmable, so you learn how they work as you would the mixer in the software. The better, more expensive ones include motorized faders, which is really, really nice when mixing. For mixing surfaces, check out Mackie Control, Avid Artist Series, or Neyrinck's V-Control for iPad. If an eight-inch screen is too small for you for a mixing surface, just wait. It is only a matter of time before large-scale multi-touch devices become commonplace.

It should be noted that there was a direct precursor to MIDI controllers, known as programmers. These devices served the same purpose but were designed to offer easier access to parameters hidden behind limited interfaces of specific devices by specific manufacturers. Roland offered a series of programmers for many of their analog synths, such as the MPG-80 used for editing the MKS-80, which was essentially a rack-mount version of the Jupiter 8. Access is known for its Virus synthesizers, but the company got its start with the Access Microwave Programmer, used to help program the powerful, but interface limited, Waldorf Microwave (a small version of the insanely powerful and very expensive Wave).

Figure 8.11 An assortment of MIDI controllers and control surfaces that I've collected over the years, together for the first time ever.

Furniture

Studio furniture can get expensive, especially when it is designed to have minimal acoustic impact on a room. While you don't need to spend a lot if you are inventive or happen to be a good carpenter, you do need to set yourself up with the right desks, chairs, and stands so you are physically comfortable, your gear is well cared for, and you can maximize productivity. Please, be sure to read the "How to Avoid RSI" section in Chapter 9.

Necessary Accessories

There are a lot of other accessories that different people will need to different degrees, although all are important, and are often left out of budgeting considerations. Don't forget to consider things like instrument stands, speaker stands and isolation pads, patch bays, good power strips and surge protectors, a variety of adapters, and plenty of extra hard drives for backing up important files.

When you know what you are doing and have some nice equipment to work with, it is time to make sure your cables are not the weakest link. As you step up your game and the quality of your tools, cables commensurately grow in importance. Which ones you choose can make a huge difference. You don't need to go nuts with pre-made Mogami or Monster at every turn, but never go with the cheapest options, either. If you are good with a soldering iron, consider buying cable in bulk and making your own. It will cost you a lot less and you will notice the difference.

Software

Generally speaking, compared to hardware, software is less expensive, doesn't break down (not counting OS problems), gets better with free or cheap updates, and takes up less space. On the downside, software offers less tactile immediacy, can be discontinued or become obsolete, and may lack sonic advantages of more expensive hardware. Software is often a more affordable virtual version of an existing tool, such as a synth, mixer, or compressor. But, a lot of software offers functionality only possible in digital that is not practical to build into a dedicated hardware device. Many audio-processing methods and tools are found in this category, such as anything that uses granular synthesis or resynthesis, as are unique interfaces for interacting with your computer.

I am not going to give detailed descriptions for categories of software like I did for hardware for two reasons. First, much of it emulates the tools listed in the "Hardware" section. Second, there is way too much software out there. Instead, here is the short list:

▷ **Digital audio workstation (DAW).** See the next section for a full discussion.
▷ **Plug-ins.** These are virtual instruments, audio processors, and utilities. The following plug-in types are available for both Mac and Windows systems: VST, RTAS, TDM, AAX. AU plug-ins are for Macs only, and DX plug-ins work only on Windows systems. A few popular virtual instruments from Germany's Waldorf and Native Instruments are featured in Figure 8.12.
▷ **Operating system (OS).** Operating systems include Mac, Windows, Linux, iOS, and Android.
▷ **OS utilities.** These are pieces of software that enhance your OS or help to keep it working properly, including programs for hard-drive maintenance and file backup/recovery.
▷ **Misc.** This includes audio editors, CD/DVD authoring tools, file converters, patch editors/librarians, and more.

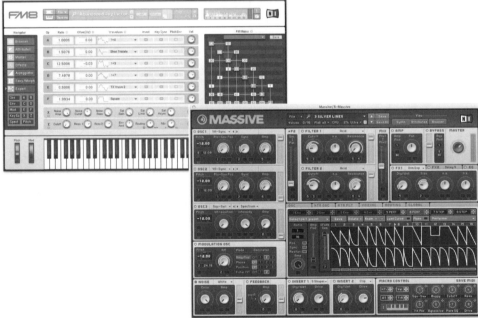

Figure 8.12 Plug-ins by Waldorf (top) and Native Instruments (bottom), each with one based on a vintage digital synth (PPG Wave and DX7, respectively) and one original design.

Sources: Waldorf Music and Native Instruments.

The DAW

There is a lot of software used in music production, but the centerpiece of your studio is your DAW. Indeed, the DAW is the producer's most important material tool. Sitting in front of your DAW should feel like being at home. You want to be very comfortable so that realizing ideas is as effortless as possible. In fact, you want to get to a point where the software is like an extension of yourself. It should become almost invisible as you work. You can effortlessly realize ideas as though you were a skilled painter splashing around different colors and hues using a variety of brushes and brush strokes.

In Chapter 4, I suggested that beginners should learn one DAW really well before trying to learn too many other pieces of software. There are two main reasons for this:

▷ All DAWs are deep, complex pieces of software with their own personality.

▷ You need to know one really well to be able to effectively compare it to other DAWs.

There was a time when there were huge differences between the capabilities of various companies' products, but nowadays the established ones are all quite good and full featured—even sharing most of the same features. Yet, they do all have fortés and shortcomings, their own personalities and quirks, their own ways of doing things, and yes, different visual aesthetics. So how does one decide which to use, and why?

Basic Considerations

The following three points tie back into the discussion in Chapter 2, "Point on the Space-Time Continuum," of what we mean when we say "professional," and also to Chapter 3, "What Is Your Plan?"

▷ **Professional.** If you want to take on clients as a music producer, you need to know at least one popular, industry-standard DAW. Many professionals are experts in at least one, and very comfortable with another one or two. For the highest-quality productions of your own music, some DAWs are better than others depending on what you are doing, so it is highly likely you will use the same one for your personal creative works as for your client-based projects. Keep in mind that DAWs that meet professional needs will also be able to meet personal and collaboration needs.

▷ **Collaborations.** If you regularly collaborate with the same people, it is highly recommended that you all use the same DAW to make it easier to send ideas back and forth—in other words, to collaborate. As long as you and your collaborators agree, use whatever works.

▷ **Personal.** If you are only producing your own music, then use whatever DAW you like and are most comfortable with. If you get good results and are earning a living, just keep using what you are using. Over time, you will likely learn a thing or two about other DAWs anyway.

Specific Considerations

The idea behind the following list is for you to determine which of these considerations are most important for you:

▷ **MIDI recording and editing.** Some DAWs are much better at MIDI than others, especially if you are integrating external hardware.

▷ **Composing and scoring.** There are dedicated notation packages, but some DAWs include decent notation functionality, others not at all.

▷ **Audio recording and editing.** For basic recording and editing, most DAWs are quite good. But if you are working with large, multi-track sessions then only a few are up to the needs for professional environments.

▷ **Mixing.** For professional mixing, you need to be sure that the DAW has features dedicated to efficient workflows for large projects.

▷ **Mastering.** Some DAWs are known for their high-quality, neutral audio engines. Although there are dedicated CD-mastering DAWs, a few full-featured ones also enable you to lay out a CD and add the necessary codes for authoring.

▷ **Video and post production.** Just because a DAW can import video does not mean it has the features needed for professional post production.

▷ **Performance.** If you need to go on stage with your DAW, there are very few options.

▷ **Creativity.** Some DAWs are very powerful, but may be slow and clunky. Others just make it easier to get your ideas down quickly and efficiently. How much can you customize a given DAW to fit your needs and style?

▷ **Mac/PC.** Most of the big DAWs work on Mac and PC, but a few are for only one or the other. Linux and iOS are future possibilities, if not now in some cases.

▷ **Stability.** DAWs are very complicated pieces of software. There are going to be some bugs. But how often does it crash? Is it just you, or is the DAW's forum full of people with the same issues? How responsive is the company when it comes to releasing bug fixes?

▷ **Learning curve.** Some DAWs are just easier to learn than others.

If you want people to pay you for any variety of your skills, some DAWs stand heads above others. Depending on where you are in the world, different DAWs are more popular than others. There are many differing opinions on the matter, some being educated opinions and others just based on someone's personal taste and experience. I am sharing my opinion here, knowing that it is just that, but these are educated opinions based on 20 years of experience. Also, realize that I am not telling you to avoid other options; I'm only sharing what has worked for me and what I see working for others—creatively, but more importantly, professionally (that is, for income).

Selecting Your DAW

Assuming you are in North America, as of 2013, there are three DAWs that you should seriously consider if you want to maximize your chances of getting work: Avid Pro Tools, Apple Logic, and Ableton Live. I use all three of them, with Pro Tools and Live being my personal tools of choice depending on specific workflow. The following sections explain why.

Avid Pro Tools

Users have had a love/hate relationship with Pro Tools (PT) since the beginning: Love the software, hate the company. Since Avid dissolved Digidesign in 2011 and opened the software to third-party hardware, things have improved quite a bit, especially for users of their native systems. Regardless, Pro Tools is the industry standard for recording studios and audio post production. When it comes to multi-track editing, and to audio editing in general, Pro Tools is king. PT is also great for mixing, and is actually quite good with MIDI, too. If you have any interest in working on commercial music in an audio-engineering capacity, especially in North America, Pro Tools is a DAW you want to know.

> ▷ **Most appreciated by:** Audio engineers, recording musicians, producers of all sorts, anyone doing sound for picture work.
> ▷ **Key strengths:** Recording, editing, mixing, and file management. Once mastered, Edit Window workflows are second to none. Powerful feature set for efficiently managing large–track count projects. Industry standard in music-recording studios and audio post production facilities, which means big potential for paying work. HD systems offer superior audio quality, DSP cards for plug-in processing and I/O, scalable I/O options, and latency free monitoring during audio-recording sessions. ICON series control surfaces offer immediate tactile control over every parameter.
> ▷ **Key weaknesses:** Audio engineer–friendly design can frustrate musicians with the learning curve. Included virtual instruments are functional at best, so third-party plug-ins are necessary for electronic music production. HD systems and ICON surfaces are too expensive for most independent producers. Parent company Avid has gone through major restructuring in the last few years, even selling M-Audio, so it would not be surprising if Pro Tools ends up owned by someone else in the future.
> ▷ **Plug-in formats:** TDM, RTAS, AS, and as of Pro Tools 10, AAX. (TDM and RTAS are discontinued and replaced by AAX as of Pro Tools 11.)
> ▷ **Noteworthy competition:** Logic, Nuendo, Sonar, Sequoia/Samplitude, Pyramix, SADiE.
> ▷ **Quick history:** Started as audio only in 1991, added MIDI in version 5 in 1999, but it was not until version 8 (2008) that MIDI in Pro Tools became good.

Apple Logic

When Apple bought Emagic in 2002, for obvious reasons it dropped development for Windows. Logic is incredibly popular with composers and electronic musicians for good reason. Its deep MIDI functionality is paralleled only by the likes of Max/MSP, and it includes a great bundle of powerful and really good-sounding virtual instruments. Logic is also very good for mixing, editing, and post production.

> ▷ **Most appreciated by:** Composers who need a DAW, electronic music producers, anyone with a lot of MIDI hardware, and recording musicians who don't like Pro Tools.
> ▷ **Key strengths:** Long-time favorite of electronic music producers and composers worldwide. Included virtual instruments and audio effects are great, and can compete with many third-party plug-ins. Object-oriented design makes it incredibly flexible and customizable. Deep MIDI functionality, including the ability to build and import custom mini-apps in the Environment (much like a basic version of Max/MSP). Solid recording, editing, mixing, and post production features. In 2011, Apple dropped the price to $199!
> ▷ **Key weaknesses:** Mac only. Very quirky. (People used to jokingly call it "Illogic.) Deeper functionality has very steep learning curve. Low priority for parent company.
> ▷ **Plug-in formats:** AU.
> ▷ **Noteworthy competition:** Cubase, Pro Tools, Digital Performer, Sonar, Samplitude.
> ▷ **Quick history:** Started as Notator in 1988 and was MIDI only. Added audio functionality in 1994 in version 1.7, although it was not until version 4 (1999) that audio was decent and not until version 8 (2007) that it was good.

Ableton Live

Ableton Live was founded by two Berlin-based electronic musicians who hit the limits of using custom-built Max patches and Logic environments for live performance. More precisely, as Robert Henke states the following on his website, in addition to himself, "Ableton was founded by my former Monolake partner Gerhard Behles, together with a developer, Bernd Roggendorf and a finance person, Jan Bohl." As of version 9, Live is still the only DAW on the market designed for live performance. It is also excellent in the studio for many producers, and can even be a primary DAW for some. Because it is so good for live performances, a lot of established acts need an Ableton Live person. Knowing Live can translate into work as a supporting musician on stage or as a consultant to help artists figure out how to best integrate it into their performances.

▷ **Most appreciated by:** Electronic music producers, improvisational musicians, DJs, and performing artists of all sorts.

▷ **Key strengths:** You can take Live on stage and perform with it. Non-linear workflows are very musician friendly, and allow for incredibly easy and intuitive realization of ideas. Creativity factor is off the chart. Audio warping (everyone has it now, but Live was first to make it useable in real time). Fast flexible signal routing, signal processing, and virtual-instrument customization. Most everything in the software can be quickly custom mapped for tactile control. Max for Live (through a partnership with Cycling '74) offers unlimited options for extending and interacting with Live. There is a variety of powerful hardware- and iPad-based controllers designed just for Live, including Ableton Push (a collaboration with Akai), which blurs the lines between instrument and controller. Produced by a relatively small company, employing mostly musicians, that is known for being responsive to its user base.

▷ **Key weaknesses:** Requires purchase of more expensive Suite option to get decent collection of virtual instruments. Primitive features for many of the workflows used in recording studios, such as efficiently managing large–track count projects, multi-track editing and recording, comping, timeline editing, post production, and mixing.

▷ **Plug-in formats:** AU (Mac only) and VST.

▷ **Noteworthy competition:** None at the moment. Though, Bitwig was founded by former Ableton employees and looks promising. They announced Bitwig Studio in January 2012, and then showed a working beta at Winter NAMM 2013 (January). It is the first DAW to build on the non-linear innovations unique to Live's Session View up to this point. We will have to wait and see if Bitwig becomes a player or turns out to be the BeOS of the DAW world. As of August 2013, Bitwig Studio was still a no more than a private beta with no release date yet announced, and the latest news update on its site dated back to Musilmesse in April.

▷ **Quick history:** Started as audio only in 2001, added MIDI in version 4 in 2004.

A Few Other Considerations

If your client-based needs are already covered, or you are simply looking for some other ways of working, then you may also consider Studio One, Digital Performer, or Reaper. There are also options that are either not quite a DAW or are simply not industry standard. These handle various portions of the production process that may be lacking in your primary DAW. They include Maschine, Reason, Fruity Loops, Audition, and Acid Pro.

Finally, make sure to find out what is going on in your scene of producers. There may be something popular in some communities that are not well-known in others. If you see an opportunity, whether locally or otherwise, go for it and don't be concerned if it is "industry standard" or not. It is also a good idea to peruse forums and respected rumor sites for additional information on companies that may be on their way out the door. With regard to the latter point, remember that rumors are just that, rumors. The demise of Apple Logic at version 9 was "common wisdom" right up until Apple released Logic Pro X.

Subjective Terms and Hype Words

If you look at Figure 8.13, you will notice a list of words commonly found in press releases and other marketing materials: powerful, intuitive, ultimate, huge, fat, groundbreaking, advanced, unique, vintage, analog, futuristic, professional, easy, warm, expressive, ultra, highly anticipated, new era, next-step, next-generation, state-of-the-art, cutting-edge, inspiring, classic. Just remember that these words are either subjective adjectives or claims that will require feedback from the community before validated. Whenever you see these terms in marketing materials—which often also includes reviews in print and online—your initial perceptions can be biased. Always consider the source. Are they appealing to your hopes, dreams, and wishes by referencing how it will somehow improve your music or your ideas? Consider the reputation of the company or developer, and most importantly, make decisions based on your own experience.

What does is mean when we say "sounds good" or "sounds better than"? What are you actually comparing?

▷ **Character.** This is the most subjective category and the least precise term. It might be thought of as a parallel to words like "flavor" or "style" or "taste." Some devices just add something to a sound or generate it with characteristics that are more or less desirable. Character can refer to a wide range of sonic causes or results: a stylistic plug-in effect used in a specific genre, different types of reverb algorithms, the differences between analog synths that use integrated circuits instead of more expensive discrete components, and different tonal colorations added to a sound by germanium transistors in a preamp, iron toroidal transformer in a compressor, or tubes in a guitar amp. It is very common for inexperienced producers to make important creative decisions based almost solely on character at the expense of the following items in this list.

▷ **Timbral richness.** Timbre traditionally refers to the tonal quality of different types of instruments, based on our subjective perception of what objectively might be referred to as a sound's time-varying spectra. Consider the following list of adjectives that can help you discern differences between options: full, detailed, complex, vivid, lush, creamy, detailed, intelligible, crisp, and defined. Even given very similar devices with very similar parameters, you will notice that some are just timbrally richer than others. In the world of electronic instruments and devices, I find that this variable is almost always crucial when comparing synthesizers, sample libraries, and reverbs.

Figure 8.13 An author-generated tag cloud showing common words used to describe and market audio tools. When are they accurate and when are they just marketing?
Source: wordle.net.

▷ **Clarity, detail, depth, and precision.** These characteristics usually come most into play when considering mics, speakers, amplifiers, preamps, converters, and other audio-engineering tools such as EQs and compressors. There are many scientific measurements and specifications that offer a significant amount of objective information, but ultimately you will have to make subjective decisions about what you prefer. A limited budget helps make the decision easier.

▷ **Stereo field.** How is the stereo field affected? A lot of plug-ins and cheap hardware either widen it at the expense of phase-cancellation issues or make it smaller and more closed. One way to tell a really nice compressor from ones that just add a lot of character is to hear what happens to the stereo field with just moderate compression. Does it close in or open up?

Listening Decisions and A/B Comparisons

When you are making comparisons between different sorts of equipment or software, it is crucial that you control for as many variables as possible. (Though, don't waste too much time getting sucked into comparisons between the "quality" of various DAWs' audio engines. It is almost impossible to control for all the variables in any given real-world scenario.) Some things to watch out for—or at least be aware of—when evaluating or comparing audio products include the following:

▷ **Fancy GUI.** Don't look, listen!
▷ **Hyped sound.** Steer clear of exaggerated, bombastic, layered, or FX-drenched presets.
▷ **EQ, gain, and compression.** Does it sound better just because it got louder, or did it improve something? Is it boosting or cutting any frequencies?
▷ **Weird processing.** Are there exciters, enhancers, or other uncommon processes hidden somewhere? These can add a sheen that seems really nice at first listen, but ultimately sounds artificial or causes other issues later.

The best way to compare different tools is through an A/B comparison. That means you quickly switch back and forth between the two options. For this useful approach to be effective, you need to control for variables as best as possible. If you do not do so, you may not be making the best decision. Because your final decision will almost always be based on a combination of objective and subjective differences, make sure you have at least accounted for objective differences.

▷ If at all possible, try to listen in a room you are familiar with—ideally, one that is also well-treated—on speakers or headphones that you are familiar with, too.
▷ Pay close attention to differences in gain, because increasing SPL changes how you hear across the frequency spectrum.
▷ Don't listen too loud or you may not be able to trust what you are hearing even a few minutes later, depending on SPL levels.
▷ Especially when comparing high-quality products, differences in cables, converters, speaker placement, and even where you are standing in the room can skew the comparisons one way or the other.

> NOTE: Some of the photos in this chapter are from Vintage King's LA appointment-only showroom. Although there are a variety of great pro audio shops around the U.S., it is a first of its kind due to its ground-up design for optimal A/B comparisons of a wide variety of high-end products.

Your Setup

The production studio is in and of itself a powerful tool, and is an extension of you. Your studio should fit you and reflect your personality and style. It needs to be physically comfortable for you, your collaborators, and your clients. As you gain experience and develop as a producer, you will cultivate deeper understanding of what these statements really mean for you. Equipment and acoustic treatment are crucial, but never underestimate the importance of vibe and physical comfort. Simple things like flexible lighting options and inspiring decoration can make a big difference when you are in the same room for long periods of time. Think about how you enhance the optimal mood given the phase of the production process that is ongoing.

As you develop your own setup, try to avoid the following all-too-common patterns:

▷ **Buy, sell, buy.** You want item X, but you can't really afford it right now, so you get item Y. A few months after getting item Y, you realize you really need item X. It is either not possible or too late to return item Y, so you sell item Y used for less than you just spent on it and go get item X. Rather than succumbing to this pattern, just wait. Be patient. Save up for what you need. See if someone you know has what you want and if they are willing to let you check it out. Software is often available as a demo, so look into that option first.

▷ **Tool jumping.** Don't let frustration cause you to jump from one tool to the next unless the frustration is an actual limitation of the software or hardware. Be sure the limitation is not your mood, patience, or skill level. When just getting going, expose yourself to as much as possible as long as you are not overwhelmed. But, do not become a novelty addict—someone who becomes a software collector. There are many excuses for not working on your ideas, and always messing with new stuff is an easily rationalized way to avoid dealing with the actual sources of your creative blocks. Instead, as before, just wait. Be patient. Make sure to spend enough time learning about your new tools. Maybe you need to focus on some theory for a while. Find a good teacher to help you if need be.

Sufficient Versus Necessary: Sufficient means "good enough," while necessary means "must have." If something is necessary it is also sufficient, but the opposite is not always true. For example, having an Apple Macintosh computer is sufficient for running Pro Tools, but it is not necessary, since one could also use a PC. It is necessary to have a Mac to run Logic Pro X, however, because Logic does not work on Windows. By meeting the requirement of "must have" it is therefore also "good enough." So the relevant questions is this: Is gear/software x just one way to accomplish a production goal, or is it needed?

The following two examples illustrate how extremely different combinations of ideas, music, aesthetic, style, and sufficient/necessary tools can equally lead to highly successful production outcomes. Let's consider the artists and albums, and then the tools they used.

Bruce Springsteen (U.S.): *Nebraska* (Columbia Records, 1982)

- ▶ Sixth album
- ▶ Solo singer/songwriter (1937–)
- ▶ Already commercially successful
- ▶ Access to major-label budget
- ▶ Recorded mostly in bedroom
- ▶ Widely considered one of top 100 albums of the 1980s
- ▶ RIAA certified platinum (1,000,000+ copies)
- ▶ Highest profile show in North America: too many huge concerts to pick one

Coil (U.K.): *Love's Secret Domain* (Wax Trax! Records, 1991)

- ▶ Third album
- ▶ Experimental electronic musicians
- ▶ Previous works ruthlessly experimental
- ▶ Indie, self-funded

▶ Recorded mostly in home studio
▶ One of the most influential electronic post-industrial albums of 1990s
▶ Sales unknown, not certified
▶ Highest profile show in North America: Mutek Festival, 2003

Both the following featured pieces of equipment are featured in *Mix Magazine*'s TECnology Hall of Fame, available at mixonline.com. Each one of them played a key role for one of the above artists.

▶ **1979 TEAC Model 144 Portastudio.** Mixonline.com describes this as "an integrated 4-track cassette recorder with Dolby B noise reduction, 3.75 ips operation and a 4 × 2 mixer with pan, treble and bass on each input." If we account for inflation, it would cost over $3,700 in 2013.

Springsteen planned to go into the studio to record *Nebraska*. It was common in those days to put some demos together ahead of time to play for others involved in the production, so he used the Teac 144 with some Shure SM57s to do so. The studio-produced version of the album with the E Street Band was never released; Springsteen and his producers ended up liking the sparse, raw, folky vibe of his demo so much, they sent it off for mastering and release.

Moral of the story: The technology fit the ideas behind the music. Even with access to a big major-label budget and studio, keeping the feel of the songs was more important to The Boss than a more produced sound.

▶ **1979 Fairlight CMI (computer musical instrument).** Mixonline.com describes the Series I as follows: "Based on two 6800 processors, the CMI provided digital synthesis with a 6-octave keyboard, 8-note polyphony, two 8-inch floppy disk drives (one for the operating system, the other for archiving/library storage of sounds), and a whopping 208 KB of RAM. The system offered onscreen displays of waveforms, which could be modified via Fourier synthesis or simple light-pen redrawing of the waveform." It also had an onboard sequencer and could pitch-shift sampled sounds. If we account for inflation, in 2013 the Series I would cost more than $100,000, as would the Series II (1980), while the 16-bit/100 kHz Series III (1985) would cost more than $200,000!

Coil's *Love's Secret Domain* (1990/1991), and its follow-up full-length album of outtakes and unreleased tracks, *Stolen & Contaminated Songs* (1992), are densely layered, timbrally rich sound-design masterpieces of their era. In addition to the Fairlight CMI Series II and Series III, they used other expensive cutting-edge equipment like the E-mu Emulator and PPG Wave. Members of Coil were not "rich kids" with trust funds, so how did ruthlessly experimental, non-commercial musicians afford such equipment? Coil's founding core members John Balance (1962–2004) and Peter Christopherson (1955–2010) were already established artists. Prior to Coil, both were part of Psychic TV, and Peter was also a founding member of Throbbing Gristle (formed in 1975, they are widely considered the first "industrial" music group). In 1973, he joined the Hipgnosis design group, known for some of the most famous record covers of all time, including classics from Pink Floyd, Peter Gabriel, AC/DC, Black Sabbath, Depeche Mode, and also more contemporary indie artists such as Vitalic and I Am Spoonbender (for the album released a few years after I departed).

Moral of the story: The technology enabled the ideas behind the music. Even without access to big major-label budget and studio, Coil gained access to the tools they truly needed to realize their ideas. Given their creative process, and the lengthy duration of time over which the music was created, it was necessary for them to have such tools in their personal "home" studio to accomplish their goals. Many aspects of their hugely influential music from the 1980s and early 1990s were way ahead of their time, and not even possible for most electronic music producers at home with a personal computer until about a decade later.

Using Software Without a License

Because software is not a physical object, when you buy software, you are mainly buying a license. The license specifies what your payment buys, such as how many computers you can use it on and if you can resell it to someone who can re-register it in his or her name. Software licenses are included with nearly all software, even if it is open source. Here you will find descriptions of the most common types of licenses.

▷ **Commercial.** This software is designed by professionals and will have the strictest licenses. This is a big category and can include everything from an operating system, to a DAW, to a synth plug-in, to a simple utility. Usually, the license features some sort of copy protection that controls the number of possible authorizations. The simplest copy protection is a serial number and/or authorization file. More common protection for audio software involves either a serial number and online authorization or the use of a hardware dongle such as a Pace iLok or Steinberg eLicenser. In the past, commercial software was packaged in a box, but now it is also often available as a download. Many companies offer a demo version of their commercial software, which is either crippled in some way (for example, you can't save any work done using the program) or expires after a period of time unless you purchase a license.

▷ **Shareware.** This is software that you can use for free for a set time or indefinitely, but will have to deal with limited functionality, ads, or nags until you pay the shareware fee. (Nags are nagging dialog boxes or pop-up windows that remind you how long you've been using the software for free.) Shareware is usually very affordable and nearly always developed by individuals or very small companies.

▷ **Donationware.** This is basically shareware, but you never have to pay the fee unless you want to support the developer or get rid of ads or nags. Developers of donationware usually suggest a fee, but you can pay them whatever you think it is worth to you—or nothing at all.

▷ **Freeware.** This is free software. Some freeware is great, some of it is weird, some of it is rough around the edges, and some of it just doesn't work. Unlike free software on mobile devices, you rarely have to deal with ads. Sometimes the developer offers a link if you want to donate, but you don't have to feel guilty for using freeware for free. The biggest downside of freeware is that it often becomes an unsupported legacy project as the developer moves on to other things. You can sometimes find commercial-quality freeware, such as little freebies from big companies, the open-source DAW Ardour, or Pure Data (PD), a graphical patching environment created by Miller Puckette, one of Max's original developers. Check out the great freeware collection available at www.dontcrack.com.

▷ **Open source.** Linus Torvalds launched the open-source revolution when he basically recoded UNIX from scratch to create Linux in the early 1990s. The idea behind open source is that the source code is available to everyone, and anyone can modify it and then recompile it to suit their needs. Most open-source software also has a license. This license specifies what is allowed for commercial use of the code, often even implementing one of the Creative Commons licenses. A great site with links to open-source software is www.sourceforge.net.

NOTE: Samples and sample libraries are also covered by licenses. Commercial sample libraries are royalty free because you own the license for the samples. Royalty free means that you can do whatever you want with the samples and will never owe the creator any more money or credits. I have never heard of it happening with a sample-library creator, but technically speaking, if you do not own the license (that is, you didn't pay for it), they can sue you for royalties if you use it in a released song just as if you sampled part of a commercially released song without clearing the sample first. Many free samples are covered by various Creative Commons licenses. That means although they are free to use, for commercial use you may have to pay for it, allow anyone to reuse it, and/or simply credit the source.

Following are a few of the important terms related to unlicensed software:

▷ **Pirating.** Illegal distribution and sale of software that was acquired legally or illegally.

▷ **Warez.** Pirated software or other copyrighted material that is illegally distributed.

▷ **Bootleg.** Warez that are bought and sold. Never, ever, *ever* pay for warez. People who make money off of other people's labor in this way are bottom feeders, unable or unwilling to create something original for themselves. This goes for anything that can be downloaded—software, music, movies, games, books, etc. It is the equivalent of someone downloading your music and then selling it for their own profit. If you are going to pay for something, pay the people who made it or their authorized resellers. (If you know someone who is bootlegging and think they are just being foolish, not greedy, then do them a favor and make sure they understand what they are actually doing.)

▷ **Cracked.** Warez that have had their code altered to bypass copy-protection schemes.

▷ **Full-version.** Warez that can be authorized without having to crack the software copy protection, and therefore are just like paid copies but without a license.

Bits Want to Travel

Software trading has been around at least since the early 1980s via Usenet, BBS systems, the U.S. Postal Service, and even in-person "floppy copy." Back then, it was mostly small or closed communities of geeks and nerds, so the scope was limited. In the 1990s, however, the Internet changed everything when it spawned file sharing via numerous peer-to-peer clients such as Hotline, KDX, LimeWire, the infamous Napster, and of course BitTorrent. Once things hit the Web in the mid 2000s, making pirated software readily accessed by anyone with a Web browser (not just those with P2P knowledge), we had hit a turning point of brazen excess. No longer did you need any real technical know-how to find or distribute unlicensed software. Any idiot could do it, and they did.

The now-infamous Chinese-based Megaupload.com was shut down by the U.S. Justice Department in early 2012, with more than $42 million worth of assets seized by Hong Kong's Customs and Excise Department. Megaupload and similar sites charge their users a monthly fee for "file storage." Just a few years earlier, in 2009, founders of Sweden's The Pirate Bay were convicted by their own government and sentenced to a year in prison with a $3.5 million fine. Unlike Megaupload-type sites, TPB is merely an information-sharing site that does not host files and is free of charge for all personal use. For those interested in the increasingly consequential zone of tension between copyright and digital freedom, make sure to check out links on this book's companion website, www.iempsg.com.

The Facts of the Matter

Every developer is all too aware that people are using their software without paying for it. Some of them are old school about it and hate the fact that even a single copy is used without payment for their hard work. No one is okay with it, but others understand the reality of the Internet and are on a spectrum of acceptance when it comes to some non-professionals—namely, that those just getting started often obtain unlicensed software they wouldn't buy even if they had the money. On the user side of things, the all-too-common half-baked argument is that it doesn't cost the companies anything because it is just software and there are no physical objects involved. Even if you buy that weak argument, unfortunately, there are a lot of people who can afford to buy it and don't—even some who are willing to spend large amounts on high-end hardware.

If you are an aspiring professional, even if you are financially challenged, you should find a way to be a responsible member of your community and support your peers so they can support you. If you make money with software, there is absolutely no excuse not to pay for it. No matter your perspective on the free flow of information, there is not a gray area when you are getting paid for your work. Even the crews who are responsible for cracking and distributing warez are very clear about this: "If you earn money with it, then buy it!" On my company's website, I list the software I use along with the following statement: "We will gladly demonstrate proof of ownership for all advertised software. Ask the same of others." If you are paying someone for any part of a production, and you notice they are using unlicensed software—especially if they advertise that they have it—then at the first opportune moment ask them for a rate reduction. If they don't want to give it to you, tell them you are totally okay with that if they simply pay for the tools that are making it possible for them to take your money.

The International Music Software Trade Association's (IMSTA) stated goal "is to promote the legal use of software and to educate the end-users on the negative effects of software piracy." Many people who use pirated software say they can't afford to buy it, yet they seem to be able to afford hardware. On IMSTA's site, they use a 2007 NAMM industry report to show that from 1996 to 2006, there was 12 × growth in sales of sound cards, but only a 2.7 × growth in software sales. That means more and more people are buying audio interfaces, but software sales are not keeping pace. For more information and analysis, check out the "piracy" and "myths" section on the IMSTA website (www.imsta.org). Then, make sure to check out IMSTA Festa when they visit your area. There you can check out all the new toys, listen to expert producers on a variety of panels, and even win software and hardware in multiple raffles.

Why You Should Care Even If You Are Broke

I am not equivocating. Everyone should pay for software they use. But I am not here to give morality speeches about "illegal" downloading. Practically speaking, there are a lot of reasons you will want to pay for your software.

▷ **Stability.** Cracked software is notoriously unstable because its code has been altered in clever but crude ways. It crashes more often, and may even unexpectedly stop working altogether. Crashes can corrupt your projects and other data on your hard drive. What will you say to a client when cracked software leads to the permanent loss of many hours of work?
▷ **Malware.** Warez are an easy way to get viruses and spyware on your computer. Sometimes, you may end up downloading malware disguised as the warez you were looking for. That InstallAwesomePlugin.exe file may simply be an installer for some spyware or worse. Keeping your computer free of malevolent software is already a serious concern, especially on Windows machines and most mobile devices.
▷ **Updates.** If you have a crack, you can't easily get bug-fix updates and upgrades. You are stuck with whatever version you happen to have.
▷ **Tech support.** If you need help from the company, you won't get it unless you have a license. Calling for tech support for warez is a slap in the face to the company whose time you are wasting. The best you can hope for is for them to simply laugh at you before hanging up.
▷ **Professionalism.** Clients and peers will not take you seriously if you are using warez for professional work. It can lead to a bad reputation. You may recall from Chapter 5, "The Social Scene," the importance of guarding your reputation.

Early in Your Career and Implications for Later On

You must feed the industry that feeds you.

—Michael White

Trading of warez among students goes on at every audio school where I've taught. Inevitably, there is someone who seems to have everything, and not so coincidentally they are not known for much else. When asked how they obtained all of it, they act as if they have access to secret hipster knowledge about the coolest VIP after parties, answering smugly along the lines of, "I have my ways." Don't be *that* guy. The fact of the matter is, the procuring of warez has not been privileged knowledge since the late 1990s. Anyone who doesn't know falls into three categories:

▷ They don't care because they buy their software.
▷ They are computer and Internet illiterate.
▷ They are just plain lazy.

In other words, by trading in warez, you will only impress the lazy and ignorant. Getting a letter of recommendation from an instructor who is aware of such an attitude will be challenging, to say the least.

Software is ephemeral and far removed from the people who made it, so it is easy to think of everything on your computer as bits and bytes of equal value. I was never *that* guy, and I have been buying the software I use from day one. But, one day, when in my 20s I had some warez with me at work. My supervisor noticed the contents of one of my hard drives and asked me about it. He then proceeded to tell me the names of the people he knew who had developed those titles, and how they used sales of that software to support their families. He told me to leave that stuff at home, and that was it. From then on, I never forgot the value of the software on my computer. It was also an awakening to the fact that I was just starting a career in an industry, and the people who made that software were potential peers, colleagues, connections, clients, and even friends.

Apple, Microsoft, and Adobe are big companies, and a lot of people use their software without a license. Does it affect their bottom line? Certainly. But some people not paying for that software is not going to put them out of business. Most software companies in our industry are small, independent shops. That goes even for many of the companies that people may think of as big, such as Propellerhead, Native Instruments, Ableton, and yes, even Waves. It is very common for companies to be run by just a few people, or even one person. Unlike bands that don't get paid when their music is downloaded without compensation, developers can't go on tour to play their code live. (I am not saying that it is okay to download music because a band has more options than developers; I am merely saying it's arguably *even worse* to download developers' code.) I would like you to think about the following developers as if they were bands or solo artists, trying to make a living doing what they love, and that their software is their art.

▷ **u-he (www.u-he.com).** Composer Hans Zimmer used u-he synths in the soundtrack for the *Dark Knight* movies. They must be huge, right? Wrong. For years, u-he was just Urs Heckmann. Recently, his company has grown to five people—the size of a band.
▷ **Audioease (www.audioease.com).** Their flagship product, Altiverb, is arguably the best convolution reverb plug-in on the market. So they must be huge, right? Again, wrong. Founded in the late 1990s by Arjen van der Schoot, Audioease now has only between five and eight full-time employees. Arjen started out offering freeware, the (unfortunately) long-discontinued Thonk.
▷ **Flux (www.fluxhome.com).** Flux makes very high-quality audio-processing software, including arguably the best cross-platform multi-band dynamics plug-in on the market, Alchemist. Flux is composed of just five people.
▷ **Five12 (www.five12.com).** Numerology for MacOS is the most full-featured step sequencer/modulation/control signal–centric app available. And it can run as an AU plug-in! Five12 is one guy, James Coker.
▷ **SoundHack (www.soundhack.com).** SoundHack is Tom Erbe, a teacher at Cal Arts. He sells a few innovative effects-processing plug-ins and recently programmed the DSP for Make Noise's Echophon synth module, but that is not why he is known by his peers. The SoundHack app has always been freeware (since 1991), and along with other software, he's been sharing free tools with the electronic music community for a long time.

Some other small software developers no bigger than a band include URS, DSP-Quattro, Fabfilter, Audio Damage, Sugar Bytes, McDSP, Brainworx, AudioMulch, Softube, Puremagnetik, and many others.

Ways to Legally Get Your Software Cheap or Free

There is a perennial irony in many industries. When you are getting started and have limited resources, you have to pay for everything. Yet the more successful you are, the more you can afford to buy your tools, the more stuff you get for free. But you don't have to be established to get not for resale (NFR) copies of software. Here are a few other avenues:

▷ **Academic licenses.** Many companies offer special pricing for students and teachers—often 50% off or more. The only catch is that if you sell it to someone else, that person will not be able to re-register it in his or her name and will not be eligible for upgrades and free tech support.
▷ **Become an expert.** Get to know the company, get involved in beta testing and product feedback, or maybe even become a demo artist at events and trade shows.
▷ **Your Web presence.** Drive a lot of traffic to your website or social media sites with tutorials, tips, and tricks. Write reviews for magazines or established blogs and link to them off of your site. Once established, ask companies if they can supply an NFR in exchange for a quality review.
▷ **Your job.** Work for a software company or an establishment that sells audio products.

▷ **Your business.** Become an authorized reseller and sell it to yourself at cost.
▷ **Trade.** Trade your skills for software. Just make sure it is either unopened or the license is transferrable.
▷ **Grants.** Apply for a grant. Many cities, states, and countries have a variety of grants available to musicians and artists to help them complete projects.

It is also possible to get hardware for cheap, but rarely free because there are manufacturing costs. The more friends you have in the industry, the more established you are as a producer, the more likely you will be offered special pricing. Even musicians who are sponsored by companies often have to pay something. Only the people who really don't need free stuff always seem to get it!

Outro

All the kit discussed in this chapter is important, but not all equally so—and not for everyone in every situation. Tools are central to what we do, but remember: They are a means, not an ends (unless you are a developer). They are meant to be extensions of you and your ideas. In this age of affordable, high-quality software and hardware, and floods of information on the Internet, it is easy for someone who is just getting started to focus too much on what's cool at the moment or on the technical bits. I regularly have students—usually the ones who are a little too smart for their own good—who get hung up on features or techniques at the expense of more productive foci of attention. Tool selection is a skill unto itself, and like the other aspects of being a music producer, it will grow and evolve over time. Now would be a good time to refer to the Bruce Lee quote at the beginning of Chapter 4.

Lifestyle Tips

9

Responsibility is the price of freedom.

–Elbert Hubbard

You can't make positive choices for the rest of your life without an environment that makes those choices easy, natural, and enjoyable.

–Deepak Chopra

Ecstasy is a complex emotion containing elements of joy, fear, terror, triumph, surrender, and empathy. What has replaced our prehistoric understanding of this complex of ecstasy now is the word comfort, a tremendously bloodless notion. Drugs are not comfortable, and anyone who thinks they are comfortable or even escapist should not toy with drugs unless they're willing to get their noses rubbed in their own stuff.

–Terence McKenna

We often forget that WE ARE NATURE. Nature is not something separate from us. So when we say that we have lost our connection to nature, we've lost our connection to ourselves.

–Andy Goldsworthy

A CHAPTER SUCH AS THIS ONE IS UNUSUAL FOR A MUSIC-PRODUCTION BOOK, and you may initially wonder why it is even here. Hopefully, you've noticed and appreciated that this is not a usual music-production book. In fact, it is as much about *being* a music producer in the 21st century as it is about music production itself. Each of the previous chapters directly addressed the requisite knowledge, skills, tools, and craft needed to survive and thrive as an independent/electronic music producer. Those topics are notable sub-holons in the holon of "you as music producer." You may recall from the sidebar about complexification in Chapter 2, "Plot Point on the Space-Time Continuum," that in any given system some holons are more fundamental (for example, building blocks) and others more significant (for example, emergent properties). If Chapter 7, "Creative Process," covered, arguably, the most significant holons, then this chapter is certainly about the most fundamental. What is more fundamental to survival than your health?

Trust Me: I'm an Engineer

Musicians, artists, and many other intensely creative or highly intelligent people are known to be a bit eccentric or "crazy." I mean this in the best way; besides, there is really no such thing as "normal" to begin with. In Chapter 7, I recounted a joke about the difference between a mystic and a psychotic being that the mystic knows who not to talk to. It is commonplace for those of us who are just a little bit (or a lot) "crazy" to, at times (or often), make questionable decisions that simultaneously have negative impacts on our overall health and add to our intellectual and creative pursuits. Sometimes these decisions are worth the tradeoff, sometimes not so much. With this reality as a given, let's approach the rest of this chapter knowing that our imperfections, quirks, vices, and guilty pleasures are what they are. Since everyone is different, each one of us must decide for ourselves what works or what is problematic. Yet, there are certain questions relevant to everyone reading this book.

Do you want to maximize your creativity, productivity, health, joy, and fulfillment? Do you want to minimize frustrations, traps, illness, dangers, and pitfalls? This chapter discusses the positive-negative spectrums of behaviors, decisions, results, and outcomes. Which ones do you want to add, increase, maximize, enhance, or embrace, and which ones do you want to subtract, decrease, minimize, detract, and avoid? Nightlife lifestyle, repetitive strain injury, diet, exercise, sleep, positive mental attitude, and altering of brain chemistry are key topics. For those of you who have been around a while, parts of this chapter will be old hat, but I guarantee that you will pick up some useful things no matter your veteran status.

> **DISCLAIMER:** Talk to your doctor or health professional about anything I say here related to your health. Everyone is different. I am not a doctor, I have never played one on TV. My younger brother *is* a doctor—a brain surgeon, actually. I've learned a lot from him, but that doesn't give me any professional qualifications via some sort of sympathetic resonance neuro-entrainment fraternal

telepathy phenomenon. The fact is, I've never needed to use a Midas Rex Legend EHS Stylus high-speed surgical drill to do a craniotomy for a glioblastoma, so having a neurosurgeon brother is not as useful as one might think when writing about "health." I am not a certified nutritionist. I am not a certified or licensed health anything. I'm just a smarty-pants geek who has learned a few things about health and healing after messing himself up with some combination of the following activities as a kid, teenager, and beyond: jumping off roofs because that is what ninjas do, pretending to know how to do tricks on a BMX bike, stage diving, stage diving near skinheads, ice hockey (with spleenectomy), Okinawan karate, wrestling, judo, Muay Thai, lugging around bass amps, and loading and unloading band vans after hours of driving said van. The worst of them all was bad posture while sitting in front of computers without any ergonomic considerations, for too many hours, without taking breaks, without enough sleep, and with too much coffee. So, to manage lower-back issues, overcome moderate repetitive sprain injury (RSI), and generally stay healthy, over the years I have applied much of the same energy to learning about health as I have to learning about music and audio.

A Fish Doesn't Know It Is Wet

King Midas gained the "Midas touch" after being granted a wish by arts patron Dionysus (a.k.a. Bacchus), the ancient Greek god of wine, nature, fertility, rage, ecstasy, and secret initiation. Run DMC said they've been told that Jam Master Jay was like King Midas because everything he touched turned to gold. Sounds great if you are a DJ with an uncanny ability to make music popular, but not so much when you turn your daughter into gold, or starve due to gold's lack of nutritional value. Too much of a good thing *does* exist. Humans mainly worry about challenges of scarcity, and understandably so. But challenges of excess can sneak up on you, and like the proverbial frog in slowly warming water, we can fail to notice the trouble we're in until we've past the boiling point.

For most people, "lifestyle" essentially is defined by their relationship to modern consumer culture and the interests and activities pursued when not at work—for example, healthy "green" living, nature and the outdoors, fancy designer clothes and table service, or perhaps family life or visiting their suburban "big box store" on the weekends. For a smaller group of people it includes additional layers of significance—for better or worse, their life is their job, by choice. Pro athletes, entrepreneurs, those who work crazy hours in hi-tech startups, and Wall Street traders are a few examples of career-as-lifestyle. If you can do music or art for a living full-time, so you don't need a "normal" job, then you too can live a unique lifestyle 24/7/365. You don't have to wait for the weekend to find blocks of time to do what you like doing. Your career, life, and lifestyle are inseparably merged. Often, there are long periods when there is minimal externally applied structure, offering much more freedom in choosing how to live from day to day, week to week. If you don't have kids, you can likely go to sleep when you want, wake up when you want, work when you want, go out or stay in when you want. Yes, you will still have personal and professional responsibilities that influence these decisions, but there is much more flexibility in your schedule. Flexibility, freedom, and independence are great. We all want more of it.

Nevertheless, for some people, structure is one of the two major upsides of a steady job that supports your music habit (steady income being the other). Yes, structure is limiting, and can stifle your career's potential, but externally enforced responsibilities can also be liberating, encourage good time management skills, and keep you out of trouble. The flexibility and freedom that come with our lifestyle is a draw unto itself, but it presents serious pitfalls, too. Accepting the responsibility that comes with this hard-earned freedom is the ideal scenario, in my opinion. Because producers are ultimately responsible for the whole project, they have more responsibilities than single-role artists. As such, there are external pressures (though unlike those that come with a "normal" job) as well as many more degrees of freedom in one's lifestyle.

Lifestyle is fundamental to your health and well-being, and is itself a major holon in your holarchy. This holon is at least as important as mastering your craft, the social scene, and the creative process. For some of us, this path is at times a lot more than just a career or a lifestyle; it is a completely immersive self-created alternate reality. As to how much of this self-created world is conscious, unconscious, or utterly taken for granted varies wildly from person to person. And just as a fish is not aware it is wet until it is no longer in the water, those who have yet to reflect on the lifestyle in which they are immersed are often equally unaware of their environment.

Fundamental Holons Versus Sex, Drugs, Rock 'N' Roll

Our lifestyle makes a lot of people jealous. Having fun is part of our job. We stay out late, travel, and get to meet interesting people. The more successful you are, the more true those statements are, and then some. No punching the clock, no nine-to-five. No boss. No unfulfilling, soul-sucking j.o.b. If you are just getting started, living this lifestyle might be your goal, but not yet the full reality of your situation. Either way, the key word here is freedom.

Everyone agrees that freedom is good—the more the better. Yet history books are littered with countless tragic cases: people who could not handle so much freedom and success. Freedom also means autonomy, and the price of admission is responsibility, whether you realize it or not—first and foremost to yourself, but then equally to your collaborators, friends, family, fans, and anyone else who has helped you along the way.

> *Punk is musical freedom. It's saying, doing and playing what you want. In Webster's terms, 'nirvana' means freedom from pain, suffering and the external world, and that's pretty close to my definition of Punk Rock.*

> –Kurt Cobain

What do all of the following people have in common: Jimi Hendrix, Jim Morrison, Jean-Michel Basquiat, Kurt Cobain, and Amy Winehouse? All were talented, famous, successful artists—*were* being the key word, since none of them made any music after the age of 27. In all cases, their lifestyle allowed for excess, and even supported and encouraged self-destructive behavior. Yes, William Burroughs was a junkie for decades and lived to the age of 83; Ozzy Osbourne went to rehab a few dozen times before getting sober for the first time in 40 years (in 2010); and Keith Richards had multiple blood changes before years later, in his late 60s, acting in Disney movies with Johnny Depp. You are not them. They are severe outliers, genetic freaks of nature.

> *I can honestly say, all the bad things that ever happened to me were directly, directly attributed to drugs and alcohol. I mean, I would never urinate at the Alamo at nine o'clock in the morning dressed in a woman's evening dress sober.*

> –Ozzy Osbourne

Although originally from a 1949 *film noir* Humphrey Bogart vehicle, "Live fast, die young, and leave a good-looking corpse" became a punk-rock cliché by the early 1980s, often tragically. Fortunately, as a music culture, we have largely outgrown the romanticization of the self-destructive, knee-jerk reactions to the adolescent angst and alienation of the Cold War, pre-Internet era. Many electronic music genres that emerged in the 1980s—synth pop, house, techno, electro, and (pre-gangsta era) rap/hip hop—seem to have emerged as life-affirming counterpoints to the widespread self-destructive hedonism of rock and punk. (Yes, I realize a whole book could be written about the previous sentence.)

Faster and Faster

But while our attitudes and outlooks on life have evolved for the better, for the most part, the fundamental structural elements of the lifestyle have not changed. Moreover, the faster pace of an omni-connected, computer-driven culture places new demands on us that need attention. In his 1999 must-read, *Faster,* James Gleick speaks to our new normal:

> *All our information sources evolve toward complexity. No software program gets simpler in release 2.01. No television-news anchor or daily newspaper holds its former central position as announcer to a whole nation. Instead citizens awaken each day with a multitude of experiences to divide one from the other—last night's five hundred channels and million Web sites....The connection between complexity and speed—between variety and time pressure—are not always obvious, but they are real.*

Given the emerging breakthroughs in life-extension science, exemplified by Ray Kurzweil's conviction that the "Singularity" will mean indefinite longevity, the new unstated maxim might as well be, "Live fast, stay young, and leave a good-looking corpse (if you do die)."

I welcome the faster pace and the new demands, but fully admit that it all can be exhausting at times. Remember, this book emphasizes the importance of the long game as much as immediate next steps. Getting your 15 minutes of fame or being a one-hit wonder are great only if healthy royalty checks follow for years to come. But if you are totally burned out, then what? Following are a few metaphors and thoughts on the topic for your contemplation. How are they all related?

▷ Don't burn yourself out in the first round of a 15-round fight.
▷ You can't run a marathon with a broken foot.
▷ Push hard when you are younger and have more time and energy.
▷ Prepare for multiple phases of a career.
▷ Don't become a zombie, as discussed in Chapter 5, "The Social Scene."
▷ Don't be afraid to make mistakes and learn from them.
▷ Enjoy the fruits of your labor.
▷ Have fun.
▷ Don't be stupid.

Balance

If I had to pick one word to characterize the music producer's lifestyle holon, it would be *balance*. Balance is subjective, and like all holons is contextually relative with fractal self-similar characteristics at all scales. Everything in moderation, including moderation in moderation.

There is no one right answer, way of doing, or way of being. One person's balance is another's boredom or insanity. But balance doesn't mean that oscillating between extreme bad habits and equally extreme healthy habits will average out. For example, heroin addiction with a strict macrobiotic diet is not balance. This is not a zero-sum game. No oscillation is not a good answer either. Extreme Puritanism's bet on repression and reliance on strict codified rules of dos and don'ts attempts to create a steady state of balance, which does not match the modern world, and therefore creates *im*balance. You don't want too much chaos or too much order. Complexity studies teach us that health is a balanced tension between the two. You've probably seen the famous photo of Albert Einstein riding a bike, which captured his philosophy: "Life is like riding a bicycle. To keep your balance you must keep moving."

Hey You! With the Short Attention Span!: If nothing else, there are three things that you really, absolutely must take seriously. I talk about each of these in detail elsewhere in this chapter.

▶ Protect your ears. Without them, you are done. Hearing loss is irreversible.
▶ Don't get repetitive sprain injury (RSI). RSI is a common problem for musicians, audio engineers, and anyone who spends a lot of time in front of a computer. You are at risk—yes, you. It will make your life miserable, and can end your career.
▶ Health in four easy steps: diet, exercise, rest, and positive mental attitude.

Not Unlike a House of Cards

In 1943, Abraham Maslow's seminal article, "A Theory of Human Motivation," appeared in the journal *Psychology Review.* His first conclusion on the research into human motivation was as follows: "The integrated wholeness of the organism must be one of the foundation stones of motivation theory." It was in this article that he first presented his now famous hierarchy of needs. Maslow's seminal work revealed important truths about the fundamental and the significant in this holarchy, which are still relevant to us.

These needs drive our motivations, and are not about our capacities or natural aptitudes. We all share four deficiency needs (d-needs) and one growth need, which is dependent on the four d-needs. Usually presented as a pyramid with the growth need at the top, I am presenting these in holarchical order from the fundamental to the significant.

▷ **Physiological needs.** These are fundamental biological requirements of the human organism: air, water, food, sleep, sex, homeostatis (for example, blood pH, body temp).
▷ **Safety needs.** These are secondary survival needs: physical safety, health, property, employment, financial stability, etc.
▷ **Belongingness needs.** These are social needs: friends, family, love, intimacy, community, etc.
▷ **Esteem needs.** These are ego needs: respect, achievement, confidence, status, self-esteem, etc.
▷ **Self-actualization needs.** These needs are only truly possible when you are no longer primarily motivated by deficiencies (for example, lack or scarcity). You are motivated toward developing creativity, morality, problem-solving, etc.

NOTE: Maslow spent a lot of time researching what he dubbed *peak experiences,* which he believed revealed a lot about the nature of self-realization. This inquiry culminated in the founding of transpersonal psychology with Stan Grof in 1969.

We have learned a lot about human motivations and needs since 1943, so Maslow's hierarchy of needs is more of a guide than a map. Integral theory shows us that there are also lines of development, so we don't need to meet all of the lower needs to realize higher motivations in different areas of life. But physiological and safety needs really do set the parameters for our higher aspirations. Whenever a lower, more fundamental need is deficient, it makes it more difficult to focus our attention on the higher, more significant motivations. If you are starving, or fending off a burglar, your immediate concern surely is not self-actualization. That said, you can be creative and socially isolated, or like the late, great Wesley Willis, even homeless and schizophrenic, and creatively successful and motivated to achieve. People figure out how to compensate and overcome adversity. On the flip side, there are a lot of people in the modern world motivated by achievement and success, but at the expense of belongingness and even safety or health. When there are imbalances caused by building on shaky ground, the stability of the structure is questionable. How easily will external stresses (perturbation) break the system—you and the structures of your creative-professional life? How much of your potential is being limited by neglected fundamental needs? Only you can answer those questions for yourself. Keep these needs in mind as I talk about how your lifestyle decisions affect your creative and professional success.

Protect Your Hearing

Do you hear constant high-pitched ringing in your ears when it is really quiet? Does this happen only after you get home from a club, and then it goes away after a day or two? Or, is it there all of the time? If so, then like me, you have tinnitus. For people reading this book, years of listening to loud music is the primary suspect (although there are other health-related causes, too). It is a first sign of hearing damage, and it is your warning to take action now. It is also important to note that there are many common causes of hearing issues in just one ear, such as cell phones, DJ monitors, and other environmental factors. I recommend getting a hearing test regardless, just so you know how well your ears work. (Should you ever attend the semi-annual AES Convention, you might even get your hearing tested for free, because the National Hearing Conservation Association is often there.) As you may recall from Chapter 4, "Master Your Craft," three of the Big Four music-production holons include ear training as a core skill. How do you train something that is broken?

Music does sound better when turned up, to a point. If you still use those cheap earbuds that came with your iPod or phone, stop using them now unless you keep the volume very low. If you are a musician and never wear earplugs at rehearsal or at shows, start now. If you are a DJ, well, it is a bit more complicated, but if you ever plan on seriously mixing or mastering, you will have to figure something out. At the end of this section I have suggestions for all of you.

> *I have unwittingly helped to invent and refine a type of music that makes its principal components deaf. Hearing loss is a terrible thing because it cannot be repaired. If you use an iPod or anything like it, or your child uses one, you may be okay…But my intuition tells me there is terrible trouble ahead.*
>
> –Pete Townsend (The Who)

There is a question asked in every Philosophy 101 course: If a tree falls in the woods, and there is no one there to hear it, does it make a sound? At first, this seems like a tricky metaphysical question, but once you define a few terms, it is easy to answer. The falling tree creates *objectively* measurably pressure waves in the air, but sound is a *subjective* perception. So, the answer is no (assuming no creatures are present with ears). For humans, sound is auditory perception of vibrations in a limited bandwidth (roughly 20 Hz to 20 kHz) and a limited dynamic range (roughly 0–150 dB SPL). We feel earthquakes, we do not hear their vibrations—even if we are there to hear the trees falling. The waveform in Figure 9.1 is a seismic wave measurement of a small earthquake that occurred below Mammoth Mountain in California in 1989. Its time duration is shown in relation to the 60 seconds long scale given at the bottom of the image. The waveform represents frequencies lower than 20 Hz, and therefore those vibrations are not in the audible range. Figure 9.2 is a screenshot of a snare drum with a measure bandwidth of approximately 100 Hz to 10 kHz, with its time duration shown in relation to the 600 millisecond (0.6 seconds) long scale given at the bottom of the image.

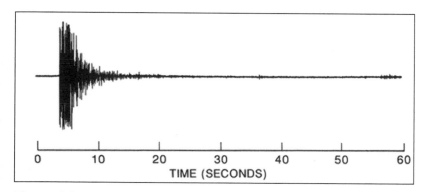

Figure 9.1 Seismogram of an earthquake, roughly 60 seconds, < 20 Hz. Courtesy of the U.S. Geological Survey.
Source: Public domain via USGS.gov.

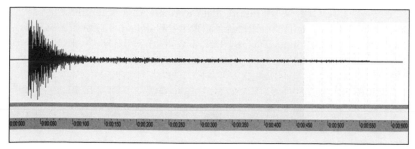

Figure 9.2 Snare drum sample, roughly 0.6 seconds, 100 Hz–10 kHz.
Source: Ableton Live.

The Science (In Brief)

Our ears are amazing, finely tuned biological, hydraulic-like, fluid-filled transducers (see Figure 9.3). They convert longitudinal pressure waves traveling through air into electrical impulses that our nervous system sends to our brain for processing and interpretation. The outer ear collects sound and helps us determine its direction, and the ear canal causes resonance amplification, which boosts mid-range frequencies crucial to speech intelligibility. The tympanic membrane (ear drum) transfers energy to three ossicles (the smallest bones in your body) that match impedance (resistance) differences between air and the fluid in the cochlea. Eventually, this energy gets to many thousands of little hair-like nerve cells, called *stereocilia*. Stereocilia have microphonic potentials, are binary (on/off), roughly correspond to the frequencies we can hear (roughly 20 Hz to 20 kHz), and are largely responsible for masking (and thus MP3s). These transducers send the energy as a chemical-electrical signal down the auditory nerve to the brain. Voilá! Sound. Too much energy, and we stress our hearing system, which for the most part is not repairable.

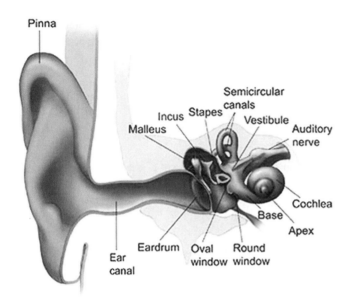

Figure 9.3 The human ear. Image courtesy of National Institutes of Health (NIH.gov).
Source: Public domain via National Institutes of Health (NIH.gov).

How do we measure sound energy? We use dB SPL (decibels, sound-pressure level) to measure *intensity*, which is an objective measurement of amplitude. Each additional dB SPL represents a tenfold increase of atmospheric pressure on our ear drum. An increase of 6 dB is a doubling of amplitude but, all things being equal, it takes a 10 dB increase to double loudness. *Loudness* is a subjective concept that refers to our perception of intensity, and it is tricky to quantify. For starters, studies show that at the same SPL, some frequencies are louder to us than others. The resulting measurements are represented as charts, such as the ubiquitous Fletcher-Munson equal-loudness contours chart seen in Figure 9.4, which are overlaid next to the newest ISO standard from 2003.

To read an equal-loudness contours chart, start by following either line labeled 40. Pick two points on it. The number at the bottom is the frequency (Hz) and the one on the left is SPL (dB). For those frequencies, the values on the left are the intensities that would make them seem equally loud. When measuring sound-pressure level, we can choose to take these differences into account and refer to decibels as A-weighted, or dBA. In essence, any measuring equipment (see Figure 9.5) would apply an EQ curve to the input before giving us a value, so it more closely resembles our perception. Consider measuring a very quiet band during sound check from the back of the club. We barely hear 20 Hz, so a dBA measurement of 40 would essentially be ignoring any 20 Hz components. A 20 Hz sine wave by itself would need to be about 100 dB to be as loud as a 1 kHz tone at 40 dB, also referred to as 40 phon. It is worth noting that in pro audio, it is common to use A-weighted measurements when dealing with lower levels and the flatter C-weighting for higher levels. (FYI, this paragraph condenses a lot of core material from the audio-engineering holon, as discussed in Chapter 4, which most of you will want to learn at some point.)

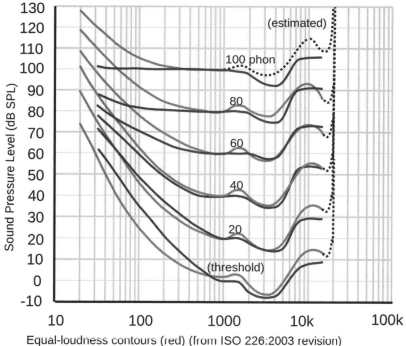

Equal-loudness contours (red) (from ISO 226:2003 revision)
Fletcher-Munson curves shown (blue) for comparison

Figure 9.4 Fletcher-Munson equal-loudness contours chart (flatter, darker) compared to ISO 2003 revision (longer, lighter), compliments of Lindos Electronics (lindos.co.uk).
© Lindos Electronics. All Rights Reserved.

NOTE: Due to the conversion of Figure 9.4 from color to grayscale, the red lines are a lighter shade of gray and go all the way to the left, while the blue ones are darker gray, flatter, and do not go as far left.

Figure 9.5 A sound-level meter set for an A-weighted, slow-response measurement of SPL.
© 2013 Brian Jackson, All Rights Reserved.

In the U.S., the Occupational Safety and Health Administration (OSHA) determines legal safe noise levels and their durations in work environments. For the most part, these regulations are most important for people who work in industries around large machines such as stamping presses, jackhammers, and jet engines. We must set our own guidelines, and using OSHA's guidelines are a great place to start, but keep in mind they are government figures so you will likely see more conservative versions of this list elsewhere. Additionally, you should make sure to take breaks every so often, not only to protect your hearing, but also to keep your ears "fresh" for optimal decision making.

Let us first look at the estimated dB SPL of some sounds, as found in Gary Gottlieb's *Shaping Sound in the Studio and Beyond*:

▷ 140 dB threshold of pain (Note: as low as 120 dB is commonly cited.)
▷ 110 dB pop group
▷ 90 dB heavy truck
▷ 50 dB conversational speech
▷ 0 dB threshold of hearing

Let us now look at OSHA's chart that specifies legal maximum duration and noise level (duration per day, hours/sound level dBA slow response):

▷ 8.0 hours = 90 dBA (Note: 85 dB is commonly cited elsewhere.)
▷ 6.0 hours = 92 dBA
▷ 4.0 hours = 95 dBA
▷ 3.0 hours = 97 dBA
▷ 2.0 hours = 100 dBA
▷ 1.5 hours = 102 dBA
▷ 1.0 hours = 105 dBA
▷ 0.5 hours = 110 dBA
▷ .25 hours or less = 115 dBA

Earplugs: Get to Know Them Well

You should use earplugs if you are exposing your ears to high SPL sounds for long durations. You have many options to choose from, so there is something for everyone. For about $20, you can get 200 disposable foam plugs. These do a good job protecting your ears with a 30 dB reduction, on average, but they block out high frequencies more than the lower ones. Just be aware that after removing them, you will want to give your ears time to readjust in a relatively quiet environment for about 25 minutes or so, since they will be more sensitive to higher frequencies. These common earplugs are not ideal for listening to music, but with some practice you can learn to place them in such a way that the sound is not so muffled, but with a bit less reduction. They are usually fine for rehearsals and such. I have a big pack of them right by my front door so I don't forget to grab some on my way out for the night. I often pocket a few extra ones in case I drop one or I run into a friend in need. The next step up is to spend about $12 for a pair of washable, reusable earplugs designed for music listeners. These try to block all frequencies equally so music sounds more natural, usually offering about 20 dB of reduction. (And, they come in a nifty little case!) If you want to get really serious about comfort and flexibility, you can get custom-molded earplugs for about $150–$200. These will fit your ears perfectly, and even match your skin color if so desired. Moreover, these usually include changeable filters that offer different amounts of SPL attenuation.

In the Crowd

There is no excuse for not having earplugs with you when you go to concerts or clubs, and even movie theatres. Don't be embarrassed for being smart. If people ask you why you are wearing earplugs or your friends poke fun at you, just tell them that your ears are your profession and that you are protecting your unrepairable assets. This often gets them thinking about their own hearing or might even lead to more interesting discussions about what you do for a living.

Performing Musician

When you're rehearsing, you should seriously consider wearing earplugs. Many musicians even wear them on stage while they are performing. In the studio, earplugs make no sense in the control room, but for musicians it is something to think about. I once worked with a professional drummer who played so loud he had to wear earplugs under his headphones so as not to go deaf during the recording process—often at the expense of the headphones. A lot of artists now use professional in-ear monitoring systems on stage, which actually can be better for your ears than the traditional stage monitor setups—as long as levels are kept within safe usage guidelines and the brick-wall limiters are functioning properly.

The Control Room

When working in the control room, which might be the only room in a home studio, you are in total control of your listening level. It is normal to vary your working level depending on the task at hand. Mixing engineers tend to significantly vary their listening levels throughout the project, depending on the task at hand. Mastering engineers tend to work at a very consistent level, somewhere around 85 dB SPL, give or take a few dB at the listening position. When writing music and recording, work at a comfortable level, and then check it nice and loud for short durations just to make sure the vibe is right.

I recommend calibrating your monitoring system to a universal standard. Many of you have likely seen features in various pieces of software that utilize K-system metering. Based on longtime standards in the film industry (SMPTE), this system of metering was devised by Bob Katz, and is intended to work hand in hand with a calibrated monitor level control setup. There is a lot of information on the Internet, including Bob's own site (digido.com), about calibrating your system. Essentially, using an SPL meter, you set each speaker to 83 dB SPL using −20 dB FS uncorrelated pink noise and mark your master monitor controller at various dB increments. In addition to more consistent results when mixing and mastering, you will have a really good idea how the metering in your DAW relates to the setting on your monitor controller (volume knob) and more importantly, the SPL in the room.

DJ

If you are a DJ, you are all too familiar with the levels often necessary to mix properly in a club. DJ headphones are designed for loud environments, usually of closed-back design, and with low impedance. The monitor in the booth is often cranked, too. In most cases, there is not a lot that you can do about the volume in the club, but wherever possible you should try to turn down your headphones and the monitor. Ultimately, if audio engineering to pay the bills is one of your goals or part of your plan, you should rethink whether being a DJ is a long-term option for you. I decided to stop DJing more than a few times a year when I realized that I wanted to seriously focus on mixing and mastering. The indie movie *It's All Gone Pete Tong* (2004) is a fictional story about a popular Ibiza DJ who goes deaf. Believe it or not, given the subject matter, it is a fun watch. In the *Music Producer's Survival Guide*'s companion book, *The Music Producer's Survival Stories: Interviews with Veteran, Independent, and Electronic Music Professionals*, you will find an interview with DJ Spun. He mentions that it is a good idea to switch your headphone ear every so often, not only to balance out any hearing loss across both ears (theoretically not as bad) but also to help minimize common neck problems that develop over time.

Earbuds and Headphones

Our ears have a few built-in protection mechanisms (including ear wax) that are largely bypassed when using earbuds (and, to a lesser extent, headphones). The ideal situation is to work with good studio monitors in an acoustically treated room. Sometimes that is just not possible. If for whatever reason you cannot use studio monitors, then you should use a good pair of professional over-ear headphones. If you must use earbuds, then make sure to get a quality pair designed for professional musicians and audio engineers. Regardless, pay extra attention to your listening levels when the speaker is right next to your ear drum. There are numerous buying guides at the various audio and music equipment retailers online.

Avoid RSI at All Costs

Repetitive strain injury (RSI) comes in many forms—and all of them, simply stated, suck. Our bodies, especially our small muscles, are simply not designed for repetitive tasks for long periods of time, day after day, year after year. Tennis elbow, writer's wrist, gamer's thumb, BlackBerry thumb, and iPod finger are colloquialisms for various common forms of RSI. Whether a minor inconvenience or an excruciatingly painful nightmare, all forms of RSI are injuries to the nervous or musculoskeletal system. The injury can be to the joints, tendons, ligaments, muscles, and/or nerves. Tendonitis, focal hand dystonia, radial tunnel syndrome, carpal tunnel syndrome, ulnar nerve entrapment, and thoracic outlet syndrome are some medical names for forms of RSI of serious concern to musicians and anyone who spends a lot of time sitting in front of a computer. You are at risk, but it is avoidable.

Even given the same activities, some people are more likely to develop RSI issues than others. While genetics are surely a variable, lifestyle decisions are a major factor. An MD who specializes in RSI once told me that even though there was not enough research to prove what makes one person more predisposed than another, he had noticed chronic allergies were a significant correlation. Allergies are inflammation. Repetitive activity causes inflammation. Too much inflammation is a major factor in developing RSI. In the next major section of this chapter, "The Four Pillars of Health," you will learn how to minimize inflammation via lifestyle decisions.

The reason this is my first book is simple: I have personally struggled with minor RSI since 2001, primarily tendonitis in both wrists. I also have close friends who have dealt with various forms, including serious nerve damage, and I've met dozens of traditional musicians, electronic musicians, and computer programmers who have had issues of one variety or another. I'd be willing to bet that you know someone with one of the forms of RSI, even if you don't think you do. In other words, RSI is an occupational hazard of our profession (and many others) that is very common.

What Are the Symptoms?

The order and severity of symptoms can vary from person to person. The first warning signs are often arthritis-like symptoms in the hands and/or regular tightness in the upper back/lower neck area (near vertebrae C7 and T1), which can feel like a knot or "pinched" muscle. This is an early warning sign that you need to make some changes, such as spending less time in front of a computer, taking more frequent breaks, and having better ergonomics. What usually follows is additional soreness (often deep and dull) and/or weakness in the forearms and hands. Weakness and dull aching sensations are a sign that there is an injury, perhaps minor, possibly serious. Make adjustments now or be sorry later. Tingling, numbness, burning, and sharp or shooting pain are advanced symptoms and must not be ignored. If you think you can work through these advanced symptoms, you are wrong. Eventually, your body will simply not be able to do what you want it to do. I've seen it get to a point where you won't even be able to write your name or hold a coffee cup.

> **CAUTION:** Once you notice you are injured, you need to stop and change your behavior, immediately. Seek professional help.

If you have symptoms, don't push it. Whatever you are doing at that time is not as important as you think it is compared to dealing with nerve damage in your arms and hands. The healing time is exponentially longer than the time spent working after you need to take it easy. A few more days can mean a few more months of recovery time; a few more months can mean additional years of recovery.

If you think you have RSI, take a break from the activities that caused it and then get an expert diagnosis from someone who regularly deals with it. Believe it or not, some doctors don't believe RSI is a real injury unless it is the type that can be fixed with surgery. Others may assume that you just want to get worker's-compensation checks and not have to go to work (even though you do pay for the insurance out of each paycheck). The situation has improved over the years as working all day on a computer has become commonplace, but there is still a lingering myth that it is "all in your head."

If the injury is work-related and you are relying on your employer-based insurance, keep in mind that some employers send you to those skeptical doctors on purpose. As a countermove, pick out your own doctor beforehand. Even if your employer is supportive, don't be surprised if the health-insurance company gives you a hard time. They may try to claim that you had a pre-existing condition or fight you on authorizing payments for doctor-prescribed treatments, and most likely on any final settlement. It is a good idea to find a good lawyer who only does worker's-comp cases and know that the legit ones don't take payment unless you win. They might even be able to help you find a doctor who has experience with RSI and will be supportive. It should go without saying, but laws differ from state to state, and I am not a lawyer, so do your own research should it be necessary.

If your symptoms are serious enough that they affect your ability to play an instrument or work on a computer, it can be frustrating and even depressing. Find others who have gone through it and know what it is like. It will not be easy, but with time you can learn to manage your issues or even heal enough to make them no more than minor inconveniences. Drummer Max Weinberg (Springteen's E Street Band and Conan O'Brien's bandleader) is an example of a famous musician who figured out how to deal with severe tendonitis and maintain a long, successful career. I personally know a professional pianist who completely retrained her body using the Alexander technique and was able to resume her career. Additionally, myofascial release therapy, Rolfing, chiropractic, acupuncture, and Pilates can significantly speed up recovery time.

Like many of life's difficulties, RSI can be blessing in disguise if you address it head on and make the necessary changes in your habits and behaviors. Immediately following my injury, I had to choose between a good-paying computer-centric job and making music with computers. I wasn't going to give up computer audio, so I decided to focus on teaching (audio engineering and music production). It also forced me to find other ways to stay productive and creative, such as integrating more hardware (and less computer) into my workflows. In addition, it put me in the position of having to learn a lot about the body, health, and healing in general. Anything you do to get over RSI is good for your overall health. So, be committed to getting better and make the Four Pillars of Health a priority. Nietzsche famously stated, "That which does not kill us makes us stronger." You may recall from Chapter 4, Nobel laureate Ilya Prigogine's definition of a *dissipative structure* as a system that maintains its structure with a constant flow of energy. When that flow is perturbed, the system either breaks down or reorganizes at a higher level of efficiency and complexity, capable of more energy throughput. You are the system and RSI is the perturbation. The required changes needed to heal from a habit-induced injury such as RSI can actually lead to a higher level of organization—that is, a structurally more healthy mind and body.

How to Avoid RSI

RSI is avoidable. I wish I knew then what I do now, so I could have avoided it. The fact that basic RSI prevention is not in the modern curricula of every audio-engineering and music-production school/program not only amazes me, but I posit that it borders on negligence. For most people, it is avoidable even if you perform repetitive tasks, such as playing an instrument or using a computer all day. If you already have early warning symptoms (as previously discussed), you can prevent it from turning into something serious that cripples your productivity for years. Just as it takes time for exercise to build strength and endurance, it can often take years of bad habits before symptoms show up. If you don't have any symptoms, don't assume that your current work habits are okay. If you suffer from allergies or any other inflammation-related issues, pay special care—especially during flare-ups.

Ergonomics and Good Posture

The position of your body is very important when working for long hours. The height and angle of your desk, chair, keyboard, pointing device, and monitor determine the position of your neck, shoulders, arms, and hands. You don't want to strain any more than needed, and you want your position to be as natural as possible. Gripping all day is no good, so ditch the mouse (1970s technology) and get a trackball or touch surface. Try to keep your wrists from facing down all the time; their most neutral position is facing each other. (Just stand up and let your arms hang to your side for reference.) If you do a lot of typing, get an ergonomic keyboard, and if needed a height- and angle-adjustable keyboard tray. For non-audio time spent on a computer, such as answering emails or writing books, look into voice-to-text software, which is now quite good on all platforms.

Be mindful of your posture. "Computer neck" comes from constantly leaning forward to get a closer look at the computer monitor. If the muscles in your neck are tight, they reduce blood flow down your arms, and inflame nerves, too. A stiff neck is one thing; the inability to hold a coffee cup is another (no hyperbole here). Also, try to keep your shoulders back and down, don't let them pinch in or creep up. You should be able to take a nice deep breath into your diaphragm without having to lift your shoulders. (If you cannot do so, find a good Pilates instructor.) Ultimately, to best ensure good posture, you need to analyze and adjust your setup as needed so you are forced into good habits.

You don't need expensive chairs or studio furniture if you know what to look for. The desk in my studio is a used IKEA Jerker, found on Craigslist for $50 plus cab fare to get it home. I added on a really nice Allsop keyboard platform for about $100. I prefer a trackball since there is no need to grip it like with a mouse, which helps minimize some common RSI problems. My preferred one is a Kensington Expert Pro Mouse four-button trackball, which goes new for about $70. The studio staple "nice" chair, the Herman Miller Aeron chair, is readily available used or from an office-furniture liquidator for as low as $250. So for less than $600, you can have a nice, professional, ergonomic setup that won't hamper creativity (once you get used to it). If you have a bigger budget, there are very comfortable ergonomic chairs such as the Steelcase Leap (my current chair), Humanscale Freedom, or the $1,200+ Herman Miller Embody, and even desks with motors that can switch the height from sitting to standing position. You might also consider "alternative" ergonomic seating such as a Balans chair ($150–$300) or a balance ball chair (under $100).

Please take the time to read up on good typing habits, as well as chair, desk, and computer monitor placement. There is readily available information all over the Internet on the basics. To get started, just do Web searches for "RSI prevention" and "ergonomics," and check out the image results too.

Breaks

Giving your overused small muscles a break is key to avoiding RSI. If you can alternate between standing and sitting, then do so, or try using a balance-ball chair so you have to mind your posture and engage your core muscles even while sitting. Regardless, make sure to drop your hands and shake them out every 10 minutes or so, even if just for 10–15 seconds. These micro breaks are very important. Every hour, you should take a 10-minute break. Get up, walk around, and drink some water. If so inclined, do some light stretching, too. The more hours you work each day in front of a computer, the more important it is that you take breaks. Because it is easy to lose track of time when working on a computer, you may even want to look into software designed for RSI prevention, starting with freeware apps such as Time Out (Mac) or Big Stretch Reminder (PC). If you have RSI or are showing symptoms, you might also consider more feature-laden commercial options such as MacBreakZ (Mac) or RSIGuard (PC). There are also simpler options for mobile devices if you don't want to run such software on your audio workstation, or perhaps even just use an egg timer.

Follow The Four Pillars of Health

This is a short preview of the next major section, which goes beyond avoiding or recovering from RSI. For now, here are a few highlights central to avoiding RSI:

▷ Drink enough water! Most people do not drink enough water every day. If you are regularly dehydrated while overtaxing your small muscles and irritating your nerves, you are asking for RSI.
▷ Be careful with caffeine and sugar intake, especially during stressful "crunch" times with tight deadlines. Stimulants tax your nervous system.
▷ Eat healthfully. Avoid dairy and processed, acid-forming foods to help minimize inflammation during work hours.
▷ Get some exercise, whether it is walking, biking, doing yoga, or playing hipster kickball (yes, that exists in Brooklyn).

The Four Pillars of Health

You gotta eat right, you gotta have healthy habits, you know, and balance out your decadence with a healthy lifestyle during the day.

—Talib Kweli

The life of a technical-creative professional is often erratic, resulting in irregular sleep schedules and questionable food and beverage choices, especially when traveling. It is often at the times when it is difficult to easily find healthy choices that it is most valuable to make them. My primary goal in this section is to help you be more creative and productive. Obviously, overall long-term health is important, but this is not a "health" book, so here I focus on topics most directly relevant to the rhythms of the music producer's lifestyle. To best accomplish this goal, I am structuring this section around four basic health topics:

▷ Diet
▷ Exercise
▷ Rest
▷ Positive mental attitude

First, however, this section discusses the usefulness of "alternative" medicine and the central role played by a few of our body's chemical messengers.

(Alternative) Medicine

Health is often defined as a lack of pain, injury, or disease. But that is too low a bar to set. Being healthy includes those things, but in our affluent, hi-tech, information society, it must also include overall well-being, able to pursue Maslow's self-actualization needs. At its best, modern medicine is truly amazing, especially when it comes to surgery and pharmaceuticals. Only recently has the mainstream started to emphasize well-being and preventative care and not just the treatment of injury, illness, and their symptoms. The MD paradigm, although powerful, quickly runs out of solutions when surgery and drugs aren't appropriate or don't work.

So called "alternative" medicine has a lot to offer when it comes to health and healing, especially the ancient and highly evolved Chinese and Indian systems. But we don't have to look to the East for holistic medicine. Europe, Russia, and the U.S. have a long history of naturopathy and herbalism, and although they offer mixed results for most people with modern ailments, they offer a lot in terms of understanding health. When an MD can't help, and herbs and acupuncture are insufficient, there are two other types of highly trained practitioners in the U.S. who share many of the basic beliefs about health and healing as the "alternative" forms:

▷ **Doctor of Osteopathic Medicine.** Someone with a DO degree has the same legal standing as an MD, a Doctor of Osteopathic Medicine believes in the body's ability to heal itself with guidance.
▷ **Doctor of Chiropractic.** Those with a DC degree also subscribe to this same basic core tenet that the body knows how to heal itself, though a Doctor of Chiropractic has a few years less schooling than an MD or DO and cannot perform surgery or prescribe drugs.

There is something valuable about all these systems, but when it comes to core philosophy, the mainstream MDs are the only ones who primarily prescribe to the insufficient definition of health as absence of disease.

Tanzt das Z.N.S.: **Do You Need a Chiropractor?:** Not only am I physically healthy in large part because of good chiropractors, they have also taught me a lot about health, including what they call the five factors of health—the inspiration for my "four pillars," with the fifth being a clear nervous system—the topic of this sidebar.

D.D. Palmer was the founder of chiropractic. His first patient had a number of problems, including hearing problems. After a number of adjustments to correct subluxated disks in the spine, the patient's hearing unexpectedly improved. We now know this happened because the adjustments relieved pressure on nerves related to hearing. Sometimes, after a good neck adjustment, it is as though cotton has been removed from my ears, which is very useful prior to a mastering session. A lot of musicians and audio engineers swear by their chiropractor for such things, in addition to the usual relief from sitting in a chair and reaching forward all day.

Contrary to popular belief, the goal of chiropractic is not to "crack your back" or repair neck injuries with forceful adjustments. It is to help ensure that your nervous system (see Figure 9.6) is clear of blockages so your brain and the rest of your body can clearly communicate, and thus heal itself as it already knows how to do. Yes, chiropractors are of course great at fixing you up if you've been in a car accident, tweak your neck, or your lower back pops out of place. I recommend having a good one in your phone book, just in case. Not all of them are great, however, so get a referral from someone you trust if possible. I've been to many chiropractors since my lower back first went out on me in 1992. There is one commonality shared by the best ones, which I stuck with for as long as possible: They all graduated from Life University's Chiropractic College in Georgia. If you are in their area, I recommend the following Life College grads: Dr. Richard Johnson (West Bloomfield, MI), Dr. Andrew Lesko (San Francisco, CA), Dr. Michael Shwartzstein (Port Washington, NY), and Dr. Adam Silk (New York, NY).

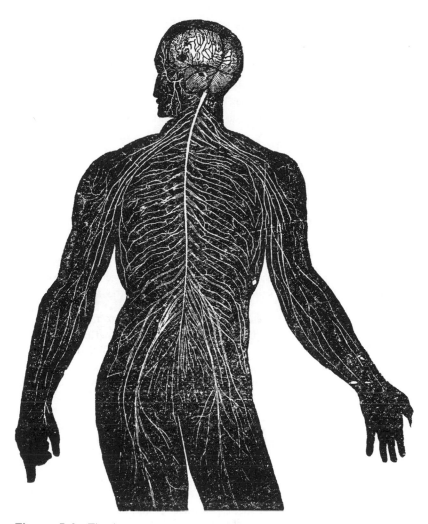

Figure 9.6 The human nervous system.

Chiropractors often get an unfair bad rap. Mainstream modern medicine frowns on their "natural" methods for a number of reasons—some reasonable, but most because they are seen as competition. Wilk *v.* the American Medical Association was a lawsuit brought by a group of chiropractors against the AMA in 1976 for violations of the Sherman Antitrust Act. They won in 1983, and it was upheld in appellate court in 1987, and again in 1990. The AMA was found guilty of an illegal, systematic attempt to eradicate chiropractors in the U.S.

Yes, there are bad chiropractors. Some are even quacks, as in any profession. But mainstream medicine is much more likely to kill you than chiropractic is to injure you. It is well known that many surgeries are unnecessary, and some studies claim the number to be as high as 60 percent. If you have back problems and see a surgeon first, you are much more likely to undergo surgery than if you see a chiropractor first. Even if the doctor does not perform surgery, he or she will prescribe pain killers, many of which are addictive or have potentially lethal side effects (such as Vioxx, which killed at least 60,000 and upward of 500,000 people before being recalled in 2004). In *Death by Modern Medicine* (2005), Dr. Carolyn Dean, MD ND explores the implications of corporate control over our healthcare system. Based on her research, she claims that from 1990–2000, more than 7.8 million people were killed by the very same medical system they turned to for healing. At the Progressive Policy Institute, David B. Kendall drafted a memo on the current state of the U.S. healthcare system entitled "Improving Health Care—By "Spreading the Mayo" (the Mayo Clinic Model, That Is)." Addressed to "the New President" and dated January 15, 2009, it states, "Peter Orszag, director of the Congressional Budget Office, estimates that 5 percent of the nation's gross domestic product—$700 billion per year—goes to tests and procedures that do not actually improve health outcomes."

When people say that the U.S. has the best health care in the world, they are right and wrong, as they are conflating two different things. It is important to make the distinction between "health care" and "the healthcare system." They use the same words, but they have little in common. So, the critique herein is not so much about our amazing medical technology and science, but instead of the mainstream medical system and many of its practitioners.

The Ambient Temperature of Your Mood

Hormones are chemical messengers that trigger changes in cellular function. Cortisol gives us an edge in "hot" situations, while serotonin helps us to keep our cool. Our diet, exercise habits, sleep patterns, attitude, and environment heavily influence the levels of these biological messengers, and vice versa. Health is a process, and these two molecules play a major role in it.

Serotonin is a neurotransmitter and hormone. It has a lot to do with the regulation of mood, immune response, gastrointestinal function, and a lot more. Serotonin is in some ways our "anti-stress" hormone. Sleep deprivation leads to a depletion of serotonin, which can cause irritability. This can also cause increases in cortisol levels, which further adds to irritability and causes more stressful feelings.

Cortisol is a steroid hormone released by the adrenal gland when we experience stress. It increases blood sugar to make sure that our brains get enough glucose to better deal with the danger at hand. To do this, it suppresses other systems that don't need energy at that moment, such as our immune system. Stress can cause weight gain, high blood pressure, insomnia, and other problems largely because of cortisol. Our ancestors needed this energy boost to survive. To them, stress often meant life or death. Now, for most of us, most of the time, not as much. Cortisol doesn't know or care if you are a hunter being chased by a lion 10,000 years ago or a musician in fear of losing your day job after getting chewed out by a jealous supervisor.

> **NOTE:** Full disclosure: Please keep the following in mind as you go through the rest of this chapter. Though I've kept a strict vegetarian diet since 1992, been practicing yoga since 1995, and do my best to stay in shape and eat healthy foods, in no way, shape, or form am I judging or preaching. My diet is far from perfect, and I've done my share of partying over the years. Coffee, brick-oven pizza, and Absinthe Supérieure are certainly enjoyable on a semi-regular basis. That said, ignore the following tips at your own peril. As with much of this book, you get to learn from my experiences, and those of numerous friends and acquaintances, which include both our successes, discoveries, and mistakes. As Will Rogers famously stated, "Good judgment comes from experience, and a lot of that comes from bad judgment."

Diet

There are four pillars of health, but diet is the most fundamental. You are what you eat. Seriously, we definitely, actually, veritably are what we eat. Most of the cells in our body renew every 7–10 years. We are biological dissipative structures, systems that maintain form even though energy continually flows through us. Where do we get this energy? Food, of course, is the source. You may have noticed that I am not prone to hyperbole and resist making absolute statements in favor of holonic contextualism. When I say that diet is everything, it is only a slight over-statement. Consistently avoiding certain foods and drinks, and making sure to choose others, can literally make you a different person over time. You can even learn to modify what you eat and drink on any given day to modulate focus and energy levels as needed.

Giuseppe Arcimboldo's brilliant proto-surrealist-meets-still-life paintings from the 16th century are evocative of how we physically are part of the biosphere. (If you have never seen them, just do a Web image search for "arcimboldo seasons.") Our bodies are truly amazing complex ecosystems, literally, with more than 200 different kinds of cells that comprise our organs, fluids, and other tissues. We are also home to countless microorganisms: bacteria, yeasts, fungi, archaea, and mites, among others. Some of these are necessary for health, such as the "good" bacteria in our guts (and yogurt), while others are parasites draining our energy and vitality. When thinking about how to approach your diet, ask yourself the following: "Do I want to feed my brain, my muscles, and the friendly symbiotic guests, or do I want to fuel the nasty invaders? Do I want to have more energy and mental clarity or feel sluggish and regularly experience mental fog?"

Say what you want about the efficacy of government agencies in the age of multi-national corporations, but there is a good reason that food and drugs are regulated by the same agency in the U.S., the Food and Drug Administration (FDA). Both are substances we put in our body that need quality-assurance regulations, both can alter physiological functions, both can alter states of consciousness, and both can heal or kill you. The main difference is that food is the source of our nutrients. Food supplies the energy needed by our cells and our organs—all of them: brain, blood, skin, heart, eyes, muscles, etc. Putting aside the parts of you that you don't think about as often, you surely care a lot about your mind. Your mind depends on your brain for optimal functioning, and making sure it gets the right nutrients can enhance learning and creativity, for starters, which should be of interest to everyone reading this sentence right now.

Who Eats What and Why?: One way to talk about how food affects our health is in terms of its pH and effect on our bodies' pH (one of Maslow's "physiological needs"). The pH scale is a spectrum of acidity (acid) to basicity (alkaline) in aqueous fluids, with acids starting around a pH of −5 and bases going up to about 14. It is a logarithmic scale, with each number representing a power of 10 in terms of the concentration of hydrogen ions. Pure water has the neutral pH of 7, so anything below 7 is acidic and anything above is alkaline. Let's consider a few common examples on the spectrum to give some perspective: hydrochloric acid pH −1, battery acid pH 0, vinegar pH 3, coffee or beer pH 5, milk pH 6, neutral pH 7, ocean water pH 8, hand soap pH 10, ammonia pH 12, bleach pH 13, lye pH 14.

Humans are not naturally carnivores or omnivores, technically speaking. We started as tropical herbivores, but as the most adaptive mammals in our planet's history, we've been able to survive and settle in every climate on the planet. To accomplish this, we often needed to act like omnivores, even though our physiology is still mostly that of a herbivore. Did you know that findings from recent genetic-mapping projects strongly suggest that humans actually evolved lactose tolerance for non-human dairy (milk) as we migrated into colder climates and became dependent on sheep, goats, yaks, and cows? People who have lived in very cold and/or high-altitude climates for generations can find it most difficult to follow a strict vegetarian diet (most notably the Dalai Lama from Tibet in the Himalayas). The following list gives some key facts about the three basic diet types.

▶ **Carnivore.** Carnivores are predators that primarily hunt and eat other animals. For the most part, carnivores have only sharp teeth, and their jaws don't move side to side, just up and down. Their saliva does not contain digestive enzymes because their stomachs are highly acidic, with a pH around 1 (as mentioned, battery acid is pH 0). Their livers can handle very high levels of the uric acid needed to break down meat into useful amino acids. They have only a relatively straight small intestine for fast elimination of food that quickly rots. Cats are carnivores. They must eat meat to live and cannot survive on plants alone for extended periods of time.
▶ **Omnivore.** Omnivores are primarily predators that eat meat and plants. They essentially have a similar dental and digestive physiology and anatomy to that of a carnivore. Dogs are omnivores. They must eat meat for optimal health but can survive on plants alone for extended periods of time.
▶ **Herbivore.** Herbivores are animals that primarily eat plants, and therefore are not predators. They have flat teeth and jaws that not only move up and down, but also side to side for grinding and crushing with an alkaline saliva containing enzymes for digesting carbohydrates (ranging in pH from 4 to about 7.4). They often have a short and a long intestine, if not multiple stomachs, so there is sufficient time to absorb nutrients and water from the plants. Herbivores eat foods high in fiber, which is needed to push waste through the long, circuitous, digestive tracts. Example: Lagomorphs (rabbits) and their physiological cousins, horses, must constantly eat a lot of plant fiber all the time to live. They do not eat meat.

Humans are not carnivores, period. We are not true omnivores either, though practically speaking the human diet is often that of an omnivore. In human-speak, an omnivore eats anything edible; a vegetarian does not eat any meat (anything with eyes or a nervous system); and vegans are vegetarians who also do not eat or drink any animal products, including eggs, milk, or cheese, and may even avoid anything that uses animal by-products such as leather.

If you are considering a vegan or vegetarian diet, but are concerned about muscle, strength, toughness, or athletic performance, just consider the following examples to put your mind to ease. Mike Tyson went vegan in 2009. San Francisco's Jake Shields is a world-class grappler and elite MMA fighter, having held championship belts in multiple organizations, and was also a contender for the UFC welterweight title. He is a strict vegan. Or, consider WWE wrestling star The Great Khali. If like me you do not watch professional wrestling, you may have seen him in action movies. Born in Punjab, India, in 1972, Dalip Singh Rana is 7 ft 1 in, and 347 lbs, making him the largest body builder in the world. He is a vegetarian. For many more examples check out www.greatveganathletes.com.

To Meat or Not to Meat, That Is the Question (Sorry, Couldn't Resist)

When it comes to your health, a good balanced diet that matches your lifestyle is more important than the specific type of diet. An omnivore with a thoughtful, whole food–based diet can be better off than a vegetarian eating mostly salad, pizza, pasta, and fake soy meats such as veggie dogs. My vegetarian/vegan friends and I share a joke to justify our veggie junk food affairs at any of the numerous vegan fast food or dessert joints in NYC: "It's vegan; it's good for you." That said, for most people, the healthiest diets are primarily, or solely, plant-based, and if you are struggling with RSI, are highly encouraged.

Even if you are a committed omnivore for life, there is a lot you can integrate into your diet based on the sound principles espoused by professional triathlete Brendan Brazier. As a vegan athlete, Brazier set out to create the ultimate vegan diet for himself, which eventually resulted in a few great books, and his Vega brand of products. He is one of the world's foremost authorities on plant-based nutrition. A regular guest lecturer at Cornell University, he has also presented to the U.S. Congress on diet and health, and regularly works with professional and Olympic athletes. Even main-card MMA/UFC fighters swear by his approach, vegan and omnivore alike (Mac Danzig and Duane Ludwig, respectively). If you don't like shelling out cash for health supplements, his books are full of recipes and tips for the DIY inclined.

What to Minimize: A Short List

We get energy from two sources: nourishment and stimulation (for example, caffeine). According to Brazier, *biological debt is* "a state that the body goes into after energy from stimulation has dissipated. Often brought about by eating refined sugar or drinking coffee to gain energy in the short term, biological debt is a state of fatigue." The more processed the food, the more likely it is to have a stimulating effect, whereas simple raw foods are more nourishing. Stimulating foods and drinks are great for energy, stamina, and mental focus at that moment, but the downsides include strain on our nervous system, kidneys, and adrenal glands, and they can even play a role in developing RSI. All these concepts are really important when you know you are going to be working long hours with less-than-ideal sleep and rest. So this section is especially important when you are on tour, are pushing to meet a deadline, or are just crazy busy working a job and trying to launch your career at the same time.

Following is a partial list of common things to avoid or minimize when possible. Note: I am not addressing most of the obvious, bad, fatty foods, or tobacco use, since there is plenty of info everywhere on those.

▷ **Corporate chain fast food.** Basically, just cut this junk out of your diet if at all possible, especially the burger joints. Why are there 20 ingredients in white bread buns? If this one is not totally obvious to you, watch the documentaries *Super Size Me* (2004) and *Food, Inc* (2008). If you have no other options for some reason, learn to make the best choice you can, which is easier these days than in the past (in large part due to *Super Size Me*). Many touring bands have this down to a science, since long stretches of the U.S. interstate system commonly offers limited possibilities.

▷ **Refined sugar.** Bleached white sugar is not your friend. It gives an energy boost, but it wears off quickly and leads to crashes. Parasites, yeasts, and other invaders in our body love refined sugar. Moreover, we have to break it down into smaller sugars (such as glucose) for use anyway, so why offer a buffet of energy to unwanted visitors? Don't feed them unless you want to be more gassy and have more acne. Quitting refined sugar can actually cause withdrawal symptoms for some people as parasites die off, so if need be, look into a good cleanse or two. Corn syrup and other industrial sweeteners, including all of the artificial chemistry-set sweeteners, are also to be avoided whenever possible. Friendly sweeteners, such as evaporated cane juice, fruit juice, agave syrup, honey, raw sugar, Stevia, and other non-processed, natural sweeteners, are much better options.

▷ **Sodas and energy drinks.** For the most part, these are full of artificial ingredients that lead to biological debt from the corn syrup, sugar, and caffeine buzz. People who drink diet caffeine-free sodas are literally just drinking a mild poison with no fun effects, which is completely backward from a logical trade-off made when the fun effects are deemed to be worth taking in a little poison, such as when drinking alcohol. There are organic, natural, and "micro-brew" versions of these drinks that have good ingredients and uncommon flavors, so just look at the label. If you need to lose weight, cutting out soda is a great place to start; drink more water, juice, or tea.

▷ **Dairy.** We are one of the only mammals that regularly drinks milk into adulthood. If you stop and think about it, it is pretty weird that not only do humans keep drinking milk after infancy, but it is the milk of other animals. Regardless, too much dairy can make you feel sluggish and tired, and can even lead to constipation and other unsexy issues. If you do partake in milk and cheese, try to stick to organic or local sources that do not pump the animals full of hormones and antibiotics, and that do not feed the animals pesticide-laden, genetically modified foods. Most pesticides are fat soluble, so they wash off of most veggies while they build up in animal fat that you eat and drink. If you need a lot of energy and are low on sleep, severely minimize your dairy intake.

▷ **Caffeine.** Caffeine is not only a natural pesticide found in plants that can ward off insects, it is also the world's most popular psychoactive/stimulant. Too much caffeine can be bad for you, but many of its sources also have health benefits, so it is more about minimizing how much you take in and how you take it in. Beyond the obvious effects, like all stimulants, caffeine stresses the nervous system, tightens muscles, can increase RSI risk, and messes with sleep cycles. When you have a long day or week ahead of you, pacing your caffeine intake and source is vital. According to an article in the February 2013 edition of *Wired* magazine, there were 13,000 caffeine-related emergency-room visits in 2009, up from 1,100 in 2005. They also stated that most caffeine is now made in chemical factories, such as ones owned by German-headquartered BASF (the world's largest chemical company), and more than 50 percent of synthetic caffeine is cooked up in just three Chinese factories. So given what we know about caffeine, from best to worst, here is the order of common natural caffeine sources that are not on the "avoid" list: yerba mate, green tea, black tea, espresso, and drip coffee. Yerba mate in particular is really good for you and is even higher in antioxidants than other teas.

NOTE: Caffeine is physically addictive, and withdrawal can cause headaches and other symptoms. A few times a year, I quit caffeine for at least three to seven days to help my system recharge and lower my tolerance to less caffeine when needed. A lot of sleep is the best way, but if needed, a little caffeine the first day or two from tea can help with any headaches. After clearing it out of your system for a while, just one cup of coffee is a serious boost.

What to Maximize: A Short List

We live in the best time in human history for readily available healthy, convenient foods. Fresh, unprocessed foods are the best. Eat a lot of fresh, leafy greens and other alkaline-forming whole foods, every day. (Look them up. Many acidic whole foods are actually alkaline forming when ingested.) Common items like avocados, bananas, coconut, and ginger are great for you too.

Here are a few other tips:

▷ Look into including "super foods" in your diet whenever possible, such as raw kombucha, wheat grass, açai berry, goji berry, chlorella, maca, rooibos, white chia, sea vegetables, and green tea or yerba mate for your stimulants.

▷ Drink enough water. We are 40–80 percent H_2O (depending on age). Assuming you have a decent diet, a good guideline is at least eight 8 oz. glasses a day. Definitely check with your doctor to see what is optimal for you.

▷ Consider a vegetarian or vegan diet, if not full-time, at least part-time. It takes time to get good at it, and a lot of people quit because they are low on energy. Just do your homework. If you do decide to go veggie, avoid the beginner's diet: pizza, pasta, ranch dressing, etc. Don't overly rely on fake meats. They are tasty convenience food, but while not as bad as normal fast food, are often heavily processed food-science product.

▷ Learn to identify ingredients on all the food and drinks you regularly consume. Take the time to look them up and don't go with intuition on this front. As an example, based on their names, you might think pyridoxine hydrochloride, ascorbic acid, and cyanocobalamin should be avoided, whereas isolated soy protein would be acceptable. But in fact, according to Brendan Brazier, it's isolated soy protein that should be avoided, as it is acid forming, is a common allergen, and can actually inhibit digestion. The other three are the vitamins B_6, C, and B_{12} respectively.

What Is a Vitamin?: Everyone knows that vitamins are good for you. All around you, you regularly see multi-vitamin pills, drinks, tablets, and powders formulated for kids, men, women, adults over 50, immune system, energy, so on and so forth. You may even know that some vitamins are water soluble, such as B and C, while A, D, E, and K are fat soluble and can build up to dangerous levels. Yet, most people have no idea why something is labeled as a "vitamin." If a substance is a nutrient that is needed in small amounts, and our body cannot sufficiently synthesize enough of it, then it is a vitamin.

For the most part, vitamins should be obtained through your diet, but to make sure you get everything in the right amounts just through food is challenging. This is why so many people use supplements. If you have a good diet and sleep well, but are still tired all of the time, you may be lacking a certain vitamin. Blood work is the only sure way to tell, so go see your doctor and get it checked out to make sure it is not something more serious. (Yes, this is the kind of thing mainstream medicine is really good at.)

A lack of Vitamin D is a common culprit for those with a music-culture lifestyle. Vitamin D is primarily obtained by sunlight, and many of us are night people, so getting enough D may require supplements more so than other vitamins. That said, D is fat soluble, so follow the instructions on the bottle. When in doubt, a high-quality nutrition shake every day is a good way to make sure you are getting everything without overdoing anything.

Note: If you are vegetarian, make sure the capsules are not made of gelatin (horns and hooves). In most cases it will be clearly labeled on the bottle or packaging if the capsules are suitable for vegetarians. Also, as with any product, not all brands are equally effective. *Bioavailability* is a term used to describe how much of the vitamin content your body actually uses. Some brands are much better than others.

Exercise

Simply stated, being active is good for you. Humans are not designed to be sedentary. It is only the industrial revolution and modern medicine that has allowed us to be so out of shape and survive. In ancient times, obesity was rare and seen as a sign of wealth or fertility. Today, it is considered a sign of laziness and illness (and it is an epidemic in the U.S.). Even if someone is not overweight, lack of exercise will limit productivity and creativity to some extent. Regular exercise not only leads to more energy, it really helps minimize the risks of RSI for most people. Exercise is not just good for your body, but is good for your mind and can even enhance creativity and learning. You don't have to join a gym or buy P90X to stay in decent shape. If you sit in a chair all day, leaning forward with your hand gripped on a mouse or trackpad, hunched over a computer screen, then you need to do something to get the blood moving and stretch out those muscles.

There are three basic types of exercise, and each one is important (although for our purposes, some are more important than others):

▷ **Stretching (flexibility).** This is the most important one while you are working. Every hour or so, you should get out of your chair and do some simple basic stretching. Just do a Web search for "desk stretches," and you will find an assortment of charts and articles. I also highly recommend learning a more serious stretching routine, which you can do each morning and evening. This can be very light, and take only 5–10 minutes. If you are new to regular stretching, take it easy and go slow. Don't worry about how deep the stretch is as long as you feel something. Just do a Web search for "daily stretching" to find a ton of info. Once this becomes a habit, it will feel weird to not stretch out every morning and night.

▷ **Aerobic (cardio).** This is the second most important one for us. Getting your blood moving will help get oxygen to all those muscles that need it after you've sat in front of a computer all day. You don't have to start jogging or hit the treadmill to get the refreshing feeling of a good aerobic workout. Walking is a great low-impact option. For us New Yorkers, walking is a way of life, since most of us don't use cars to get to work. It is not uncommon to walk a few miles a day here, and it makes it easy to get some aerobic exercise as part of your regular day. But if you live somewhere that requires a car, find ways to walk when you can. Riding a bike is also a great option and can be a lot of fun. Swimming is arguably the best option in terms of low impact, but it is not the most convenient option for most people. And yes, going dancing at a club, bar, or festival certainly counts!

▷ **Strength (muscle building).** This is the least important for our purposes unless you are really out of shape. There is no need to use weights to build strength. Some basic exercises such as push-ups and sit-ups, in tandem with a good stretching routine is a solid, old-school minimum.

Yoga

There is evidence that yoga was developed in large part so that it would be possible to sit still all day and meditate. If you want to get all your exercise at once, I can't recommend yoga more strongly. I do about 20 minutes every morning and another 20 minutes every night. There are tons of free yoga podcasts and other reputable sources online. People I know with RSI issues who still work with computers swear by hot yoga classes—once their doctor gave them the okay, of course, and with a few modifications to some postures based on their specific issues. There are classes in most every city and suburb at various times of day.

Martial Arts

Why not get your exercise while learning self defense? Any martial art is going to offer health benefits when properly taught and practiced. Krav Maga is the best all-around practical self-defense system, but for a serious workout, go to a beginner's Muay Thai class and be ready to burn as many as 1,000 calories while learning to kick butt. Some schools even offer women-only classes, led by female instructors.

Pilates

Pilates is not known for its aerobic benefits, but for core strength and flexibility, it is at the top of the list. Many male athletes have learned to appreciate this "woman's" workout, having realized first-hand how difficult it actually is. For people with bad computer posture issues, Pilates can really help correct problems. If you have RSI or early symptoms, I highly recommend taking a private session or two to help you break bad habits.

Whole Body Vibration (WBV)

To shake out your whole system, check out this technology used by the Russian space program to help cosmonauts returning from zero gravity regain bone density. Now used by many athletes and physical therapists, WBV has a ton of health benefits. Unfortunately, the really good machines (Vibraflex, TurboSonic) are commercial grade and cost $10,000 and up. There is likely a gym in your area that has them to check out. You can get a pretty good home model such as the DZT Ultra Vibe V2000 for about $750 or less (if you look around) or the Noblerex K1 for about $2,000. Don't confuse WBV with the small plates meant just for workouts. As with anything I say here, check with your healthcare provider, especially if you have any nerve damage or other health issues.

Rest and Relaxation

Work hard, play hard, relax hard…I think you get what I'm getting at here. There are natural ebbs and flows in the music producer's lifestyle, so learn to identify when you need to keep pushing and when you need to rest.

According to a 2010 CDC study, more than 30 percent of adults in the U.S. average less than six hours of sleep a night, and depending on occupation and industry, it varies from 24.1 percent to 69.7 percent. The average healthy adult needs between seven and nine hours a night for full recuperation. Not only do we rebalance our serotonin levels, but the body also regenerates cells during sleep. This regeneration process actually burns more calories during a full night's sleep than when sitting on the couch watching TV. There are times when enough sleep is just not possible. In those situations, it is even more important to pay attention to your diet if you want to function as efficiently as possible.

When it is time to go to sleep, our brains secrete the hormone melatonin (N-acetyl-5-methoxytryptamine) from the pineal gland. Melatonin production is stimulated by darkness and inhibited by light, so the darker the better for sleep, and vice versa if you are trying to stay awake. If you regularly have trouble winding down and falling asleep, here are a few guidelines:

▷ Don't exercise too close to sleep time, although light stretching can be okay.
▷ Avoid caffeine for four to eight hours before sleep.
▷ Avoid sugar two hours before sleep.
▷ See the next section on breathing.

Sleep Aids

If you need some assistance, there are a lot of commonly available over-the-counter sleep aids, although the active ingredient is usually just the antihistamine diphenhydramine or doxylamine, essentially rebranded cold medicine. I recommend that you research some of the commonly used natural options, botanicals such as valerian, hops, and chamomile, or supplements like L-tryptophan, melatonin, and GABA. There are also natural sleep aids and drinks that contain some combination of the above, often with additional herbal extracts. Even though herbs and natural supplements are generally very safe, there are contraindications for people with various conditions and prescriptions, so do your research and talk to your doctor.

While sleep is a necessity, never underestimate the importance of down time—simple rest and relaxation. Read a book. Get a massage. Stream an episode of *The IT Crowd* or *Farscape*. Go to the park and get a little sunlight, which not only helps with vitamin D production but with healthy serotonin (5-HT) levels, too. Don't get sucked into R&R mode for too long, but enjoy it when you can.

Breathe

In Hindu creation mythology, Brahma is the creator of the universe (see Figure 9.7), which cycles in and out of existence with each inhale and exhale of Vishnu. (There are various permutations of the name Brahma, each with a significantly different meaning.) Brahma is also sometimes known as the *deva* of sound and speech. Our words *breath* and *breathe* stem from the same Sanskrit root word as does Brahma. Breathing is so fundamental that we don't even think about it most of the time. It is more fundamental than food, water, exercise, and sleep. You can go days without water or sleep, and weeks without food, but just a few minutes without air and you are a goner. Consciousness of breathe is not only central to yoga, athletics, martial arts, and even archery, but to overall mood and health, too.

Stress causes a number of physiological changes, but an unconscious change in breathing patterns is one of the first. Usually this involves faster and shallower breathing, which means that you are getting rid of carbon dioxide too quickly. In the extreme, this is known as hyperventilation, but before reaching that point shallow breathing can cause other anxiety-inducing symptoms. The easiest thing you can do to better deal with stress is to be mindful of your breathing and learn how to control it.

It sounds simple, but just remember to breathe in deeply and slowly through your nose, especially when you are stressed or tired. Try not to lift your shoulders or engage any muscles in your neck as you breathe down into your diaphragm (upper stomach area). To better help blood flow through your body, elevate your feet above your heart. This can be as simple as putting your feet up on another chair. To take it further, lay on your bed or on the floor and put your feet up on the wall, using a pillow to support your back if needed. Just hang out and breathe for five, 10, 15, even 20 minutes. Just following your breath and watching your thoughts come and go is a common, basic form of Buddhist meditation. Just sit there, follow your breath, and let your thoughts flow freely, simply watching them come and go as though they were nothing more than changes in the weather.

Figure 9.7 A famous painting of Brahma on a lotus emerging from Vishnu (artist unknown).
Source: Public domain from print of Mahabharata, Ramanarayanadatta astri version via University of Toronto.

There is a well-known yogic breathing technique that has a balancing effect, which might also help you fall asleep faster. It is called "alternate nostril breathing." Just sit or lay comfortably, keep your mouth closed, don't cross your legs or arms if possible, and do the following for 10–20 cycles:

1. Use your index finger to gently press one nostril closed.
2. Slowly breathe in.
3. Move your finger over to the other side to block the other nostril.
4. Slowly breathe out.
5. Slowly breathe in.
6. Move your finger over to the other side to block the other nostril.
7. Slowly breathe out.

That is one cycle. Simple. Easy. Effective. Try it each night before you go to sleep.

Positive Mental Attitude (PMA)

If you are not failing, then you are not trying hard enough. That adage gets right to the heart of the issue. Keeping a positive mental attitude does not mean you should not be disappointed, sad, or frustrated. It does not mean you have to walk around practicing self-help affirmations or going to see motivational speakers (but if those help you, by all means keep doing what works). It does not mean you are never snarky, cranky, or cantankerous. It means you deal with whatever difficulties or challenges face you and make the best out of the situation. It means you are not normally cynical, bitter, and resentful when things don't go your way. Your general attitude from day to day has huge implications for your health, social life, and career.

As discussed in Chapter 1, "Musica Universalis," cybernetics is the transdisciplinary study of feedback loops, with applications in fields ranging from robotics to multiple schools of psychology. It is a powerful lens for understanding how our attitudes shape outcomes and vice versa. Let's start with an analogy from audio electronics. When you place a microphone right in front of a speaker, it creates a positive feedback loop: mic to amp to speaker to mic to amp to speaker, etc. Even in a quiet room, this quickly amplifies the low-level signal into a painfully loud, piercing, shrieking, ear-splitting, speaker-blowing noise. Now consider a guitar player artfully modulating feedback into useful sound by moving his or her guitar's pickups closer to and farther away from the amp and speakers. The first example is an analogy for what can happen when you lack awareness of how your attitude feeds back on itself, while the second example is an analogy for an understanding of the same loops.

Positive feedback loops amplify whatever signals are in the loop. When we talk about someone in "a downward spiral" or say a DJ or producer is "blowing up" or that his or her career is "really taking off," we are referencing the extreme ups and downs produced by positive feedback loops. Our emotions influence our thoughts, which influence our emotions.... Our thoughts and emotions influence our diet and sleep, which influence how our bodies feel, which influences our thoughts and emotions.... Our thoughts and emotions influence our attitude, which influences our behaviors (conscious and unconscious), which influence outcomes, which influence our thoughts and emotions.... Curiosity is a great way to help minimize habitually falling into the same loops. The more diverse your interests, the wider a variety of thought patterns you have, which will help put more conscious signal into the loops and less unconscious noise and error.

You've probably heard an adage along the lines of, "You get back what you put in." In this case, I am not offering up the cliché about having a good work ethic; I mean it more literally in the context of interpersonal communication. The actual words used to communicate thoughts in a spontaneous discussion can account for less than half the information actually transmitted. Depending on the context, situation, and degree of familiarity of those involved, it can be as low as just a few percent. When we talk about someone's "vibe" or "energy" to describe our impression of them, we are summing up perceptions of their body language, facial expressions, tone of voice, pitch of voice, eye movement, and numerous other non-verbal cues that are used to interpret what is being communicated (which is why hastily written emails and text messages are so easily misinterpreted). These cues communicate attitude and emotional state, regardless of the verbal intent. We naturally mirror back a lot of these cues to each other, thus creating a feedback loop. There are very obvious examples, such as feeling anger when someone is angry at you, feeling sad when around a sad person, or feeling anxiety around someone who is anxious, even though they claim to the contrary. Once you become aware of the obvious, it is easy to see that mirroring is the norm, no matter how subtle or unconscious.

The overlap of the intrapersonal and the interpersonal is yet another example of a ubiquitous complex system: a system of feedback loops inside feedback loops inside feedback loops, order at the edge of chaos displaying fractal self similarity on many scales. So what does this mean in simple language? If you work at keeping a positive mental attitude, it will become easier to stay positive, which will make it easier to minimize stress, which will make it easier to stay positive, which will make it easier to stay healthy, productive, and creative, which will make it easier to stay positive, which will lead to more contacts and more opportunities, which will lead to.... Positive feedback loops amplify the input, no matter what it is.

> **TIP:** You may want to revisit Chapter 5 after soaking in the implications of the last few paragraphs.

Unnecessary Stress and Anxiety: Cut It Out: A perfect example of unnecessary stress and anxiety has been on wonderful display with the silly hysteria about the end of the Mayan calendar on December 21, 2012 meaning the end of the world. I am literally typing this sentence at 11:10 pm on Dec 20th, 2012; I plan to type my next sentence on December 22, 2012.

[Pause for 26 hours]

So yes, here I am back at the computer typing at 1:22 am on 12/22/12. What is the point of this little exercise? I didn't waste my energy stressing about the end of the Mayan calendar and was able to complete the first draft of Chapter 4 during that little pause without worry, even though the History Channel and NatGeo were doing their best to work us into an anxiety-laden frenzy about doomsday prepping and the impending 2012 apocalypse.

There is always something to worry about, always something bad that can—and will—happen in the future. A few billion years from now, the Andromeda galaxy and our Milky Way galaxy are going to collide and merge into a new bigger galaxy, and our sun will balloon out into a red giant, swallowing Mercury and Venus before shrinking into a white dwarf, leaving Earth a scorched, lifeless rock. We are all born and we are all going to die, so stop worrying about things you can't control. I am not suggesting donning rose-colored glasses and ignoring real threats, but staying positive and not giving in to unnecessary fear, worry, and anxiety will lower your ambient stress level and keep cortisol levels low until you actually need that spike of energy and adrenalin. You are alive at the most amazing time in human history. Enjoy it!

Set and Setting

Timothy Leary coined the phrase "set and setting" in the context of psychedelic psychotherapy research he conducted at Harvard in the 1960s, before LSD, DMT, and psilocybin were criminalized. *Set* refers to your state of mind, and *setting* refers to your immediate social and physical surroundings, both of which are equally important for minimizing negative experiences during therapy (or what is commonly referred to as a "bad trip"). For our purposes, I am expanding his definitions beyond the context of psychedelic psychotherapy. Set and setting are equally pertinent considerations for avoiding undesirable outcomes from the types of positive feedback loops discussed in the previous section. At the same time, we must also consider a basic understanding of set and setting as powerful conceptual tools that can help us cultivate positive experiences, from fun or formative to transformative or life changing.

The preceding discussion of positive mental attitude addressed *set* (although not exhaustively). Adept navigation of the music producer's lifestyle most certainly also includes developed instincts about *setting*. Setting includes two parts: people and places. Chapter 5 is about people, and includes discussion about social ecologies, scenes, and their casts of characters. Everyone is influenced by the people around them. Although the nature and degree of this influence varies wildly from person to person, it is unavoidable. Chapter 3, "What Is Your Plan?," includes discussion about some places where you might choose to work or go to school. These decisions can of course determine your social circles, but also the city and neighborhood you inhabit. Do you live in a depressing or dangerous neighborhood, or is it simply boring, conservative, and homogenous? Are your roommates a constant source of petty drama or people you like going home to? Are you surrounded by smart, interesting people or narrow-minded knuckle-draggers?

You will need to get used to working with limited options for a variety of reasons, including financial limitations, health issues, family obligations, natural disasters, or an infinite variety of unpredictable events and unlikely convergences. Some of the scenarios in the previous paragraph are very likely during and just after college, when you are just getting started, although, rough patches can pop up at any time. In other words, life happens. These variables are inputs into a chaotic system of feedback loops that we simply have to deal with as best as possible. See these less-than-optimal scenarios as temporary, as necessary sacrifices made so you can reach other goals.

Although we cannot always control setting, we can learn to control how we react to it, our set. When we *can* control setting, it is that much more important to make good choices. Over time, you can learn to cultivate the ways in which you inhabit the world around you—to create a setting conducive to productive creativity. After all, many of us choose this lifestyle, with all of its challenges and pitfalls, for the freedom and flexibility it can offer. If you've actually made it through this whole chapter, the Elbert Hubbard quote at the opening should make a lot of sense.

The Stresses of Success: What follows is a Twitter discussion between a legendary Detroit techno veteran and a very popular electronic dance music producer that rose to popularity in recent years. I have not made any corrections to their tweets, and have anonymized both of these Canadians, even though it was a public conversation.

Public Twitter feed from November 14, 2011:

@newguy: i feel like i've had the best highs in life…even too high. being happy making millions happy. and the lowest lows. nothing in between.

@veteran: @newguy in the long run time brings all of these extremes into perspective and you might even feel that things balance out!

@newguy: i blame the stress. touring, music making, trying too hard to meet everyones high expectations, making relationships work, projects, house.

@veteran: @newguy welcome to the real world of touring, producing & performing…AND living THE GOOD LIFE! Don't worry, it doesn't get any easier!

Pick Your Friends with Care

We all have different kinds of friends. Some we've known since childhood, some are around only for a few years and then are gone from your life for no particular reason. We have artist friends, music-scene friends, and pro audio–world friends. There are fair-weather friends, party friends, sports friends, yoga friends, casual friends, and even friends who don't understand some of our other friends. There are friends we see all the time, and others we don't see for years. The more friends the better. The question is this: How many of them are proven, close, trusted friends?

Contrary to the title of this section, I am not so presumptuous as to think I should offer advice about how other people should make friends. But, there are a few things I've learned over the years that are worthy of your contemplation. The life of an artist or musician can be intense. We find ourselves in situations and having experiences that are so amazing, outrageous, terrifying, surreal, or just plain bizarre, most people do not understand or simply cannot relate to them. Not only will you want to share these experiences with people who can appreciate them, but there likely will be times when it might even seem necessary. The view from the top of a mountain can be a lonely one.

With just a little bit of success, people start coming out of the woodwork who want to meet you. With a lot of success, too many people wanting something from you can lead to isolation. Just consider the previous sidebar, in which a hugely successful EDM producer had a meltdown on Twitter about coping with success. Someone with a solid group of people around would not need to do such a thing unless they were simply looking for attention. There is a good reason that the very successful have an entourage. The word *entourage* literally means "surrounding" or "environment," so in a sense, an entourage is a portable setting. Yes, some have a big entourage to show off their success, but for many, it is about having a close circle of people they trust around them. This surrounding group of people are often there to act as a shield or filter. I've been on the inside of the filter on numerous occasions, and I can tell you that the entourages of rock stars, hip-hop legends, and superstar DJs I've been around were primarily groups of close, trusted, long-time friends.

Each of us can figure out for ourselves when we've outgrown certain friendships. But if you do fully embrace a music producer's lifestyle—and especially if you achieve a high level of public success—you will be happy that you've cultivated at least a few friendships with people who can relate to you and who can handle whatever craziness you may throw at them.

As artists get older and become more established, the smart ones tend to develop a circle of friends who are creative and inspiring. As the years go by, also connecting with like-minded people from different arts, fields, or professions can make it easier to avoid jaded and bitter people—people who, just a few years earlier, might have been optimistic friends or inspiring peers at the outset of a career path but simply have not dealt well with challenges and failures. Staying inspired and avoiding bitterness and cynicism is hard enough as it is.

Why Is Good Music So Often in Shady Places?

Back in the early 1990s, one of my bands played at an infamous underground club in Muskegon, MI, the Icepick. After loading in and sound checking, we went to find some food. The owner/promoter told us to be careful because we were in a really bad part of town. We told him we were from Detroit, so we shouldn't have anything to worry about in Muskegon. His response: "A bad neighborhood is a bad neighborhood." Fortunately, nothing bad happened to us that night, other than people throwing beer cans at us on stage (a custom there, as we discovered), but looking back I realize we were naïve and lucky.

Warehouse parties, underground clubs, and even many legit venues that emphasize edgy or extreme styles of music are often in a bad part of town, and commonly in somewhat desolate or light-industrial areas that are devoid of people at night and on weekends. Once inside the venue, many promoters are really good at creating a safe, even fantastical environment that allows you to completely drop your guard. Adding this sense of security to altered consciousness often equals a lack of judgment and awareness of one's surroundings when stepping back out into the "real world." Most of the people I know who have been mugged or assaulted by strangers underwent those horrible experiences early in the a.m. on their way home from a music event or party, sometimes even within a block or two of their apartment. When in unfamiliar terrain, especially in these shady areas, try to never leave a party alone. And even when with a few people, just keep your wits about you until you are somewhere where there are a lot of people around or home.

The Leading Edge of Gentrification

Most of the remaining people I know who have been jumped on the street fall into another category common to people with our lifestyle. In a search for affordable rent, musicians and artists often find themselves moving into less-affluent, working-poor, or just straight-up sketchy neighborhoods. Of course, many of these neighborhoods are über-hip, and in a few years will gentrify into a safe place to live. No matter how "up and coming" or hip a neighborhood may be, however, most every gentrifying neighborhood goes through a transition phase when tensions between the new residents and those who are being chased out of their neighborhood by rising rents leads to problems (see Figure 9.8). Artists and musicians are not the cause, are usually also negatively affected by rising rents, and may even try to assimilate into the existing community. Yet, they do inadvertently help pave the way for developers, landlords, and other business owners to take things to the next stage of gentrification. As visible symbols of these changes, the skinny white hipster musician living across the street is seen as the cause of the problem. Whether in San Francisco's Mission District in the mid to late 1990s or Brooklyn's Williamsburg in the mid-2000s, teens and other troublemakers will vent their frustrations with vandalism and even physical violence toward the perceived "invaders." This dynamic is nothing new, and dates as far back as Roman Britain, although modern usage of the word gentrification stems from the 1960s.

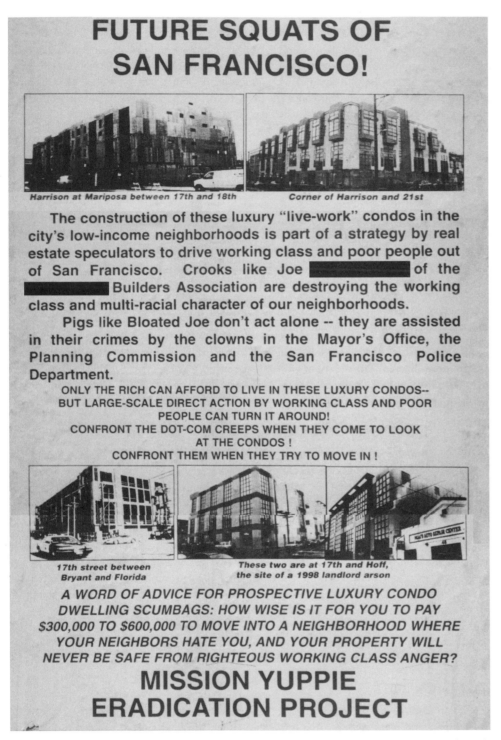

Figure 9.8 Evidence of the anger caused by gentrification. I took this photo of a wheat-pasted poster in 2000 or 2001, in San Francisco's Mission District on Valencia St. near 16th St.

This Is Your Brain On...

Humans like to alter their consciousness. Kids spin around in circles to get dizzy. Joggers get hooked on the "runner's high." Coffee is only outdone by oil on the global commodities market, not to mention sugar and cocoa. Alcohol has a significant place in human history, with evidence of fermented drinks going back 10,000 years. There are even other mammals known to get drunk on rotted, fermented fruit. The role of mind-altering substances in the evolution of many religions is well documented, such as in the origins of Hinduism and the mystery religions of ancient Greece. The relationship between humans and mind-altering substances is as fundamental as it is complex.

Artists and musicians, in particular, are known to imbibe and ingest, often as part of their creative process (see the discussion in Chapter 7). Whether through direct experience or otherwise, mind-altering chemicals are the inspiration and/or subject matter of untold songs, albums, books, films, and paintings. Here are a few examples: Edgar Degas' "L'Absinthe" (1893), Aleister Crowley's *Diary of a Drug Fiend* (1922), The Memphis Jug Band's "Cocaine Habit Blues" (1929), The Beatles' "Lucy In the Sky with Diamonds" (1967), Velvet Underground's "Heroin" (1967), Black Sabbath's "Sweet Leaf" (1971), Hunter S. Thompson's *Fear and Loathing In Las Vegas* (1971) and Terry Gilliam's subsequent film adaptation (1998), Eric Clapton's "Cocaine" (1977), Butthole Surfers's "Bong Song" (1989), Coil's "Love's Secret Domain" (1990), Irving Welsh's *Trainspotting* (1993) and Danny Boyle's subsequent film adaptation (1996), Alex Grey's *St. Albert and the LSD Revelation Revolution* (2006), Gaspar Noé's *Enter The Void* (2009), and countless others.

Some artists and music styles are clearly associated with various substances and the states of consciousness they are known to induce; dub/ reggae and ganja come to mind as an obvious example. In many cases, the music, the altered perceptions characteristic of the substance, and the culture surrounding the drug merge and inform each other, as exemplified in genres such as "stoner" rock or "psychedelic" trance. Substances are so prominent in music culture that whole genres, styles, and even historically significant cultural movements evolved in tandem with specific ones—most notably the hippies with LSD starting in the 1960s, and rave culture with MDMA in the 1990s. In fact, some music barely makes sense outside of the context in which it evolved. In other words, such music is best appreciated when in a certain state of mind, most commonly through experience with the substance that inspired its creation (though for some people drugs are not necessary to "get there").

Regardless of your personal position on drug use, recreational or otherwise, one of the biggest casualties of the failed war on drugs is research into legitimate medical applications, and the truth. By the truth, I mean good, scientific information. Decades of concerted, often racist, xenophobic, and political misinformation campaigns about various drugs, combined with bans on FDA-approved research, have created an information deficit. In theory, with FDA-approved drugs, there is a body of research explaining the various positive and negative effects to a wide variety of users, including contraindications. (For example, don't take x with y, or if you suffer from condition z). Even if you think you know what you can and cannot mix, most street drugs are either cut with other substances or completely misrepresented. Assuming that a high-quality sample of the desired chemical is procured, most users have no idea about proper dosage or contraindications. The most popular drug, alcohol, does not mix well with other substances, especially prescription meds. Speaking of prescription meds, cocaine was once a very popular medical remedy, and is only a schedule II controlled substance since it still is occasionally used in modern medicine. Most people are totally unaware that a third potentially more dangerous substance, cocaethylene, is created and can build up in the liver when you mix alcohol with cocaine, especially over a long period of time. Thanks to the drug war, that information is not readily available.

NOTE: Two of the best sources for good information on this section's topic are www.erowid.org and www.drugpolicy.org.

DIY Testing and Science: Even though I've been to my share of all-night electronic music parties, I was never a raver in the classic sense. What I have always appreciated about the old-school promoters and members of those communities was their DIY attitude. DanceSafe started in the Oakland/SF Bay area in 1999 to help people in their scene have fun in as safe a way as possible. Now a national non-profit with local chapters throughout the U.S. and Canada, they are at the forefront of spreading good, harm-reduction information on many of the topics in this chapter: getting home safely, hearing protection, safe sex, and responsible use of recreational "party" drugs.

DanceSafe, along with MAPS.org and Erowid.org, helped to launch EcstasyData.org in 2001. They are an independent lab that publishes test results on the contents of street ecstasy/Molly. They found that in 2012, less than 25 percent was pure MDMA, down from 50 percent in 1999, and almost 40 percent contained no MDMA. The other detected ingredients were an assortment of other substances, ranging from the relatively innocuous MSM and caffeine to a variety of dangerous stimulants such as dibenzylpiperazine (DBZP) and illegal tryptamines such as 5-MeO-DIPT (a.k.a. "foxy methoxy").

Even assuming a safe setting, it is important to understands that "drugs" is a huge category, covering substances with sizable variances in toxicity and possible side effects. As briefly discussed in Chapter 7, some drugs are not physically addictive and have low toxicity (THC, LSD) but can be problematic in other ways, especially for those predisposed to mental illness. Others can lead to addiction or even death on first use (heroin, crack, meth). Also, never forget that many dealers misrepresent their product. For example, blotter "acid" is now more likely to contain a potentially dangerous synthetic cannabinoid, such as 25I-NBOMe, than to actually contain LSD.

Don't for a second assume that a pharmaceutical-grade prescription drug is necessarily safer; they actually cause more death and addiction than all the aforementioned combined. The now-infamous "hillbilly heroin," OxyContin, has created a black market unto itself, and has actually led users to turn to heroin when they can no longer afford to illegally obtain the more-expensive FDA-approved pharmaceutical.

Leaving aside issues of legality, altering your brain chemistry is serious business and should never be taken lightly. Moreover, many of these substances are known to cause other physiological reactions, separate from the desired change in consciousness, that can be problematic. You have to find reliable sources of information and do your research. Don't be a guinea pig, and don't play Russian roulette. Never make decisions based on what other people do. I am not talking about peer pressure here; each of us has a different physiology and psychology, different tolerances, and different genetics. Physical fitness and age seem to be poor indicators when it comes to drug use. At age 23, Len Bias was the second overall pick in the 1986 NBA draft; two days later, he overdosed on powdered cocaine while celebrating with friends (although it was reported he was smoking crack). Supposedly, it was the first time he tried it, and he died of a heart attack. On the other end of the spectrum, William S. Burroughs was a long-time junkie (heroin addict), and died of a heart attack at the age of 83.

Fortunately, research bans are loosening a bit. Marijuana is the most researched, and as of 2012, medical marijuana is legal in 18 states, with Colorado and Washington fully decriminalizing small amounts for personal use. In recent years, research has also resumed in very limited cases on MDMA, LSD, psilocybin, and ibogaine, leading to promising medical and therapeutic uses for post-traumatic stress disorder (PTSD), cluster headaches (way worse than migraines), and yes, even curing drug addiction. But I digress, so check out www. maps.org if this topic interests you.

My point here is not about whether you choose to use or not use substances that alter your consciousness. I only want everyone to think about what they are putting into their bodies and know why they are doing it. I also hope that anyone who chooses a lifestyle that regularly includes exposure to drugs, legal or illegal, is educated on the topic. This education is not only for yourself, but also for, and about, those around you. I have barely scratched the surface on this vast subject, so as with other topics in this chapter, I urge you to do your own research. If you don't know where to start, check out www.erowid.org or www.drugpolicy.org.

There is no question that a lot of people are drawn to dance clubs and other music events for an experience that includes swallowing some sort of pill at the beginning of the night. Good music, good chemicals, a good sound system, and a good, safe venue are a powerful combination. That said, those who do this for a living regularly change their relationship to that aspect of the culture as they get a little older and wiser, and realize that they need to get more serious about their art and career.

Berlin-based Ellen Allien is a successful veteran DJ and music producer. She also founded the highly respected BPitch Control label in 1999. In a 2004 interview for *Exberliner Magazine*, interviewer Elizabeth McGrath asked her a question about the evolution of her career—one that is very germane to our current discussion.

Elizabeth McGrath: You mean it took you a while to respect the life and culture you had chosen for yourself? You felt you were doing something wrong?

Ellen Allien: Yes, because it was nightlife, it was underground; it was playing to drug people. It was not easy to respect that part of my life, I always thinking that maybe I am not doing the right thing, that I am choosing the wrong system and lifestyle for myself. And it took me years to respect that. But after I started my label and made more things, I see that it's right. And now I see I am in a system I can live with and I am respected. And it's not only drugs—it's art.

Last Call

Being a music producer means your whole life is about your art. Your passion is your career, and your career includes easy access to a lifestyle that is a lot of fun but can be bad for your health and thus your career. Knowing when to push the limits and when to pull back is a sophisticated life skill and display of professional acumen. Attaining mastery of one's craft is more than just technical skill, creative potency, and networking dexterity. Mastering the art of balance is a never-ending challenge, but cultivated instincts in its pursuit helps the practitioner get the most out of life as a music producer.

10

Dénouement

Chance and destiny are merely the agencies which release the intensities in ourselves which are ready for manifestation. It is these intensities that cause the decisive events to "happen by chance" or "destine" these events for us. The intensities manage the chance and destiny so that the possibilities for their own manifestation occur. In a word, we are our chances and destiny.

–Jean Gebser

Cultivate in yourself a grand similarity with the chaos of the surrounding ether.

–John Cage

Technical skill is mastery of complexity, while creativity is mastery of simplicity.

–Erik Christopher Zeeman

Adapt what is useful, reject what is useless, and add what is specifically your own.

–Bruce Lee

The presence of those seeking the truth is infinitely to be preferred to the presence of those who think they've found it.

–Terry Pratchett

What do you think an artist is? An imbecile who only has eyes if he's a painter, ears if he's a musician, or a lyre at every level of his heart if he's a poet, or even, if he's a boxer, only muscles? On the contrary he is at the same time a political being constantly awakened by the terrible, ardent or sweet events in the world, molding himself to their image. How could it be possible to not be interested in other fellow human beings, and in the name of what isolationist values detach oneself from a life they bring to you so copiously?

–Pablo Picasso

NOTE: The preceding Picasso quote is from a publication of the National Front, *Les Lettres Françaises*, March 24, 1945, "Picasso n'est pas officier dans l'armée Française." It was translated from French to English by Jean-Luc Cohen, a New York City–based music producer, electronic musician, audio engineer, and educator.

A S THE TITLE OF THIS BOOK SUGGESTS, *The Music Producer's Survival Guide: Chaos, Creativity, and Career in Independent and Electronic Music* is about a career in music production. But it is about a lot more than just the words in the title. It is about figuring out how to make a living while pursuing one's passion for music and production. It is about choosing a life that is meaningful and rewarding, even if it is a constant balancing act full of ups and downs. It is about making your mark. It is about surviving in a constantly shifting landscape. It is about having fun and following your heart. It is about taking what you do seriously without taking yourself too seriously. It is about patience and persistence. It is about taking part in the creation of a collective soundtrack to life and history. It is about collaborators, scenes, communities, peers, mentors, teachers, students, fans, friends, and a lot of other people. It is also about the big picture.

The Producer's Mindset

Consumers consume what is available. Producers decide what is on the menu. Dedication to being a professional, independent, and/or electronic music producer means that a career is more than just a way to make a living. It is the persistent pursuit of one's passion—it is as much a lifestyle as it is a profession. As you may recall from the sidebar in the introduction, "Magic Might Make Machine Mechanism, *Moegen Macht*," the verb *produce* means to make, to create, to bring forth, to bring into being, to give form or shape to, to oversee the making of. All true artists, no matter their skill level or preferred media, evolve their own unique internalization of a producer's mindset. The producer's mindset is nothing less than a paradigmatic wellspring that guides one's inception of attitudes and perceptions of the world around them. Simply stated, how do you perceive the world around you, and how do you want to express your perspective through your art? Although I might be preaching to the choir here, even so, we all benefit from a refresher course every so often.

#Trending

The National Association of Music Merchants (NAMM) releases a global retail sales report every year. Its 2011 report includes 10-year sales trends for a wide variety of musical instruments and recording products. The "fretted products" market, which includes guitars, basses, ukuleles, amps, strings, and other related accessories, was down more than 6%. The "recording and computer music" market, which includes digital multi-track and handheld recorders, sound cards and related hardware, audio software, and other related products, was up more than 108%. (Pro audio and DJ equipment are each their own category.) Total retail sales of fretted products is still more than double that of recording and computer music products, but the trend is pretty clear.

Prior to the big electronica wave of the mid to late 1990s that kicked off a huge boom in aspiring DJs, way more kids wanted to shred like Eddie Van Halen or mimic the alternative stylings of Kurt Cobain than make music on their home computer. Even though guitars still sell like crazy, the significant rise in computer-centric music production over the last decade suggests that the preferences of teens and young adults is changing. This point is supported by Guitar Center's recent reorganization of products in some of their stores. Now, upon entering the store, you immediately notice the prominent placement of computer music and production products, having been promoted from downstairs or in back to where guitars once took center stage.

Like a Flock of Birds

As discussed throughout this book, chaos is a fundamental feature of our universe. Our increasingly complex civilization's proliferation of networks and feedback loops, and subsequent accelerated rate of change, is escalating the role of chaos in our daily lives. This dynamic is exemplified by the dual explosion of social media in tandem with hyper-connectivity via mobile devices. Humans have always been embedded in a variety of networks, but the immediacy of communication and exchange of information characteristic of our era is geometrically unprecedented. Atemporal, non-local, and near instant cybernetic social interaction is part of our new normal, and is intensifying the prevalence of self-organizing social patterns. Sometimes these patterns reveal themselves as contrived fun activities, such as a flash mob, though most chaos-driven self-organized movements of any group are more organic in origin.

Once a sufficient number of individuals (parts) connect to one of these ephemeral social networks (a whole), the emergent patterns often resemble those of a giant flock of birds. Bird flocking behavior is a quintessential chaos theory example of self-organization in nature. Large flocks in particular are truly an amazing thing of beauty. (Do a Web search for "flock of birds video," watch a few of them, and then do an image search for "strange attractor.") In most flocks, there is no leader guiding the group's behavior; instead, each bird reacts to the movements of its direct neighbors. Order literally emerges out of chaos based on just a few simple rules. Our new communication technologies enable immediate flocking behavior, locally and globally. This new cultural emergence is powerful, and is a positive and/or negative influence depending on the context. Most sociological interactions are unconscious but producers need to be conscious of the ways that group think–flocking behavior influences their career and creative decisions. Use these insights to the benefit of yourself and your community. When it comes to career-related creative decisions, unlike birds in a flock, we can go our own way anytime we choose.

Trends, Innovation, and Individuation

If something is "trending," it must be important, right? Trends in music are nothing new, nor are bandwagons to jump on, and there is no indication things will be different anytime soon. Some styles are historically known for trendiness much more than others. Specifically, in the case of electronic dance music and other club-oriented genres, an emphasis on continuous novelty paired with an intense trend-following disposition is largely functional. A near pathological predilection for a constant flow of novelty and innovation actually makes a lot of sense given the desire of producers and DJs to feed their crowd's insatiable appetite for new dance-floor adventures and mind-blowing experiences. With the fairly recent full-on mainstreaming of electronic music in the U.S., particularly EDM, trend-following has gone off the rails. This trend of increased attention to what is trending can exist only because of the new normal of hyper-connectivity.

There are now waves of new, young aspiring music producers (mostly self-producing) who have grown up with the Internet. This generation is coming of age in an era when Kurt Cobain and Eddie Van Halen are their parents' music, and Jimi Hendrix and The Beatles are ancient history. It is not a coincidence that EDM's mainstreaming in the U.S. has occurred in tandem with the nascent dominance of the digital and information revolutions. So, it is no surprise that the first generation to grow up surrounded by all of this technology is also the first to find itself having to wake up to the formative influence of the technology, and therefore, the implications at the onset of a career. These dynamics effect all of us, but watching them emerge as an adult is a whole different story than it is for the generation forming their identities in the midst of it all.

Autonomy Continuum

As you may recall from Chapter 4, "Master Your Craft," a holon is a whole/part that simultaneously displays degrees of dependency and autonomy, which vary according to the given context. Everyone works within a cultural context, and everyone has influences, as discussed in the "Influences and Originality" section in Chapter 7, "Creative Process." Whether the intended audience is niche or as mainstream as possible, all good producers put their unique stamp on their productions. When producing other artists, this stamp should be appropriate to the project, so that it may be integral to the final aesthetic or might even be almost invisible. When self-producing, even if you choose to work within the very narrow parameters of a given subgenre, there is no valid excuse for omitting your musical and sonic perspective.

Could you be satisfied acting just like any other bird in the beautifully chaotic, self-organizing metaphorical flock of the music culture world? If so, then why do you want to be a producer? Countless amazingly talented, successful, and creative people are very happy as supporting artists, artisans, and/or technicians, and are also often influential and able to express themselves through their craft. So, too, were many producers at the onset of their career, before they were a producer. Moreover, many producers comfortably assume the role of supporting artist if a given project offers sufficient incentives, whether creative, personal, financial, for simple enjoyment, or otherwise. When making the conscious decision to be a part of something bigger than one's self, the tradeoff is giving up some degree of autonomy. Simultaneously, we can also make decisions that increase our autonomy in other endeavors, perhaps by focusing our attention on a single element of a project or on another project altogether.

The Challenge

The challenge is to figure out how to find success financially (at least enough to make a comfortable living) and also creatively (that is, to produce something that truly expresses who you are). There is no reason not to try to have it all; indeed, you *should* try to have it all. Take this opportunity to figure out not only what you want to do, but why you want to do it. If you are really cut out to produce mainstream music with widespread commercial appeal—if that is who you are—then go for it. If you are meant to push the envelope and break new ground possibly at the expense of more widespread acclaim—if that is who you are—then go for it. It doesn't matter that most of us are somewhere in the middle of those two extremes. Regardless, don't sell yourself short and settle for a career guided by "#trending."

Music Business and Personal Finances

There was so much to talk about in this book that we didn't get into business or finances at all. I did not avoid these topics because they lack importance. Indeed, I highly recommend that you take the time to learn about publishing, copyright, licensing, and royalty collection. Start with the free information found at Christopher Knab's website, www.musicbizacademy.com, or the sites of the music royalty collection agencies: Harry Fox Agency (harryfox.com), BMI.com, SESAC.com, ASCAP.com, and/or SOCAN.ca. If you prefer books, also check out the latest editions of *This Business of Music* by M. William Krasilovsky, et al., and/or *All You Need to Know About the Music Business* by Donald S. Passman. If you prefer multimedia, a three-part series by music professor Dr. Paul Bissell is streamable at askvideo.com and macprovideo.com. Because laws change and contracts are not intuitive, obvious, or easy to understand, knowing a trustworthy entertainment lawyer is highly desirable.

As an independent professional, it is also strongly recommended that you develop basic small business and personal finance skills. Start with free information as is found at sites like www.freelancetaxation.com, or perhaps shell out a few bucks for Martha Retallick's e-book, *Finance for Freelancers*. Working with a good accountant is never a bad idea; just make sure he or she understands creative freelance professions if for no other reason than to make sure you learn how to best maximize your tax write-offs. If you don't know where to find such an accountant, or lawyer, ask for a referral from a friend, peer, or your local musician's union.

There Is Always More

There is something about an intense fascination with sound, acoustics, psychoacoustics, music, music production, electronic music, digital technology, and music culture that is conducive to big thoughts and deep insights about people, culture, and the universe in general. This sentiment might be your cup of tea, but some of you just want to make music and are not so concerned with the big picture. That's totally fine; everyone is different. That said, much of this terrain is unavoidable for anyone who dedicates himself or herself to the career and lifestyle that is the topic of this book. Irrespective of where you are on the spectrum of interest in such matters, inevitably and often, each of us, in our own way, must figure out where to draw the line that demarks borders of relevancy.

A Promethean Network: Augusta Ada Byron, Countess of Lovelace (1815–1852), is widely considered to have authored the first algorithms for a computer (1843), and is therefore considered to be the first computer programmer. Ada wrote her historic algorithms for Charles Babbage's (1791–1871) proposed general purpose mechanical computer, the Analytical Engine. (If realized it would have been the first Turing-complete computer.) These algorithms were for calculating Bernoulli numbers, named after Jacob Bernoulli (1654–1705), one of many famous brilliant mathematicians from that Swiss family. Ada was the only legitimate child of English poet Lord Byron (1788–1824) and his wife, Anne Isabella Byron (who worked with Babbage). While in Switzerland, Lord Byron befriended fellow English poet Percy Bysshe Shelley (1792–1822) and Mary Wollstonecraft Godwin (1797–1851), his future wife. Later, on a group vacation to Geneva with the Byrons, Mary Shelley had a waking dream, which was her first conception of the Frankenstein story. The full title of her famous book is *Frankenstein; or, The Modern Prometheus* (1818). She drew inspiration for the subtitle from Immanuel Kant's (1724–1804) reference to Benjamin Franklin (1706–1790) as "the Prometheus of modern times" because of his experiments with electricity. Edison Studios produced the very first film adaption of *Frankenstein* (1910). Thomas Edison (1847–1931) didn't just invent motion pictures, but also commercial transmission of direct current (DC), the light bulb, and the phonograph. As discussed in Chapter 1, "Musica Universalis," Karlheinz Stockhausen (1928–2007) was not only one of the very first electronic musicians, he was arguably the first person to create a purely electronic composition. His music was literally produced by electricity. At the onset of his career, Stockhausen's mentor was author Herman Hesse (1877–1962), husband to Maria Bernoulli (1868–1963), a direct descendent of Jacob Bernoulli's brother.

Speaking from experience; the more you know, the more you realize you don't know. There is always another detail, another technique, another approach, another perspective, another combination, another context, another connection in another node of another system. Opening up to the implications of complexity, chaos, and holonic contextualism is usually mentally stimulating, often exciting, occasionally intoxicating, and at least at first, always disorienting. Regression or retreat as an attempt to regain stability is rarely successful in the long run. You simply have to make it through the jungle to find the open field on the other side. Some of us prefer to hang out for as long as possible and might get lost in the chaos, while others make a beeline for the nearest exit. (For discussion on getting lost in "holonic space," refer to the "Holons" section in Appendix B, "Integral Theory Primer"). Often emerging from experience in these terrains is a sense of humility that is not at odds with confidence, accomplishment, wisdom, knowledge, nor skill. On the contrary, humility is a natural extension of wisdom, which develops over time with the confidence, knowledge, and skill garnered through accomplishment.

As discussed in the previous sidebar, Ada Byron is widely considered to be the first computer programmer, and is held in the highest regard among very smart people. As quoted in Harry Henderson's 1995 book, *Modern Mathematicians (Global Profiles)*, Ada confessed the following:

> *I never am really satisfied that I understand anything; because, understand it well as I may, my comprehension can only be an infinitesimal fraction of all I want to understand about the many connections and relations which occur to me, how the matter in question was first thought of or arrived at, etc., etc.*

Confidence and humility are not the only seemingly contradictory or paradoxical pairings central to this book's themes. There are many others, such as patience and persistence, analysis and intuition, technical and creative, plans and instincts, logical and irrational, conscious and unconscious, order and chaos, complexity and simplicity, and parts and wholes. Hidden behind the obvious emphasis of a book focused on each individual's career and skills is another faux-contradiction, closely related to "parts and wholes"—that of attention to one's own individual improvement, advancement, and development as "selfish," and therefore at odds with that of the greater good. Marie Curie (1867–1934) is one of the most universally respected and inspirational scientists. She was not only the very first female Nobel laureate, but also the first and only person awarded the Nobel prize in multiple sciences (physics and chemistry). Curie once said:

> *You cannot hope to build a better world without improving the individuals. To that end, each of us must work for our own improvement and, at the same time, share a general responsibility for all humanity, our particular duty being to aid those to whom we think can be most useful.*

Finale

Everyone's life is an exciting journey. Some paths offer greater potential for excitement than others, and pursuing a career in any creative field is one of those paths. This factor is amplified when the career includes an immersive lifestyle, such as found in the worlds of DIY, independent, and electronic music, production, and culture. We don't know what unexpected opportunity is just around the corner or where we will end up. Further adding to the excitement, we have no idea what it is going to be like in a few decades—though most of the fundamentals should be relevant into the foreseeable future. But let us never forget the first rule of futurology: Predictions about technological advances and their impact tend to significantly overestimate the short term and even more so underestimate the long term, commonly in epic fashion. As Nobel laureate physicist Niels Bohr once put it, "Prediction is very difficult, especially if it's about the future." At least there is one thing we can all be sure about: that we can expect the unexpected.

Keep the Conversation Going: Make sure to check out this book's companion website, www.iempsg.com. In addition to supplemental resources, errata, and updates, it also includes a forum. The forum is designed for social networking and further discussion on the book's core topics.

Chaos Theory and Complexity Studies Primer

T HROUGHOUT THIS BOOK, I have referred to a number of ideas and concepts from chaos theory and complexity studies. Over the last 30 years, these ideas have found their way into a growing number of fields outside of mathematics and the hard sciences from which they originally emerged. Psychology, education, and visual art are just a few of the fields to benefit from these insights, so it seemed to me that their application to music production, and to being a music producer, is overdue.

Complexity Studies

Complexity studies is the broadest intellectual umbrella for the various fields of inquiry related to chaos and complexity, although systems theory is the official branch of science connecting them. Taken as a whole, these theories represent a paradigm shift. I am using Thomas Kuhn's original meaning of the word paradigm, described in his 1962 classic *The Structure of Scientific Revolutions*, as a change in science's basic assumptions. A paradigm of complexity avoids reductionist, atomistic, simplifying thinking and science. Early on, it laid the foundation for numerous holistic movements that emerged in the mid 20th century, then evolved beyond the subtle reductionism of holism, and to this day continues to revolutionize our understanding of our universe. Needless to say, one could spend a lifetime exploring the world of complexity, so here I present merely brief definitions of these overlapping fields as background on my thinking throughout this book.

Systems Theory

Systems theory is the formal branch of science that might be thought of as the parent of chaos theory and complexity studies. It is the transdisciplinary study of any self-regulating system—for example as found in the fields of thermodynamics, electronics, computing, biology, psychology, ecology, sociology, and even history. Systems theory can be thought of as the first "holistic" modern field of science. Ludwig von Bertalanffy is the founder of general systems theory (1930s) and is the most prominent pioneer of the field.

Cybernetics

Cybernetics is the transdisciplinary study of feedback loops in self-regulating systems (1960s). Norbert Wiener derived the term from the ancient Greek words for "helmsman" or "steersman," in reference to the feedback loop of captain > wheel > boat > current > boat > wheel > captain. Cyber also shares etymology with *kyma*, meaning wave, or wave-like. Feedback loops are commonly discussed with the terms *recursive, iteration,* and *iterative.*

> **NOTE:** Tangent of interest: Also derived from *kyma, cymatics* is a term coined by Hans Jenny in the 1960s to describe his study of wave phenomena, especially emergent patterns created in a variety of particulate matter with sound vibrations. Notable influence on 20th century music includes works by Alvin Lucier, who is known for integrating not only acoustic and psychoacoustic phenomena in his pieces, but also EEG measured brainwaves (as discussed briefly in Chapter 9, "Lifestyle Tips").

Emergence

Emergence refers to the common phenomenon of complex patterns or behaviors emerging from interaction between simpler parts. Very complex outcomes are often created by nothing more than feedback and iteration of very simple rules. An emergent property or behavior is commonly described with the idiom "the whole is more than the sum of its parts." Your personality is not just all of your brain cells, it is something more than just the parts. In Chapter 7, "Creative Process," you will find these ideas illustrated in a few sidebars: "The Creative Power of Chaos, from Simplicity to Everything" and "Third Mind, Post-Dada/Surrealism for the Multimedia Age."

Bifurcation Theory

Bifurcation theory is a historical precursor to chaos theory and fractal geometry. Henri Poincaré is widely considered the godfather of chaos theory. In the 1880s, he coined the term bifurcation (Figure A.1). Catastrophe theory is a subset of bifurcation theory, and is the mathematical study of sudden or unpredictable qualitative changes in the topological structure of a dynamical system (1960s).

Figure A.1 This image shows a bifurcation diagram (top) and the fractal Mandelbrot set (bottom).
Source: Georg-Johann Lay, public domain.

Set Theory

Classical set theory (1870s) is not complex at all, and is the only item in this appendix not directly related to systems theory. A set defines basic, clear, logical, binary relationships between categories, as can be illustrated in Venn diagrams (see Figure 4.1 in Chapter 4, "Master Your Craft"). Here's an example: All A are B, and some B are C, but A cannot be both a member of B and not a member of B. *Fuzzy sets* (1960s) are sets with members that have degrees of membership. They are relevant when dealing with incomplete information or uncertainty, and when making predictions about certain chaotic systems (such as the weather). Georg Cantor invented set theory, and as Poincaré is to chaos theory, Cantor is to fractal geometry. Cantor is also famous for a mathematical proof showing there are infinite infinities, and coined the term *transfinite* to refer to numbers that are bigger than all finite numbers but are not the ultimate infinite (which to him could only be God).

L-systems

L-systems, which get their name from Aristid Lindenmayer (1968), can be considered as a very close cousin of fractal geometry. They are used to generate self-similar branching patterns, as seen in biological systems. Computer modeling of realistic-looking plants and trees relies on the iterative math of L-systems' algorithms. Unlike the infinitely complex Mandelbrot sets, which require computers for visualization, we can manually draw L-systems, making them easier to grasp as visual metaphor. (See Figure 1.4 and Figure A.2.)

Figure A.2 A bush/tree generated with an L-system algorithm.

Chaos Theory

In episode 3 of the science mini-series *The Code*, "Prediction," produced by BBC Two, host and math professor Marcus du Sautoy offers a nice definition of chaos as "the behavior of a system which is governed by cause and effect but is so unpredictable as to appear random."

Chaos theory is the mathematical study of non-linear, unpredictable behavior of complex deterministic systems (1960s). *Deterministic* means that even though results are not predictable, they are not random, and when plotted in phase space (an X,Y plot of all possible positions) can reveal shapes known as strange attractors. The Lorentz attractor, discussed in Chapter 3, "What Is Your Plan?," is the best-known one because it was named by meteorologist Edward Lorentz, arguably the most prominent chaos theory pioneer (see Figure A.3). Among other contributions to the field, his application of computing to Poincaré's work on "sensitive dependence on initial conditions" resulted in what is commonly known as the "butterfly effect."

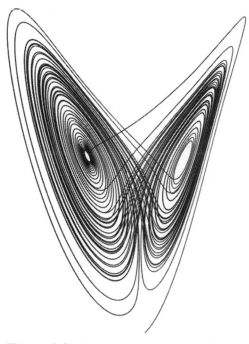

Figure A.3 The Lorentz attractor, the most famous "strange attractor," is closely associated with the butterfly effect. (Image modified by author.)

Order Out of Chaos

Ilya Prigogine was awarded the Nobel Prize in Chemistry in 1977 for showing how disorder can lead to order, and in 1982 published a book entitled *Order Out of Chaos*. Central to his discoveries are what he calls *dissipative structures*. If you've ever witnessed a tornado, seen a hurricane, or watched a whirlpool in an emptying bathtub, you've seen one. Basically, any system that continually moves energy through it but maintains a stable shape is a dissipative structure. The human body is one, too. We are continually renewing the cells in our bodies, yet we maintain the same structure. Our biology is full of self-organizing systems at the edge of chaos. If we get sick, our immune system either fails and we die or it fights off the invaders and we become immune to that strain of infection. Health is a balance of chaos and order. The opposite of chaos is a steady state, which is not healthy, because in biology it means death. (See biologist Brian Goodwin's *How the Leopard Changed Its Spots: The Evolution of Complexity*.)

Prigogine discovered that if a dissipative structure is perturbed, it will either break down or restructure at a higher level of organization. We can apply this knowledge to many aspects of our personal, professional, and creative lives. Understanding that order emerges from chaos, and that it is governed by cause and effect (even if not predictable), can help to cultivate instincts for making good decisions and coping with life's rough patches. Embracing the chaos in our social and cultural ecosystems can even enable us to position ourselves to best take advantage of unexpected opportunities and emerging trends.

Fractal Geometry

A subset of chaos theory (and set theory), fractal geometry explores mathematical sets with fractional (non-integer) dimensions, which display self-similarity at multiple scales. The term *fractal* was coined by mathematician Benoît Mandelbrot (1970s), and the most common images of computer-generated fractals are derived from what is known as the Mandelbrot set, which is a graphical plotting of results from recursive iterations of $z = z^2 + c$ (refer to Figure A.1). Fractal self-similarity has even been found in the works of painter Jackson Pollack. Many of the images in this book show fractal patterns, such as every image in the preface, Figure 4.3, and Figure 9.6.

Please set aside any hippie/new age associations or preconceptions you may have about fractals. Most people know of fractals as visually stunning psychedelic computer-generated images or animations, possibly through Scott Drave's *Electric Sheep* (a distributed computing freeware screensaver). *Fractal* means having fractional dimensionality and describes the roughness around the edges of the natural world. This math shows how nature repetitively uses just a few shapes in an iterative process to create an infinite variety of forms. The key characteristic of fractals is *self-similarity* (see the next section). In other words, similar patterns commonly appear at vastly different sizes and scales. Zoom in, zoom out—we find similar patterns in trees, broccoli, lungs, river systems, nervous systems, cardiovascular systems, coastlines, and even galactic superclusters. Ideas from fractal geometry are employed at numerous points in this book, so it is important to realize that the concept of fractional dimensionality is not an abstraction.

If you ignore all those tiny extra dimensions in string theory and just consider the world as you see it, there are three spatial dimensions. A rectangular room is measured as L(ft) × W(ft) × H(ft), and the volume is expressed as something like 1,500 ft^3. One side of a normal sheet of 8.5 × 11-inch paper has a surface area of 93.5 in^2. Whether cubed (^{3}) or squared (^{2}), we are dealing with integers, or whole numbers.

Yet, a piece of paper is not really just the two dimensions of width and length, as it is also about .004 inches thick (height), so you might say it is somewhere between two and three dimensions. To help make sense of this, crumble the paper up into a ball. See all the texture and the craggy channels? It is still not quite three dimensions; it is 2.x dimensions. If you know the mass of the sheet of paper, you can actually do some math to get an exact value. A crumpled-up ball of paper is a simple example of the fractional dimensionality all around you.

> **NOTE:** Do not confuse the three-dimensional space surrounding an object with its dimensionality, especially when considering measurements of outlines or borders. If you are having a hard time understanding how crumpled paper that exists in three-dimensional space is itself less than three dimensions, perhaps the following example will help.

What about a less simple example? Here's one: How long is the coast of Britain? As discussed in Chapter 1, "Musica Universalis," the answer is that it depends on the size of the smallest increment used for measurement. Weird, right? Mathematician Benoît Mandelbrot coined the term *fractal* to describe what was previously known as "the coastline paradox." If you try to measure the coast of England, you get hugely divergent answers depending on how you measure it. Imagine you have an impossibly resizable ruler. Set it to 1-kilometer increments, then change it to 100-meter increments, then to 1-meter, then to 100-centimeter, then to 1-centimeter. The 1 km measurement is considerably shorter than the 1 cm measurement! With the larger size, you miss small bays, harbors, and inlets. But as you get smaller and smaller, you have to follow all the waterways and their branching rivers, streams, tributaries, canals, etc. Get the point? A one-dimensional, integer measurement (that is, length) is a human construct and simply not up to the task for measuring nature, which is fractal.

Fractals are most obvious in the natural world when there is something right in front of your eyes. The same geometric relationships also exist in more abstract ways, and data visualization helps us to notice such patterns. Whether looking at statistical sociological data or considering the evolution of music genres and the seemingly endless branchings of subgenres and micro-genres in electronic music, or the potentially endless options in creative decision-making, there is a lot there to help us understand the dynamics of being a music producer. Anytime we round off, offer a precise definition, or simplify, we do so for convenience and should keep our minds open to the additional dimensionality in most everything we do.

Self-Similarity

Self-similarity is a term to describe a specific type of relationship between a whole and its parts. If something is self-similar, it means that its parts are of a similar shape or pattern as that of the whole. As seen in Figures A.1 and A.2, L-systems, bifurcation diagrams, and the Mandelbrot set are great examples of self-similar shapes. Additionally, because all fractals are self-similar, every image in the preface, Figure 4.3, and Figure 9.6 are also good examples. Another great example of self-similarity is the Internet. Ruslan Enikeev, creator of internet-map.net, was kind enough to grant me permission to use the following images. If you go to internet-map.net and click the About link, the first paragraph states the following:

> Like any other map, The Internet map is a scheme displaying objects' relative position; but unlike real maps (e.g. the map of the Earth) or virtual maps (e.g. the map of Mordor), the objects shown on it are not aligned on a surface. Mathematically speaking, The Internet map is a bi-dimensional presentation of links between websites on the Internet. Every site is a circle on the map, and its size is determined by website traffic, the larger the amount of traffic, the bigger the circle. Users' switching between websites forms links, and the stronger the link, the closer the websites tend to arrange themselves to each other.

As you consider the images in Figure A.4, Figure A.5, and Figure A.6, notice that similar patterns appear at each zoom level. We are using wordpress.org and google.com as our navigational references. As we zoom out and the text that indicates wordpress.org becomes too small to read, you can locate it by identifying the largest circle to the left of facebook.com and above google.com (at about 1 o'clock). Keep in mind that you can go to internet-map.net and explore for yourself, since it is searchable and interactive.

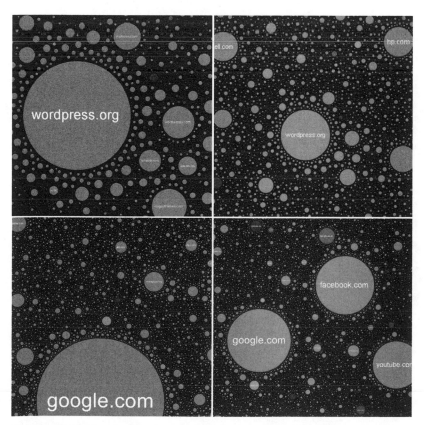

Figure A.4 Starting in the upper left, move clockwise to zoom out of the Internet Map.

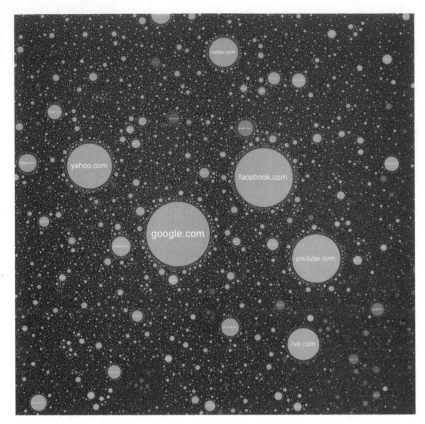

Figure A.5 Zooming out a bit further, wordpress.org almost disappears in the distance as only the most popular sites' text is readable.

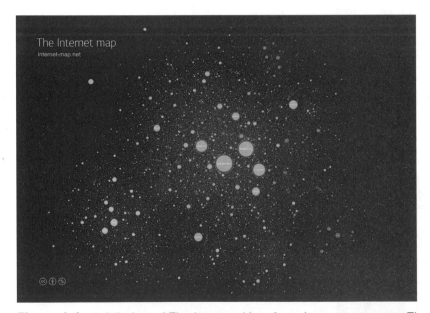

Figure A.6 A full view of The Internet Map, from internet-map.net. The first level of zoom shows text in a few of the circles, the most popular sites.

If you would like to learn more about chaos theory and complexity studies, make sure to check out recommendations at www.iempsg.com.

Integral Theory Primer

I N THE PREFACE, I briefly introduced Integral theory, and mentioned that is a major influence on my thinking. I also explained that Integral theory is mostly supporting architecture, so explicit discussion is largely absent from the chapters that it informs. I did bring it up in a few key places, so this appendix is for those of you that are interested in knowing a bit more. What follows is a brief overview of Ken Wilber's Integral map. As Integral philosophy's premier theorist, Ken is also keen to remind us that "the map is not the territory."

Part of Ken Wilber's work focuses on his AQAL model (pronounced *ahkwool* and an abbreviation for "all quadrants, all levels, all lines, all states, all types"). This model has five fundamental aspects:

▷ Quadrants of knowing and being
▷ Levels of development
▷ Lines of development
▷ States of consciousness
▷ Personality types

These five elements generate and support a universe that is composed of holons, or whole-parts. *Holon* is Arthur Koestler's term for capturing the fact that everything we see (and all that we are) is composed of wholes that are themselves parts of larger wholes. (Consider your organs, which are wholes that are also a part of your body.) I explain this in a moment. For now, to assist in keeping a potentially long explanation rather short, Figure B.1 artfully shows these five elements, courtesy of Steve Self of Formless Mountain Integral Atelier. As you read through the sections, refer back to this image as needed.

Holons

This element of Integral theory should sound familiar to you, since it is the one most explicitly employed in the previous chapters, especially Chapter 4, "Master Your Craft." In his 1967 book, *The Ghost in the Machine*, Arthur Koestler coined the terms *holon* and *holarchy*. Although there is such a thing as a hierarchy of power or control, what most people think of as a structural hierarchy is better considered as a holarchy, a nested system of holons. In his 1978 book, *Janus: A Summing Up*, Koestler tells us that each member in a holarchy "is a sub-whole or 'holon' in its own right—a stable, integrated structure, equipped with self-regulatory devices and enjoying a considerable degree of autonomy or self-government…[holons] are Janus-faced. The face turned upward, toward the higher levels, is that of a dependent part; the face turned downward, toward its own constituents, is that of a whole of remarkable self sufficiency."

Consider the following example: Your brain is a stable, integrated structure dependent on your body, but self sufficient from each individual brain cell. When you move, your brain and all of its cells necessarily move with you. If one single brain cell dies, your brain function is not altered and the rest of your body is completely unaffected. But if enough brain cells are damaged, they cause a loss of functionality that cascades through the holarchy (from the fundamental to the significant).

Ken Wilber first presented the AQAL model in his 800+ page, 1995 magnum opus *Sex, Ecology, Spirituality: The Spirit of Evolution*, or *SES* for short. AQAL represented a major evolution from his previous models, in large part because of this emphasis on holons and quadrants. Toward the beginning of *SES*, Wilber tells us that the book is about holons and then goes on to explain the laws of holon dynamics and interaction in 20 tenets. Fundamental to Wilber's 20 tenets is knowledge and insights garnered from systems theory, complexity studies, and even set theory (see Appendix A, "Chaos Theory and Complexity Studies Primer"). So, understanding complexity is essential for understanding holons is essential to understanding complexity…[insert feedback loop here].

During his exposition of tenet 1, Wilber shares a story:

> *"There is an old joke about a King who goes to a Wiseperson and asks how is it that the Earth doesn't fall down? The Wiseperson replies, 'The Earth is resting on a lion.' 'On what, then, is the lion resting?' 'The lion is resting on an elephant.' 'On what is the elephant resting?' 'The elephant is resting on a turtle.' 'On what is the…' 'You can stop right there, your Majesty. It's turtles all the way down.'*

> *"Holons all the way down."*

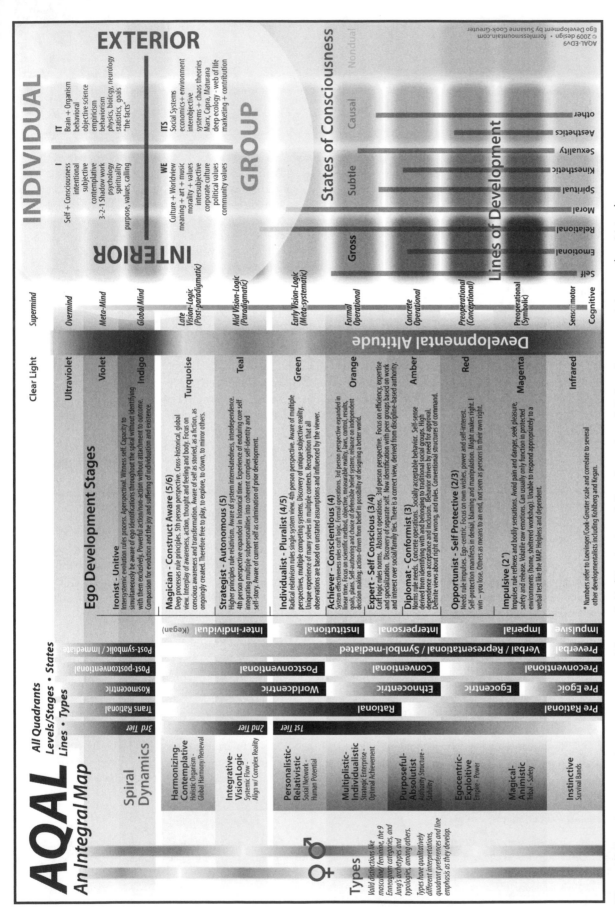

Figure B.1 AQAL Integral map, courtesy of Steve Self. (To obtain a full-color print, visit formlessmountain.com/aqal.htm.)

This book, too, is about holons. So what *is* a holon? If you can give something a name, it is a holon. Although holons are whole/parts, in any given context we can choose to define something as the whole or a part. If the context changes, wholes become parts or parts become wholes. In the relativism common to postmodern thought, this "sliding" of contexts can lead to murky confusion and an inability to make value judgments. Integral consciousness builds on the important contributions of postmodern relativism, but transcends its deficient modes. Have you ever wondered what comes after postmodernism—*post*-postmodernism? Cultures and civilizations essentially are dissipative structures, so if postmodernism deconstructed (perturbed) the system, integralism restructures it at a higher level of organization.

I realize there is a high likelihood that some of you may feel intellectually ungrounded by some of the ideas presented herein. Opening up to the implications of chaos and holonic contextualism is always disorienting at first. But there is no point getting lost in what Wilber calls "holonic space." There is a perspective that can encompass uncertainty, infinite relativity, and the "sliding" contexts characteristic of post-modern thought. In Chapter 5 of SES, Wilber points out: "That all perspectives interrelate, or that no perpsective is final (aperspectivism), does not mean that there are no relative merits among them." Later, in Chapter 14 of SES, in one of the many lengthy footnotes, he further tells us that:

> *Contexts slide, but they often slide in relatively stable ways; meaning is context-bound, but many contexts are common or shared (and can be so disclosed in mutual understanding); contexts are boundless, but that doesn't prevent them from being fixed in relative but stable ways; that sociocultural reality is largely constructed does not mean it is constructed arbitrarily, for linguistic meaning is itself exposed to extralinguistic restraints (in both I, we, and it domains), and that allows meaning to be tied to validity claims that can be redeemed in the intersubjective circle, validity claims of truth, truthfulness, cultural justness, and functional fit.*

Quadrants

The quadrants in AQAL Integral theory represent four basic dimensions of each holon, distilled to I, We, It, and Its. To help you grasp this, consider what each of the following lists have in common:

▷ Sensations, emotions, thoughts…
▷ Traditionalism, modernism, post-modernism…
▷ Cells, organs, organisms…
▷ Villages, empires, nations…

You could say that each list represents a hierarchy, or better yet, a holarchy of I, We, It, and Its, respectively. These can be presented in quadrant form:

▷ **Upper left (I):** Intentional (subjective)
▷ **Lower left (We):** Cultural (subjective systems)
▷ **Upper right (It):** Behavioral (objective)
▷ **Lower right (Its):** Social (objective systems)

To be clear, each quadrant represents what each holon "looks like" from that perspective. Holons are not "in" quadrants; each holon minimally includes these four quadrants. Refer to Figure B.1 so you can see the quadrants with common examples.

▷ **Left:** Interior
▷ **Right:** Exterior
▷ **Top:** Individual
▷ **Bottom:** Group

The quadrant aspect of Integral theory inspires much of this book's underlying structure. Given the holon of "you as music producer," each quadrant is expressed in various chapters or sections of chapters. Here is a non-hierarchical list for each quadrant:

▷ **Upper left (I):** Creativity, learning, motivations, aspirations
▷ **Lower left (We):** Culture, music/art meaning, shared values, context
▷ **Upper right (It):** Tools, data, technology, who/what/when/where
▷ **Lower right (Its):** Objective social ecologies, music/art products, systems and chaos theories, economics and law

If the second and fourth bullets seem like they are the same, just keep in mind that the We perspective is subjective (interior), while the Its perspective is objective (external).

Levels (Stages) of Development

This facet of Integral theory is a distillation of the most researched and accepted knowledge from a number of fields, although primarily Western psychology (developmental, cognitive, humanistic, transpersonal), sociology, anthropology, and Asian wisdom traditions. Essentially, we are talking about the evolution of consciousness, which applies to individuals and groups. I am going to attempt a single-sentence definition of such developmental models. If it seems like gibberish to you, just pretend you are watching that scene in *The Matrix: Reloaded* when Neo meets The Architect. (YouTube it if you need a refresher…ergo, concurrently, assiduously, inevitably, integral anomaly….)

> *Developmental model of consciousness: A model of psychological growth based on empirically measurable and qualitative differences in one's capacity to simultaneously hold perspectives. The data from these empirical studies corresponds to the progression of a demonstrably discrete sequence of developmental levels, stages, and/or structures of consciousness, whether individual or collective.*

If nothing else, consider these crucial points:

▷ Stages cannot be skipped.
▷ Stages are not about motivations, styles, or types.
▷ Most importantly, although higher stages are desirable and tend to correlate with what most cultures consider being a good person, there are also pathologies that correspond to each level.

Thus, here we are concerned with form, not content—how information is organized, not the information.

Throughout the book, I presented stages of various processes, but I did not explicitly address this part of Integral theory because its influence and implications saturate the world of the 21st century music producer, individually and culturally. When referring to Figure B.1, keep in mind that *stages* and *levels* are often used interchangeably, even though they are not exactly synonymous terms.

Example 1: Stages of Cognitive Development

A true pioneer of developmental psychology, Jean Piaget (1896–1980) conducted research that revealed four basic stages of childhood development, to adulthood:

▷ Sensorimotor (to age 2)
▷ Preoperational (ages 2–7)
▷ Concrete operational (ages 7–11)
▷ Formal operational (ages 11–16 and beyond)

As an infant, we are only aware of basic sensations. Soon we become aware of our body. Then we become aware that there are others around us, even if they only exist when we see them. We come to understand that others have emotions too. Eventually, we can deal with objects such as numbers and letters, then definitions, then concepts. Finally, if all goes well, we develop the capacity for abstract thinking.

Example 2: Structures of Consciousness

Not only do individuals evolve through stages over the course of a lifetime, but groups, cultures, and civilizations follow similar trajectories. When referring to a culture or subculture, the term "center of gravity" is used when approximating its stage. Sociologist Paul Ray utilized representative national surveys sponsored by the Fetzer Institute, The Institute of Noetic Sciences, the EPA, and the President's Council on Sustainable Development to gather evidence for co-existing cultural consciousnesses in the U.S. (1995, 1999). After presenting initial findings in various journal articles, in 2000 he published a book, *The Cultural Creatives: How 50 Million People Are Changing the World*. According to Ray's model in 2012, most Americans share values and preferences with one of four worldview populations:

▷ Traditionals
▷ Moderns
▷ Transitionals
▷ Cultural creatives, which include a small, but emerging Integral sub-culture (transmoderns)

According to data on his website, culturalcreatives.org, the percentage of U.S. adults who are cultural creatives grew from 23.6 percent in 1996 to 34.9 percent in 2008, with moderns at 39.7 percent, traditionals at 15.4 percent, and transitionals at 10.1 percent. Based on Ray's research, we could say that the "center of gravity" is late-stage modernism, or what Jean Gebser refers to as the mental structure of consciousness.

In his magnum opus *The Ever Present Origin* (1949/1953), Jean Gebser eruditely presents evidence that humanity has evolved through four structures of consciousness, with a fifth emerging:

▷ Archaic
▷ Magical
▷ Mythical
▷ Mental
▷ Integral

Let me illustrate with just one example: the increasing dimensionality of our relationship to time. The archaic structure is timeless. Magical consciousness perceives time as point-like, the primal now of nature. Mythical time is circular, based on the change of seasons and lunar orbits. Mental time is linear, mechanically measurable, going from the past to the present to the future. Integral time is atemporal—all of the above and relative, *vis à vis* Einstein's special theory of relativity.

What about our relation to space? Humans once believed that the sun ate the moon during an eclipse, and that angry sky gods caused drought and flood. We once knew that Earth was the center of the universe and that the sun, the moon, Mercury, Venus, Mars, Jupiter, and Saturn revolved around us. It was not even 100 years ago that we believed the universe was just the Milky Way galaxy, which was in a static steady state. In the early 1920s, Edwin Hubble discovered that the Milky Way was but one of countless galaxies, and moreover, that these galaxies are accelerating away from each other, revealing a vast, expanding universe. We now know that black holes are at the center of most every mature galaxy, and that the structure of the visible universe resembles a sponge. In mainstream science, there is mounting evidence that our universe is actually part of a multiverse, and that there might even be an infinite number of parallel universes.

Lines of Development

Your style of learning includes multiple overlapping lines of development. These represent different capacities and aptitudes that develop through stages in each of the quadrants. When you take a standardized test such as the SAT as part of a university application, you are scored on reading, writing, and arithmetic. You are scored on each section and given a total score. Think of this as a profile of sorts. Three different test takers can achieve the same total score but have drastically different scores in each area. Some people do very well in math but not so well in writing. Similarly, you may know someone with advanced cognitive abilities who is relatively immature morally or emotionally.

In Chapter 4, I discussed Howard Gardner's theory of multiple intelligences as it relates to different learning styles. For example, some people are naturally more visual, others more kinesthetic. AQAL Integral theory includes more than 12 developmental lines in three loosely defined categories: cognitive, self-related, and capacities-talents, as listed in Figure B.1. At times, I refer to lines of development when discussing the skills and knowledge of music-production holons—for example, music, sound design, audio engineering, etc. My usage of this terminology strays from the intended usage in AQAL theory because in reality, our capacity to develop skills is framed by our stages of development in various lines, such as cognitive, creative, and aesthetic.

States of Consciousness

I am assuming that you are awake right now, and later you will go to sleep and dream, and then fall into a deep dreamless sleep. Some states are spiritual and some are mundane. When a lot of people first look at a map of the levels of development, they mistakenly assign spiritual to the higher levels and think, "Hey, are you saying you have to be at a high stage to have a spiritual experience?!" The answer is, of course not. Whether you use the term spiritual, peak, religious, or otherwise, let's call them "extraordinary" for now. Based on thousands of years of meditative, contemplative, and psychological knowledge, there is more or less universal consensus that we all experience three basic states of consciousness: waking, dreaming, and deep dreamless sleep. In the Eastern traditions, these are commonly referred to as gross, subtle, and causal. With enough practice meditating, you can experience all of these while awake and aware. So, there are at least three different flavors of extraordinary experiences.

Looking at the AQAL map, you see nine developmental stages. An extraordinary experience can happen at any stage, and is interpreted according to the structure of that stage. That means there are at least 27 different kinds of extraordinary experiences (the Wilber-Combs matrix). Interestingly, there are numerous written accounts for nearly all of them. On a side note, in the early days of transpersonal psychology, there were two camps of researchers arguing with each other about all this. Those who gave primacy to states tended to utilize substances (psychonauts), and those who emphasized stages tended to be meditators. We now know they are both equally relevant.

Types

Types recognize that humans are very diverse, with different preferences for and experiences of reality. Types are discussed in terms of the four quadrants. For example, the upper left includes personality types, such as those specified by the Myer-Briggs Type Indicator (MBTI) assessment. The upper right addresses different body types, the lower left different cultural types, and the lower right different biomes (climate, ecosystems, etc.).

If you would like to learn more about Integral theory and Integral philosophy, make sure to check out recommendations at www.iempsg.com.

Interview with Hank Shocklee

T HE FACT THAT THIS INTERVIEW IS IN AN APPENDIX SHOULD NOT DIMINISH YOUR PERCEPTION OF ITS VALUE AND IMPORTANCE. The knowledge, wisdom, and experience shared here is solid gold. The selection of questions was carefully considered for this book's primary goal of helping you with your career.

> **NOTE:** This interview serves as a preview to this book's companion title, *The Music Producer's Survival Stories: Interviews with Veteran, Independent, and Electronic Music Professionals.* Each interview in that book covers a different perspective on this book's topics—for example, that of a DJ/promoter/musician, an electronic music producer turned mastering engineer, and an indie rock bass player turned electronic music producer.

Hank Shocklee is a legendary producer, DJ, composer, remixer, culture evolver, and self-described sonic architect. It is not uncommon to see the words "innovator" and "visionary" next to his name in books and press. Artistic and commercial success at the level of the groundbreaking Public Enemy records of the 1980s and 1990s, which he co-produced, would be a capstone of accomplishment for most producers. In 2004, *Rolling Stone* put Public Enemy at #44 in a list of the top 100 greatest artists of all time. In 2012, Public Enemy was inducted into the Rock and Roll Hall of Fame. Yet, Hank is about a lot more than just Public Enemy. Whether producing superstars like LL Cool J, Ice Cube, Mary J. Blige, Yoko Ono, or indie artists like Emika (Ninja Tune); composing for records and movies; or sharing his knowledge as a panelist at countless industry-related events, Hank is an optimistic force of nature. Shocklee.com, Shocklee Entertainment Universe • The Future Frequency, is the online hub for his music, culture, and media company, which is also a steady source of inspiring and well-curated news, tips, and multimedia.

Hank and I first met at the 2011 AES convention in NYC and shortly thereafter started collaborating as organizers of the NYC Ableton Advanced Users Meetup group. The following interview happened on April 11, 2013 via Skype, with Hank in Long Island, NY and me in Brooklyn, NY. In Part I, we discuss key aspects to the art, science, and philosophy of music production. In Part II, we talk about some of the major changes in music culture, the role of authenticity in modern music, and the importance of experimentation. Part III gets into the value of collaboration, the need for a renewed emphasis on musicality, dynamic performances, and a few final thoughts.

Part I

Brian: There is a lot online about your time with Public Enemy, The Bomb Squad, and Spectrum City, so tell us a bit about what you do now.

Hank: I consult, I manage, I executive produce, I produce music for film, for artists, for myself as well. I guess I'm still doing the same things, but I also do a lot of marketing and promotional stuff too. It's brought me full circle. I pretty much fill in all the areas where record companies and management companies really don't fill in for artists, and also do productions for projects that are new and up and coming.

Brian: One of the other things I noticed that is keeping you busy too is Shocklee Entertainment in general, but also your website shocklee.com, The Future Frequency. What's the idea behind it, with the terms frequency and spectrum? Is it a full-circle idea from where you started, but in a bigger way?

Hank: Exactly. It encompasses everything that I've been doing, and I think a website is something that you need to have today. I think that all producers, all artists have to have a means of broadcasting. You have to have some sort of presence, some sort of home base now. Before, there used to be an industry where people could get in contact with you, because it's a small-knit industry. Therefore, everybody knew the producers and knew how to get in touch with them directly, you know? Now, we're dealing with an international business, and we're also dealing with a business that's 24 hours a day, 7 days a week. You've got to have some sort of major online presence in order for people to know that this is where you are, this is your home, these are the kinds of things that you're into and this is what you're about, so that you can sensitize your fans and the people that want to do business with you. They know where you are and what you're doing, at any given moment.

Brian: How did you get into music production?

The Music Producer's Survival Guide

Hank: From a technical standpoint, what got me so into the music was always reading liner notes. The first thing I recognized was that there always seemed to be a pattern, and the pattern was developing from when you read that this record was produced by this guy, you sit there and go, "Okay, this record sounds like this other record," and then you realize, "Okay, those two records were produced by the same guy." For example, I love *The Psychedelic Shack* by The Temptations. I said, "Damn, this record is hot," but I also loved *Smiling Faces*, by Undisputed Truth. These two records were incredible, then I looked down and said, "Okay, who produced these records?" I realized they were both produced by Norman Whitfield. Now, when I look back and see that production credit, that, to me, is what spawned me into producing. It made me look at the producer as the guy that oversees the musical structure, or the content or the flow, or the color, or the flavor of this particular track.

Brian: Like the director and the cinematographer.

Hank: Exactly. He's the guy that's there to keep the music consistent, because the one thing that you noticed back in the day is that when groups used to self-produce themselves, you'd hear a noncontinuity. One record sounded one way, and you might like that sound, but you would never hear that sound again. You'd hear 10 other songs that sounded totally different, and all these 10 records don't sound like they should have been on the same record. They sound like they should have been on separate albums somewhere, or compilation records.

Brian: They were no more than a collection of songs.

Hank: Exactly. The producer is the guy, that entity, if you would, that oversaw the process and made sure that the record sounded cohesive, and then also made sure that that record hit a certain targeted demo. For example, if I wanted to reach Juan Atkins' electro crowd, so to speak, I couldn't make a record that had a breakbeat in it, that was 90 beats per minute. I had to go and make a record that pretty much had the same instruments, the same vibration that that record had, but in my way. Thus, the producer not only became the person that was responsible for the cohesiveness of the particular record, but also the direction of it, and where does it go? Where is it going to be played? For example, you would know, if I have a record that has a breakbeat on it and an MC, and then I also have that same record with more of a dance beat and a rapper on it, I'm going to take those records to two different places. I may take one to a New York City rooftop or the Latin Quarters, and the other one, I may take to the Warehouse in Chicago. You know those records are going to be played in different places. That created your fan base, or the kind of music you were going after and that, to me, is when music started becoming more artistic, because now, the producer is shaping the sound. It's not only shaping the sound, but it's also shaping the artist on top of it. How should this artist sound on this particular record? Should they sound sad? Should they sound powerful? Should they sound big? Should they sound small? Should the emotion be happy or angry? Now you're getting into the areas of artistic crafting, and that's the area that the producer is responsible for. A light bulb went off in me, because I'm not a guy that can be in front of the camera or in front of the microphone. I'm the guy that's behind it, you know? I've got to be backstage.

Brian: The architect.

Hank: Exactly. I think that you have to create an environment with your artists, in whatever project that you're trying to convey, and I think, in creating that environment, the more you create that environment, the more you pull people into your world. You do that through various means. Of course, we know that it's done through the beats, it's done through the rhymes or the singing, or whatever the case may be, but it's also done through the mood.

Brian: When you're working with an artist and you have an idea in mind, a lot of people, when they think of creative process, they think of specific steps. When you think of creative process, what are the first things that come to mind before even considering tools or technologies? You were starting to say it's something like a mood would be the first step.

Hank: To me, the first thing is finding out the strengths and limitations of your artists, because that's the area where I think a lot of people go wrong. As a producer, yeah, you have an idea of what you want to produce and how you think this thing should sound, but if you have an artist that can't deliver…You have to know what their limitations are. You're going to have to restructure your situation to be able to mask their weaknesses. Because a lot of times, with the artists, the whole idea for a producer is that they're like an editor. You're not supposed to hear or see the edit. It's supposed to be seamless and invisible. Therefore, the artist has to shine, and if the artist shines, then the producer has done their job, and that's the area that a lot of people that are producing today should understand. I hear a lot of producers forcing artists to do things that are out of their zone, so to speak. For example, let's say it's a singer. In their highest range, they can kick you a nice F. Now, if you decide that you want to push that, you can push that to the G. Well, if you push it to the G, what you're going to get is the artist's vocal starting to crack.

Brian: It's straining.

Hank: Yeah, at that level. I'll hear producers who would have a song already written in G, and will have an artist who's best note is in F, trying to sing the G. They maybe can hit it, but the problem is that now you have no headroom. You can't go up a notch from there. All you can do now is come back down. What I would do is I would sit there and say, "Okay, I know I've got this artist that can sing and give me a good F note. Why don't I start this artist out in the key of E?" Let them sing a song in E, because now the artist has room to go. Now I can create a change into the F, and now we're climbing, you know? I can even go to an F#.

Brian: But you can't start there?

Hank: No, because if you start there, you've got no headroom. A lot of times, it's all about knowing the strengths and limitations of your artists, and then understanding the character of the artist's vocals.

Brian: In any creative process, it's about understanding the parameters you're working with.

Hank: Yes.

Brian: And not trying to force things or make something happen because you have an idea in mind.

Hank: Exactly, no. And to me, you want to make sure that that artist always sounds at their best, and doesn't show their weaknesses, so to speak. When you have that artist singing in that G, you're already exposing weaknesses, meaning that the artist can't go up higher. Now, people listening are going to notice. They're going to say, "Oh, this artist can't go any higher than that." They're going to perceive that that artist really cannot sing, when that's not the case. This artist can sound amazing, you just need to bring that key down. You bring that key down, and then that artist will sound good. The other thing you have to also listen to is the character and tonality of the vocal. For example, you can't take Janet Jackson and have her singing a song about how she got dumped by her man, because that takes an artist to have power in their vocals, because they have to get across anger. They have to get across hurt. That emotion has to come out, and Janet has a light voice. She's not going to sound good singing words that are angry. You have to know that, well, you have to tailor the song around tonal aspects of your artist. If your artist has an airy vocal, then you have to create a song that's going to take her tonality and make it work for the song.

Brian: Yes, I think that's right. I think a lot of people now, they're so busy writing everything in the box, they have every sound possible, they forget that their singer needs room to sit in the mix, and to feel comfortable, and every singer's going to be different.

Hank: Yes, yes. Every singer is going to be different, and then the other aspect of it is, the artist also has a thing where you want to make sure that they sound comfortable, that they sound relaxed, that the song fits them and their tonal characteristics. Bell Biv DeVoe, for example. Here's guys who's normal speaking voices have a Bostonian accent. I don't know if you're familiar with that. Bostonian accents sound like the Kennedys.

Brian: Yes, I'm very familiar with it.

Hank: Therefore, what happens is this. You have to be careful of having a lot of A's.

Brian: So, they're going to go to the baah in a caah?

Hank: Yeah, in the caah. O's and A's, you've got to be careful. They can be in there, but they can't be long notes. They've got to be short notes. That's another characteristic that cats don't understand. For example, Whitney Houston, she was a long note singer, meaning that, if you gave her a song like "Somewhere Over the Rainbow," she'd destroy it, but if you gave her "Every Little Step I Take," she'd kill that song in a bad way, because she's great with vowels, big vowels, but ridiculous with short hard consonants. Beyoncé, for example, can sing short, staccato notes and make that sound amazing. You have to understand the writing of the artist, not just the tonal value, but also the rhythmic capacity of that artist. If you take Mary J. Blige and give her short little consonant sounds, she's not going to sound good. She has to have bigger vowels, longer notes.

Brian: I imagine there's similarities among all the different musicians, even if it's a drummer or bass player or DJ or someone who just does sequencing.

Hank: Exactly. For example, a rock drummer cannot do a soul ballad. It's like, dude, you've got to know that, coming into the game. If somebody just says, "Hey, I need a drummer," and then somebody will come up, "Hey, I'm a drummer. I can play." Well, what kind of a drummer are you? There's a difference. The same thing is if I'm doing a rock record. I don't want a jazz drummer. The power won't be there. You get a jazz guy that's not used to beating hard. That takes a lot more energy than to just play musically. A lot of jazz cats are really great with making the drum sets sound like percussion, as opposed to it sounding like a drum kit. That's the difference. The other difference is going to be in the area of the cymbals. The jazz guys are going to make the cymbals sound musical. That's not for rock. You don't want musical-sounding cymbals.

Part II

Brian: Music is not only a reflection of our culture, but it's also often ahead of people. What do you see, what we're doing now, that might be a preview of where the culture might catch up to in a little bit?

Hank: I think that the one thing that we have to realize today is that music has now become the universal language. What I mean by the universal language is that everybody gets the music, no matter where you're from today. It used to be, when we talked about it back in the day, music was regional and there was a big difference between a New York sound and a Detroit sound. Well, that's not the case anymore.

Brian: It finally has really become the universal language?

Hank: Exactly. For example, that latency isn't there anymore. What used to happen was, by the time a particular music got to South America, it was three, four, five years old. Now, that latency is a lot closer, because now people can vibe on that music instantaneously, you know? There used to be a thing where we used to go over to London and used to have to wait three months before the movie played out here and you were like, "Damn, that shit's late." Now, movies are released at the same time. We have this one-world culture happening, you know? The beautiful thing about what's happening with music now is that music is the only place where you can time travel. Meaning that I can come up with a 70s disco record or 70s funk record, or a 60s record today. Amy Winehouse was the classic example of that. She took a very 60s approach to music.

Brian: Very Motown.

Hank: Exactly, but it didn't feel like Motown. Adele did the same thing. She took a very 60s format in her musical structure, and brought it into today. See, we can time travel with music, which was what you couldn't do before. Music is also the unifying factor of creating culture today. For example, the only way that you're going to notice a difference between someone that's from Japan versus someone from Brooklyn, New York, is going to be by the musical elements that are embodied in your particular music. All of the cultures now have become assimilated. We now have this normalcy thing that's happening, where everybody's becoming the same. We have this model culture going on today, which is the B-Boy is in South Africa, at the same time as the B-Boy is in Ireland, at the same time the B-Boy is in LA.

Brian: And Tokyo.

Hank: And they've all got their Yankee caps on, they've all got their pants sagging, they've got their Jordans on, you know? They all look the same. Everybody's feeling the same. They all listen to the same record. The thing that separates the differences today is culture. If I take ancient music from South Africa, and I embed it into my hip-hop beat, I'm creating a different vibration now, on my hip hop, so to speak. Now, I'm giving it culture. Now, I can feel that this music is from South Africa. The same is if I add some Irish bagpipes on that hip-hop record. I might feel like, "Oh, this record's from Dublin," you know? That vibration now is doing a lot to keep the lineage of culture together, because it makes you have to go in and think about it. "Oh, this guy, he just took his whole frequency and changed up its whole tone." Now, instead of he's coming in the Western scale, they're doing a totally different scale. That's something that you might hear in Baghdad. You may hear those same instruments and sounds that you hear from there, and you're getting that feeling and that vibration. That's giving it character today, and that's what's also accentuating culture. That's how culture is being kept alive today, through the musical art form.

Brian: Even though we have all these different styles of music, now everything is cross-pollinating, and there's a lot of awesome music. Do you think that people are playing it a bit more safe in some ways, even if they're drawing on more influences than, say, people back in the 80s?

Hank: I tend to think that people are taking more risks today than they did back in the 80s. The reason why I'm saying this is because back in the 80s, everybody had to assimilate. Let's think about the rise of new wave. New wave was basically rock music that was trying to find a way to get into the disco/urban world. Thus, what did they do? They added synths and drum machines, and created vocals that were non-descriptive, if you would. You didn't hear any British accents, you know what I'm saying? You didn't hear any French accents or German accents. What you heard was an American assimilation and so that's why those records got across. If you asked anybody, about the Thompson Twins, cats wouldn't know where they were from. They'd be like, "Damn, they could have been from the Midwest or they could have been from anywhere," you know? It's like, "Where are you from?" Today, you've got more range now, because you can be from Brixton, and somebody will know the difference between Brixton as opposed to Bristol. It's like, "Oh, that's that Bristol sound. Oh, that's that Berlin sound." People are a lot more acute to understanding where your techno is coming from today. I can hear the difference between where your techno was made at. I can tell, "Oh, okay, this techno was made out of Denver, Colorado," because there's a different vibe that it has. There's a different vibe, whether it's a dubstep record made in LA, as opposed to that same dubstep record made in London. They're going to sound different. They're going to be different. I think that there's a lot more diversity going today. I think you have to be diverse in order to stand out, because we all have the same tools.

Brian: So, they're a bit more educated, and there's more information everywhere. But much of that information is also going to be a lot of noise and negativity and banality. Over time, how does a producer avoid getting distracted or jaded or cynical, and stay focused and inspired?

Hank: Well, I mean, that's basically on the person today. To me, I still have to sit there and say, "What are you into it for?" It's still a labor of love, and you have to love the music. It can't be about, "Well, I want to make the music because I want to make money and hopefully I can pay my bills." That's not what it's about. The fact that there's more music out there than ever means that you have to be that much more dedicated to cut through. The other thing you have to also understand is that music today has another component to it that you have to take into consideration, which is visual. The visual aspect of music hasn't even begun yet. To me, it's still at the stage of it being two-dimensional, and what I mean by that is that I hear the music and I can see the artist singing the music. That's two-dimensional. Well, the third-dimension is the media aspects of it. There's still another aspect of music that has to get across, which is just starting to kick into the marketplace, which is "What is the personality of the person that's singing?" "What is the personality of the drummer that's on the drums?" Those things are going to be key, today, because we have so much access now to convey so much information. Now, I want to know not just the fact that yeah, I know you're a great keyboard player, but I want to know, are you an asshole of a person?

Brian: Yeah, so you're not talking about celebrity, you're talking about genuine knowledge of what someone's like.

Hank: Exactly, and I think that that's another factor that's going to separate you from the rest. For example, if people know that Brian is a good dude, and they like you as a person, they're going to like your music much, much more, you know what I'm saying? That's another factor that's just starting to kick in, so you don't have to be graded on how you look, singing the record, and how the song sounds. Now you've got not only how those two things look and sound, but what is the kind of person that you are? Now, that puts pressure on your songwriting. For example, if somebody sees you eating a ham sandwich, and all of a sudden, you're singing about being a vegan, now people are going to be like, "Yo, this dude is not…." You know what I'm saying?

Brian: Sure.

Hank: In the two-dimensional world, that can get over. But now, when you add the third dimension to it, it's a different aspect now. Now it becomes, "Okay, you're not true to the game, you're just doing this to try to get over." People are feeling that now. That's why, have you noticed that the gangsta music has quieted down? The reason for that is now I can peep who you really are. Oh, you ain't a gangsta, so now you can't front. You can't sing about something that you ain't about, because that third dimension is going to kick in, and when that third dimension kicks in, I'm going to find out, "Oh, you ain't no gangsta. You didn't do this. You don't have any of these things that you say, and you didn't do any of those things that you said, because you're not that dude."

Brian: Right, they're just trying to sound like the people that they liked, growing up. It's like, back in the day, you'd have people that said they were experimental musicians, but really what they meant is they sounded like other experimental musicians.

Hank: Exactly. Now you're starting to see, for example, somebody's sitting there, telling you that they're a fluent musician and they've got this and got that. And when you go to see them do their shows and they're using Ableton Live's Chord or Scale devices to keep them within a certain boundary. You say, "Well, I thought you were a fluent musician. What happened?" These are things that people are starting to see come out, and that's going to affect how you view and feel about the music, because now you're going to feel that the music is not authentic, because the artist is not authentic. It doesn't matter what you're about, it just needs to be authentic.

Brian: So, even given all the homogeneity of corporate culture blanketing everything, simultaneously, there's this explosion of people wanting sincerity and authentic experience.

Hank: Of course. There's always going to be that. It's always going to be an antidote to the virus, and as the virus becomes more known… see, the beautiful thing about something becoming mainstream is that you know that it's at its end, because it can't go anywhere else. Therefore, there's going to be something new that people are going to vibrate to, just around the corner. Now, the question is, are you chasing the thing that's already dying, or are you on the cusp of creating something that's new? That's the area where music, to me, becomes exciting. It's not exciting if you're chasing the rainbow. It's exciting if you're creating something new, and you have something new to offer. Then you'll never get bored of it, because now, you're constantly experimenting to see what will get across to people. I think that's an area that's just going to start to open up. For example, I was playing in Denver this past weekend, and one of the things that I noticed is that in DJ culture today, cats don't experiment, because everybody is so afraid to be wack. They end up working within a small bandwidth. They don't go outside that box, because outside that box is the land of "I'm not sure. I didn't practice that, so I don't want to introduce that, because I don't want to look bad." Now, the audience can feel that. What's happening is that the audience is feeling restricted because the DJs are being restricted. They're restricting themselves.

Now, if you add more experimentation, what experimentation means is that you are now charting areas that you didn't practice, you didn't rehearse. You just want to see what would be the vibrations, if you go outside that zone. The audience can feel that. They can feel you going outside the boundaries. They can feel you taking chances. They don't mind you taking chances, because here's the next thing, the thing that people need to understand: It's okay to have mistakes, because mistakes create a humanistic vibration. If all the records are perfectly segued into each other, then that record could be made by a drone. You could put an android up there, and tell the machines what record to play at what BPM, at what point did you want the segue to happen, and then you could just sit there and watch that happen. You can create an algorithm for that, and that's not what people go out for. People still want to be entertained by other human beings, and I think that that's why you've noticed that the collaborations are going to come back into play. That's what Ableton Push is all about. It's an instrument that's not really designed just for being in the studio. It's designed so that you can collaborate with someone else, in the studio or on stage. That's when you're going to really feel its intensity, because a lot of people are looking at it and going, "Okay, well, what's the next vibration?" The next vibration is always going to be collaboration, because we've got to go back to the band.

Part III

Brian: What are your thoughts not only on the importance of being involved in a community, in a scene, but then also the next step, close collaboration with other intense people?

Hank: Well, I think community is necessary today, because what's happening is computers are making it so that everybody's isolated. You can make a whole record by yourself. I can make a record by myself, but what fun is that? The fun comes in, to me, when you're working together, because the areas that I'm deficient in, you may pick up at. The areas that you're deficient in, I'm going to pick up for you at. That's what true synergy is all about, and that's why people love bands today. That's why you can't beat the early 70s records, because if you think about those records, man, some of those groups…. For example, take The Beatles. Ringo wasn't the greatest drummer, nobody ever mentions Ringo being the greatest drummer on the planet. But he was the greatest drummer for The Beatles, and what did that mean? Well, that meant that the one thing that Ringo did very, very well was, his amazing use of toms. He knew when to bring in the right tom for the right part of the record. The other thing that he had better than anybody else was incredible fills. His fills were amazing. If his back beat was just basic and so what, he would have a fill that would accompany that back beat that would be amazing. Then when he comes back to the back beat, you're like, "Oh, this dude is dope." His fills, not only were they intricate and creative and musical, but the timing of them was impeccable. A lot of cats rush over fills just to get back to the back beat, and you can feel that. "Okay, I'm back to the back beat." No, Ringo's stuff was placed, almost orchestral-like. His fills meant so much to that record, just as important as that bass line, just as important as that background vocal.

Brian: Yeah, that gets him into the collaboration aspect of it. Ringo, by himself, he was okay.

Hank: Yeah, just like George Harrison by himself, John Lennon by himself.

Brian: Right, they had their moments, but it wasn't the same.

Hank: But together? They were phenomenal, and why is that? Music collaboration, it's not an additive process. It's a geometric process. What happens is that me and you could get together, and it's not just one and one. We may create something that's equivalent to 10 times 10, you know what I'm saying? It's like, wow. What you guys are doing is working very well together. Or, we may create something that's just worse than both of us could ever be.

Brian: Yeah, so, long-term collaborative projects, at some point, most of them fall apart. Most of them fall apart before people even get successful, and sometimes the more successful they are, the quicker they fall apart. What do you say to somebody who's thinking about collaborating, and they're only seeing the breakups, or they're thinking about the stories of how this person screwed over that person? What are the positive things they should try to keep in mind when their egos start getting in the way?

Hank: Well, that's a hard process. You have to understand that in order to get to the vibration of where those guys were, back in the 80s and the 70s and the 60s and the 50s…the thing that they had as a positive was the fact that they didn't have an alternative. It wasn't like a thing where me and you got together and said, "Hey, if this thing doesn't work out for six months, then I'm going to try something else."

Brian: Sure, I can go home and do it by myself on my computer.

Hank: And I think that that's the area that hurts the music, or when you get together and you're putting so much pressure on it to be successful. You have to look at music. It's not like making shoes. It's not like being in a bank, where you know that I'm going to lend you money, and I've got to get it back at 10 percent. It doesn't work that way. It works like, me and you, we're just going to vibe, and we have to vibe and see whether or not our personalities work. What I mean by personalities, I'm talking about our musical personalities. You might be impatient. I might be patient. Those two processes might work if my patience is going to fill in the areas that you are not filling in. If I become dark matter and I'm patient to your playing, then there's a nice harmonic vibration, because you're impatient and you're rushing, but I'm filling in the background. I'm patient, but I'm not playing where you played already.

Brian: Right, it works together. The difference is, work together.

Hank: Exactly, and I think a lot of times, that doesn't happen with cats. You see two cats trying to do the same thing, like two drummers trying to make a record together. It's not going to work, man. Somebody's got to play bass. You've got cats today that are not willing to do those things. For example, how many cats do you know that ended up playing keyboards, because they were really a guitar player, but the band already had a dope guitar player, so they said, "You know what? I'll play keys."

Brian: Instead of being a really good rhythm guitar player.

Hank: Instead of saying, "Well, I want to be a guitar player, too. Yeah, I know he's dope, but I'm good, too."

Brian: We'll just be different.

Hank: But see, that's the problem that we have today. People are trying to be the same thing, and no one understands that you can't be the same thing. You can't have two lead guitar players. You can only have one lead, and if you're going to have to have a second guitar player, somebody has to be rhythm, but you can't have two leads. What you've got today is that everybody wants to be the lead, because music is something that no one studies anymore. For example, I was talking to an R&B group. There were four guys in the group, and so I asked a guy, "What do you sing?" The guy says, "Lead." I said, "No, no, what are you? Are you a baritone, tenor?" "I'm lead." They don't understand, in musical form, what they are. So what happens is, you get groups that are put together like Destiny's Child, where the girls pretty much all sing the same frequency. They're all what would be the female equivalent to tenors, but all three of them are hogging that same position. That's why you can take Beyoncé and pluck her out and make her the star, because the rest of them, all they're doing is backing up the lead. There's not enough of a difference to the point where I knew the difference when the group was there, than when they weren't. Back in the days, that was never the case. You would have a soprano, a tenor, and a baritone. Those three girls would end up creating a group, and they would sound phenomenal. Not only that, they could sing three different types of songs, because each one of them could take the lead. The baritone could take the lead on a couple of songs, and the soprano could take a lead on some songs, and the tenor could take some leads. It's like, when you're covering frequency range—you know how that is—that's another thing that no one thinks about. They don't think of music as covering frequency ranges.

Brian: Just good, old school instrumentation choices.

Hank: And I think that's an important aspect of when you're trying to put together a group or a band or anything. You have to look at what you're dealing with, and be flexible enough. Back in the day, you had cats that were flexible. You had a someone that was a great keyboardist, but the guys didn't have a bass player, so the guy would be like, "I can play bass." You had people that played multiple instruments. Cats could pick up for each other. Now you've got cats with no specializations who are like "I only play bass, and only these types of songs." Now you're like, "Wow, dude, you're really giving us no flexibility." Flexibility is key in music. It's key, and that's the area that I find that's not being picked up in the differences of today's artists versus yesterday's artists.

Brian: I think you read my mind, because the last couple questions you already kind of answered a bit, but I want to give you a chance to think big picture. Somebody who's just getting started in all of this, whether they're a musician producer, an engineer producer, or any of it, what are the things that they should try to avoid and what should they always try to keep in mind?

Hank: I think that today, you have to be a jack of all trades. I think that producers have to know engineering. I think that producers also have to know instruments, some form of an instrument, or at least understand the idioms of these instruments. I think that it's important for anybody that's a musician to also understand not only from the electronic musician perspective, but from the acoustic instrument perspective as well, understanding what a trombone does, and understanding what its idioms are. Once again, what's its frequency range, and what are its limitations? What you end up hearing a lot of is a lot of music sounds that don't correlate to the idioms. What does that mean? If you're playing a trumpet, you and I both know that a trumpet cannot hold a note for two minutes, a minute. The other thing that you also know is that you're not going to get more than one note at a time. You get cats that make a chord out of it and then wonder why people have got a frown on their face, like "What's that?" I understand that sometimes you want to be creative and you want to be outside the box, but I think that what happened was, that between the DJ culture and the producers basically coming into the game not knowing anything about music, I think that we went too far outside the box. I think that everything has become super spectacular, to the point where you're hearing kick drums that are impossible to be done by a human being. You're hearing bass lines impossible to be done by a bass player. It's okay for those special moments, if you want to be outside the box, but if nothing is inside the box, then how will you ever know whether anything's outside the box? I think we have to move toward getting back inside the box again, and at least have an understanding of what the traditional instruments were like, and what are their limitations.

Brian: But now we're in a much bigger box, because we've done all this exploration, and now we're realizing the value of the roots.

Hank: Exactly, it's like anything else. It's like basketball. You can never forget how to shoot a free throw, you know? You can't forget how to do a layup.

Brian: The fundamentals.

Hank: Right. I know that we want to do the 360 tomahawk dunks and the alley-oops and all that, but at the end of the day, if you can't hit a free throw, you can't hit a simple 12-footer, it just gets to the point where it's like, "Dude, you've got to go back into the gym and study the basics." I think that music has to do the same thing. I think that people have to keep in mind what an orchestral arrangement is like, so that this way, you can do things that create tension and release on your records. You can do things like build up certain portions higher than you can build it up without…if I hear another rise, that keyboard rise to give you some sort of build up…. Yeah, that's one way of doing it, but the problem is, it's become so widely used because people forgot how to do that same buildup without necessarily using that keyboard rise. You can build up by just adding other instruments on top. That will give you the same kind of tension without necessarily using the same parameters, and I think that those are the kinds of things that you have to learn today. I still think harmony is another area that's gone by the wayside.

Brian: Definitely. Harmony, more than anything else.

Hank: Yeah, because there's something with harmony. Even though when I started out, there was so much harmony and the idioms of music were done to perfection, that I wanted to break that rule. It got to the point where I said, "Wait a minute, I want to destroy that. I want to get away from that." But now what's happening is that everybody's gotten away from it. Now you have to bring it back, you know? Now you have to bring back traditional forms of making music again. We can have not only tension, but also release. The thing that we're not having today is that there's no buildup. There's no crescendo at the end. Everything starts out at a crescendo, at the top, and it doesn't go anywhere. It just stays there. Even DJs do that. How many DJs start out by playing something mellow? It's like being with a girl and never having any foreplay. It's like, "Dude, take her out to dinner. Give her a rose."

Brian: Create some mood, some vibe, some context.

Hank: Right, before we're already jumping into the peak. I think that what's happening now, when you get cats that are playing out together, or bands, bands think that they've got to compete with each other all the time, or DJs competing with each other, to the point where everybody feels that they've got to outshine the next, rather than they should add something to make you want to hear the next guy. If you're coming on at 10:00 and people are just getting to the venue, why are you killing them over the top of the head with the peak? Let them get in the place, let them experience something. What ends up happening is that people start leaving at 11:30.

Brian: All the great DJs are masters at dynamics.

Hank: Right.

Brian: They know how to bring something up and then down. Richie Hawtin would play only a filtered kick drum for four minutes in the middle of his set, so you just hear this muffled thing, so when he would bring everything back in after he'd been playing for five hours, it was like he was starting all over and building back up again.

Hank: Exactly. How many people know how to clean your ears out from the character that was on before? That's an art form in itself.

Brian: Musicians can learn a lot from that, just the dynamics, the builds and drops.

Hank: Yes, and now, keep in mind, we talked about the DJ aspect. Okay, I want to come on and I want to play a totally different type of music. You just got on, you just played an hour and a half of techno. I want to come on and play an hour and a half of reggae. How do I do that? Well, the first thing is, I've got to have something that segues between you and where I'm going to go.

Brian: Right, don't just drop a heavy reggae beat right away.

Hank: Yeah, because then it becomes like somebody's snatched your pants down in the middle of the club.

Brian: [laughs] "Where am I? I just got teleported, what happened here?"

Hank: Exactly. The other thing is, you've got to let people clear their ears out. Not every time you have to come with something back to back. You can come in, like you said where Richie Hawtin did the filtered kick drum. You could come away with a "jank-jank-a-jank" for a long time, for a minute and a half, two minutes, to get people to understand, "Okay, we're going into a new vibration, everybody." These are things that people don't even do today, because they're so busy trying to bang everything upside everyone's heads.

Brian: When Memory Systems would perform, we would open up our set with a 1 kHz sine wave in the right channel and another sine wave in the left channel, 7 Hz off from each other, so you heard and felt a 7 Hz beat pulse. We let that play for two or three minutes, where everyone's like, "What's going on?" and then you can tell it's a new set.

Hank: And what you've done was you refreshed everybody. Because the problem that I have, is nobody's refreshing the crowd. I remember when we used to stay at gigs for hours. Now, I can't stay there for an hour. It's like I've been there for five hours, and I'm sitting there, going, "I didn't even really experience anything."

Brian: Yeah, so if you were going to sum that up for somebody who really wants to be good at this, they really want to do this and they want to distill this down to something, what would be a couple words that you can leave them with, that would help them stay on track?

Hank: The first thing, to me, is you've got to have an open head. You guys know music so well that you have to get away from it being programmed. I see cats force their set down, regardless. They're going to shove this set down, because they've already practiced this set at home 50 times, so they're going to go through that set, no matter what. The crowd's not into that. The other thing is some sort of eye contact with your audience. I think that what happens is that everybody's so worried about being great, that they forget about being entertaining, and I think that the first rule of thumb is that we're in this game for entertainment, and if people are bored out of their minds, I don't care if you're playing phenomenally well, the crowd is yawning. If you've got people in the front that look like they're disinterested, and you're still doing your thing, what are you looking for? They came to see something. They came here to be entertained. You have to entertain the audience, first and foremost, not just perform. I just see so much performance going on that I see very little entertainment.

Brian: Awesome. Thanks.

Hank Shocklee.

© Hank Shocklee.

Index

Index

Index

Index

Index

Index

Index

Index

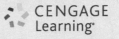

  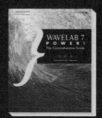